FREE APPROPRIATE PUBLIC EDUCATION

The Law and Children with Disabilities

4th Edition

H. Rutherford Turnbull III
The University of Kansas

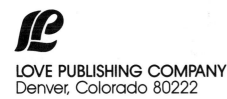

LOVE PUBLISHING COMPANY
Denver, Colorado 80222

Library of Congress Catalog Card Number 92-072338

Copyright © 1993 Love Publishing Company
Printed in the U.S.A.
ISBN 0-89108-225-5

Revised Printing 1994

CONTENTS

II THE SIX MAJOR PRINCIPLES   31

3 Zero Reject   33

6 Least Restrictive Appropriate Educational Placement   157

IV FREE APPROPRIATE PUBLIC EDUCATION AND THE AMERICAN VALUE SYSTEM   289

11 Objections to the IDEA and Answers to Them   291

12 Underlying Beliefs and Values in Right-to-Education Laws   301

PREFACE

The goal of American education is to value each child as equally an individual and entitled to equal opportunity of development of his own capacities, be they large or small in range. . . . Each has needs of his own as significant to him as those of others are to them. The very fact of natural and psychological inequality is all the more reason for establishment by law of equality of opportunity, since otherwise the former becomes a means of oppression of the less gifted.

—Thomas Dewey

Dewey's sentiments have a familiar ring to those of us who have been working to establish the rights of children with disabilities to a free appropriate education. He admonishes us to value all individuals, whomever and whatever they are, recognize their needs and satisfy them, establish equal educational opportunity by law, and change a system that oppresses some because of their inequalities. How surprised Dewey would be to learn that his views have become so widely accepted!

This book tells the story of the initial rejection and ultimate acceptance of those ideas. It also shows how law adopts these ideas and enacts them as the idea of equal educational opportunities for children with disabilities. Its essential teaching is legal. Its essential message is moral: A person who is less able is not less worthy.

How the nation's public schools have dealt with the challenge and opportunity of educating these children in the past, and how they must do so under present law, is this book's initial focus.

The book next analyzes in detail the six principles of special education law: (1) zero reject, or the right of every child to be included in a free appropriate publicly supported educational system; (2) nondiscriminatory classification, or the right to be fairly evaluated so that correct educational programs and placement can be achieved; (3) individualized and appropriate education, so that an education can be meaningful; (4) least restrictive placement, so the child may associate with nondisabled students to the maximum extent appropriate to his or her needs; (5) due process, so the child and child advocates may have an opportunity to challenge any aspect of education; and (6) parent participation, so the child's family may be involved in what happens in school.

Recognizing that these six principles generate widespread resistance, the last part of the book represents the most common objections to these principles. It also attempts to answer those objections on two major grounds: (1) the beliefs that support the principles, and (2) the system of values that undergird the principles.

This fourth edition discusses all of the major cases interpreting the federal special education law (through the middle of 1992). This law, originally called the Education of the Handicapped Act (EHA), is now entitled the Individuals with Disabilities Education ACT (IDEA).

This edition also discusses the 1990 amendments to IDEA and the Americans with Disabilities Act (ADA). Thus, it represents the most current analysis of the relevant court decisions and federal statutes and their implications for students, families, and educators.

H.R.T. III
September 1, 1992

*To Jay, for whom these rights have meant
    so much;
Amy and Kate, who teach and learn
    from Jay;
Ann, our best teacher; and
Ruth W. Turnbull, gone but everlasting.*

SECTION I
Introduction to the Law

1
Introduction to the American Legal System

FEDERALISM

The law serves many purposes, among them ordering the public affairs of individuals and their governments and resolving disputes between them. These seemingly simple purposes are accomplished through an intricate network. To explain the workings of that network, we will use some familiar images.

Public law can be thought of in terms of three parallel ladders—descending rungs of parallel authority affecting the relationships between individuals and their governments and between various levels of government. At the top of the federal ladder is the United States Constitution; in the middle are laws enacted by Congress pursuant to constitutional authority; and on the bottom are regulations issued by federal agencies pursuant to congressional authority. Next to this ladder stands one representing the state governments, and it has similar rungs of parallel authority: state constitutions, state statutes, and state agency regulations. Finally, next to the state ladder is the local ladder with its three rungs: the charters of local governments, local ordinances, and local regulations.

The whole picture shows that the highest source of law in each "ladder" is the fundamental government document: the federal Constitution, the state constitution, and the local charter. Federal, state, and local statutes are next in line, followed by federal, state, and local agency regulations:

Federal	*State*	*Local*
Constitution	Constitution	Charter
Statutes	Statutes	Ordinances
Regulations	Regulations	Regulations

This system of parallel governments (federal, state, and local) is known as the *federal system*. As a form of government, it is known as *federalism*.

Two major principles are involved in the form of government known as federalism. First, there is the sharing of responsibility and power between the federal, state, and local governments. As pointed out later in this chapter, the responsibility for and power over the education of children with disabilities is shared between those governments. Traditionally, local and state school boards (or other governing bodies) had the greatest responsibility and power. Recently, however, responsibility and power have been allocated in greater part to the federal government. This shift is the result of the court cases that began with the desegregation cases in 1954, and it gathered force with two cases decided in 1972 (as pointed out later in this chapter and in chapter 2). It also is the result of legislation—the Individuals with Disabilities Education Act, which is reviewed in detail later in this book.

Second, there is the supremacy of federal constitutional and statutory law. Early in the history of this country, the Supreme Court, in *Marbury v. Madison*, made it clear that the Constitution of the United States and laws passed by Congress to implement the Constitution are the supreme law of the land. This means that state and local school boards must comply with federal law if, among other things, they receive federal funds (as they do when they educate children who have disabilities with money allocated to them under the Individuals with Disabilities Education Act) or if their laws are in conflict with federal constitutional law or federal statutes. Clearly, the supremacy doctrine has permitted the federal role in the education of children with disabilities.

LAWMAKERS: WHO MAKES THE LAW?

For each source of law there is a lawmaker—a group of persons who make the law. For the federal Constitution and its amendments the initial lawmakers were the delegates to the constitutional convention and subsequently the legislatures of the various states that acted to ratify constitutional amendments (other than the first ten, the Bill of Rights, which were drafted by delegates themselves). The delegates were representatives of the franchised citizens of the states. Thus, the source of the federal Constitution was the citizenry of the United States. This is generally true, too, with respect to the constitutions of states and charters of local governments.

This is not true, however, of statutory law. In that case, the lawmaker is not the citizenry but, rather, its elected representatives serving in Congress or in state legislatures. The Congress and the legislatures may not enact laws that violate provisions of the federal Constitution or the constitution of the state in whose legislature they serve. All federal and state laws are subject to "testing" to determine if they are "constitutional" under the federal Constitution and the applicable state constitution because the federal Constitution provides that the Constitution shall be the supreme law of the land, protecting all citizens of the United States and regulating all state and local governments. Also, the fundamental law of each state is its constitution, and no state law or state agency regulation has the effect of law unless authority for it can be found in the state constitution. There is, then, a lawmaker for each source of law, a fundamental law that has greater authority than any other, and a hierarchy of law in each of the three governments.

Although it may appear that all lawmakers are alike (that there are no basic differences between legislatures and legislators and regulations and regulators), there is a fundamental difference. Statutes are enacted by legislatures whose members are elected by the franchised citizens. Regulations are made by regulatory agencies whose staffs are not elected but, rather, are appointed by the legislatures or with the consent of the legislature or by the chief of the executive branch for which the person works. Agency regulations must be based on authority given to them by the legislatures. The regulators are both executives, persons who execute or carry out the legislature's statutes, and legislators—in the limited sense that they write regulations designed to carry out legislation.

We obviously have a complex system for enacting and carrying out laws. This is especially true in the area of education for children with disabilities. The system can be illustrated as follows:

1. *Constitutional law*
   Federal Constitution (especially Fifth and Fourteenth Amendments)
   State constitution (especially provisions about education)
   Local charter (especially provisions creating schools or school boards)
2. *Legislature (legislative body)*
   Congress (e.g., the Individuals with Disabilities Education Act)
   State (e.g., equal educational opportunities legislation)
   Local (e.g., school board policies establishing programs for children)
3. *Regulations (executive agency)*
   Federal (Special Education Programs, Office of Special Education and Rehabilitative Services)
   State (e.g., North Carolina State Board of Education, Department of Public Instruction, Division of Exceptional Children)
   Local (e.g., director of pupil services or coordinator of special education)

CASE LAW AND THE COURTS

One important type of law and lawmaker has not yet been identified: case law (judicial decisions) and the courts. When the delegates to federal and state constitutional conventions wrote those constitutions, they created three branches of government—legislative, executive, and judicial. The function of the legislature is to make law, and the function of the executive is to carry it out. The function of the judiciary is to resolve disputes between citizens or between a citizen and his or her government. Courts do this by applying law to a given set of facts and interpreting the meaning of the law in that factual context. It is their unique function to say what the Constitution or a federal statute or regulation means in a given case, to issue a decision setting forth the facts that underlie their interpretation, and to enter an order commanding the parties in the case (or other courts, if the case is on appeal) to take certain action.

Within the overall federal system are three parallel systems: trial courts, U.S. circuit courts of appeals, and the U.S. Supreme Court (the court of last resort). State and local systems also consist of trial courts, appellate (appeals) courts, and a court of last resort. It is a matter of great complexity why a case may be tried in one court, appealed or reviewed by another, and finally disposed of by yet another. We do not need to enter that thicket. A brief discussion of court jurisdictions will serve our purpose.

The terms used to describe trial and appellate courts vary from state to state and sometimes are different from the terms that describe the United States courts. This makes it difficult from time to time to understand precisely which court is deciding a case. For example, United States trial courts are called district courts, but trial courts in the state system are called circuit courts, district courts, or even supreme courts. Likewise, the United States appellate courts are called circuit courts or circuit courts of appeals, with the country divided into eleven circuits (regions) over which the appeals courts have jurisdiction. In some states the appeals courts consist of intermediate courts of appeals, together with courts of final appeals. And states use different terms to describe the intermediate courts and courts of final appeals.

The U.S. Supreme Court is the court of last resort for all cases, whether from the state court system or from the federal courts, and its decisions are binding throughout the United States. The U.S. circuit courts of appeals have appellate power over cases decided in the trial courts in their circuits. Their decisions are binding throughout the circuit but may be only persuasive, not binding, in other circuits and in all district courts. The U.S. district courts are the trial courts in their respective districts; their decisions are generally binding in the district only (not throughout the appellate circuit in which they are located) and may be only persuasive, but not binding, on circuit courts and other district courts.

The state court systems are parallel to the United States court system. Each state has a court of final appeals or last resort, whose decisions are binding throughout the state. The diagram on the following page illustrates the relationships between the courts in a federal system.

Note that decisions may be appealed to the U.S. Supreme Court from the U.S. circuit courts of appeals and from the courts of final appeals (or last resort) of the states. Again, it is a matter of great complexity as to when a case may be taken to the U.S. Supreme Court. Several special education cases have gone to the U.S. Supreme Court from the U.S. circuit courts of appeals.

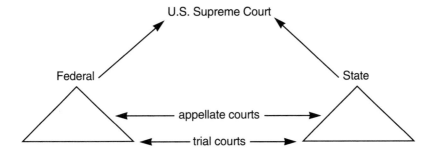

BROWN v. BOARD OF EDUCATION

In the field of education law, the following diagram is well reflected by the original school desegregation case, *Brown v. Board of Education. Brown** was not one case, but four that were consolidated and heard as one by the U.S. Supreme Court. Three of the cases were on appeal from federal district courts (the appeals went directly to the Supreme Court, bypassing the circuit courts of appeals, because, under the Federal Rules of Civil Procedure, a federal constitutional issue was an indispensable element of the case). One was on appeal from a state appellate court after having been heard first in a state trial court. Thus, *Brown* can be illustrated as follows:

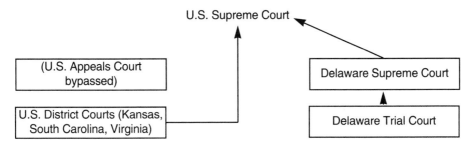

Aside from the structural (functional) aspects of the case, *Brown* was a landmark because it had an impact on so many aspects of educational law and procedure:

1. *Brown* illustrates the principle that the federal Constitution, as interpreted by the U.S. Supreme Court, is the supreme law of the land, is binding on all federal, state, and local governments, and is the precedent that must be followed by all federal and state courts in subsequent similar cases.

---

*Typically, cases are given a shortened name, usually the name of the appealing party, for easy reference in discussions. The name—in this case, *Brown*—is italicized to indicate the case, not the person being discussed.

2. *Brown* is a nearly perfect example of one of the major lessons of this book: All educational issues (such as the educational rights of disabled students) are essentially political policy and social issues cast in the guise of constitutional litigation (should disabled students be educated and, if so, how and by whom?) and, because they are presented in the garments of the law, ultimately are resolved by the courts.

3. *Brown* also demonstrates that the truly difficult educational issues are fought on various civil rights battlefields. Just as *Brown* was the first case on the battlefield of racial desegregation of schools, it was the seed that gave birth to other civil rights battles and to grounds for successful challenges to governmental discrimination against certain persons because of their unalterable personal characteristics (such as race and sex). *Brown* gave rise to the *right-to-education* cases, and they in turn helped establish other rights for disabled persons. The point—so obvious, but so important—is that judicial resolution of educational issues on constitutional grounds becomes precedent for judicial resolution of related civil rights issues on similar constitutional grounds.

4. *Brown* gave immense comfort and support to civil rights activists, legitimizing their legal arguments and furnishing them with a powerful tool for persuading legislatures, particularly Congress, to enact antidiscrimination legislation. Case law frequently is the underpinning of legislation, and federal cases and legislation frequently precede state case law and legislation. Nowhere has this been more true than in establishing the rights of disabled pupils to an education.

5. *Brown* caused a fundamental change in the federal system. As precedent for other federal school desegregation cases and as the legal foundation for federal school and other civil rights legislation, *Brown* heralded the entry of the federal government into public education in the United States. Thus, it made significant inroads into an area that had been reserved almost wholly by state and local governments as their province. Over the long run, its effect has been to shift the balance of the federal system heavily toward the side of the federal government. Right-to-education cases and legislation also have shown us that the areas of state and local autonomy in education are quickly diminishing. According to current interpretation, it is questionable if there is any such thing as a "purely local" concern in education. Are all educational concerns truly national, requiring national leadership in the form of case law precedents and legislation enacted at the federal level? This surely is the conclusion that has been reached in the right-to-education movement.

6. In *Brown* it was proven that although the U.S. Constitution never once refers to a public education, its principles of equal protection and due process under the Fifth and Fourteenth Amendments have a significant effect on public education. Nowhere is this fact clearer than in the right-to-education cases. This is significant because, as noted, the federal Constitution does not guarantee the right to an education. State constitutions do guarantee it. But if a state denies (as many had) an education to some students, usually those with disabilities, but provides it to others, the state violates the equal protection doctrine of the federal Constitution and, depending on the provisions of the state constitution, its own constitution as well. The essential point of *Brown*, however, is that the states were violating the equal protection clause of the federal Constitution. Chapter 3 discusses this point in detail.

7. *Brown* illustrates one kind of lawsuit—the *civil action*—that is typical of litigation between citizens and their governments. This type of suit is brought by a citizen who alleges that a government or a governmental official denied him or her rights or benefits to which the person is entitled under the law (constitution, statutes, or regulations). In this case, the plaintiff, *Brown*, sued the defendant, the Topeka Board of Education. In two of the consolidated cases, other citizens sued governmental officials who represented school agencies. A civil action is typical of the right-to-education cases. Criminal actions—in which the state prosecutes a person accused of a crime—are alien to educational law.

8. *Brown* is almost ideal for teaching someone how to read a case and how cases are decided, particularly in the right-to-education area. If "disabled" is substituted for "Negro" and "nondisabled" for "white" wherever those words appear in *Brown*, it is fairly easy to understand why *Brown* is important to education of the disabled and how the Fourteenth Amendment became the constitutional basis for the rights of the disabled to be educated. Appendix A gives excerpts from the U.S. Supreme Court opinion on *Brown*.

   a. What are the *controlling* (or *dispositive*) facts of the case? Blacks are denied admission to schools attended by whites under laws requiring or permitting segregation according to race, and racial segregation in public education is inherently damaging to the educational opportunities of black children.

   b. What are the *allegations*? The facts constitute a denial of equal protection of law as guaranteed by the Fourteenth Amendment because segregated public schools are not and cannot be made equal, and the "separate but equal" doctrine should be set aside.

   c. What are the *issues of law* the Court must resolve? The Court must determine whether the separate but equal doctrine applies to public education, and whether segregation, under that doctrine, violates the equal protection clause.

   d. What is the Court's *holding* (answer to the issue)? Segregation solely on the basis of race in the public schools violates equal protection and denies minority (black) children an equal educational opportunity.

   e. What is the Court's *reasoning*? Equal educational opportunities are denied when, in light of (1) the importance of education, (2) the stigmatizing effects of racial segregation, and (3) the detrimental consequences of racial segregation on the education of those against whom segregation is practiced, a state segregates by race.

   f. What is the Court's *order*? The cases are to be argued again before the Court, and the argument should focus on the nature of the remedy that the Court should order.

   g. What is the *principle* of the case? State action in segregating the races in public education violates equal protection, and, by extension, any state-required or state-sanctioned segregation solely because of a person's unalterable characteristic (race or disability) is usually unconstitutional.

   h. What are the *implications* of the case? They are massive, and will be discussed throughout this book.

   i. What is the *public policy* in the case? State-created stigma or badges of inferiority based on race (or other characteristics, such as disabilities) are constitutionally intolerable because they mean that the state acts invidiously (i.e., discriminatorily, by denying equal opportunities) with respect to persons who have certain traits. In brief, invidious (discriminatory) action is unconstitutional.

j. Whose *interests* are at issue? The interests or *claims* of blacks to an equal educational opportunity are at issue.

k. Finally, what *functions* of government are at issue? At issue are the functions of education—namely, cultural assimilation, preparation for participation in the political process, and training so that economic opportunities might become available. Given the interests, the functions could not be parceled out or denied solely according to race.

Brown is worth an extended discussion here because it speaks directly to public schools, special education, and disabled children. There are undeniable similarities between the *Brown* plaintiffs and children with disabilities. Both can prove they have been denied equal educational opportunities; both allege an unconstitutional denial and base their arguments on equal protection principles; both challenge separateness in education; both find comfort in the holding of *Brown* and the right-to-education cases concerning denials of equality; both are strengthened by the reasoning that relies on concepts of stigma and detrimental educational consequences; both successfully advance a public policy against invidious state action; both have similar interests in obtaining an education; and both lay claim to the functions of the schools to meaningfully educate all students.

2

Introduction to Law and Free Appropriate Public Education

EGALITARIANISM AND NORMALIZATION

A major legal development in this decade has been the extension of the principle of egalitarianism to people with disabilities. This principle says that all persons, however unequal they may be in terms of their abilities, should be treated equally by being granted equal opportunities. Many professionals, including educators, have argued for egalitarianism in the treatment of disabled citizens. Their arguments are couched in terms of *normalization* or *social role valorization,* a term given by Wolf Wolfensberger,[1] one of the originators of the normalization principle, to clarify the intent of normalization.

Normalization stands for the proposition that persons with disabilities should live and be treated like nondisabled persons as much as possible and that their differences from nondisabled people can be reduced by minimizing the degree to which they are treated differently. Social role valorization means that people with disabilities should be given opportunities, including education or special education, to have socially valued roles. Those roles include being students (and thus being included in schools), associating in all aspects of life with people who do not have disabilities, and having real jobs for real pay. Like normalization, social role valorization seeks to minimize the differences between how people with disabilities are viewed and treated by those who do not have disabilities. One step in minimizing those differences is to acknowledge that disabled persons do, in fact, have an equal right to an education.

With the foundation of a political ideology (egalitarianism) and a human-service ideology (normalization), it became feasible and desirable to extend those ideologies into the law and thereby to ensure that they had the force of law. This extension of ideologies—and their combination with a legal doctrine—occurred through the doctrine of equal protection and the refinements that began with *Brown.*

EQUAL PROTECTION: JUDICIAL PRECEDENTS

In the eyes of the law, egalitarianism invokes the concept of equal protection and gives rise to the argument that limiting the civil liberties of disabled students violates their constitutional rights to equal protection under the Fourteenth Amendment because there is no rational reason for imposing special burdens or limitations on them. This argument also asserts that the educational opportunities granted to nondisabled pupils are constitutionally required to be granted to disabled pupils.

"Equal protection of the laws" is such a simple phrase, but it is by no means as simple to understand and apply as one might think. As chapter 3 shows, simplicity in interpretation and application is hardly the case when the educational rights of disabled students are involved. Long before those rights were affirmed under the doctrine of equal protection, however, other disadvantaged persons were successfully arguing that their rights had been infringed upon unconstitutionally. Establishment of their rights was the indispensable foundation for establishing the educational rights of students with disabilities.

The high-water marks made by the equal protection doctrine on the shore where the disadvantaged waited can be delineated by looking first to *Brown* (see chapter 1) and its progeny—the many cases that held that equal educational opportunities may not be predicated (granted or limited) upon race. Under the equal protection doctrine, a person's financial status also cannot be used as a basis for denying benefits to him or her. For example, the Supreme Court has held that the right to vote,[2] ensured access to court to settle disputes with others,[3] and entitlement to financial assistance from a state a person has the right to move into[4] are rights that may not be denied to those who cannot afford them. Equal protection, the Court said, requires that the poor be treated as though they were not poor; they must have free access to the franchise, to courts, and to interstate movement.

Other disadvantaging characteristics have been added to those of race and poverty. The fact that a person is illegitimate,[5] an alcoholic,[6] a narcotics user,[7] a convict,[8] or a female[9] has been held by the Court to be improper grounds upon which to base legislation if the result of the legislation is to discriminate against such persons but not against others in similar circumstances. Chapter 3 discusses more fully the equal protection doctrine and its application to people who are disabled.

The point here is to highlight a series of cases that indicate a strong egalitarian movement—a movement that, despite recent cases, furnished a solid foundation for extending the concepts of egalitarianism and equal protection to people with disabilities. This line of cases did more than provide precedents that were adapted and tailored to remedy unhappy conditions the public schools were imposing on disabled children. It also, and perhaps just as significantly, made law reformers realize that they should—and could success-fully—move from other civil rights battlefields to the school grounds and work to extend the equal protection doctrine to children with disabilities.

THE HISTORY OF FEDERAL LEGISLATION

It takes more than a cursory review of constitutional developments to explain how disabled children's rights to an education were established. To be sure, the case precedents were in-dispensable (as later chapters demonstrate), but a slowly evolving federal role that turned into a massive involvement in the education of disabled children was an equally indis-pensable ingredient.

The earliest federal role—creating special schools for those who were mentally ill, blind, and deaf between the 1820s and the 1870s—paralleled a similar movement at the state level, in which state schools for the disabled were established as early as 1823. No further significant federal activity occurred until World Wars I and II spurred the govern-ment into vocational rehabilitation programs and aid for disabled veterans and other disabled persons. Public assistance programs were evidence of increasing federal concern for the disabled. Application of the Social Security Act to blind, disabled, aged, and dependent persons, the grant of benefits under Medicare and Medicaid programs, the payment of Sup-plementary Security Income, and a host of programs under Title XX of the Social Security Act all give testimony to the federal government's concerns.[10]

The parent movement was typified by formation of the Association for Retarded Citi-zens of the United States (formerly the National Association for Retarded Children/Citizens) in the 1950s and its increasing clout on the federal and state scene in the 1960s. It was en-hanced in the early 1960s when President John F. Kennedy and Vice President Hubert Humphrey used their influence to advance the interests of mentally retarded persons by es-tablishing the President's Committee on Mental Retardation.

Congress first addressed the education of children with disabilities in 1966, when it amended the Elementary and Secondary Education Act of 1965 (P.L. 89-750) to establish a program of federal grants to the states that would assist them in initiating, expanding, and improving programs and projects for the education of children with disabilities. In 1970 Congress repealed the 1966 law but established a grant program that had a similar purpose (P.L. 91-230). Both the 1966 and 1970 laws tried to stimulate the states to develop special education resources and personnel.

By 1974 Congress had become dissatisfied with the states' progress and was con-fronted with the courts' decisions in two pioneering special education cases, *Pennsylvania Association for Retarded Children (PARC) v. Commonwealth of Pennsylvania* and *Mills v. D.C. Board of Education* (both are discussed in full in chapter 3). Those cases ruled that dis-abled children should be given access to public education. Accordingly, in 1974 Congress substantially increased federal aid to the states for special education and required them to adopt a goal of providing "full educational opportunities to all handicapped children" (P.L. 93-380). Congress also recognized that its 1974 law was an interim measure only and would have to be supplemented. Thus it was that Congress enacted the Education for All Handicapped Children Act (P.L. 94-142) in 1975.

The 1975 law was the most significant amendment of the Education of the Handicapped Act (EHA) to that time. But it has not been the only amendment. Congress amended the EHA in 1978 by P.L. 95-561, in 1983 by P.L. 98-199, in 1986 by P.L. 99-372, in 1986 by P.L. 99-457, and again in 1990 by P.L. 101-476.

Congress also had an effect upon special education in other ways. The Elementary and Secondary Education Act itself was the springboard for the EHA. The Vocational Education Amendments of 1968, the Economic Opportunities Act of 1972 (Headstart), the Rehabilitation Act of 1973, the Higher Education Amendments of 1972, and the Developmental Disabilities Assistance and Bill of Rights Act of 1974 not only contributed to the political feasibility of the 1975 amendments to the EHA (the Education for All Handicapped Children Act, P.L. 94-142) but also underscored the federal concern for people with disabilities.

The 1990 amendments renamed the law, which is now called the Individuals with Disabilities Education Act (IDEA). The amendments also made the following changes in the law (the section affected by each change is noted in brackets):

- They made it clear that students with autism and traumatic brain injury are included as "children with disabilities" [20 U.S.C. Sec. 1401(a)(1)]. This is not a change in the law so much as it is a clarification. These students were covered by the law previously, but now the law identifies them as a separate and distinct class entitled to the law's benefits.
- They include therapeutic recreation and social work services as related services, and they make it clear that rehabilitation counseling is also a related service [Sec. 1401(a)(16)]. Again, this is not so much a change as a clarification. Before the amendments, recreation was a listed related service; the amendments indicate that recreation includes therapeutic recreation. Similarly, before the amendments, "counseling services" were designated related services. The amendments indicate simply that "rehabilitation counseling" is a "counseling service" and thus emphasizes that counseling for vocational rehabilitation is a related service. This change is consistent with the Act's emphasis on transition and expectation for vocational outcomes as a result of special education. This change also reflects Congress's awareness that transition planning should anticipate three elements of life: work, residential living, and recreation/leisure time activities.
- They add a definition of "transition services." This book will discuss transition services in chapter 5, as part of the discussion of appropriate education.
- They make it clear that students in Bureau of Indian Affairs schools are entitled to the benefit of the EHA if they are qualified as students with disabilities [Sec. 1401(a)(24)]. This clarifies the EHA and is not a major substantive amendment.
- They add two new definitions, namely, "assistive technology device" and "assistive technology service" [Sec. 1401(a)(25) and (26)]. These definitions are the same as used in P.L.

100-407, Technology-Related Assistance for Individuals with Disabilities Act of 1988. Under that Act, states are given federal funds in order to develop statewide systems of technology-related assistance for individuals with disabilities. That Act leaves it up to each state how it will develop that system and who will benefit from it. If a student with a disability, however, needs technology-related assistance and the student's IEP calls for such assistance (either "devices" or "services"), the student may obtain them from the student's LEA or from the statewide system. This amendment makes it clear that assistive technology services or devices are to be considered as part of the student's educational program, where appropriate, and that a student's IEP should call for these services and devices, where appropriate, in order to be regarded as legally sufficient. In other words, if a student needs those devices or services, the student's IEP should call for them and the student may obtain them from the LEA or from the statewide system, if one exists.

- They add a new definition of "underrepresented" to include minority populations, the poor, individuals with limited English proficiency, and individuals with disabilities [Sec. 1401(a)(27)]. This emphasis on outreach to underrepresented groups is consistent with the Act's "service priorities" (those not served get the first crack at the federal funds; those with the most severe disabilities get the second crack).
- They permit the secretary of education to conduct or make grants or contracts for studies concerning the education of students with serious emotional disturbances [Sec. 1426].
- They redefine "deaf-blind" and make it clear that students who are deaf-blind are entitled to programs, services, and supports as they transition from school to life-after-school, and that these supports include assistance related to independent living and competitive employment [Sec. 1422]. This amendment is consistent with the "service priorities" provisions of the Act and indicates that Congress expects the SEAs and LEAs to provide an education to deaf-blind students that includes a transition plan and an expectation/curriculum that prepares them for independent living and competitive employment. This is a significant expectation of outcomes, given the Act's previous reliance on process (not outcome) measures as a way of holding schools to a standard of performance.
- They amend the special provisions for the early education of students with disabilities [Sec. 1424] by making it clear that early education (ages three through five) includes the education of the child's parents; that adult role models with disabilities should be included in early childhood education programs; that early education programs should focus on the transition of infants and toddlers into early education and of young students from early education into elementary education; that the programs should promote the use of assistive technology devices and services; and that the programs should promote the understanding of and address the early intervention and preschool needs of children exposed prenatally to maternal substance abuse. Here, the amendments reiterate the Act's emphasis on parental roles and education of parents (consistent with Part H and the entire concept of "parent participation"). Moreover, they also indicate that infant/toddler and preschool programs should employ "role models" (people with disabilities), and they strengthen the Act's requirements that, in programs funded under the Act, there should be employed people with disabilities. These amendments also address the transition issue, suggesting

that if parents and students learn transition skills at the infant/toddler and early education stage, they will be able to practice them later (such as, at age fourteen or sixteen as part of transition from school curriculum and plans). The amendments make it clear that infant/toddler and early intervention programs should acquire assistive technology for young children, just as other special education programs should. Finally, the amendments state that programs should work with students whose parents are substance-abusers (the so-called "crack kids"), thus indicating that those children are covered by the Act if they need special education and should not be excluded from its benefits simply because of the cause of their disabilities.

- They authorize the secretary of education to create model programs of extended school years (that is, twelve-month programs, not the usual nine-month programs) for students with severe disabilities and require the secretary to emphasize ESY programs that integrate children with and without disabilities [Sec. 1424]. This amendment gives special emphasis to the integration/mainstreaming programs and strengthens the "least restrictive education" doctrine for students in ESY programs.
- They emphasize that transition services should aim toward independent living, full participation of youth with disabilities in community programs, and use of assistive technology devices and services [Sec. 1425].
- Finally, they change the term "handicapped student" and similar "handicapped" usage to "child/student/individual with a disability" and rename the Education of the Handicapped Act to the "Individuals with Disabilities Education Act" [Sec. 1400(a)]. This amendment is consistent with the "people first/characteristic second" approach of the disability field: emphasize the person before the trait.

School Practices

As a general rule, the nation's public schools were highly ingenious and very successful in denying educational opportunities, equal or otherwise, to disabled children. Their success was evidenced by data showing how many children were excluded: Congress found that approximately one-half of the nation's eight million children with disabilities were not receiving an appropriate education and about one million were receiving no education at all. The multitude of exclusionary practices that the courts found in violation of educational rights of the disabled was also proof of the problem. Among these practices, two dominated: exclusion and classification.

Exclusion. Exclusion occurs when children are denied education (denied access to all public educational programs or provided an inadequate education for their needs). *Total exclusion* may involve the school's refusing to admit a child or placing him or her on a long waiting list. Exclusion also occurs when programs are inadequate or unresponsive to students' needs, as when Spanish-speaking children are given an English curriculum and no special provision is made to accommodate the fact that they do not understand English. Another example of exclusion occurs when children are put in large regular classes and given little or no training or education. Practices such as these constitute *functional exclu-*

sion; although the child has access to a program, the program is of such a nature that the child cannot substantially benefit from it and therefore receives few or none of the intended benefits of education.

The schools excluded school-aged children with disabilities individually and as a class.[11] They admitted some but not all of the students with the same disability.[12] They inadequately funded tuition-subsidy programs that would have enabled families to purchase appropriate education from alternative sources (such as private schools) when appropriate education was not available in the public schools.[13] When appropriate programs were not available, the schools placed disabled pupils in special education programs that were inappropriate for them.[14] When faced with a shortage of special education programs, schools created waiting lists for admission to the few available programs, thus excluding many eligible pupils.[15]

Also, the schools created different admission policies for children with disabilities.[16] They placed disabled pupils in situations with virtually no programs of instruction available.[17] They excluded retarded children on the grounds that they created behavioral or disciplinary problems.[18] Finally, they limited the number of students that could be enrolled in special education programs by using incidence projections that bore little relation to the actual number of disabled children in the school district[19] or by restricting state-level funding for hiring special education teachers by establishing artificial quotas such as one state-paid teacher for every twelve pupils in each special education class.[20]

Classification.   Classification is at issue when children are misplaced or wrongly tracked.[21] Misclassification denies children the right to an equal educational opportunity because it results in their being denied schooling that will benefit them.

Past challenges to school placement criteria were often accusations of racial discrimination as much as they were complaints about denial of education. The objection was that the tests used to classify children were biased toward knowledge of English and familiarity with white middle-class culture. Accordingly, test scores resulted in minority children being placed in special education programs in far greater numbers than were other children. The result was a dual system of education based on race or cultural background.

Other Practices

A host of other practices, not easily categorized, also denied education to disabled students. State and local appropriations for special education were shamefully sparse. Institutionalized children often were denied even the barest programs of care and habilitation. The responsibility of state and local governments was fragmented, and competitive bureaucratic structures within the school or institutional agencies rarely undertook any cooperative efforts. The result was that meager resources (money and personnel) were diluted, gaps existed in service, services often overlapped, and accountability was nearly impossible.

Architectural barriers, the lack of adaptive materials and materials for vision, speech, and hearing impaired children, and the inability or unwillingness of school personnel to teach some children (emotionally disturbed, learning disabled, mentally retarded) likewise contributed to their exclusion. It was not unusual for teachers to be uncertified to teach children with disabilities or to be the least skilled teachers in a school system. Teachers often were required to use the oldest, least adequate facilities, located far from the classrooms of nondisabled students. The separateness and devaluation were underscored by separate financing, administration, and organization of special education services.[22]

Once a child was placed in a special education program, the placement often became permanent. For the child it was a terminal assignment, and reconsideration or reevaluation was out of the ordinary. The assignment usually was carried out without parental participation and without opportunities for due process. Frequently, schools failed to identify the children with disabilities in their districts; child census procedures were rare, and the school's target population was not known, planned for, or served.

Early intervention programs were the exception, not the rule. Placement in private programs was encouraged, because it relieved the school of any responsibility for serving children whose families were able or desperate enough to pay for private school opportunities. Local noncompliance with state law requiring education of children with disabilities was rarely punished. Preschool, elementary, and secondary school programs— when they existed at all—were unequally available. Finally, the schools' longstanding discouragement of pupils ("don't call us—we'll call you") made many parents weary of trying to rectify wrongs, kept them in ignorance of their children's rights, and reinforced the unbalanced power relationships between the powerful schools and the less powerful parents.

Many readers may object to these generalized characterizations, possibly being able to point to specific circumstances in which some or all of these practices did not exist. But the generalizations have been true more often than not, and the practices have been the rule more often than the exception. Some of the better studies of school practices substantiate the generalizations;[23] court decisions have set forth facts that support the generalizations;[24] and Congress itself has filed a broad-based indictment of the public schools based on findings of many of these practices.[25]

Reasons for the Practices

Schools have followed these practices for many reasons. Not only is the cost of educating or training a disabled child normally higher than the cost of educating a nondisabled child, but manpower, money, and political clout for children with disabilities are also limited when compared with the same resources for nondisabled children. Many educators have not considered disabled pupils, particularly mentally retarded ones, educable in the traditional sense. The time-honored "reading-writing-arithmetic" philosophy has been a reason for exclusion. The fact that special education has been separated from the mainstream of education and that both special educators and educators in programs for nondisabled students have desired this separation has also tended to diminish educational opportunities for individuals with disabilities.

As pointed out before, a disabled child, once placed in a special education program, often has had little chance to return to a normal program. Placement in special education has tended to be permanent because there were no requirements for periodic reevaluation and the schools understandably were reluctant to question their own decisions.

Special education has served as an important escape hatch, permitting schools to classify as disabled those children they considered undesirable: the racial minorities, the disruptive, and the different. Behind this practice (indeed, underlying all of the discrimination) was the widely held attitude that governmental benefits, including education, should be parceled out to the most meritorious—a belief that equates merit with average intelligence or nondisabling conditions and asserts that the less able are less worthy.

The three ideologies or principles—egalitarianism (a political ideology), normalization (a human services ideology), and equal protection (a legal doctrine)—play important roles with respect to the reasons for the practices. First, they are based on a different value system. The new value system holds that although a person is less able, the person is not therefore less worthy. Second, they shape the legal and educational practices embodied in and required by IDEA. Third, they demonstrate that values are as effective as politics, economics, and science in shaping how people with disabilities are treated. Indeed, given the resistance to the education of all children with disabilities and their inclusion, to the maximum extent appropriate for them, in the regular school programs, these ideologies demonstrate that values prevail over other forces.

THE IDEA AND SECTION 504: ONCE OVER LIGHTLY

The Relationship of the Two Laws

The IDEA provides federal funds to states and local education agencies if they agree to comply with certain conditions set out in the law and the regulations that implement the Act. Thus, the law is a federal grant program with conditions attached.

> References to sections of IDEA that are cited in the text in brackets [] are references to the Act itself, as passed by Congress. The Act has been codified at 20 United States Code, Sections 1401-1468. The Department of Education has issued regulations implementing the Act. They are codified in 34 Code of Federal Regulations, Parts 300 and 303, and are cited in the text as, e.g., Sec. 308.
>
> The Rehabilitation Act, of which Section 504 is part, is codified at 29 United States Code, beginning at Section 706. Section 504 is codified at 29 U.S.C., Section 794. The Department of Health and Human Services has issued regulations implementing Section 504, which are codified at 30 Code of Federal Regulations, Part 104, and are cited in the text as, e.g., Sec. 104.2.

By contrast, Section 504 is federal antidiscrimination legislation. It prohibits any state or local government or any private organization that receives federal funds from discriminating against an "otherwise qualified handicapped person" solely on the basis of the person's handicap. It does not provide funds to state and local governments or private organizations and therefore is not a federal grant program with conditions attached (as is IDEA). Instead, it is civil rights legislation that reaches all recipients of federal funds and prohibits them from discriminating against people with disabilities. In both its language and intent it is like other federal civil rights laws that prohibit discrimination by federal recipients on the basis of race or gender.

The State Plan

Any state desiring to receive IDEA funds must apply for them by submitting an application from its state education agency (SEA) to the U.S. Secretary of Education. The application is called the *annual program plan*. The plan must be submitted when required by the secretary of education and must indicate how the state will comply with the IDEA and its regulations.

Regardless of whether an SEA or LEA (local education agency) receives federal funds, it must comply with Section 504 and its regulations. The law prohibits any recipient of *any* federal financial assistance from discriminating against a disabled person solely because of disability. Because Section 504 is intended to prohibit the same discrimination in the education of disabled children that the IDEA prohibits, its regulations are consistent in concept and policy with the regulations under the IDEA. They apply to any SEA, LEA, or any state or local agency that receives funds from the Department of Education. Thus, an SEA or LEA that does not receive IDEA funds but receives other federal funds from the Department of Education or other federal agencies must comply with essentially the same regulations (under Section 504) as for funds under IDEA.

IDEA applies to more than SEAs or LEAs receiving IDEA funds. Assume that an LEA chooses not to receive funds but that the SEA does. Is the LEA exempt from IDEA? No—not entirely. If an LEA elects not to receive funds, it does not have to comply with requirements of the IDEA; however, the SEA, as a recipient of funds, is required to ensure that the children with disabilities residing in the LEA's jurisdiction are granted all of the rights and protections of the IDEA. The IDEA's requirement that the SEA must provide special education directly to children with disabilities when an LEA refuses to do so has been reaffirmed by the United States Supreme Court in *Honig v. Doe*, a 1988 decision. Moreover, if the LEA receives any other federal funds, it must, of course, comply with Section 504.

The SEAs and LEAs are not the only state and local agencies affected by IDEA. All state and local agencies (including LEAs) that furnish "special education" and "related services" to disabled children, such as state departments of mental health, welfare, or corrections (hereafter called *public agencies*) are treated as though they were SEAs or LEAs. There are two reasons for this.

First, the IDEA requires the SEA to assure the federal government that the Act is carried out statewide. It assigns the SEA the responsibility for general supervision of all educational programs for children with disabilities in the state. Thus, requirements of IDEA are binding on the state itself, not just on an agency or a department of the state.

Second, because the basic rights granted disabled pupils under the IDEA are also included in the regulations for Section 504, *any* recipient of federal funds has to comply with these provisions. Accordingly, IDEA provides that the regulations apply to each *state* (not just to an agency or department thereof) that receives IDEA funds. The SEA submits an application for funds on bidealf of the state as a whole. As a consequence, the Act and the regulations apply to all agencies and political subdivisions of the state involved in educating children with disabilities.

The effect of IDEA and Section 504, then, is to assure that children with disabilities receive a free appropriate education and are not discriminated against in or by any public agencies furnishing special education services. Together, the two laws cover all disabled children without regard to where they live in the state (whether in the community or in an institution, for example) or which state or local agency serves them (whether a department of public education or a department of human resources, for example). There is no real escape from these Acts for state and local agencies. The two Acts seal all the cracks in services and carry out policies of zero reject and nondiscrimination.

Children with Disabilities: Definitions

For purposes of the IDEA, disabled children are those who are mentally retarded, hard of hearing, deaf, speech or language impaired, visually disabled, seriously emotionally disturbed, orthopedically impaired or other health impaired, autistic, deaf-blind, multihandicapped, or who have specific learning disabilities or traumatic brain injury. All must need special education and related services because of any one or more of these disabilities.

Under Section 504, which prohibits discrimination against an otherwise qualified disabled individual, and for the purposes of special education only, the term "disabled person" means any person who has a physical or mental impairment that substantially limits one or more major life activities, has a record of such an impairment, or is regarded as having such an impairment.

"Physical or mental impairment" means (1) any physiological disorder or condition, cosmetic disfigurement, or anatomical loss affecting one or more of the following body systems: neurological, musculoskeletal, special sense organs, respiratory (including speech organs), cardiovascular, reproductive, digestive, genito-urinary, hermic and lymphatic, skin, and endocrine; or (2) any mental or psychological disorder, such as mental retardation, organic brain syndrome, emotional or mental illness (including addiction to alcohol or drugs), and specific learning disabilities.

"Major life activities" means functions such as caring for oneself, performing manual tasks, walking, seeing, hearing, speaking, breathing, learning, and working.

"Has a record of such an impairment" means the person has a history of or has been classified as having a mental or physical impairment that substantially limits one or more major life activities.

"Is regarded as having an impairment" means the person (1) has a physical or mental impairment that does not substantially limit major life activities but is treated by a recipient of federal funds as constituting such a limitation, (2) has a physical or mental impairment that substantially limits major life activities only as a result of the attitudes of others toward such impairment, or (3) has none of the impairments listed above but is treated by a recipient of federal funds as having such an impairment.

With respect to public preschool, elementary, secondary, or adult educational services conducted by public schools other than universities, a qualified disabled person is someone who is (1) of an age at which nondisabled persons are provided such services, (2) of any age at which it is mandatory under state law to provide such services to disabled persons, or (3) guaranteed a free appropriate public education under the IDEA.

The Supreme Court clarified the meaning of otherwise qualified disabled person in its 1979 decision, *Southeast Community College v. Davis* (see Appendix B). In that case, Frances Davis, who was hearing impaired and had a degenerative hearing disability, applied for admission to the college's nursing program. After being examined for her ability to hear, she was denied admission and sued to be admitted, claiming that she was discriminated against because she is a person with a disability, in violation of Section 504.

The Supreme Court ruled that she is not "otherwise qualified" and thus is not entitled to the protection of Section 504 and could not be discriminated against in violation of the law. The Court interpreted "otherwise qualified handicapped person" to mean one who is able to meet all of a program's requirements in spite of the disability. Because Frances Davis could not meet all of the requirements of the curriculum in nursing, she was not "otherwise qualified." If she could have met them in spite of her disability, even with some accommodations the college made for her, she would have been "otherwise qualified" and would have been the victim of discrimination.

The Court's decision is notable for reasons other than that it offers the first definition of "otherwise qualified." First, it makes clear that Section 504 is an antidiscrimination statute, one that requires some accommodations to be made by a recipient of federal aid; but it is not an affirmative action law that requires substantial accommodations, such as Title VI (race discrimination) or Title IX (sex discrimination) of the Civil Rights Act.

Second, it recognizes the need to balance the rights of a person with a disability (Frances Davis) against the rights of other people—namely, the patients who would be cared for by a nurse who may not be able to hear adequately, and the institutions of higher education, which have a claim to control their curriculum and make independent judgments concerning the suitability of a person for the curriculum. As chapter 3 points out, balancing the interest of people with disabilities against the interests of others is a matter that affects the interpretation of Section 504 and its application to the education of students with disabilities.

The language of Section 504 provides that no recipient of federal funds shall discriminate against an otherwise qualified person solely on account of a disability. The regulations for implementing this law make it clear that Section 504 applies to preschool, elementary, and secondary public education programs that receive *any* federal assistance from the Department of Education or other federal agency. They also make it clear that the schools must adopt a zero-reject policy (chapter 3 discusses zero reject), provide a free appropriate public education to each disabled person who is a legal resident of the recipient's jurisdiction regardless of the nature or severity of the disability, conduct nondiscriminatory testing (see chapter 4), place disabled children in the least restrictive environment (see chapter 6), and guarantee due process for disabled children (see chapter 7). Thus, Section 504 and its implementing regulations accomplish largely the same results as IDEA in prohibiting exclusion and discrimination against children with disabilities.

Despite a similarity to the IDEA, Section 504 and its regulations differ in several important respects:

1. Section 504 includes those persons who are so defined by the IDEA, but it also includes many others, such as persons addicted to the use of drugs and alcohol (not for employment discrimination purposes). The two laws take different approaches to the issue of who has a disability. The IDEA basically relies on a *categorical* approach and anticipates the continuation of categorical labeling of children. A child has "MR" or "LD" or "ED."

   Section 504, however, relies on both a categorical approach and an entirely different approach, best described as *functional*. Under that approach, a child has a disability if he or she functions as though disabled, or if a state or local government receiving any federal funds acts as if the child were disabled. There is an impairment in major life activities, a record of an impairment, or the child is treated as having an impairment.

2. Section 504 prohibits discrimination not only in preschool, elementary, secondary, and adult public education, but also in the employment of persons with disabilities and in social and health services. By contrast, IDEA addresses only preschool, elementary, secondary, and adult education. Both laws, however, speak to the problems of architectural barriers and access to facilities and, in a limited sense, to the employment of people with disabilities by the public schools (see chapter 3).

3. Section 504 does not require individualized education programs for disabled children; IDEA does. Both require appropriate education.

AMERICANS WITH DISABILITIES ACT

At this point, it is appropriate to give a summary of the Americans with Disabilities Act, P.L. 101-336. It is the most important disability law enacted since at least 1975 (when Congress enacted Education of All Handicapped Children Act, P.L. 94-142) or, arguably, ever. The ADA's purpose is to provide clear, strong, consistent, and enforceable standards prohibiting discrimination against individuals with disabilities, without respect to their age, nature of disability, or extent of disability. ADA recognizes that discrimination occurs in many ways, for many reasons, and in almost all sectors of society; that the proper goals of the nation for individuals with disabilities are to assure equality of opportunity, full participation, independent living, and economic self-sufficiency.

Obviously, the amendments to IDEA (described above) and the ADA should complement each other. They do, in ways set out below.

General Coverage

Consistent with its goals, the ADA extends its civil rights/nondiscrimination protection to the following sectors of American life: employment in the private sector; privately owned public accommodations (for example, theaters, hotels, restaurants, shopping centers, and grocery stores); services provided by state and local governments, including public and private transportation services; and telecommunications services (for people with hearing or visual impairments).

Consistent with the 1990 amendments to IDEA, the ADA anticipates certain outcomes for people with disabilities. These are that they will enjoy equal opportunity to fully participate in the life of the community and will have equal opportunity to live independently and to achieve economic self-sufficiency. Accordingly, IDEA's transition-services provisions speak about independent living and full participation in community programs. These outcomes cannot be ensured unless the community ceases to discriminate on the basis of disability. ADA now prohibits that discrimination, thus opening up the possibility that students (as students) and individuals with disabilities (as citizens, not just as students) will not be barred from participating in the community because of their disabilities and the community's barriers. Just as IDEA's zero-reject rule (see chapter 3) is a rule of inclusion and against exclusion, so too is the ADA a rule of inclusion and against exclusion: it prohibits the physical and attitudinal barriers that kept people out of the "mainstream" and from participating in the community and thus makes it possible for them to participate because they cannot be excluded and must be included.

Protected Individuals

Those who are entitled to ADA's benefits are "individuals with disabilities" as the term is defined under Section 504 of the Rehabilitation Act: a person who has, has a history of having, or is regarded as having an impairment that significantly limits one or more of life's major functions. This also is the same definition used in the Fair Housing Act Amendments, prohibiting discrimination in housing on the basis of disability. Generally speaking, a student who is entitled to the benefits of IDEA (that is, to special education) will be covered under ADA as one who has a disability. But there may be more people covered by ADA than by IDEA: A person may have a history or be regarded as having a disability but still not need special education and thus not be covered by the IDEA.

For the purposes of the ADA, homosexuality and bisexuality are not impairments and are not disabilities under the Act. Also, the term "disability" does not include transvestitism, pedophilia, transsexualism, exhibitionism, voyeurism, gender identity disorders or other sexual bideavior disorders, compulsive gambling, kleptomania, pyromania, and psychoactive substance use disorders resulting from current illegal use of drugs.

Although an individual who currently uses illegal drugs is not "disabled" under the ADA, the Act does prohibit discrimination against an individual who has successfully completed a supervised drug rehabilitation program and is no longer using illegal drugs. The ADA also allows testing for illegal drugs. It prohibits discrimination against users of illegal drugs if they are otherwise entitled to health services or other services related to drug rehabilitation. ADA also amends the Rehabilitation Act of 1973 to make it clear that an individual who is currently using illegal drugs is not "disabled" under the Rehabilitation Act when a covered entity acts on the basis of the individual's use of the drugs, and the person may not be denied rehabilitation benefits on the basis of current drug use if the person also is otherwise entitled to those services.

Persons with AIDS are covered by ADA but the Act makes it clear that a person with a contagious disease or infection may be excluded or denied a job or benefit if the person poses a significant risk of transmitting the infection to others through the receipt of a position or benefit, and, if no reasonable accommodation by the employer or service provider can eliminate such a risk, the individual may be denied the position or benefit.

The ADA states that in disciplining children with disabilities who are using illegal drugs or alcohol, educational agencies may use their regular disciplinary procedures, applicable to all students, and are not required to use the due process procedures of the IDEA.

Employment Discrimination

With respect to employment, the ADA prohibits discrimination against a person with a disability who is "otherwise qualified" to perform the essential functions of the employment position, with or without reasonable accommodation.

This rule has important consequences in the education of children with disabilities. As noted above, the IDEA now is both process-oriented and outcome-oriented. The outcome, as set out in the new provisions on transition plans as part of the student's IEP, is independent living, vocational training, integrated employment (including supported employment), or community participation. They also require instruction, community experiences, the development of employment and other post-school adult living objectives, and acquisition of daily living skills. In short, the IDEA anticipates an outcome of employment during and especially after the student exits from school. That outcome cannot be achieved in many cases as long as there are barriers to employment. These barriers are the targets of ADA's employment provisions, which make them illegal.

It is now illegal to discriminate against an otherwise qualified person with a disability who can perform the essential functions of a job with or without reasonable accommodations. A "reasonable accommodation" includes making existing facilities used by employees readily accessible to and usable by individuals with disabilities, job restructuring, part-time or modified work schedules, reassignments to vacant positions, acquisition or modification of equipment or devices, appropriate adjustment or modifications of examinations and training materials or policies, the provision of qualified readers or interpreters, and other similar accommodations.

An employer is not required to make these accommodations if they would impose an "undue hardship" on the employer, that is, a significant difficulty or expense when considered in light of the nature and cost of accommodation, the overall financial resources of the facility or facilities involved, the number of persons employed at the facility, the effect on expenses and resources or the impact on the operation of the facility; the overall financial resources of the employer, the size of the business with respect to the number of its employees, the number, type, and location of its facilities; and the type of operation of the employer.

Employment practices that are covered include application procedures, hiring, advancement, discharge, compensation, job training, and other conditions of employment.

The rules on employment discrimination do not apply to religious organizations, small businesses (fewer than twenty-five employees until 1994, and fifteen or fewer employees after 1994). Employers may not discriminate against people with contagious diseases but employers may reject applicants or fire employees who pose a direct threat to the health or safety of others in the work place, and applicants or employees are not protected if they currently use illegal drugs.

The ADA makes it likely that individuals with disabilities can expect that discriminatory barriers in employment will be coming down. Accordingly, they, their families, and their educators should prepare for work in competitive settings, for comparable wages, and for accommodations to their disabilities. The role of special education is now clear: to prepare individuals with disabilities to take advantage of the new opportunities available in employment.

Public Services and State/Local Governments

Many opportunities for employment and participation in a community are provided by state and local governments. These governments operate numerous programs, such as recreational activities, libraries, health services, social services, and so on. Although Section 504 of the Rehabilitation Act prohibited these governments from discriminating against otherwise qualified persons with disabilities if the governments received federal financial assistance, there were many functions of state and local government that were not federally supported and thus still could (under federal law) discriminate against people with disabilities. These functions—employment and services including transportation, as well as facilities—now may not do so. The consequence of this change in law is to ensure that people with disabilities will have access to those functions and be able to participate in the community as service-users. The role of special education is to prepare them to participate and take advantage of these functions.

All state and local governments are prohibited from discriminating against any qualified individual with a disability. Such a person is one who meets the essential requirements for eligibility for receiving the services or participating in the activities and programs of the government and who meets those requirements with or without reasonable modifications to governments' rules, policies, or practices, the removal of architectural, communication, or transportation barriers, or the provision of auxiliary aids and services. Such a person may not be excluded from participating in or receiving the benefits of the services, programs, or activities of that government or be subjected to discrimination by it.

Public Accommodations and Services Operated by Private Entities

The ADA also bans discrimination in public accommodations such as restaurants, hotels, theaters, doctors' offices, pharmacies, retail stores, museums, libraries, parks, recreational programs and facilities, private schools, and day-care centers. Private clubs and religious organizations are exempt from that ban. Just as in the case of employment and state/local government functions, the ADA removes barriers to community participation and anticipates that the role of special education is to prepare students with disabilities to take advantage of the opportunities for participation.

Public accommodations may not discriminate against otherwise qualified individuals with disabilities. Discrimination consists of denying them participation in programs and operations, denying them participation of equal benefit, offering only separate benefits, and not offering programs and operations in integrated settings. Public accommodations must make reasonable changes in their policies, practices, and procedures, to avoid discrimination. This includes providing auxiliary aids and services to individuals with vision or hearing impairments or other individuals, unless the provision would result in an undue burden. Physical barriers must be removed if that can be accomplished without undue expense or difficulty. If the barriers cannot be removed, alternative methods of providing services must be available, if readily achievable. "Readily achievable" means accomplishable and able to be carried out without much difficulty or expense. Factors to be considered in determining what is "readily achievable" include the nature and cost of the action required, the overall financial resources and size of the facility and the covered entity, including the impact of compliance on the facility's or entity's expenses, resources, and operations, and the type of operation carried on by the entity. All new construction and alterations must be handicap-accessible.

Here, again, ADA opens up new opportunities for individuals with disabilities. The role of special education is equally clear as in the employment field: preparation of students with disabilities to participate in and use the public accommodations. This may mean much more community-based, community-referenced curriculum.

Transportation

As a general rule, ADA bans discrimination in public and private transportation on the basis of disability. It creates separate rules for complying with this ban for various types of transportation systems ("demand responsive systems," "designated public transportation," and "fixed route systems"). It has special rules for public bus systems, public rail systems, and privately operated bus and van companies. It permits paratransit systems to operate as a complement to fixed route systems. It bans new construction that is not handicap-accessible and requires alterations to be handicap-accessible.

The implications for special education are, simply put, that one role of special education is to provide instruction to students with disabilities—no matter the nature or extent of disability—on the use of public transportation systems. There is no reason to prohibit discrimination in the systems if, at the same time, students are not taught how to use them.

Telecommunications

The ADA requires all telecommunications services to offer relay services for hearing-impaired and speech-impaired individuals, as well as the closed-captioning of public service announcements. Thus, companies offering telephone service to the general public must offer telephone relay services to individuals who use telecommunications devices for the deaf (TDDs) or similar devices.

Here, again, the role of special education seems clear: to provide instruction on the use of telecommunications systems to all students, especially those with hearing or speech impairments.

Enforcement and Remedies

The ADA creates separate enforcement procedures and remedies for each of the major areas in which it prohibits discrimination.

In employment, an individual may file a complaint with the Equal Employment Opportunity Commission and take appeals from it to court. If the individual wins the complaint, the remedies include back pay and court orders to stop discrimination.

In public services (state and local government operations), an individual may file a complaint with federal agencies that the attorney general will designate or bring private lawsuits to recover actual damages and obtain court orders to prohibit further discrimination.

In public accommodations, an individual may seek a court order to prohibit discrimination but may not obtain money damages; the individual also may file a complaint with the attorney general, who then may file a lawsuit to stop discrimination and also to obtain money damages and penalties. In transportation, individuals may file complaints with the department of transportation or bring private lawsuits to prohibit discrimination. In telecommunications, the individual may file complaints with the Federal Communications Commission to prohibit discrimination.

The ADA and IDEA are similar in their approaches to remedies. Both require a complainant to use administrative, quasi-judicial remedies and both open the federal courts' doors to complainants.

Attorneys' Fees.   Any individual who prevails in any complaint or lawsuit against an entity covered by ADA may recover the attorneys' fees incurred in connection with the complaint and lawsuit. This is the same rule adopted by IDEA (under the Handicapped Children's Protection Act, discussed in chapter 9).

Alternative Dispute Resolution.   The ADA encourages but does not require the use of alternative means of resolving disputes, including settlement negotiations, conciliation, facilitation, mediation, fact-finding, minitrial, and arbitration. The IDEA also encourages alternative dispute resolution in two respects: it permits the states to use them (Part B) and it even does so explicitly (Part H).

Exemptions.   The insurance industry is exempt from ADA's provisions.

State Immunity.   The ADA makes it clear that no state is immune under the Eleventh Amendment to the Federal Constitution from any lawsuit filed under ADA; remedies may include injunctions prohibiting further discrimination and damages for past discrimination. IDEA also makes it clear that a state is not immune from a lawsuit; the 1990 amendments reverse the Supreme Court's decision in the *Dellmuth* case (discussed in chapter 9).

Effective Date.   The ADA becomes effective in 1992, and regulations have been issued by the federal agencies responsible for enforcing the law.

The Dream

Senator Tom Harkin of Iowa was the sponsor of the ADA in the 101st Congress and its chief manager. What he said on the floor of the Senate on the date the Senate enacted ADA is worth restating here:

"All across our Nation mothers are giving birth to infants with disabilities. So I want to dedicate the Americans with Disabilities Act to these, the next generation of children and their parents. With the passage of the ADA, we as a society make a pledge that every child with a disability will have the opportunity to maximize his or her potential to live proud, productive, and prosperous lives in the mainstream of our society. We love you all and welcome you into the world. We look forward to becoming your friends, your neighbors, and your coworkers. We say, whatever you decide as your goal, go for it. The doors are open and the barriers are coming down."

NOTES

1. Wolfensberger, "Social Role Valorization: A Proposed New Term for the Principle of Normalization," *Mental Retardation* 21 (Dec. 1983):224.

2. Harper v. Virginia Board of Elections.

3. Boddie v. Connecticut.

4. Shapiro v. Thompson.

5. Weber v. Aetna Casualty and Surety Co.; Levy v. Louisiana.

6. Wisconsin v. Constantineau.

7. Robinson v. California.

8. Martarella v. Kelley.

9. Reed v. Reed.

10. LaVor, "Federal Legislation for Exceptional Persons: A History," in *Public Policy and the Education of Exceptional Children,* edited by Weintraub et al. (Reston, VA: Council for Exceptional Children, 1976); and Boggs, "Federal Legislation Affecting the Mentally Retarded," in *Mental Retardation,* vol. III, edited by Wortis (New York: Grune & Stratton, 1971).

11. *See, e.g.,* Children's Defense Fund, "The Exclusion of Children with Special Needs," ch. 4 in *Children Out of School in America: A Report of The Children's Defense Fund, Washington Research Project, Inc.* (Washington, DC: The Fund, 1974); Mills v. D.C. Bd. of Ed.; PARC v. Commonwealth; Wolf v. Legislature of Utah; MARC v. Maryland; North Carolina ARC v. North Carolina; and Tidewater Ass'n. for Autistic Children v. Tidewater Bd. of Ed.

12. Mills; PARC; and Tidewater Assn. v. Tidewater Bd. of Ed.

13. PARC; MARC v. Maryland.

14. MARC v. Maryland.

15. Mills; LeBanks v. Spears; David P. v. State Dept. of Ed.

16. PARC and Mills.

17. PARC; MARC v. Maryland.

18. Mills.

19. David P. v. Dept. of Ed.

20. North Carolina's Department of Public Instruction allocated funds to local units, for use in hiring special education teachers, on the basis of 12 TMR disabled children per classroom.

21. Hobson v. Hansen; Larry P. v. Riles.

22. Milofsky, "Why Special Education Isn't Special," *Harvard Education Review* 44(1974): 437-58.

23. *Supra* n. 12.

24. *See infra,* chs. 3, 4, 5, 6, and 7.

25. P.L. 94-142, Sec. 1402(b).

SECTION II
The Six Major Principles

3
Zero Reject

CONSTITUTIONAL FOUNDATIONS

The Fourteenth Amendment provides that no state may deny to any person within its jurisdiction equal protection of the laws. As indicated in chapters 1 and 2 and interpreted by the courts, this amendment has produced a remarkable series of judicial results that have effectively prevented government from denying governmental benefits to persons because of their unalterable and uncontrollable characteristics (such as age, gender, race, or disability) and in many cases require affirmative or other positive or remedial steps to redress the unequal treatment those people have experienced at the government's hand. Inequalities have existed in the opportunity to be educated, and children with disabilities have been among the victims of educational discrimination. The Fourteenth Amendment has recently become the vehicle for redressing that inequality.

Brown as Precedent in Right-to-Education Cases

Judicial attacks on the many exclusionary practices of schools focused on the importance of education, its protected status under *Brown*, and its claim to favored treatment under the Fourteenth Amendment. In holding that racial segregation in public education violated the Fourteenth Amendment, *Brown* stressed the importance of education in terms that have been quoted or cited with approval in nearly every subsequent related case. "The importance of education to our democratic society" and the relationship of education to "the performance of our most basic public responsibilities" were the grounds on which the Court reached the conclusion that the opportunity of an education, "where the state has undertaken to provide it, is a right which must be made available to all on equal terms."

Representatives of disabled students, relying on *Brown*, have claimed that these children have the same rights to education as nondisabled children. Their complaint has two major elements. First, they complained that there was differential treatment among and within the class of children with disabilities—that is, some children were furnished with educations while others were not. They sought the remedy that all excluded children with disabilities be given an education. Second, they complained that some disabled children were not furnished an education while nondisabled children were. They sought the remedy that all children, including children with disabilities, be included in the public education system.

The basic argument of *Brown* was that the equal protection doctrine protected a "class" of persons—in this instance, a racial minority. In applying the equal protection doctrine, the courts have asked whether a state's action in distributing benefits and burdens (such as educating some but not others) was based on a "classification" of persons with apparently equal characteristics, and whether that classification resulted in some members of the "class" being treated less equally than others. For example, in the school desegregation cases the class to be protected was all students, whether white or black. When a state treated black students differently by requiring them to attend segregated schools, the courts found that black students had been denied equal protection of the school laws on the basis of an unalterable and uncontrollable trait—their race.

In the right-to-education cases, the class is all students, whether disabled or not. A state undertakes to provide a free public education system for its school-age citizens. When the state treats disabled students differently by denying them an opportunity to attend school or by inappropriately assigning them to special education programs, the courts have found that these children had been denied equal protection of school laws on the basis of their unalterable and unchosen traits—their disabilities.

The Evolution of Equal Protection Analysis

Until the advent of the Warren era of the Supreme Court, the Court generally held that governmental action alleged to be discriminatory and in violation of the equal protection doctrine was not unconstitutional. When the traditional equal protection analysis applied in these cases failed to correct abuses of individual rights, the Warren Court applied a new equal protection analysis. The application the Court used depended principally on who the complaining party was, the nature of his or her interest or what right was being infringed upon, and the ability of the government to justify its action.

Under the new equal protection concept, if the case involved a "suspect classification" (such as a person being classified by race) or a "fundamental interest" (such as the right to vote), the Court subjected the classification to "strict scrutiny" and required the state to show a "compelling interest."[1] The Court also required the state to prove that the distinction drawn by the law was necessary, not merely convenient, in order to achieve the government's purpose.

If no fundamental interest or suspect classification was involved, the Court resorted to the "rational basis" standard, asking only whether the ends or purposes sought were legitimate state purposes and whether there was a rational relationship between the ends or purposes and the particular classification. A state practice was much more likely to

survive an equal protection attack under the rational-basis test than under the strict scrutiny test.

Even more recently, the Court has developed an "intermediate" or "middle-tier" approach to equal protection. In cases involving women and aliens (but not racial minorities)
or in cases involving important personal interest (but not one that is "fundamental" in the
sense that it is explicitly guaranteed by the Fourteenth Amendment or is necessarily implied by explicit guarantees, as is the right to privacy), the Court has given some protection
to disadvantaged people, but not as much as it has given in the race segregation cases. Thus,
a state must show an exceedingly important or special justification for a law that puts
women or aliens at a disadvantage. This middle-tier approach has enabled the Court to
strike down some laws that discriminate against people who have been traditionally excluded from the political process (and thus unable to correct the laws that single them out).
But it also has not required the Court to create any new suspect classes (such as racial minorities) or to imply any new fundamental rights from the explicit guarantees of the Bill
of Rights.

Understanding basic equal protection analyses is necessary to appreciate how a claim
of equal protection is generally made and resolved in right-to-education cases, despite the
fact that recent right-to-education cases generally lack a clear or formal equal protection
analysis. Until recently, the courts deciding those cases typically have cited the equal protection clause and added an accompanying reference to *Brown*. But they have failed to state
that education is a fundamental interest and that the disabled plaintiffs are a suspect class,
and they usually have not specified which equal protection tests finally apply.[2]

Under a 1985 decision of the U.S. Supreme Court, involving a local ordinance that
excluded group homes for people who are mentally retarded from a nonresidential zone,
people who are retarded, and apparently all disabled people, were held not to fall into a
suspect or quasi-suspect class and therefore are not entitled to special protection under the
equal protection doctrine.[3] The impact of this decision, in *City of Cleburne v. Cleburne
Living Center, Inc.*, is not entirely clear. On the one hand, the Court seems unwilling to
give people with disabilities any special protection under the equal protection doctrine; it
says it does not want to do so. Yet it also uses language and an approach indicating that it
has special concerns for those people and reaches a result that strikes down the exclusionary
zoning ordinance as blatantly discriminatory, thereby granting them some protection under
the equal protection doctrine. (See *Cleburne* discussion under ADA in chapter 2).

In addition, the Court seems to give great weight to legislative judgments, saying that
they are presumed to be valid. But it also strikes down the particular legislative judgment—
the exclusionary ordinance—on the grounds that discrimination against people with mental retardation had no valid reason.

In sum, the Court seems to be saying one thing and doing another. On the face of the
opinion, however, it appears that the Court will not give any special protection under the
equal protection doctrine to people with disabilities. If this result holds over the period
of years, *Cleburne* will have marked a clear retreat from an activist or liberal use of the
equal protection clause—that is, away from the suspect class/fundamental interest or

intermediate/middle-tier approach to protecting minority populations from majoritarian decisions.

PARC and *Mills*

Although *Brown* established the right to an equal educational opportunity based upon Fourteenth Amendment grounds, it was not until *Pennsylvania Association for Retarded Children (PARC) v. Commonwealth of Pennsylvania* and *Mills v. D.C. Board of Education* that *Brown* became meaningful for children with disabilities. In both *PARC* and *Mills*, the courts relied on legal and educational authorities to support their finding that education was essential to enable a child to function in society and that *all* children can benefit from education. They applied the equal protection and due process guarantees of the Fifth and Fourteenth Amendments to furnish this important right to students with disabilities. Neither court engaged in careful legal analysis; each was content to make the assertion of fundamental interest and strike down school policies denying education to children with disabilities. *Mills*, citing *Brown* and *Hobson v. Hansen*, concluded:

> In *Hobson v. Hansen*, . . . Judge Wright found that denying poor public school children educational opportunities equal to that available to more affluent public school children was violating the Due Process Clause of the Fifth Amendment. *A fortiori*, defendants' conduct here, denying plaintiffs and their class not just an equal publicly supported education but all publicly supported education while providing such education to other children is violative of the Due Process Clause.

Subsequent cases closely followed the arguments made in *PARC* and *Mills*, and the form of the decision and the relief granted have been similar. *PARC* relied on the following findings (the so-called *PARC* syllogism):

> 1. Expert testimony in this action indicates that . . . all mentally retarded persons are capable of benefiting from a program of education and training; that the greatest number of retarded persons, given such education and training, are capable of achieving self-sufficiency and the remaining few, with such education and training, are capable of achieving some degree of self-care; that the earlier such education and training begins, the more thoroughly and the more efficiently a mentally retarded person will benefit from it; and, whether begun early or not, that a mentally retarded person can benefit at any point in his life and development from a program of education and training.
> 2. The Commonwealth of Pennsylvania has undertaken to provide a free public education to all of its children between the ages of six and twenty-one years, and further, has undertaken to provide education and training for all of its mentally retarded children.
> 3. Having undertaken to provide a free public education to all of its children, including its mentally retarded children, the Commonwealth of Pennsylvania may not deny any mentally retarded child access to a free program of education and training.
> 4. It is the Commonwealth's obligation to place each mentally retarded child in a free, public program of education and training appropriate to the child's capacity, within

the context of the general educational policy that, among the alternative programs of education and training required by statute to be available, placement in a regular public school class is preferable to placement in a special public school class and placement in a special public school class is preferable to placement in any other program of education and training.

One important premise is absent from the court's findings: It is generally true that educators have the ability to educate and train children with disabilities. Without both the ability of disabled children to learn and the ability of educators to help them learn, it would be a futile expenditure of public money to attempt to teach them in the public schools. Instead, it would be rational and arguably constitutional for the state to exclude them from school if they could not benefit from it and if there were no educators competent to teach them. It was significant that the defendants in *PARC* and *Mills* did not deny that they were under a duty to educate *all* children or that mentally retarded or other disabled children could be educated.

Unlike *PARC, Mills* was not resolved by a consent decree but, rather, by judgment against the defendant school board. Also unlike *PARC*, the suit was brought on behalf of children who had disabilities other than mental retardation. Like *PARC*, however, *Mills* resulted in a court order stating that before any child with a disability eligible for a publicly supported education may be excluded from a regular school assignment, the child must be furnished adequate alternative educational services suited to his or her needs, including (if appropriate) special education or tuition grants. The District of Columbia school board was required to provide each disabled school-aged child a free and suitable publicly supported education, regardless of the degree of mental, physical, or emotional disability. The school board was also enjoined from making disciplinary suspensions for any reason for longer than two days unless school authorities gave the child a hearing before suspension and continued the child's education while he or she was suspended.

Uses of Equal Protection for Zero Reject

The equal protection doctrine was put to many uses in the context of zero-reject policy. It was used to prevent (1) the total exclusion of all or some children with disabilities in the schools, (2) the total exclusion of some children when others with the same disability were included, and (3) the total exclusion of all persons with one kind of disability (such as autism) when persons with a different type of disability (such as a physical disability) were included. In each of those instances, the class of persons entitled to equal protection was "students," not just *some* students.[4]

A fourth use of equal protection came into play when children with disabilities were included in school programs on a different basis than nondisabled students. For example, it applied when disabled children's parents were required to pay tuition for attending public schools but the parents of nondisabled children were not.[5] It also applied to disabled children who were ruled medically ineligible to attend school (because they were nonambulatory or not toilet-trained) when nondisabled children were not screened out because of their medically related characteristics.[6] And it also operated for disabled children who were denied free transportation to school when nondisabled students were given such service.[7]

The fifth way the equal protection doctrine has been applied in right-to-education cases is in establishing a new doctrine of equality—the equal access doctrine. *Brown* and other school desegregation cases interpreted the equal protection doctrine as requiring that black students be given *equal access to the same resources* as whites. Typically, the courts ruled that when a school system provides facilities to white children, exactly the same facilities (not an equivalent separate set of facilities) must be made available on the same terms to black children.

Equal Access Doctrine

In right-to-education cases, the theory of equal protection was quite different and was best understood in terms of claims for students with disabilities to *differing* resources for *differing* objectives.[8] Under this approach, the right to education meant that the schools must furnish *all* children with disabilities equal opportunities to develop their own capabilities. Thus, schools were required to provide different programs and facilities for pupils with different needs, according to those needs.

It is now clear that the "equal access doctrine" is quite different in 1992 than it was when it was first developed in 1975. There are several new laws that reflect the doctrine established by Congress.

The 1990 amendments make it clear that supported employment, use of assistive technology devices and services, full participation in community life, and integration into regular education program are high priorities. The 1988 Technology-Related Assistance for Individuals with Disabilities Act funds statewide assistive technology programs in order to increase the independence, productivity, and integration of individuals with disabilities. The 1986 amendments of the Rehabilitation Act create the supported employment initiative. The 1986 and 1990 amendments to the Developmental Disabilities Assistance and Bill of Rights Act clarify that the purpose of the law is to help individuals with disabilities become independent, productive, and integrated into society. The 1988 amendments to the Housing Act prohibit discrimination in housing, while the 1990 enactment of the Americans with Disabilities Act, P.L. 101-336, prohibits discrimination solely on the basis of disability in state and local government services, including transportation, privately owned public accommodations, communications, and employment.

As noted above, the equal access doctrine required that students with disabilities have equal access to different resources for different purposes. That doctrine was essentially established in 1975 when the Education of the Handicapped Act was amended by P.L. 94-142 and the Rehabilitation Act was amended by adding Section 504 (prohibiting discrimination). The doctrine, as established in 1975, assumed that, as a rule, individuals with disabilities would not be able to do what nondisabled people can do, even with support. Thus, although they should have equal access to different resources (to take into account their needs), they should have them in order to produce different results—that is, a life different from that of nondisabled individuals.

Today, in 1992, however, the equal access doctrine means something quite radically different. It means that individuals with disabilities should have equal access to different and the same resources for different and the same results. Thus, the doctrine, as amended by the laws cited above, assumes that individuals with disabilities will have the same or different kinds of life as nondisabled individuals, depending on the extent of their disabilities, the degree to which society accommodates to their disabilities, their choices, and the availability of support to meet their needs. To obtain these results, the doctrine assumes that equal access to the same resources—that is, to regular education services and to other public and private services and networks—will occur, with support. It also assumes that equal access to different resources—that is, special education, vocational rehabilitation, assistive technology, and special support systems—will occur, but for the purpose of enabling those with disabilities to have access to the "nondisabled" or "generic" world as well as to a world that is primarily disability-oriented.

Thus, federal law no longer assumes a limited life for individuals with disabilities—one limited because it is lived separate and apart from people without disabilities. Instead, it assumes that individuals with disabilities will have opportunities to live in the "regular" world and be educated in regular programs, work in regular jobs, live in regular housing, and otherwise be more like than different from nondisabled people.

FEDERAL LEGISLATION

Nothing is clearer in the IDEA than the intent of Congress that no child with a disability be excluded from school and that all involved agencies follow a policy of zero reject. Finding (as the courts did) that both total and functional exclusion existed [Sec. 1400(b)(3) and (4)] and concluding that it was in the national interest to provide programs to meet the needs of children with disabilities and thereby assure them equal protection of the law [Sec. 1400(b)(9)], Congress declared that the purpose of IDEA was to provide a free appropriate education to them [Sec. 1400(c)] and acted in numerous ways to implement the zero-reject policy.

Free Appropriate Public Education (FAPE)

By the 1975 amendment (P.L. 94-142), Congress required the states to provide full educational opportunities to all children with disabilities between the ages of three and eighteen ("ages-certain" requirements) by September 1, 1978 ("dates-certain" requirements) and to all children with disabilities between the ages of three and twenty-one by September 1, 1980.

There was, however, an exception. If a state law or practice or court order were inconsistent with the ages-certain and dates-certain requirements, the state was not required to follow those requirements. This provision recognized that the states themselves should have some autonomy to continue to educate certain age groups. In a very real sense, the exception paid deference to the tradition, engrained in some states' laws, of state and local autonomy over education. But the exception also was a political necessity: The act probably would not have passed or it would have been substantially weaker with such a provision in it.

Early Intervention and Special Education

Subsequent amendments expanded the age coverage. Under the 1983 amendments (P.L. 98-199), Congress emphasized the need for more early education. It authorized incentive grants to states for special education and related services to children with disabilities from birth to three years of age. It also expanded the early childhood state implementation grant program enabling states to receive grants to plan, develop, or implement a comprehensive system of services for children with disabilities from birth to five years.

By P.L. 99-457 (adding a new Part H), enacted in 1986, Congress extended the federal role in education of very young children. It did this by two separate additions to Part H: Title I (birth through age two) and Title II (ages three through five). (Title I is new law and is codified at 20 U.S.C. Sec. 1471 and following; its regulations are codified in 34 Code of Federal Regulations, Part 303. Title II amends previous law and is codified at 20 U.S.C. Sec. 1412 and following.)

As members of Congress made clear when they were introducing P.L. 99-457, the legislation is a "pro-family" bill. Thus, the focus of P.L. 99-457's Part H—infants and toddlers—is on the person with a disability and the person's family. This is very different from the other major provisions of IDEA—namely, those in Part B that provide for the free appropriate public education of children with disabilities—because Part B focuses on the person and then on the parent, not the family.

Moreover, Part H is motivated by concerns that are broader than those that persuaded Congress to enact Part B. For one thing, it is perfectly clear from the legislative history that Congress has been convinced that early intervention services are cost-effective. Similar evidence was simply not available when Congress enacted P.L. 94-142 and Part B.

In addition, Part H sets four goals that are different and more comprehensive than Part B, which deals only with free appropriate public education as a goal. The Part H goals are to develop the capacities of infants and toddlers, to reduce the costs of special education, to minimize the likelihood that people with disabilities will be institutionalized, and to enhance families' capacities for working with their children. Although human development and family/parent–child interactions are subsumed as goals of Part B, they are explicit goals of Part H. Moreover, the goals of preventing institutionalization and reducing special education costs are distinct to Part H. With these observations in mind, it is now appropriate to describe Part H.

With respect to Title I (birth through age two), it provided separate funding for the education of disabled infants and toddlers. Those infants and toddlers who qualify for the services must need early intervention because they either (a) experience developmental delays or (b) have diagnosed physical or mental conditions with a high probability of causing developmental delays. In addition, each state has the option of serving infants and toddlers who are "at-risk" for developmental delays. Developmental delays must be in the following areas of development: cognitive, physical, language and speech, psychosocial, or self-help. The states may otherwise define "developmental delay" but must include delays in those areas of development.

Under Part H, early intervention services are those that are designed to meet the infant's needs in any one or more of certain areas of development (physical, cognitive, language and speech, psychosocial, and self-help), comply with state standards, include at least ten different types of intervention, and are provided by qualified personnel. Also, early intervention services are those that are designed to meet the family's needs related to enhancing the child's development in the stated areas, are selected in collaboration with the parents, are provided under public supervision by qualified personnel, are provided in conformity with an individualized family service plan (IFSP), and are free unless the state establishes a sliding fee scale of payment.

The ten different types of intervention include family training, counseling, and home visits; special instruction; speech pathology and audiology; occupational therapy; physical therapy; psychological services; case management services; medical services only for diagnosis and evaluation; early identification, screening, and assessment services; and health services necessary to help the infant or toddler benefit from the other intervention services.

The regulations make it clear that professionals have new or expanded roles and responsibilities with respect to families. They are expected to consult and train parents, participate in the assessment of a family and the development of the IFSP, provide case management services, provide psychological and social work services, and offer special instruction to the child and information to the parents about special instruction. The regulations also say that the list of services is not exhaustive; other services, such as respite and other family support services, may be provided. In addition, parent-to-parent support personnel, not just professionals or paraprofessionals, may provide those services. Finally, services to families also may include family training, counseling, and home visits. In short, the regulations not only expand what professionals must offer but also who may offer it.

The personnel authorized to provide these services include those who have qualified as special educators, speech-language pathologists, audiologists, occupational therapists, physicians, physical therapists, psychologists, social workers, nurses, and nutritionists.

Each state that has not yet mandated early intervention or preschool special education as a matter of its own law has the option to participate in Part H (infants and toddlers, birth through age 2) and in the early childhood programs for children from ages three through five. As of March 1989, each state had elected the option of participating in Part H.

It is important to contrast the broad eligibility provisions of Part H with Part B (ages three through twenty-one). Under Part H, those infants and toddlers who have or may experience developmental delays or are at-risk for such delays are entitled to receive services. Each state may determine which children are "at-risk." The federal law does not define those children.

But, under Part B, only those children and youth who have disabilities that cause a need for special education are entitled to the law's benefits. This means, for example, that a student who has AIDS but who experiences no adverse effect in education because of the disability is not entitled to the IDEA. Very few students are in this category, but there are some.

Moreover, although Part B provides for services free of charge to parents, Part H allows the state and local agencies to establish a system of payments for early intervention services, including a schedule of sliding fees. Some services must be free; they include child-find, evaluation and assessment, case management, and certain administrative and coordinative functions. If state law, however, provides for free early intervention services, the state law prevails and a state may not use the federal law as permission to charge fees.

Title II of P.L. 99-457 relates to children ages three through five and essentially broadens the previous law relating to them, as enacted by the 1983 and 1975 amendments to IDEA. The 1983 amendment relating to children ages three through five authorized incentive grants to states for special education and related services for those children—but only for those children, not their families, and only on behalf of children who traditionally qualify as handicapped under the IDEA. The 1983 amendments also expanded the early childhood state implementation grant to enable states to plan and implement comprehensive systems of services for children birth through age five.

Transition Out of School

Also under the 1983 amendments, Congress paid special attention to a new problem—the transition from school to adulthood (also called "aging out"). First, it gave the secretary of education, who acts in special education matters through the assistant secretary, Office of Special Education and Rehabilitative Services (OSERS), and principally through the Office of Special Education Programs (OSEP), authority to enter into contracts with SEAs to develop and operate and to disseminate information concerning specially designed programs of postsecondary education [Sec. 1424(a)]. Second, it provided for secondary education and transitional services for disabled youth [Sec. 1425]. Third, it authorized the creation of a national clearinghouse on postsecondary education for the purpose of providing information about available services and programs in postsecondary education [Sec. 1433]. Finally, it authorized SEAs to make transition services available to deaf-blind children upon their becoming twenty-two years old [Sec. 1422].

The decision to emphasize transition and postsecondary educational programs is consistent with Congress's later decision in 1986 to amend the Rehabilitation Act to create a program of supported employment for people with severe disabilities. Supported work substantially changes the notion of vocational rehabilitation services. Traditionally, those services were targeted for people with mild to moderate disabilities, who, with short-term interventions (basically, evaluation and training), could return to work and not require much, if any, further vocational rehabilitation services. Under the supported work program, however, vocational rehabilitation services were focused on people with severe disabilities, who, with ongoing or continuous vocational rehabilitation services (as contrasted with short-term services), could work with support from a nondisabled worker or "job coach," in competitive employment.

The 1986 amendments to the Rehabilitation Act, which created supported employment programs, did not do away with the traditional vocational rehabilitation programs. Instead, they added new programs. And they were consistent with the 1983 amendments to IDEA, creating transition and postsecondary programs, in that they recognized the need for special education to concentrate on the future of students who first benefited from IDEA and who were leaving special education ("aging out" or "transitioning") and entering the world of work and adult services. By combining IDEA's focus on transition with the Rehabilitation Act's focus on supported employment, Congress attempted to ensure that special education would have lasting benefits for all students, especially those with severe disabilities.

Coverage: LEAs, IEUs, Residential Facilities, and Private Schools

Congress applied the full-service goal to public elementary and secondary LEAs and IEUs (intermediate educational units) [Sec. 1412], private schools [Secs. 1412 and 1413], and publicly operated residential facilities that provide elementary or secondary education [Sec. 1412]. By providing for such extensive coverage, Congress obviously intended to prevent "service gaps" or "cracks." It attempted to reach all children without regard to the nature of the educational system by which they are, might, or should be served. As noted in chapter 2, Congress was able to affect the LEAs, IEUs, and state residential facilities by requiring compliance with the requirements of the law as a condition for receiving funds and by applying Section 504 to them.

There are other reasons—besides closing the gaps or cracks—behind the coverage requirements. First, students with disabilities are citizens of the state; if the state receives federal funds, they should benefit, wherever they are served or live within the state. Otherwise, they are not treated as full citizens of the state. This concept of treatment of full citizens also has a strong equal protection flavor because it ensures equal treatment of comparable citizens (those with disabilities). Second, it allows advocates for children with disabilities to concentrate their efforts on a single state agency and state program—the SEA (state education agency) and the state school system, with its component local school district. (This desire for accountability is also part of the "single-agency responsibility" provisions described later in this section.)

Placement by Public Agencies. Congress distinguished between two types of private school placement. One type concerns children referred to or placed in private schools by public agencies. Each state's annual program plan contains policies and procedures to assure that, to the extent consistent with the number and location of disabled children in the state who are in private elementary and secondary schools, the plan will provide for their participation in the state program by furnishing them special education and related services [Sec. 1413].

There are additional requirements for children placed in private schools by public agencies. They must (1) be provided with special education and related services (2) in conformance with an individualized education program (3) at no cost to their parents if the public agency refers them to such schools or facilities as a means of carrying out requirements of the law [Sec. 1413]. Moreover, when the agency makes such a placement or referral, the state must have determined previously that the private school or facility meets the standards set by the state and that the child retains all rights under the law [Sec. 1413].

Placement by Parents. A second type of private school placement is one made by the child's parents. As a general rule, if a free appropriate public education is available to a child in a public agency but the parent chooses to place him or her in a private school, the agency is not required to pay for the education. The agency must, however, make services available to the child, as described previously, if he or she attends the private school. If the agency and the parents disagree about whether an appropriate program for the child is available or whether the agency is financially responsible for the private school fees, either may initiate a due process hearing. (Exceptions to the general rule about unilateral placement are discussed in chapter 7.)

Clearly, Congress intended for zero reject to apply to disabled children placed in private schools by their parents or by school authorities. Congress keeps pressure on the public sector to remain responsible for them, thus attempting to answer its findings that "because of the lack of adequate services within the public school system, families are often forced to find services outside the public school system, often at great distance from their residence and at their own expense" [Sec. 1400(b)(6)].

Finally, the secretary of education may bypass SEAs in providing special education to children attending private schools in states where there is a state constitutional prohibition against public-private sharing of educational services [Sec. 1413].

Rationale. The reasons for applying the Act to private schools are easy to understand. If an LEA places a child in a private school as its way of discharging its duties to the child under IDEA, the child's rights to a free appropriate education should follow him or her to the private placement because the child is a citizen of the state and entitled to benefit from IDEA in the same manner as any other citizen of the state; the place of education is irrelevant to the child's rights. Moreover, the LEA is not allowed to divest itself of its duties to the child by making a private school placement when it cannot discharge those duties by educating the child itself. Finally, because LEAs are not always able to provide an appropriate education to every child and enter into contracts with private schools to educate some of the children, the children in the private schools become the beneficiaries of the contract between the LEA and the private school. In that capacity, the children retain the rights they have with the LEA, and the LEA should not be able to deprive them of their rights by contract.

Direct Services by SEA

The IDEA [Sec. 1414(d)] provides that an SEA must use the federal funds otherwise available to an LEA to provide services directly to children with disabilities whenever it determines that an LEA is unable or unwilling to do so or to be consolidated with another LEA, or has students who can be served best in a state or regional center. The purpose of the direct services provision is to ensure that all eligible students in a state receive a free appropriate public education; it is another one of the "gap-closing" provisions of the law.

Although use of the direct services provision was before the Supreme Court in *Honig v. Doe*, a 1988 decision, the Court did not rule on it and instead left standing the court of appeals decision that ordered the SEA (California) to provide services directly to two students who had been suspended illegally from an LEA (San Francisco).

A similar result—court-ordered direct services—was reached in *Doe v. Rockingham County School Board* when a child had been suspended and received no hearing on his suspension and no services during the suspension, which was for twenty-nine days. The irreparable detriment (which the student experienced during the twenty-nine days) and the LEA's refusal to make a hearing available were decisive facts. Similarly, when an LEA has failed to comply with a decision by a hearing officer (see chapter 7 for a discussion of hearing officers and due process protections) for eighteen months and when the SEA's withholding of funds from the SEA has not produced LEA compliance with the decision for still another eighteen months, an SEA may be compelled to provide services directly, under the holding in *Wilson v. McDonald*. These cases suggest that advocates will succeed in seeking direct services if there is a long period of time of interrupted education, bad faith on the LEA's part (refusal to convene a hearing), or illegal action (suspending in violation of the IDEA).

Child Census

Each SEA and LEA must conduct an annual program to identify, locate, and evaluate all disabled children residing in their respective jurisdictions, regardless of the severity of their disabilities [Secs. 1412 and 1414]. Congress recognized that a zero-reject policy would be meaningless without a child identification program. It also realized that identification of disabled children was a necessary prerequisite to planning, programming, and appropriating for them to attend school.

In light of past school practices that excluded the most severely disabled children, it is significant that Congress specified that the programs must identify *all* children regardless of the severity of their disability. The requirement of a child census is consistent with Congress's findings that many children are totally excluded from schools and are denied "a successful educational experience" because their disabilities are undetected [Sec. 1400(b)(4) and (5)].

The purposes of the child census are to ensure that no children are denied a free appropriate education because they have not been found or located, to ensure cooperation between the educational agencies and others (such as health, mental health, developmental disabilities, social services, corrections, and even private agencies), and to enable the SEA and LEA to appropriate funds, plan and deliver programs, and be held accountable to all children with disabilities.

Service Priorities

Realizing that many excluded children are the most seriously disabled and that they usually do not receive an appropriate education, Congress required recipients to use federal aid for two service priorities [Secs. 1412 and 300.320-.324]. First in line are children receiving no education ("first priority" children). Next are children with the most severe disabilities within each disability group who are not receiving an adequate education ("second priority" children).

The policy was designed to overcome the total exclusion of some children [Sec. 1400 (b)(4)] and the inadequate education or functional exclusion of others [Sec. 1400(b)(3) and (5)] as a method of implementing a zero-reject policy [Sec. 1400(c)]. Apparently, Congress intended to make sure that funds would be distributed across the whole spectrum of disabling conditions and prevent them from being spent wholly on one class of severely impaired children (e.g., the seriously emotionally disturbed). There is a strong equal protection flavor in this approach.

In addition, Congress has emphasized transition services for deaf-blind children [Sec. 1422]. Congress obviously recognized that service priority requirements should have special attention when severely disabled youth are "aging out" of school and "aging in" with respect to adult services—i.e., when they are in "transition."

The purpose of the service priorities is to ensure that the children who are most likely not to be served because of the severe nature of their disabilities are, in fact, given a claim on federal funds so that they may be served. Considering that the schools historically had excluded students (total exclusion) or served only those with mild to moderate disabilities (partial exclusion), it makes sense for the IDEA to require federal funds to be spent first on unserved and then on harder-to-serve students.

Naturally, the service priorities have a strong equal protection flavor to them, and they clearly support the principle of zero reject. But they also raise the issue of competing equities—namely, to what extent some students (those with mild to moderate disabilities) should be disadvantaged (by having lower claims to federal dollars) in order to provide an advantage to other students (those with the most severe disabilities). Of course, the issue of competing equities is not new. All policy decisions, whether by Congress or by state legislatures, and all legal decisions by courts (resolving the complaints of some people against others) involve the balancing of competing claims.

Finally, the service priorities illustrate a familiar approach by Congress—which is often to prefer to fund programs for persons with severe disabilities if a choice must be made between funding programs for all people with disabilities or only those with severe disabilities. This approach exists, for example, in the Developmental Disabilities Assistance and Bill of Rights Act, in the 1986 amendments to the Rehabilitation Act (creating the supported work initiative), and in various programs under the Social Security Act (such as Medicaid and Medicare). This approach attacks a problem (here, the need to provide an appropriate education to all students with a disability) from the bottom (a "bottom-up" approach) rather than from the top (a "creaming" approach). The bottom-up approach focuses funds on those with the greatest disabilities; the creaming approach focuses funds on those who are the easiest to serve because they have the mildest disabilities.

Appropriate Education and Functional Exclusion

Congress answered the problem of functional exclusion by requiring SEAs and LEAs to provide an *appropriate* education [Sec. 1400(c) and Sec. 1412(1)]. It defined appropriateness in two ways.

First, appropriate is defined generally in terms of the procedure schools must use: (1) The child must be furnished with an individualized education program, (2) must be evaluated on a nondiscriminatory basis, (3) and is entitled to a due process hearing if the appropriateness of his or her education is in doubt; (4) the parents are entitled to be included in the development of their child's individualized education program; (5) the child is entitled to appropriately and adequately trained teachers, (6) has the right of access to his or her school records, (7) is entitled to a barrier-free school environment, (8) and may be included in preschool programs; and (9) the child's representatives (parents or others) are entitled to participate in and be given notice of school actions affecting special education programs and the child's own education. Although separately provided for by the IDEA, as a whole these requirements are intended to answer the problem of functional exclusion and to assure an appropriate education.

Second, Sections 300.4 and 300.300-.307 of the regulations defined *free appropriate education* to mean special education and related services that (1) are provided at public expense, under public supervision and direction, and without charge; (2) meet the standards of the SEA, including requirements of the IDEA; (3) include preschool, elementary, and secondary school education in the state involved; and (4) are provided in conformity with the child's individualized education program.

Chapter 5 discusses the details of appropriate education. The point here is that IDEA and Section 504 both attempt to prevent functional exclusion by requiring that the disabled child be given an education appropriate to his or her conditions and needs.

Hiring People with Disabilities

Congress pushed the zero-reject principle a step further than the courts did by requiring that a child's education be meaningful after he or she leaves school. SEAs and LEAs were charged with making positive efforts to hire and promote qualified disabled persons in programs receiving IDEA funds [Sec. 1405]. Thus, an SEA or LEA must take affirmative action on employment of people with disabilities in IDEA programs (such as hiring a blind teacher to teach disabled children or promoting an orthopedically impaired person to supervise special education programs funded under IDEA). Of course, the emphasis on transition in the 1983 amendments reflects Congress's concern with employment.

All of the education and training the schools provide is meaningless to students unless they have a realistic opportunity to make later use of it. Zero reject in special education should not be an empty promise. Equal protection should be meaningful to its intended beneficiaries. And, of course, economic benefits will accrue to the public if disabled individuals are hired. The employment provisions in Section 1405 dovetail with Sections 503 and 504 of the Rehabilitation Act [29 U.S.C. Sec. 706(7) and Sec. 794] to prohibit discrimination in employment.

Comprehensive System of Personnel Development

To provide a sufficient number of adequately trained teachers and related-services personnel to educate all students appropriately and to ensure that regular education faculty members in the schools are trained to accommodate students with disabilities in their programs (in the least restrictive environment), the IDEA requires SEAs and LEAs to have programs for personnel development [Secs. 1412 and 1431 through 1435]. Without sufficient adequately trained personnel, the zero-reject principle (as well as principles relating to appropriate education and least restrictive environments) could not be implemented.

Single-Agency Responsibility

Congress sought to make the zero-reject principle effective by providing for one, and *only one*, point of responsibility and accountability. It required a *single* state agency, the SEA, to be responsible for assuring the U.S. Department of Education that requirements of IDEA are carried out. In addition, all educational programs for disabled children within the state, including programs administered by *another* state or local agency (such as social services, mental health, mental retardation, human resources, public health, corrections, or juvenile services), were placed under the *general* supervision of persons responsible for special education programs in the SEA, must be monitored by the SEA, and must meet the SEA's educational standards [Sec. 1412(6)].

To buttress the single-agency device for zero reject, Congress enabled the SEA to preempt LEA programs [Sec. 1414(d)] and to require LEAs to consolidate their services [Sec. 1414(c)]. Section 1414(b) provides for a complaint procedure for local and state agencies. There is no doubt that these provisions were designed to close the service gaps and prevent the buck-passing and responsibility-shuffling that resulted in some children not being included in educational programs in the past.

As the states attempted to implement IDEA with the limited federal and state dollars (IDEA has never been funded by Congress at the full limit it authorizes—see chapter 10 for a description of the authorization of federal funds), they found that they were facing huge expenses. Not only did they increase their own appropriations, but so did LEAs. And still funds were not sufficient, particularly for people with severe disabilities.

A major funding stream, however, existed outside of IDEA: the Medicaid and Medicare programs created by the Social Security Act. Those programs provided federal funds to pay for some of the medical or medically related expenses of people with severe disabilities who usually are required to be poor to qualify for the medical assistance funds.

To tap into the Medicaid and Medicare funding streams, some states created programs that combined the special education personnel and funds under IDEA with the medical personnel and funds under the Medicaid and Medicare programs. By taking this approach, they could ensure enough funds in the aggregate to pay for the education and related services (such as physical therapy, occupational therapy, medical evaluations) required to provide an appropriate education to students with severe disabilities. In short, they sought to prevent either total exclusion or functional exclusion, either of which would violate the zero-reject principle.

The federal agency that administers Medicaid—the Health Care Financing Agency, Department of Health and Human Services—refused to reimburse Massachusetts for Medicaid dollars that it had spent in the jointly administered IDEA-Medicaid program of education for students with severe disabilities who lived in a Medicaid-approved facility (an intermediate care facility for the mentally retarded—ICF/MR). Massachusetts sued the federal government for reimbursement, and the Supreme Court, in *Bowen v. Massachusetts*, approved the use of the Medicaid funds for joint education of ICF/MR residents.

Shortly after that decision was rendered in 1988, Congress enacted the Medicare Catastrophic Coverage Act of 1988. This law prohibits Medicaid agencies from refusing to pay for medical services covered under a state's Medicaid or Medicare plans that are provided to children with disabilities, as long as the services are included in the students' individualized education programs (IEPs are discussed in chapter 5).

Under the 1988 amendments, Section 1903 of the Social Security Act [42 U.S. Code; Sec. 1396b] was changed by the addition of a new paragraph. That paragraph provides that nothing in the Medicare title of the Social Security Act shall be construed as prohibiting or restricting payment for medical assistance for covered services furnished to a handicapped child because those services are included in the child's IEP or are furnished to an infant or toddler as part of the IFSP.

The Congressional committee that sponsored this amendment has added clarifying language. The committee reported that the amendment clarifies that the federal Medicaid matching funds are available for the cost of health services, covered under a state's Medicaid plan, that are furnished to a child with a disability or to an infant or toddler under the IEP or IFSP even though those services are included in the IEP or IFSP. The committee added that, although the SEAs are financially responsible for educational services, the state Medicaid agencies, in the case of Medicaid-eligible handicapped children, remain responsible for the "related services" identified in the child's IEP or IFSP if they are covered under the state's Medicaid plan. These services can include speech pathology and audiology, psychological services, physical and occupational therapy, and medical counseling and services for diagnostic and evaluation purposes.

The effect of the *Bowen* case and the Medicaid Catastrophic Coverage Act is that a new funding stream for related services will exist for states that decide to combine educational programs (funded under the IDEA) with medical programs (funded under the Social Security Act's Medicaid or Medicare programs). This will relieve the pressure on the state's educational dollars but increase the pressure on its health-care dollars. In the case of students who have medical complications or are primarily in health-care delivery systems (such as those in ICFs/MR or in early childhood programs administered by departments of health), the prospects are good that they will receive jointly operated services. This will have the ultimate effect of ensuring no violation of the zero-reject rule by their total or functional exclusion from special education.

Use of Private Insurance; Free Education

One way in which the schools traditionally excluded students with disabilities was by charging them fees for services. The fees often were very high (because the services were expensive or because they were set high to discourage the students' enrollment). Therefore, IDEA implements the zero-reject rule by providing that education must be furnished free to the students and their parents. If an LEA charges any fees to all students, it may charge students with disabilities, too; uniformly assessed fees are permissible. But expenses for transportation may not be billed. In addition, parents who have insurance policies that reimburse for medically related services may not be required to make a claim on their insurers if the services are provided to comply with IDEA,[9] and states may not charge for the living expenses for students whom they place in public or private residential programs to comply with IDEA.[10]

Architectural Barriers

Physical barriers can cause some disabled children to be excluded from school (whether they are mobility impaired or not—e.g., blind or in wheelchairs; some children with mental retardation also have physical disabilities). Therefore, Congress has authorized the secretary of education to make grants to and enter into cooperative arrangements with SEAs to remove architectural barriers [Sec. 1406].

Section 504

Regulations implementing Section 504 make it clear that Section 504 applies to preschool, elementary, and secondary public education programs receiving any federal assistance. They also make it clear, especially in Section 104.33(a), that a zero-reject policy is required by the schools. Section 104.32 requires the schools to undertake a child identification program. Section 104.33(b) requires them to provide an appropriate education to each disabled person who is a legal resident of the recipient's jurisdiction, regardless of the nature or severity of the person's disability. Section 104.33(c) ensures that the program will be without cost to the child's family.

As pointed out in chapter 2, Section 504 and its implementing regulations differ in important respects from IDEA. There are other differences related to the zero-reject principle.

Section 504 applies to public schools not only as providers of educational services [Subpart D of the regulations] but also as providers of health, welfare, and social services [Subpart F], and as employers [Subpart B]. It applies to school facilities as well, requiring them to be accessible to disabled persons [Subpart C]; the IDEA authorizes grants of federal funds to SEAs and LEAs to enable them to comply with federal architectural-barriers legislation [Sec. 1406]. Under the Section 504 regulations, as of 1977 all new school construction had to be barrier-free [Sec. 104.23] and all other programs had to be made accessible within three years [Sec. 104.22].

Section 104.22 of the regulations provides that SEAs or LEAs do not have to make each existing school accessible to students with disabilities if programs for them are "on the whole" accessible. Schools may redesign equipment, reassign classes or other services from nonaccessible to accessible buildings, make aids available to students, or provide services at other sites, including the students' homes. Each building in a school district need not be completely accessible, but the district may not make only one facility or part of a facility accessible if the result is to segregate students with disabilities from their nondisabled peers. In choosing between alternative acceptable methods of accessibility, an LEA or SEA must give priority to those that offer programs in the most integrated settings appropriate for the students with disabilities (see chapter 6 for a discussion of the principle of integration and least restrictive environments).

Subpart D also sets forth requirements for nondiscrimination in preschool, elementary, secondary, and adult education programs, including secondary vocational education programs. "Adult education" refers to educational programs and activities for adults operated by elementary and secondary schools. The provisions of Subpart D apply to both public and private state and local education agencies that are federally assisted.

The basic requirements of Section 504's regulations, which parallel the cases and IDEA, are that disabled persons, regardless of the nature or severity of their disability, must be furnished a free appropriate public education, and educational agencies must undertake to identify and locate all of them. These requirements are designed to ensure that no child is excluded from school on the basis of a disability. Thus, a funding recipient that operates a public school system must either educate disabled children in its regular program or provide them with an appropriate alternative education at public expense.

CASE LAW

It was entirely predictable when the IDEA was enacted that its efforts to prevent the absolute exclusion of disabled children from a free appropriate education would not be entirely successful. By the same token, it was predictable that courts would be called upon to interpret the IDEA and its regulations in cases in which school districts attempted to exclude disabled children completely or subject them to conditions that the IDEA was intended to correct. Yet, the scope of the courts' involvement is surprising, and the issues they have been obliged to resolve are manifold and sophisticated.

Expulsion

The most pressing issue early on was whether school districts may expel disabled children or whether the IDEA prevents them from doing so because expulsion is a denial of special education. The courts seemed to speak with a unanimous voice: The IDEA prevents a school district from expelling a disabled child if the behavior that triggered the expulsion proceedings is related to the child's disability. Instead of expelling the student, a school agency may change his or her placement from a less to a more restrictive one—but only after notifying the parents and giving them an opportunity to protest through due process proceedings, and only after reevaluating the child and preparing a new IEP for him or her. Short-term suspension is allowed. So too is expulsion when the child's behavior is not causally related to the disability.

This result was confirmed by the Supreme Court in *Honig v. Doe*, a 1988 decision that followed the language of the IDEA and the line of reasoning established earlier by lower courts. In *Honig*, the Court ruled that the "stay-put" provisions of the IDEA (see chapter 6— the stay-put provisions prohibit an LEA from moving a student from the current placement during the time of a dispute before a hearing officer or court concerning the student's rights under the IDEA) prohibit school authorities from unilaterally excluding disabled children from the classroom or appropriate programs because of dangerous or disruptive conduct that grows out of their disabilities, at least while the dispute is under way. The Court found that the IDEA is clear and unequivocal in its language that the student must "stay put." Moreover, it found that Congress intended to prevent school authorities from making unilateral changes of placement.

Of course, if parents and school authorities agree on a change while a dispute is being contested, the student's placement may be changed. The effect of this part of the Court's decision was to affirm the stay-put rule and prevent unilateral expulsions if the behavior grows out of the student's disability.

Yet the Court did not leave the LEA defenseless. It said that school authorities may use normal, nonplacement changing procedures (including temporary suspensions of up to ten days) if a student poses an immediate threat to the safety of others. It also said that the IDEA [Sec. 1415(e)(2)] allows school authorities to file a lawsuit for "appropriate" relief if the parents and the school authorities cannot agree on an interim placement. In such a suit for relief, the IDEA creates a presumption in favor of the student's present placement. But the presumption can be overcome if the student's present placement and behavior are substantially likely to result in an injury to self or to others.

The effect of the *Honig* decision is difficult to predict, especially so soon after it was rendered. Some effects seem likely, however. First, the case may encourage schools to seek injunctive relief—an order that the student's placement be changed, even during hearings on the dispute. Before the *Honig* decision it was not entirely clear whether LEAs could do this. Now that it is clear, they may well go to court for relief. Second, given the ten-day rule (no suspensions for more than ten days), the case may prevent not just a simple expulsion of more than ten days but also "serial" or "tacking-on" expulsions of fewer than ten days that, in the aggregate, amount to more than ten days.

Third, the case may have the effect of encouraging schools to find ways to intervene to prevent student dangerousness other than expelling a student. By putting pressure on schools to intervene during the stay-put period, the case may create both good and bad results, depending on the type of intervention. For example, some school authorities may seek to prevent dangerous conduct by positive interventions such as increased rewards for good behavior. Or they may resort to aversive or negative interventions such as corporal punishment, physical restraint, in-school suspensions by means of time out, or the use of noxious substances. Special educators, behavioral and other psychologists, lawyers, ethicists, and families are engaged in heated debate concerning the use of these aversive interventions. It is not settled law that aversive interventions—particularly when used to prevent dangerous behavior—are illegal. There are strong arguments that they are or should be illegal, but no court had prohibited them under the IDEA and one federal district court has held that time-out does not violate the IDEA.

Finally, the *Honig* case may encourage school authorities to prosecute students for dangerous behavior. The LEAs have resorted to the criminal process to handle disruptive or dangerous students and may try to do so again, when faced with *Honig*'s confirmation of the stay-put rule and the difficulty and expense of seeking an injunction to get the student's placement changed. Whether the courts would see that use of the criminal process as an attempt to escape the stay-put rule, and thus a violation of the IDEA, is unknown.

Honig dealt only with use of the stay-put provision and expulsion of students with disabilities. It did not address the expulsion issue in its broader sense—whether any expulsion is permissible under the IDEA. As noted, a long line of cases does establish the following rule: Students with disabilities may not be expelled if the cause of their behavior is their disability.

S-1 v. Turlington was the leading case on expulsion. Seven retarded students were expelled from high school early in the 1977–78 school year and for the entire 1978–79 school year because of alleged misconduct. Two other disabled children, not under expulsion orders, contended that they had not been properly evaluated and placed. All sought due process hearings, alleging that their retardation was the cause of their disorderliness and that the IDEA prohibits their expulsion, even for disciplinary reasons. The schools refused to give them any hearings, contending that the students lost their right to a free appropriate public education and hearing opportunities under the IDEA when they were expelled because of their misconduct, that their misconduct was not related to their disability, that only if they had been classified as "seriously emotionally disturbed" would their conduct have related to their expulsion, and that disciplinary procedures are independent of and should not be limited by the IDEA.

The court rejected the schools' argument that disciplinary procedures are totally independent of and may supersede the rights granted under the IDEA. It stated that only specialists, not school boards, are competent to determine the relationship between behavior and disability. And it agreed with the holding of *Stuart v. Nappi* that expulsion is a change in placement within the meaning of the IDEA. Cases reaching the same result include *Doe v. Koger, Stanley v. School Administration Unit, Adams Central School District v. Deist,* and *Kaelin v. Grubbs*, holding that expulsion is a change of placement. A student may be suspended temporarily without using IDEA procedures and may be expelled if no causal relationship exists between the student's behavior and the disability and if the school follows IDEA procedures.

Stuart v. Nappi, first of the expulsion cases, held that a school may not expel a disabled child, only change the placement pursuant to parental notice and IEP conference provisions of the IDEA if the disability is causally related to the behavior for which the school seeks to expel the student. Similarly, *Blue v. New Haven Board of Education* cast doubt on the legality of suspensions that are for more than ten days and found that homebound instruction or private school placement violates the least restrictive educational placement rule. *Howard S. v. Friendswood Independent School District* had a similar result.

But short-term removal seems permissible, according to *City of Peoria Board of Education v. Illinois State Board of Education*, which held that a five-day suspension of a disabled child is not an expulsion, a change of placement, or a termination of services under the IDEA. Likewise, in *Mrs. A.J. v. Special School District No. 1*, the federal district court held that a student who had not been formally classified as disabled but who was simply suspected of being disabled was not entitled to additional hearing procedures (other than those provided all students under Minnesota law) before being suspended for fifteen days. In a footnote, the court said that the temporary disciplinary measure of suspension does not change or alter a student's educational placement and therefore apparently is not prohibited by the IDEA, citing *Stuart v. Nappi*.

It is likely that causality will be difficult to disprove (i.e., there will be a presumption that causality exists) in cases involving seriously emotionally disturbed children, learning disabled children, and children with mild disabilities. This is so because in those cases the definition of the disability or a fair view of its characteristics will tend to support a finding of causality. In other cases, however, the nature of the disability most likely will not justify a presumption in fact that there is causality. Motor, hearing, speech, or vision impairments, for example, do not usually give rise to maladaptive or other troublesome behavior.

Students who physically threaten other students or staff at a school, have attacked and threatened to kill them, damage property, and are disruptive may be removed from their present placement and put into a more restrictive one (from special education classroom placement to homebound placement) while a due process hearing is being conducted on the student's proposed new placement (*Township High School District Board of Education v. Kurtz-Imig, Texas City I.S.D. v. Jarstad,* and *Binghampton City School District v. Borgna)* or even before a complaint and request for a hearing are filed (*Prince William County School Board v. Wills,* and *Stafford County School Board v. Farley).* Clearly, some courts are using the *Honig* exception (a school may seek relief from the stay-put rule in appropriate cases) in order to maintain order and safety in schools but also are holding that total expulsion is not permitted and the student's services must be continued.

What if a school district places one special education student in harm's way by putting him in a program with other special education students who are dangerous to him? Is the district liable to the endangered student? Ordinarily, a school does not have a duty to protect any student from harm by other students since there is no general duty on any governmental agency to protect its clients from harm [*DeShaney v. Winnebago County Department of Social Services*, 489 U.S. 189 (1989)]. But where the school takes the affirmative action of placing one student in danger by requiring him to be educated in a setting with other, dangerous students, then the school will be liable to the student who suffers harm from those other students (*Stauffer v. Orangeville School District*).

Educability

Another important issue involves the expense of residential placement for a disabled child for whom residential or private school education is appropriate. In seeking to avoid the full expense of residential placement, school districts generally have been unsuccessful. But in challenging their duty to pay, school districts have raised a troublesome issue: Are any children totally ineducable and therefore not entitled to protection of the IDEA? Until 1988, the courts were reluctant to hold that there is a child who cannot learn anything and therefore is not protected by the Act. That is, until *Levine v. New Jersey* and *Matthews v. Campbell* first put the question up for debate.

In *Levine v. New Jersey*, the parents of severely retarded children challenged New Jersey's practice of charging parents for residential care provided for their children. The New Jersey Supreme Court held that the state constitutional mandate for a free public education does not apply to mentally disabled children who are so severely impaired that they are unable to absorb or benefit from education. The court also found that the residential care such children require for day-to-day well-being does not qualify as education. The court based its interpretation on a finding that the "thorough and efficient" education clause of the state constitution was intended to provide children with an education that will prepare them to function politically, economically, and socially in a democratic society. Because profoundly impaired children will never be able to exercise that franchise and vote intelligently, they are not included within the constitutional guarantee of education.

This interpretation of "education" casts doubt on the purposes of special education, which are not always to make all students capable enough to vote. More than that, it suggests that some children do not qualify for special education under federal or state law because they cannot attain the competence to vote. Such children could be regarded as ineducable in the important sense of not qualifying for special education benefits under the law.

A 1988 decision by a federal district court in New Hampshire, in *Timothy W. v. Rochester School District*, reached the conclusion—for the first time on the merits of a case—that if a child is unable to benefit from special education, he therefore has no right to be included in schooling or to any of the benefits of the IDEA.

In *Timothy W.*, the court reviewed conflicting testimony concerning a 13-year-old boy. According to the testimony accepted by the court, he is blind and deaf, has cerebral palsy, is spastic and subject to frequent convulsions, lacks carotid tissue, is profoundly retarded, has no communication skills, operates "at the brainstem level," has acquired the highest degree of reflex behavior (some ability to respond to external stimuli—light and noise) but has made no progress in about a year. Further, he seems to be regressing, has not achieved a level of response to stimuli beyond his original baseline (first measured response), engages in only passive and nonvolitional activities, must have his hands and feet completely manipulated in order to move them, and, for these reasons, is "not capable of benefiting from special education" at the present.

Given these facts, the legal issue for the court was whether the student is entitled to benefits and rights under IDEA. The court engaged in curious reasoning to reach the result that he is not. Although it quoted the IDEA's purpose [Sec. 1400—to ensure that *all* children with disabilities have a free appropriate public education] and the eligibility requirements for the states' receipt of federal funds [Sec. 1414(a)—to ensure that "all handicapped children residing in the state, regardless of the severity of their handicap, and who are in need of special education and related services" are identified and evaluated for special education], it nonetheless disregarded the clear and absolute language of the IDEA and instead relied on the Supreme Court's decision in *Board v. Rowley.*

The district court stated that the Supreme Court said that the IDEA's purpose is to promote the education of children who (according to the district court) "otherwise would be glossed over in the scheme of public education, as a result of their inability to attend 'regular classroom' instruction due to the nature of their handicap." The district court quoted a footnote in *Rowley* relating to the effect of the *PARC* and *Mills* cases on Congress's intent: According to the Supreme Court's footnote, *PARC* holds that the school systems are to provide "access to a free public program of education and training appropriate to (the student's) learning capabilities." The district court also cited with approval the Supreme Court's *Rowley* language that the term *free appropriate public education* means "educational instruction specially designed to meet the unique needs of the handicapped child, supported by such services as are necessary to permit the child to 'benefit' from the instruction."

On the basis of these statements in *Rowley*—which seem to some to deal only with the standards for the type of services to be provided and not to be justifications for the exclusion of any child—the district court said:

> It logically follows that a handicapped child who cannot "benefit" from special education, or who does not have learning capacity (*Mills*, 334 F. Supp. at 1258), was not intended to receive education under the (EHA). Surely, Congress would not legislate futility.

Holding that in "rare" cases a child is not able to benefit, the district court interpreted the IDEA as allowing the exclusion of some children. But it did require that the child be subjected to "continuous, but periodic evaluations, intended to identify any development which illustrates a capability to benefit from special education."

In holding that a certain child is ineducable, the court attacked the underlying premise of *PARC*. In *PARC*, the federal district court found that all children are educable and that there is therefore no reason to exclude any of them from an educational system. If, however, it appears that some children are not educable, there would be no reason to include them in an educational system. The system would be asked to do that which it cannot do (by definition, the children are not able to benefit from the system's efforts), and no purpose would be served in including them in the system. Indeed, their inclusion would cause an unjustifiable expense to the educational system. Public policy would justify their exclusion from that system, then, on two grounds: (1) The system cannot benefit them, and (2) the expenditure of funds cannot be defended.

The court of appeals reversed the district court in *Timothy W.* and held that IDEA was enacted to ensure that all children with disabilities are provided an appropriate public education. Indeed, "not only are severely handicapped children not excluded from the Act, but the most severely handicapped are actually given priority under the Act." In short, the court of appeals affirmed the zero-reject principle of the Act. Moreover, there is no prerequisite in the Act that the student be able to benefit. Instead, the Act speaks about the state's responsibility to the child.

As the court noted, "The language of the Act in its entirety makes clear that a 'zero-reject' policy is at the core of the Act, and that no child, regardless of the severity of his or her handicap, is to ever again be subjected to the deplorable state of affairs which existed at the time of the Act's passage, in which millions of handicapped children received inadequate education or none at all. In summary, the Act mandates an appropriate public education for all handicapped children, regardless of the level of achievement that such children might attain."

The court cited the congressional history to support its contention that the Act is intended to benefit all disabled children, "without exception," and that an "educational benefit was neither guaranteed nor required as a prerequisite for a child to receive such an education."

Moreover, the court noted that Congress has amended the Act four times since it was enacted in 1975 and that Congress not only has "repeatedly reaffirmed the original intent of the Act—to educate all handicapped children, regardless of the severity of their handicap, and to give priority attention to the most severely handicapped—but it has in fact expanded the provisions covering the most severely handicapped."

Next, the court noted that Congress relied on the *PARC* and *Mills* cases when enacting the Act; both cases establish a zero-reject principle. Moreover, "the courts have continued to embrace the principle that all handicapped children are entitled to a public education, and have consistently interpreted the Act as embodying this principle." It noted that the trial court's reliance on *dicta* in several cases involving educability was "misfounded," since those cases did not hold that the Act permits a school to exclude a child whom it regards as ineducable.

And, the court observed, the courts have construed "education" in a very broad way, so that the trial court's conclusion that "education must be measured by the acquirement of traditional 'cognitive skills' has no basis whatsover in the 14 years of case law since the passage of the Act. All other courts have consistently held that education under the Act encompasses a wide spectrum of training, and that for the severely handicapped it may include the most elemental of life skills."

Accordingly, the court found that the district court had misconstrued the *Rowley* decision. That decision, the court held, focused on the level of services and the quality of programs that a state must provide, not the criteria for access to those programs. The Supreme Court's use of "benefit" in *Rowley* was a "substantive limitation placed on the state's choice of an educational program; it was not a license for the state to exclude certain handicapped children." And the Supreme Court even explicitly acknowledged the congressional intent to ensure public education to all disabled children without regard to the level of achievement that they might attain, since the Supreme Court said that the Act's intent was to open the doors and not guarantee any particular level of education once they are open.

Finally, the court of appeals relied on the *Honig* case, in which the Supreme Court ruled that school districts may not exclude dangerous children from schooling altogether.

The *Honig* decision from the Supreme Court relied on the language and legislative history of the Act, and the court of appeals did likewise in *Timothy W.,* to reach the result that the school must provide special education to the student.

In language that is destined to be litigated again and again, the court of appeals also seems to have established a duty on schools to use state-of-the-art procedures for educating children with severe disabilities:

> The law explicitly recognizes that education for the severely handicapped is to be broadly defined, to include not only traditional academic skills, but also basic functional life skills, and that educational methodologies in these areas are not static, but are constantly evolving and improving. It is the school district's responsibility to avail itself of these new approaches in providing an education program geared to each child's individual needs. The only question for the school district to determine, in conjunction with the child's parents, is what constitutes an appropriate individualized education program (IEP) for the handicapped child.

The problems with concluding that some children are not educable are manifold. First, no conclusive research data, to date, justify that conclusion; indeed, there is strong debate on both sides of the educability issue. A conclusion that some children are not educable, then, seems scientifically debatable. Second, there is the problem of where to draw the line. Once a child is found not educable, the tendency may be to open up the class of ineducable children so as to include some children who are simply difficult or expensive to educate but who can be educated or benefit from training. Third, the special education profession would be relieved of the pressure to find ways to educate the more profoundly disabled children. Lacking an incentive to find ways to train them, the profession may not try to find any ways. A result might be that development of new knowledge that could benefit some children would be stifled.

Notice that the debate about educability and the problems with expulsion are related. Both seek to define who is disabled for the purpose of special education. If a school may expel a child who is receiving special education because the child's behavior was not caused by the disability, it is no longer responsible for the child. In a very real sense—i.e., in the sense of being entitled to special education—the child is not "disabled." Likewise, if a school may find as a matter of fact that a certain child (or group of children) is ineducable, it too may argue that it is no longer responsible for the child (or group), since the IDEA is intended to benefit only those who are capable of learning. Again, children who are incapable of learning are not "disabled" in the sense of being entitled to special education. Thus, some educators and school systems are attempting to limit the meaning of *disabled* by excluding children who violate certain rules and children who are ineducable and by creating disincentives to classification as "disabled."

Another, similar effort is underway to limit the meaning of *disability* by making it more difficult to classify certain "borderline" children as entitled to special education under federal law. The effort to tighten up on classification takes several forms. Some states are redefining *learning disabled* and *mildly retarded*. Likewise, some are creating new procedural hurdles that schools and parents must leap before a child may be classified (e.g., "preassessment" before the child is referred for IDEA nondiscriminatory evaluation).

Students with AIDS

As the nation faced the grim prospects that AIDS would become a widespread disease, the schools faced three issues: first, whether students with AIDS are entitled to special education as disabled or to the protection of the nondiscrimination statute [Sec. 504]; second, whether to exclude students with AIDS; and, third, if not, where to educate them.

As you consider these issues, recall that in chapter 2 you encountered the argument that all educational issues are basically social policy issues. You faced that argument in the discussion of *Brown*, the school desegregation case, and you met it again in this chapter in discussions of how the courts wrestled with the problems of expulsion/suspension and educability. Now you see it again in the ways in which the AIDS issue is answered in the context of special education and nondiscrimination law.

The First Issue: Is a Person with AIDS "Disabled"?   The first question was whether students with AIDS are entitled to special education under IDEA as "disabled" or to nondiscrimination in education under Section 504 (see chapter 2 for a discussion of Section 504). The Supreme Court seems to have answered that question, with the result that students with AIDS are entitled to IDEA and Section 504 protection.

In *Board v. Arline*, a 1987 decision, the Court ruled that a person with a contagious disease (tuberculosis) is disabled under the meaning of Section 504. The Court relied on the intent of Congress to cover people with contagious diseases under the protection of Section 504, the regulations issued by the Department of Health and Human Services to implement Section 504, expert testimony that Arline (a public school teacher) has a significant physical impairment and a record of such an impairment (having been hospitalized for TB treatment), and the clear intent of Section 504 to prohibit discrimination based on the effects that Arline's disability may have on others (such as the effects generated by fear alone). It held, accordingly, that Arline is disabled, but it did not hold that she is "otherwise qualified" to be a teacher. That issue remained unsettled by the case and is being retried by the lower courts.

The disability community, school authorities, and public authorities generally had looked to the *Arline* case to settle, once and for all, whether a person with AIDS is disabled under Section 504, and therefore entitled not only to protection from discrimination but also to special education under IDEA if the disability causes the student to need special education. Knowing that the *Arline* case was to be the harbinger of law involving AIDS-affected people, the Court said in a footnote, "This case does not present, and therefore we do not reach, the questions whether a carrier of a contagious disease such as AIDS could be considered to have a physical impairment, or whether such a person could be considered, solely on the basis of contagiousness, a handicapped person as defined by (Sec. 504)."

Notwithstanding this disclaimer, many people have concluded that the *Arline* case does compel the result that some, if not all, people with AIDS are protected under Section 504 and, if they are students, under the IDEA. This conclusion rests on the nature of AIDS and on the similarities between TB and AIDS—disease coupled with contagiousness.

The Nature and Effects of AIDS.   AIDS is caused by a retrovirus now commonly called the human immunodeficiency virus (HIV). Physicians (to whose expert judgment the courts must defer, as long as that judgment is reasonable and professionally defensible, said the Supreme Court in *Arline, Davis,* and *Youngberg v. Romeo*) use three categories to classify the nature and effect of HIV infection.

1. An infected person is diagnosed as having full-blown AIDS if he or she manifests one of the "opportunistic infections" listed by the National Center for Disease Control. These infections signal that the retrovirus has seriously damaged the person's immunological capability.
2. Another person may manifest lesser symptoms collectively referred to as AIDS-related complex (ARC), ranging from swollen lymph nodes and simple fever or lethargy to more serious neurological disorders.
3. Still another person, typical of the vast majority of people who have been infected with the virus, is not presently ill with AIDS or ARC and is asymptomatic. In such a person, the virus cannot be routinely isolated, but the fact that it is present can be inferred from the presence of antibodies stimulated by the virus. Prevailing medical opinion is that these "seropositive" people have been infected with the virus at one time, are presumed to have the virus dormant in their systems, and certainly are presumed to be able to transmit the virus to others.

The modes of transmission are limited and, by and large, include sexual intimacy involving the exchange of bodily fluids, transmission of blood via shared needles among intravenous drug users, or transmission of blood that is contaminated (as by way of blood infusions after surgery). The overwhelming evidence is that the AIDS virus is not transmitted by casual contacts.

Section 504 and AIDS.   It is beyond doubt that people with full-blown AIDS and with ARC are disabled for the purposes of Section 504. Whether a carrier (a seropositive person) also is "disabled" under Section 504 was not addressed by the Supreme Court in *Arline*.

Indeed, the Court's footnote, quoted previously, is precise proof that the Court avoided deciding about the application of Section 504 to seropositive people.

Section 504 defines a person to be disabled who has a mental or physical disability that substantially limits one or more of the person's major life activities, has a record of that impairment, or is regarded as having that impairment. Clearly, people with full-blown AIDS, ARC, and seropositive diagnoses are covered by Section 504 as having a disability or as being regarded as having such a disability. Whether those who are seropositive also are covered as having a record of such a disability is not as clear. But a person with full-blown AIDS or ARC clearly is covered under that standard; the person has a record of a disability.

Many lower courts have concluded that people who test seropositive and are carriers are covered by Section 504. (The American Bar Association's publication, *Legal, Medical, and Governmental Perspectives on AIDS as a Disability, 1987*, catalogs and analyzes those decisions.) The same result seems to apply in the few cases involving AIDS-affected students and the IDEA.

The Second Issue: May an AIDS-Affected Person be Excluded?

The Courts and AIDS. The New Jersey Supreme Court, in *Board of Education of City of Plainfield v. Cooperman*, decided in 1987, approved regulations of the state commissioners of education and health that determine when children with AIDS may be excluded from public schools. The regulations provide that students with full-blown AIDS, ARC, or seropositive diagnoses will be admitted into regular school unless they are not toilet-trained, are unable to control their drooling, or are unusually physically aggressive toward other students. A panel of medical experts must review all decisions in which an LEA decides to exclude a child from school on the basis of AIDS. The LEA bears the burden of proving that the child meets the criteria for exclusion. There must be a full hearing before the LEA and medical panel, with a right to appeal to the state commissioner of education.

Other courts have followed the principles approved by the New Jersey Supreme Court. That is, there is a presumption in favor of inclusion and against exclusion (a principle of zero reject), medical judgment is controlling as long as it is reasonable, and individualized determinations—on each student's case, not all of the "AIDS kids" as a group—must be made.

New York City school authorities adopted a policy that children with AIDS would not be automatically excluded from schools but, rather, reviewed on a case-by-case basis to determine if their health and development would permit them to attend school in an "unrestricted setting." A panel of medical experts was charged with making those determinations.

When a child who was diagnosed as having or suspected as having AIDS and who had remained well for several years was allowed by the medical panel and school commissioner to enter a neighborhood school, the local school board sued to overturn the commissioner's decision. The state court, in *District 27 Community School Board (Application of) v. Board of Education of New York City*, ruled that the child should be admitted and that the student is protected by Section 504. Because the student did not need special education, however, the court did not have to decide whether the IDEA applied.

The case-by-case, individualized decision making that characterizes the New Jersey and New York approaches is followed in other states as well. For example, a federal district court in Oklahoma overturned the SEA's attempt to implement a regulation that no child with AIDS, and certainly not any individual child whose rights to attend school have been determined to be valid by the LEA, may be permitted in the state's schools.[11]

IDEA and AIDS. The rights of the child to special education do not automatically arise upon the finding that the child has AIDS. That was the decision in the New York case and in an Illinois case as well.[12] Both courts made it clear that the student with AIDS, although protected by Section 504, does not automatically qualify for special education and IDEA protection. Unless the student's condition requires special education [Sec. 1401(a)] or adversely affects his or her educational performance, the child does not meet the standard for being a "health-impaired" child [Sec. 300.5(b) of the regulations] and the child is not entitled to IDEA rights. To meet these standards, the Illinois court held, there must be evidence of limited strength, vitality, or alertness because of chronic or acute health problems; these limited conditions must adversely affect the student's educational performance; and the child must require special education or related services.

The Third Issue: Where Must an AIDS-Affected Student Be Educated? Once a student meets the test of needing special education or related services, the issue shifts from whether the child qualifies under the IDEA to what services the child is entitled to under the IDEA.

Thomas v. Atascadero USD, a 1987 decision of a federal court in California, prohibited the LEA from excluding a student with AIDS who has bitten a classmate unless he has received an opportunity to protest his exclusion. The case did not determine that the student is disabled under the IDEA but, rather, that he is disabled under Section 504. Because there was no evidence that he posed a "significant risk of harm to his kindergarten classmates or teachers" and because the LEA failed to meet its burden to show that he is not "otherwise qualified" to attend a regular-school kindergarten class, the court ordered that he be retained in that class.

Although the decision did not involve an interpretation of the IDEA, it may be followed by courts applying the IDEA. This is because the regulations and burden of proof under Section 504 are substantially the same as under the IDEA. Thus, placement in the regular class, unless there is proof of dangerousness, is presumed to be correct.

But where the student's behavior or condition is or can be dangerous to others, an LEA is permitted to exclude the student from the otherwise appropriate placement. A federal district court, in *Martinez v. School Board of Hillsborough County, Florida*, held that a student who is incontinent and has been observed drooling and sucking her thumb continually, and who has a diagnosis of "trainable mental retardation," should not be allowed to be in the TMR classroom. This is because those behaviors increase the risk of AIDS transmittal by the exchange of bodily fluids from the student to others. Instead, the student should be provided homebound instruction. Permanent and total exclusion is not allowed.

Conclusion and Rationale.   The AIDS cases to date clearly demonstrate that there must be individualized determinations (not a "meat-ax" approach that covers all students or persons affected by an AIDS condition); there must be a basis in the public health interests for exclusion (there must be a close connection between the child's condition and behavior, on the one hand, and the safety of students and teachers, on the other); and the exclusion must rest on defensible and reasonable medical testimony. These results were obtained for several reasons:

1. People with AIDS are considered to be disabled under Section 504 and may be considered disabled under the IDEA if the disability causes them to need special education or related services.
2. The zero-reject principle and the equal protection doctrine prohibit discrimination and exclusion, as long as the person is found to be handicapped under Section 504 or the IDEA.
3. The doctrine of the least restrictive alternative/environment (see chapter 6) creates a presumption that those with AIDS should be educated in the regular programs. The presumption may be overcome when dangerousness to others is demonstrated, but the LEA has the burden of proof in seeking to overcome the presumption.
4. The due process clause of the Fourteenth Amendment (see chapter 7) requires not only individualized determinations but also opportunities for the student to protest any planned exclusion; and the regulations implementing Section 504, as well as the IDEA and its regulations, codify the principle of due process and procedural protections.
5. The public's fear—"fear itself"—does not justify exclusion of the student any more than fear justified an exclusionary zoning ordinance that prohibited group homes for people with mental retardation *(City of Cleburne v. Cleburne Living Center, Inc.)* or permitted a person who is not dangerous to himself or others to be incarcerated in a mental hospital involuntarily *(O'Connor v. Donaldson).*
6. Education is an especially valuable public service, and access to it should not be denied except for the most serious of reasons *(Brown v. Board of Education* and *Plyer v. Doe).*
7. Exclusion, coupled with identification of the student as having an AIDS condition, creates special stigma and can, in the words of the Supreme Court in *Plyer v. Doe,* cause "lifetime hardships on a discrete class of children not accountable for their disabling status."
8. Homebound or hospital-based special education is an appropriate alternative to total exclusion for the student whose dangerousness has been proved and for whom the presumption of inclusion in regular programs or in nonspecial classes has been overcome.

Section 504's Requirements: Reasonableness and Cost

Reasonableness.   With respect to the reasonableness issue, the U.S. Supreme Court has made it clear in *Davis* that Section 504 is a nondiscrimination statute, not an affirmative action one—i.e., it addresses discrimination and prohibits it so that people with disabilities will have opportunities comparable to the opportunities of people without disabilities.

In this respect it differs from an affirmative action statute, which typically requires special accommodations, over and above those made under equal opportunity approaches, for people with disabilities.

Thus, in *Davis*, the Supreme Court held that the community college was not required to make substantial modifications in its nursing curriculum to accommodate as a student a licensed practical nurse who sought admission to the nursing program and who was severely hearing impaired. The Court noted that such extraordinary modifications would change the character of the school's curriculum in such a way that patient safety and academic standards might be seriously jeopardized. It also stated that the modifications would change the character of Section 504 from one of nondiscrimination to one of special opportunity or affirmative action. It did make it clear, however, that Section 504 does require some, but not all, accommodations for persons with disabilities and that the cost of the modifications is a legitimate factor for courts to consider in deciding whether and how many accommodations are required.

Cost. Taking *Davis* as their lead, several courts have applied it to students with disabilities who have sought various types of accommodations under Section 504, as applied to their public school education. Thus, *Troutman v. School District of Greenville County* held that an appropriate education can be provided at a "satellite" school, not a neighborhood school (where the expense would be considerable and possibly beyond what *Davis* requires). In *Troutman*, the cost was a factor in the court's decision about reasonableness of the accommodation required.

By the same token, in *William S. v. Gill*, where an issue was whether the school district is required to send a child to a private residential program whose costs greatly exceed those of a public school program that has not benefited the student, the court noted that the district has no responsibility for residential programs that represent a new service not available to nondisabled students, as distinguished from a modification of existing services available to nondisabled students. The court cited *Davis* for the proposition that the district is not required to fund such programs, their cost apparently being a factor in the decision as to whether they are required by Section 504: "Sec. 504 does not obligate a school system to finance a private placement *under any circumstances.*" The court cited *Colin K. v. Schmidt, Turillo v. Tyson*, and *Kruelle v. New Castle County School District* for authority.

Similarly, *Pinkerton v. Moye* held that the IDEA does not require unreasonable accommodations. The court said that Congress intended a balancing test between cost and the claims of disabled children (to self-contained classes for emotionally disturbed children in the local programs). And in *Roncker v. Walters*, the district court stated *in dicta:* "Cost is a proper factor to consider since spending on one handicapped child deprives other handicapped children. . . . Cost is no defense, however, if the school district has failed to provide a proper continuum of alternative placements for handicapped children. The provision of such alternative placements benefits all handicapped children."

Other cases have different views of cost. In *Jose P. v. Ambach*, the district court rejected the state's argument that the "affirmative action" it ordered in an earlier phase of the case (granting a class action, appointing a master, and ordering broad-based relief involving classification and programming in learning disabilities) was not warranted, despite *Davis*. Finding that disabled children are "otherwise qualified" under Section 504 and have never been considered "unqualified" to receive an education, the court held that the children have a right to an appropriate public education and, thus, the extensive modifications that might be "substantial" in other contexts may be wholly reasonable efforts to educate the children in this context.

Likewise, *Hawaii Department of Education v. Catherine D.* rejected a *Davis*-based challenge to the relief sought for the children, and *Department of Education v. Katherine Dorr* held that private school placement and tuition reimbursement were due to parents of a cystic fibroic child where the child's mother could perform the cleaning and reinsertion of the child's tracheotomy tube more conveniently at the private school than at a public one and the expense of having that service done by the child's mother was lower than having it done by school employees. The case involved a choice between homebound placement, proposed by the school, and private school placement, sought by the parents.

In *Georgia ARC v. McDaniel*, another case that clearly confronts *Davis*, the Eleventh Circuit Court of Appeals held that certain disabled children are entitled to an education beyond the state-prescribed 180 days. The limitation is contrary to the obligations of states and local school districts, under IDEA and Section 504, to provide individualized education. In that case, the state asserted that a 12-month program is not required under *Davis*, it being too great an accommodation and too great a cost to the schools. The court of appeals distinguished *Davis* on two grounds. First, unlike the plaintiff in *Davis*, the mentally retarded children in the Georgia case could benefit from the special accommodations they sought (extended-year programming). Second, the year-round programming did not amount to a change in the scope of services provided by the schools, as the change in the nursing programs would have in *Davis*.

It thus appears that in the *Davis*-type situation the amount of the accommodation ordered will be contextually determined—which is as the Supreme Court indicated it should be in *Davis*. Not all accommodations, however costly, will be excused, although some will.

Costs remain a valid defense for LEAs that object to certain programs that parents and students seek: *Burke County Board of Education v. Denton*, containing dicta that costs are a relevant factor; *Clevenger v. Oak Ridge School Board* and *Matta v. Indian Hill Exempted Village School Board of Education*, noting that costs may be taken into account when devising an appropriate program for an individual student and in choosing among several appropriate education options; and *Kerr Center Parents Association v. Charles,* permitting a court to order a remedy that nonetheless impacts on state and local budgets.

Compensatory Education

Compensatory education cases continue to favor disabled children. In the early cases, the trend was firmly established. For example, *Capello v. D.C. Board of Education* ordered education to age 21 of a disabled child to whom the school district was slow in providing an appropriate education. A subsequent order in the case required the child's education in a residential school, at school district expense. A case that concurs is *North v. D.C. Board of Education*. Similarly, *Campbell v. Talladega County Board of Education* awarded two years' compensatory education beyond the child's 21st birthday because of a school district delay in giving the child an appropriate education. And *Bennett v. D.C. Board of Education* awarded compensatory education under the IDEA, basing the decision on the fact that children's rights cannot be safeguarded, retrospectively, by the procedural safeguards in the Act or by injunctive relief. But the court denied compensatory education under Section 504 because that statute applies only prospectively. Likewise, *Adams Central School District v. Deist* awarded compensatory education for a student who was illegally expelled from two schools and denied any education for 18 months.

The more recent cases continue to award compensatory education. *Max M. v. Thompson* upheld a student's right to compensatory education beyond the 21st birthday, noting that if the school could avoid compensatory education beyond age 21, there would be an incentive to deny any services to the child. The same court also rejected the doctrine of *Anderson v. Thompson* that compensatory education can be ordered only if a school district acts in bad faith.

The Supreme Court itself laid to rest the notion that no compensatory education could ever be ordered, by holding, in the *Burlington v. Department of Education* case, that compensatory education is the equivalent of a tuition reimbursement that itself may be ordered if an LEA defaults in its obligation to a student. Other cases approving compensatory education are *Miener v. Missouri* and *Helms v. Independent School District No. 3 of Broken Arrow*.

Compensatory education is still a powerful remedy for students who have been denied their rights under the statute, especially where the LEA has failed to provide an appropriate placement within a reasonable amount of time, such as two-and-one-half years (*Lester H. v. Carroll*). But compensatory education is not a viable remedy when the school provided some appropriate educational program for the student, although the student did not make any progress as a result of those programs (*Brown v. Wilson County School Board* and *McDowell v. Fort Bend ISD*).

Also, if a student waits too long to claim compensatory education, the student will lose the right to it. In *Murphy v. Timberlane Regional School District*, a federal court in New Hampshire threw a student's claim for compensatory education out of court under these conditions: the student was 23 years old when he and his parents filed a claim for compensatory education; the parents had withdrawn the student from school for two years before filing the claim (in 1982 and 1983 school years); and their waiting for six years before filing the claim was simply too long—they failed to exercise their rights in a timely manner and thus lost them. If they had exercised them promptly, the school might have been able to correct its failure to provide an appropriate education. The late claim was judged unfair (and thus prohibited or "barred" by the legal doctrine of "laches," the doctrine that requires claims to be filed promptly).

Participation in Sports

The cases reach contradictory results in deciding whether disabled children are entitled to the protection of Section 504 when seeking to engage in contact sports. Factual differences most likely explain the results in these cases. In one case in which a student won a court decision requiring a school district to allow him to compete, the evidence was persuasive that contact sports posed no unusual risk of injury and the student and his parents were willing to assume a risk of injury.

Kampmeier v. Nyquist held that Section 504 does not entitle a student to participate in contact sports. But *Poole v. South Plainfield Board of Education* ruled that the student may participate in contact sports, under Section 504, if he and his parents knew of the risks and decided in a rational way to participate. Likewise, *Grube v. Bethlehem Area School District* found a violation of Section 504. A high school student was excluded from the football team on which he had played for three years. His only physical problem was the absence of one kidney. The exclusion was ordered despite expert medical opinion that the risk of injury was slim and there was no medical reason for nonparticipation. The court found that the exclusion violated Section 504, particularly when the student's participation would require no substantial adjustments to the program and would not lower the standards of the team as a whole.

Where a student has had a kidney removed (as a result of an automobile accident injury) but his parents are aware of the potential medical risks and legal consequences if he participates in interscholastic sports, and where two physicians have testified that the student would be reasonably safe if he participates in sports, a school district may not exclude him from sports participation (*Pace v. Dryden Central School District*). This case adopts a risk-benefit approach, as do *Poole* and *Grube*.

Qualification for Services

In addition to the cases involving students with AIDS and the cases on educability, several other cases have decided who is "disabled." It is clear from them that a child will not be afforded the protection of the IDEA unless and until the child has been formally classified as disabled and found to be in need of special education services, all according to procedures and standards of the IDEA. Thus, *Johnpoll v. Elias* held that unless and until a child is classified under the IDEA as disabled, that child is not entitled to the Act's protection (here, a change in placement).

Akers v. Bolton held that not all school-aged children with epilepsy are entitled to special education services as a matter of course because not all (only some, as individually determined) are disabled in the sense of needing special education. And when children are improperly classified (children not mentally retarded although placed in MR programs, without testing or parental consent), they are entitled to the protection of Section 504, which protects children "regarded" as disabled (*Carter v. Orleans Parish Public Schools*).

Wolff v. South Colonie Central School District held that a student with congenital limb deformities (legs approximately one foot in length, deformed hand on natural limb, and prosthetic arm) was not "otherwise qualified" under Section 504 to participate in an out-of-country tour (in Spain) that required much ascending and descending of stairs, extensive walking tours, crossing congested streets, and so forth. The tour also was found dangerous to her safety.

The issue of qualification for services also surfaces when the question is whether a child is too old or too young to claim the benefits of IDEA. In a case involving the "coverage" provisions of the IDEA (all disabled students receive the benefits of the Act without regard to the governmental agency that has custody or jurisdiction over them), *Green v. Johnson* held that inmates in prison who are not yet 22 years old have a right to special education under the IDEA.

VanderMalle v. Ambach held that a 21-year-old person still qualified for services under the IDEA notwithstanding the fact that he was an adult under state law. And in *Helms v. Broken Arrow*, the court held that a school may not exclude a disabled child who reaches the age of 19 but has completed 12 years of school. According to IDEA, states do not have to provide special education to children ages 18 to 21 if that requirement would be inconsistent with state law or practice. That means the state may not apply different standards for disabled children that will deprive them of educational opportunities enjoyed by nondisabled children. In Oklahoma, nondisabled children may attend school until they are 21. Accordingly, under the IDEA, disabled children may do so, too, even if they have already completed 12 years of schooling.

But once 19 years old, a person may be prohibited from interscholastic wrestling, as are all 19-year-olds under state policy, even though disabled, protected by Section 504, and receiving special education *(Cavallaro v. Ambach)*. Such a student experiences the same age limitations as nondisabled students and therefore does not suffer discrimination.

A case that threatens the special education of older students is *Merifield v. Lake Central School Corporation*, in which a federal district court has ruled that a state may terminate the special education services of a 19-year-old student because state law does not entitle any student to receive an education beyond age 19. The IDEA covers students ages 3 to 18 or older unless state law is inconsistent with the "or older" provision [20 U.S.C. Sec. 1412(2)(B)]. Since Indiana (state) law terminates the school eligibility of all students at the age of 19, it is not inconsistent with IDEA and thus a student beyond age 19 may be excluded from special education without violating federal or state law. Obviously, a state may now amend its education laws to provide a cut-off (such as at age 19) and thus escape IDEA responsibilities for students aged 19 or older.

Minimum Competency Testing

Recent national concerns about the quality of education have prompted states to take steps to measure how well their schools are teaching their students. One step is the minimum competency test (MCT). The test, sometimes administered during the student's primary and middle school years and almost always during the last year or two of high school, determines whether a student has mastered the minimum competencies for functioning in an adult world.

A legal issue is whether the MCT may be given to disabled children and whether students' failure of the test may be the basis for schools to withhold their graduation or other diplomas or certificates. As a rule, courts have allowed states to administer the tests as long as they do so in ways that accommodate students' disabilities (e.g., longer time to take a test if a child is learning disabled or the assistance of an aide if a child is communication impaired) and as long as the states give adequate notice to all students, including those who have a disability, that they will be required to take the tests.

Thus, the federal district court in *Brookhart v. Illinois State Board of Education* held that the administration of state-required minimum competency tests to disabled children and the withholding of graduation diplomas from disabled children who fail the test does not violate Section 504 or the IDEA as long as the manner of administration of the tests accommodates students with physical disabilities. Students who fail the test are not denied due process of law (see chapter 7) because they have not been educated in the test's subject matter where lack of exposure to subject matter results from a determination, in preparing their IEPs, that exposure is inappropriate in view of their disabling conditions. But notice of the test is required under due process.

On appeal of *Brookhart*, the court of appeals held that: (1) denying a diploma to special education students who fail the MCT does not deny their right to a free appropriate education under the EHA, (2) use of the MCT does not violate the nondiscriminatory evaluation requirement of the EHA when the MCT is one of three requirements for graduation, (3) denial of a diploma does not violate Section 504 because a disabled student is not "qualified" for graduation in spite of a disability, and (4) adequate notice of the MCT and graduation requirements must be given lest a substantive due process violation occur (because students have a liberty interest in the diploma). The court of appeals reversed the district court on the grounds of a violation of procedural due process, which requires notice and adequate time to prepare for the new diploma requirement.

A similar result was reached in *Board of Education v. Ambach*, wherein the failure of disabled students to pass the MCT and denial of their diplomas for that reason did not violate Section 504 because the children were not "otherwise qualified." The IDEA does not prevent the denial of a diploma to a child who has received an appropriate education according to the child's IEP. And the New York Court of Appeals (the highest appeals court in the state) has upheld a state law requirement that all students, including those with disabilities, must pass an MCT before they are entitled to high school diplomas. The case is *Board of Education of the Northport-East Northport Union Free School District v. Ambach.*

Children's Residence

Some parents of disabled children have "gone shopping" for appropriate programs and, in the process, raised questions about the legal residence of the child and the identity of the school district responsible for the child's education. As a rule, the courts have not been sympathetic to the parents.

A good illustration is *Connelly v. Gibbs*, in which the court found that when the parents and child have their principal residence in one school district and a secondary residence in another, the second district is not required to educate the child. The plaintiffs were unable to show any reason other than education of their disabled child for establishing a second residence. Likewise, in *Fairfield Board of Education v. Connecticut Department of Education*, a state appeals court held that a town board of education was not liable for the costs of placing a disabled child at a residential center. The child's natural parents, who had moved to Vermont, had transferred guardianship to another couple to maintain the child's placement. The transfer of guardianship was termed a "sham."

A student does have bona fide residence in a state and school district when the student's parents (who live outside of the United States and are not citizens) have transferred the student's guardianship to relatives who are residents of the state and citizens, when the student herself is a citizen of the United States (having been born here), and where there is proof that the guardianship was established legally and in good faith and not just to obtain special education in a certain state or school district (*Sonya C. v. Arizona School for the Deaf and Blind*).

Free Education

Because the cost of special education and related services are quite high (certainly higher on average than the costs of educating a child without a disability), LEAs have sought to spread or share the costs with other parties. In one instance, for example, they attempted to require parents to use their Medicaid funds for the student's placement in a private group home, but the court held that the LEA may not impose that requirement on the parents because the student's placement was for educational purposes (*McClain v. Smith*). In another case, the LEA successfully resisted the parents' claim that the LEA should pay for in-home behavior modification training of the student and parents, the court holding that the LEA was not required to pay for that training because it was not necessary in order to provide the student with an appropriate education (*Burke County Board of Education v. Denton*). In these two cases, the deciding factor is the appropriate-education standard. If the services are for an appropriate education, the LEA must pay for them; otherwise, it need not pay.

Finally, insurance companies may exclude from their benefits and resist paying any expenses that are covered under the IDEA, because the IDEA does not prohibit the insurance companies from writing certain contracts, only from having to pay once a contract is written that covers IDEA expenses or from escaping liability to pay if a contract covers expenses that the IDEA does not pay (*Chester County Intermediate Unit v. Pennsylvania Blue Shield and Capital Blue Cross*). Accordingly, it is likely that insurance companies will write policies that exclude IDEA-reimbursable expenses, as well as other governmentally paid expenses (such as Medicare). This is not an illegal practice under IDEA or even under ADA, since ADA explicitly excludes insurance companies from its provisions.

EFFECTS OF THE ZERO-REJECT RULE

Having reviewed developments that led to adoption of the zero-reject rule by the courts and later by Congress, and having examined provisions of the IDEA and their interpretation by the courts, it is now appropriate to discuss briefly the major effects of the zero-reject principle.

New Definitions for Equality

The debt that disabled children owe to the civil rights movement is enormous. Without doubt, *Brown* (the first school desegregation case) is the most important case ever decided by any court insofar as the education of disabled children is concerned. At the very least, it established the doctrine of equal educational opportunity, attacked the dual system of education and law that had relegated blacks, disabled children, and other minority children to second-class status, and laid a foundation in the Constitution's Fourteenth Amendment (the equal protection clause) for *PARC, Mills*, and the other early special education cases.

The early cases and the IDEA began to fulfill the promise of the *Brown* case—that no schools or other government agencies may establish lawfully the second-class citizenship of any children. Extension of the civil rights movement from one discrete minority (blacks) to another (disabled children and adults) was the fulfillment of the Supreme Court's principle of equality under the eyes of the law.

Right-to-education cases following *Brown* deliberately and creatively expanded *Brown*'s equal opportunities doctrine by establishing that the exclusion of disabled children from any opportunities to learn—much less from any reasonably beneficial opportunities—is unconstitutional under the equal protection clause. More than that, those cases established a new equal access (or equal opportunity) doctrine. They articulated the proposition that disabled children require different types of opportunities—namely, access to different types of resources for the same, not different purposes—in order to have opportunities for education that are equal to those of nondisabled children.

This notion of equality is different from the customary one. The usual meaning of equality is (per *Brown*) equal access to the same resources for the same purposes. The new meaning, in disabilities law, became *access to different resources for the same, not different purposes* by disabled ("different") children. There is an important reason that equality means something different for disabled children than it does for nondisabled children and, thus, one major reason that the new equal access doctrine was worthy of being recognized and legitimized by the courts. The major reason is that *the child's disability is a distinction that usually justifies a different approach.*

The fact is best illustrated by examining the cases of three different disabled children. One child is mobility impaired; his spina bifida condition has crippled his legs. He seeks to follow a college preparatory curriculum in his local high school. For purposes of that curriculum only, it is entirely consistent with the doctrine of equal opportunity to admit him into classrooms with nondisabled students and to make no adjustments in his education. In *most* classrooms (a biology or chemistry lab or a physical education class may require adjustments) equal opportunity for him consists of being treated *exactly equally*.

A second child is hearing impaired but is not so disabled that she needs an interpreter. She uses a hearing aid, which the school must be sure is in working order. She is placed in the front of the room. The teacher distributes outlines of the course, frequently writes on the chalkboard, and directly faces the class, thus enabling the child to be instructed both verbally and with written materials. For this child, some accommodations are required in order to provide equal educational opportunity. The new equal access doctrine now is in play, and equality consists of *equal treatment plus accommodations*.

A third child is severely mentally retarded and has cerebral palsy, resulting in speech and mobility impairments. Clearly, neither "exactly equal" nor "equal-plus" treatment would provide this child an opportunity to benefit from instruction. In this case, special and different accommodations are required—typically, education by specially trained teachers, a curriculum that is substantially different from that offered to nondisabled children, and perhaps extra services (the "related services" of the IDEA—see chapter 5). In this child's case, equal educational opportunity consists of *different (but favorable) treatment*.

Thus, one important effect of the early zero-reject cases and Congress's enactment of a zero-reject rule was to redefine the doctrine of *equal educational opportunity* as it applies to disabled children and to establish different meanings of *equality* as it applies to disabled and nondisabled people. These fundamental redefinitions—based on the fact of the disability, which is the distinction that makes a difference—remain apparent in the zero-reject cases that have followed enactment of the IDEA and are based on interpretations of it.

Precedent Setting by Early Cases

The early cases were precedent setting in still other ways (besides redefining equal educational opportunity). They clearly led to enactment of the IDEA. They also established the six principles of law—zero reject, nondiscriminatory evaluation, appropriate and individualized education, placement in the least restrictive environment, procedural due process, and parent participation—that comprised the foundation of the IDEA. And, of course, they were precedent for other cases involving educational discrimination and disabled children. Moreover, those cases represented a massive judicial response to patterns and practices of gross education discrimination against disabled children. They resulted in court-ordered remedies that directed systemic, institutional reform, and nothing less.

Change of Locus of Control of Education

By attacking patterns of conduct that went to the very heart of education—exclusion from educational opportunity and improper educational assessment and placement—the early cases and, later, the Congress and the courts that interpreted the IDEA graphically demonstrated that schools and their officials are not immune from judicial examination. Each case has brought the conduct of schools—traditionally a matter of state and local control—under significant judicial oversight. Frequently that oversight was by federal judges, supervising the actions of state and local elected or appointed officials.

For example, *Brown* established federal control over *where* students were to be educated. But *PARC, Mills,* and the other early cases established federal control over *which* students are to be educated ("All children can learn . . . all children shall be educated") and the *terms* on which they are to be educated (the new equal access doctrine). When it enacted the IDEA, Congress simply validated the courts' rulings.

While *Brown* related to *where* students will be educated and *PARC* and *Mills* related to *which* students will be educated, IDEA, especially as interpreted by the United States Supreme Court in *Rowley* and particularly with respect to the transition provisions (the Individualized Transition Program, discussed in chapter 5), affects *what* the students will be *taught* and *where* they will be taught—it affects the nature of the *curriculum* (appropriate education, chapter 5) and the *place* it is delivered (chapters 5 and 6).

Like *Brown*, the special education cases and the IDEA together have had an enormous impact on state and local education budgets. They caused state and local legislators and school administrators to redirect the flow of funds within education so as to benefit disabled children. They also caused those same officials to seek new money for the education of disabled children. And, because the IDEA itself authorized Congress to spend money to help the states implement the IDEA, the cases, once they were enacted into the IDEA, caused a massive shift in federal educational aid.

Cost-Effective Education

A related but somewhat tangential effect of the zero-reject doctrine has been economic in nature. There always have been—and probably always will be—people who argue that it is not a wise expenditure of public money to fund the education of disabled children. Indeed, the *Davis* and other cases involving the education of disabled children explicitly relieve educational agencies of some of the especially high costs of accommodating disabled children or adults in educational systems.

These arguments and cases notwithstanding, early childhood education for disabled children clearly is cost-effective. And, as the data are developed and experiences in post-secondary programs of special education graduates are recorded, it has become clear that special education at the elementary, middle school, and secondary levels is cost-effective. Special education is regarded as cost-effective because it reduces the number of persons classified as disabled, prevents or reduces grade retention, makes it possible for some disabled people to acquire skills that make them less dependent on others, and enables some to become wage earners.

The fiscal contribution of zero reject and the equality doctrine is important not only for disabled persons but also for the larger public. More than that, the naysayers of equality have been answered with doctrine and dollars. The response is, indeed, powerful.

Parent Participation

The zero-reject rule has had an impressive effect on still other people. It has revolutionized the relationship of parents and school officials. By providing for nondiscriminatory evaluation, individualized appropriate education, and procedural due process, the rule has created a new doctrine (or, arguably, resurrected an old one): parent participation in the education of disabled children. In doing so, it legitimized *parent advocacy*—parents' assertion of the rights of their disabled children against the educational system (i.e., to gain access to it, to be admitted to it) and within the system (i.e., to be given an appropriate, useful education once admitted).

Family Services and Relationship to Other Federal Policy

The 1986 amendments, creating the Part H program for infants and toddlers (P.L. 99-457), extend the notion of parent participation in several significant ways. First, they recognize that parents not only have the right to participate in their children's educational process, but that they also are highly influential in their children's development, particularly in the very early years (birth to age five). That is why the amendments provide for development of an individualized family service plan (IFSP): to ensure that parents are involved in their children's development and education.

Second, the amendments recognize the inextricable link between the child with a disability and other members of the family. Whatever happens to the child with a disability affects the child's family and its members, albeit in different ways—some positive and some negative. By acknowledging this reality and providing for an IFSP, the 1986 amendments recognize that families themselves are systems and that any intervention in the life of one member has effects on the others and on the system as a whole. The family-systems approach to special education and other interventions[13] takes a holistic view of the family and of the effect of a disability and disability-related interventions. The IFSP does this, too, by providing for multidisciplinary, interagency, family-focused assessments and interventions.

Third, the 1986 amendments reject the notion—once prevalent under the medical model or the behavioral model of remediating a disability—that a disability is caused by and therefore is able to be ameliorated by one, and only one, discipline. By calling for multidisciplinary interventions and providing for interagency approaches to service delivery, the amendments recognize that a disability can have medical, behavioral, psychological-psychiatric, or environmental (socioeconomic) origins. Accordingly, a disability can require a combination of approaches and interventions.

Fourth, the amendments relax the criteria by which a child is classified as disabled. For example, they use the criteria of developmental delay or probability of developmental delay. By contrast, the IDEA requires not only a confirmed diagnosis of a disability but also a clear need for special education because of that disability (see the previous discussion of AIDS cases, which illustrate this point). Similarly, the amendments permit states to serve at-risk children. By relaxing the criteria, the amendments not only may substantially enlarge the number of children served, but they also may assure that the larger numbers either (a) are diverted from special education because their disability or potential disability has been remediated to the point that they do not need special education, or (b) are given a head-start in school, in special education or not.

Fifth, either of these effects would be consistent with the purpose of the amendments. Those purposes are to (a) enhance children's development or minimize potential developmental delays, (b) reduce the educational costs related to disability, (c) minimize the likelihood that children with disabilities will be institutionalized and maximize the likelihood of their living independently, and (d) enhance families' capacities to meet their children's needs.

Sixth, the very purposes of the amendments and the means by which they are carried out—the child's IEP and the family's IFSP—signal that the government (federal, state, and local) not only will enter the private lives of families but that it should do so. If a litmus test of policy in the 1980s has been whether and to what extent government has a legitimate role in the private sector and the lives of families as symbolic of the private sector (and surely the debates around abortion, Pledges of Allegiance and school prayer, intervention in decisions about treatment of newborns with disabilities, and the extent to which child care and parental leave will be federally subsidized reflect that debate), the 1986 amendments proclaim, loudly and clearly: Government is here to stay, even in your family life.

Finally, the 1986 amendments also clearly demonstrate that Congress has adopted a largely consistent policy affecting people with disabilities and their families. That policy includes, among other things, incentives for community-based, family-based living; for integration of disabled and nondisabled people; for family support; for the policy of avoiding institutionalization; and for the policy of independence, as represented not just in a person's ability to do things without help or with only the amount of help necessary to the task, but also in the person's and the family's ability to participate in decisions that affect daily life. Other federal legislation (principally the Developmental Disabilities Assistance and Bill of Rights Act, the Rehabilitation Act, and the Social Security Act, in its Medicare and Medicaid programs) declares these purposes.[14] Now, it is beyond argument that the IDEA and particularly its most recent restatement (Part H) make the policy abundantly clear.

So it is that the rationale for the zero-reject principle is expressed in Part H: to establish equal protection of comparably situated citizens (those with or at risk of a disability); to ensure that exclusion in school, which is a cause of exclusion in other life activities, is replaced by a practice of inclusion in school as a means for inclusion in other life activities; to educate early and well and thereby, one hopes, avoid a lifetime of dependency caused by disability and the failure to ameliorate it; to respond to the horrible economic and human costs associated with a disability; and to establish an equality—an equity—between those with and those without a disability.

New Growth Industry

The early cases—especially once they were enacted into the IDEA and Congress began to channel money to the states, colleges, and universities for teacher education and research—

had a dramatic impact on personnel preparation. Together, the courts and Congress created a new growth industry in America: special education. Not only did they give tremendous impetus to that discipline, but they also affected the education of regular education teachers by requiring them to be competent to teach disabled children in the mainstream (in least restrictive or more integrated settings).

Expanded Practices and Individualization

In short, the cases and the IDEA have pushed hard at the limits of public educational systems. They have demonstrated the plasticity of the system. They have shown that seemingly intransigent systems can change (albeit slowly—never underestimate the power of inertia), that there is a (sometimes fragile) consensus about the inherent rightness of special education of special children, and that the limits of educational systems are a great deal more expansive than they sometimes appear. The early cases, coupled with the IDEA, thus have had the effect of both commanding and enabling change, and of requiring and facilitating expansion of the educational system so that it can provide equal educational opportunities to disabled children.

One of the most significant changes in school practices has been in the methods of instruction. By addressing functional exclusion as an aspect of pure exclusion, the zero-reject principle has individualized educational services for disabled children. More than that, it has caused educators to extend the individualization practice to gifted and talented children (and enacts special education laws that grant to such children substantially the same rights as are granted to disabled children). It also has caused educators and policymakers to be particularly aware of the deficits in educating slow learners (children who are not formally classified as disabled under the IDEA but who still require special education attention). The megapolitics of the zero-reject doctrine, then, have been to extend to others the benefits (individualized education) that disabled children have as a matter of right.

The Integration Impetus

On still another level, the legal cases and the IDEA have begun to integrate disabled children into the mainstream of American life. The courts and the Congress both asserted the value of integration in requiring that, to the maximum extent appropriate, disabled and nondisabled children should be educated together.

The integration principle also has had an important effect on state mental retardation centers, psychiatric hospitals for children, and schools for deaf or blind children. The children in those institutions have been given an opportunity to be deinstitutionalized. They have been given a right to education in the public school system, with the result that, in many cases, they have not been placed in the institutions to begin with, have been discharged from institutions, or have been kept in the institutions but given more adequate and effective educational services there or in cooperating local school districts.

The integration principle in education was developing at the same time that the institutions—psychiatric hospitals and mental retardation facilities—were experiencing a reduction in the number of children admitted. This reduction had at least several related and important causes. First, state legislatures were tightening up the procedures by which people could be committed to the state institutions. They were requiring much more due process, thereby discouraging commitment. Similarly, legislatures were enacting stricter criteria for commitment, requiring that the usual standard of "dangerousness" be met more obviously.

Second, the U.S. Supreme Court ruled in *Addington v. Texas* and in *Parham v. J.R.* that states must prove dangerousness by fairly strict procedures and that states must provide for neutral review of admission decisions when children are candidates for institutionalization. Both cases had the effect of putting real or perceived clamps on the ease of institutionalization. Third, the states were developing more community-based treatment programs for children and using institutional placements less and less.

The cumulative effect of these three developments was to accelerate the integration impetus. In conjunction with the IDEA provisions for zero reject, least restrictive placement, and service priorities that favored previously unserved and severely disabled children, these developments significantly changed the character of the public schools.

Lifetime Service

The court cases and the IDEA also have forced health, mental health, social services/welfare, and educational systems to begin serious efforts, separately or in cooperation, to provide community-based services. These include child-find, educational placement, cost-sharing, facility-sharing, and family support services. These efforts represent the first long-range efforts, on a large scale, to secure community integration and at-home placement of disabled children. They also represent the beginnings of a lifetime service system for disabled people.

Given the early childhood initiative, the requirement for related services, and the "transition" or "aging out" initiatives, the IDEA set into motion a linkage between schools and other agencies, in which the schools are the primary service providers during a disabled person's school years and other agencies are secondary providers but thereafter take over the principal-provider role. Accordingly, the change wrought in schools also effected a change in adult service systems (which are regulated by Section 504, just as the schools are).

"Defective" Newborns

At the same time that *Brown* and the zero-reject rule were applied to disabled students, there developed an awareness within the public and especially among the professionals dealing with disabled people that gross discrimination has been and is being practiced against newborns who have birth defects. The practice of withholding medically appropriate treatment from "defective" newborns has been the center of a major policy and legal debate. The policy issue is whether the withholding of treatment (or other practices that jeopardize the child's life) should be condoned by families, physicians, and the public. The legal issues, on the other hand, center on the constitutional rights of newborns, the enforcement of child abuse and neglect laws, the application of nondiscrimination laws (particularly Section 504) to their treatment, and the tolerable zones of privacy that families and physicians may establish to fend off external review of their treatment/nontreatment decisions.

In a very real sense, the constitutional doctrines of *Brown* and the special law cases are applicable by analogy to the Baby Doe cases (so-called because of the name given to unidentified newborns in lawsuits involving their treatment). If equality before the law means anything, it means that "defective"newborns are entitled to appropriate medical treatment. And if that treatment is given and is lifesaving, the medical and other interventions must be forthcoming: A society that compels a life to be saved is one that also must compel services to the person. Thus, special education is involved in the Baby Doe cases in two ways—first, by extension of the equal treatment doctrines; and second, by providing early childhood education.

Personal Growth

At the same time that the cases and the IDEA have commanded and enabled schools and other governmental systems to change their ways of operation and their definitions of equality, they have enabled people to change and to overcome tremendous personal limitations. Students who once were regarded as subtrainable or ineducable have begun to acquire learned skills. Parents who once were regarded as the permanent custodians of their children (even into their children's adulthood) have been given massive help from the educational and other systems of government. Parents who once were regarded as trouble-making radicals because they advocated for their children have been given the green light to participate in their children's education. Nondisabled students, who would have been excluded from education with disabled students (who would have borne the brunt of the exclusion by being denied any education), have had an opportunity to learn about their disabled peers, to develop accepting attitudes toward them, to regard them as valuable, and to develop ways of thinking about disabled people that will carry into their adult lives.

New Norms and Pluralism

The "norms" of children in school have changed in important ways. The norm now is not nearly so "nondisabled." The presence of disabled children in school has changed the complexion of the schools. In a very real sense, their presence has augmented the cultural diversity and pluralism of the schools.

This enrichment undoubtedly will have important effects on the lives of adults. A result of the integration impetus is greater diversity in society. And professionals who once regarded some children as unworthy of an education or unable to benefit from training are now engaged in educating and training those same children. Not only have systems changed, but so too have people. On the whole, the change has been much for the better.

NOTES

1. E.g., Frontiero v. Richardson, Graham v. Richardson, Levy v. Louisiana, and Loving v. Virginia, to the effect that, respectively, race, alienage, illegitimacy, and race (again) are suspect - classifications.

2. E.g., Mills and MARC v. Maryland.

3. City of Cleburne, Texas v. Cleburne Living Center, Inc.

4. For other zero-reject cases not discussed elsewhere in this chapter, see, for example, Association for Mentally Ill Children v. Greenblatt, Beauchamp v. Jones, Brandt v. Nevada, California ARC v. Riles, and North Carolina ARC v. North Carolina.

5. For other tuition cases not discussed elsewhere in this chapter, see, for example, Crowder v. Riles, Davis v. Wynne, and State of Wisconsin ex rel. Warren v. Nussbaum.

6. Reid v. Board of Education of City of New York.

7. Davis v. Wynne.

8. Weintraub and Abeson, "Appropriate Education for All Handicapped Children," *Syracuse Law Review* 23(1972):1037, 1056.

9. Seals v. Loftis.

10. Parks v. Parkovic; Jenkins v. Florida.

11. Parents of Child v. Coker.

12. Doe v. Belleville Public Schools Dist. No. 118.

13. Turnbull, Turnbull, Summers, Brotherson, and Benson, *Families, Professionals, and Exceptionality: A Special Partnership* (Columbus, OH: Charles E. Merrill, 1986).

14. Turnbull and Barber, "Future Policy Issues in Mental Retardation," in *The Future of Mental Retardation*, edited by Meyen (Reston, VA: Council for Exceptional Children, 1984); Turnbull, "Legal and Policy Issues in Community Programs," in *Community Services: Here to Stay*, edited by Krauss, Seltzer, and Janicki (Baltimore: Paul Brookes, 1987); and Turnbull, "Law and the Mentally Retarded Citizen: American Responses to the Declarations of Rights of the United Nations and International League of Societies for the Mentally Handicapped: Where We've Been, Are, and Are Heading," *Syracuse Law Review* 30(1979):1093–1142.

For 1994 Update on Zero Reject please see page 391.

4

Testing, Classification, and Placement

CONSTITUTIONAL FOUNDATIONS

Constitutional arguments against certain types of educational evaluations and the resulting classifications of children turn on the Fifth and Fourteenth Amendments. Both provide that a person shall not be deprived of life, liberty, or property without due process of law. Denying an education is arguably tantamount to denying an opportunity to develop the ability to acquire property.[1] Classifying children as disabled when they are not, or classifying them inaccurately with respect to their disabilities, can result not only in denying them their rights to an educational opportunity[2] (not to mention their rights to an appropriate education) but also in unjustifiably stigmatizing them. It follows, then, that substantive due process has been violated when a pupil is misclassified on the basis of invalid criteria and thus placed in an inappropriate "track" in school.[3]

The Fourteenth Amendment is involved in still another way. By requiring that states treat citizens equally (the equal protection clause), the Fourteenth Amendment has become the traditional bulwark against state-imposed racial discrimination. Inasmuch as special education classes (particularly for the mildly disabled) have been filled with a disproportionate number of minority students (racial minorities—principally blacks—and cultural minorities—principally Latin Americans), there is at least an arguable claim of discrimination based on race or cultural background. The following discussion will show how the substantive due process rights under the Fifth and Fourteenth Amendments and the equal protection rights under the Fourteenth Amendment came into play in school testing and classification before the IDEA was effective.

Pre-IDEA Criticisms of Testing

The alleged violations have involved the use of IQ or aptitude tests. These tests supposedly are objective and allegedly do not depend on irrelevant variables such as teacher prejudice or social class, but they nevertheless have been subject to criticism, particularly when test results are the primary basis for assigning a disproportionate number of minority pupils—black or non-English speaking—to special education programs for educable mentally retarded (EMR) or trainable mentally retarded (TMR) children. Reestablishment of racially dual systems of education is threatened by such assignments, but the constitutional doctrine of equal protection under the Fourteenth Amendment comes into play to prohibit segregation by race in any school program, including special education.

One basis for criticizing the tests has been that they have been used to determine the intelligence of children unfamiliar with the language or with the white middle-class culture that underlies the test questions.[4] In short, it has been argued that tests based on a white middle-class socioeconomic group should not be used with persons not of that group because the tests put them at an initial disadvantage and may lead to their mistakenly being classified as disabled. There have been other criticisms of the tests or the ways in which they are administered or used. In some cases, they have not been administered in the child's native language (e.g., Spanish).[5] Or they have not measured adaptive behavior—a child's ability to cope and get along in his or her *own* cultural environment.[6]

Misclassification resulting from inappropriate testing arguably imposes on students the stigma of being retarded or different. It can isolate them from normal school experiences and cause them to be rejected by students and adults alike. Sometimes it sets up stereotyped expectations of behavior and can lead to self-fulfilling prophecy—all of this to the student's irreparable harm.[7] Often the label is permanent and cannot be escaped, outgrown, or rebutted.

Moreover, the label can limit (or increase) the resources available to the child, since public and private agencies tend to serve only persons identified as belonging within their categorical clientele. Misclassified children might be placed in special education programs whether they need it or not, or they might be placed in inappropriate special education programs or be inappropriately institutionalized. Being placed in a special education program does not necessarily ensure that the child will receive training that will be effective in overcoming the disadvantages of being classified as disabled. Assignment to a special education program can become permanent, despite an original intention to make it temporary.[8]

Testing alone is not sufficient for developing an accurate picture of a child's abilities and disabilities, but it has often been treated as if it were. In some cases,[9] a single test has been used as the sole criterion for classification and placement. Testing results, when not supplemented by other evaluation techniques (e.g., medical information, parent conferences), are particularly subject to misinterpretation. Parent conferences to determine adaptive behavior have been rare, and parent participation in classification decisions has been negligible. Procedural due process concerning evaluation and periodic review of the placements has been the exception, not the rule.[10] Misclassification tells a child that he or she is deficient; the injury to self-esteem is incalculable.

Pre-IDEA Court-Ordered Remedies

Given these criticisms of the nature, administration, and use of classification and testing procedures, it is not surprising that judicial response, based on substantive due process (Fifth Amendment) and equal protection (of racial or cultural minorities under the equal protection doctrine of the Fourteenth Amendment), has been massive. Only since 1972 have the courts become embroiled in classification issues. Their traditional posture had been to find that mere classification does not of itself deprive a group of equal protection[11] and that there is no constitutional prohibition against assigning individual students to particular schools on a basis of intelligence, achievement, or other aptitudes upon a uniformly administered program.[12] Because of the criticisms of testing—criticisms centering on the permanent and stigmatizing consequences of being labeled as mentally retarded and on the racial differentiation that results from testing—courts in the early and mid-1970s began to make inroads on the testing practices and procedures of schools.

Accepting the argument that intelligence tests bear little relationship to the intelligence they are supposed to measure when there is language or cultural unfamiliarity, some courts have held that IQ tests may no longer be used to place children in ability tracks.[13] They have forbidden schools to use biased (unvalidated) tests that do not properly account for the cultural background and experiences of the children being tested.[14] They have enjoined school authorities from placing minority students in classes for the educable mentally retarded on the basis of IQ tests if using the tests brings about racial imbalance in the composition of such classes. They also have ordered the dismantling of EMR classes in which Chicanos were overrepresented.[15] They have given the schools the burden of proving that a test is a valid measure of intelligence and does not discriminate because of race or culture if the test is the primary basis for classifications that are resulting in racial imbalance.[16] In addition, they have ordered that pupils be tested or retested in their primary language or be given bilingual instruction.[17] By ordering these remedies, the courts have made it clear that they have adopted as fact the presumption that statistical imbalance (racial imbalance) would not occur unless there is some sort of discrimination based on race.[18]

The courts have ordered that factors such as socioeconomic background, social adaptation, and adaptive ability be considered in making an evaluation for appropriate placement.[19] Use of the IQ test alone was found to violate substantive due process, since the basis for the school's action—the IQ score—was not reasonably related to the purpose for which it was used—namely, to determine a pupil's ability and what would be a "suitable" or "appropriate" education for him or her.

Just as the criteria must be related to what they are supposed to measure (that is, that they not be arbitrary), the standard for evaluation may not be arbitrarily applied. Thus, when white and minority students with similar abilities are assigned to remedial classes and classes for the educable mentally retarded, it is discriminatory to put the white students in the remedial classes and the minority students into the classes for the retarded. Accordingly, schools have been prohibited from having a disproportionate number of minority students in classes for the educable mentally retarded[20] and must justify their reliance on tests that have resulted in an imbalance.[21] And schools were required to furnish disabled children with intensive training to help them attain their peers' skill levels. Finally, the courts have ordered compensatory education for adults who were improperly classified, thus being denied an equal educational opportunity as children.[22]

Why Testing Is Required

It is obvious that testing, classification, and placement in special education programs must be continued, for several reasons. The schools must be able to identify and evaluate disabled children in order to (1) plan, program, and appropriate funds for them, (2) provide appropriate services for them, (3) comply with federal and state laws requiring that disabled children be counted and served, (4) evaluate their own efforts to educate children, and (5) serve their bureaucratic interests in maintaining and expanding their own services.

Classification can assist in measuring the results of special education efforts.[23] Classification also can create educational opportunity for the disabled, supply a common denominator to create and stimulate activities of volunteer or professional interest groups, assist in the enactment of legislation to aid individuals in a specific category, provide structure to governmental programs, and serve as a basis for financial appropriation decisions.[24] Classification is useful for determining incidence and prevalence data, which is helpful in planning how many professionals will be needed for a wide variety of services and assuring accountability in programs and services. Some of the reasons students perform poorly on standardized tests—such as slow work habits, emotional insecurity, low motivation, lack of interest, and culturally related conditions—also account for their below-average performance in school. Thus, testing can provide an early warning of probable or possible future problems.

Nevertheless, classification remains a powerful political tool,[25] capable of regulating people, degrading them, denying them access to educational opportunity, excluding them as "undesirables," and, in the case of minority persons, forcing dominant cultural values and mores on them.

The label of "disabled" also often has the effect of excluding a person so labeled from an appropriate education and, in some instances, from any education at all. The label itself emphasizes the disability and underscores the differences between "them" (the disabled) and "us" (the nondisabled). It creates not only a dual system of services but also a dual system of law—law for "them" and law for "us."

For all of these reasons, it is important to establish procedures to protect children from improper testing, misclassification, and inappropriate placement. That is the principal thrust of current federal legislation. Federal legislation seeks to minimize labeling and to ensure that labels, when necessary, accurately describe the disabilities and become useful devices for appropriately serving disabled children.

FEDERAL LEGISLATION

A school's failure to detect disabilities can prevent children from receiving an appropriate education [Sec. 1400(b)(5)]. Misuse of classification data can result in discrimination, and erroneous classification represents a major obstacle to a child's receiving an appropriate education.[26] Recognizing these problems, Congress sought to accomplish *nondiscriminatory evaluation*. Its effort is broad-based and multifaceted.

Nondiscriminatory Evaluation Procedures

Congress required certain strategies be followed to assure nondiscriminatory evaluation. The SEAs and LEAs must establish procedures to assure that testing and examination materials and procedures used for evaluating and placing disabled children will be selected and administered so as not to be racially or culturally discriminatory [Secs. 1412(5)(C) and 1414(a)(7)]. Next, each SEA and LEA must provide and administer such materials or procedures in the child's native language or mode of communication unless it is clearly not feasible to do so [Secs. 1412(5)(C) and 1414(a)(7)]. The term *nondiscriminatory testing* applies to evaluation materials and procedures used with all disabled children, as the regulations make clear [Sec. 300.530-.534].

In response to the requirement for racially and culturally nondiscriminatory testing and evaluation, Section 300.532 requires that:

> (a) Tests and other evaluation materials
> (1) Are provided and administered in the child's native language or other mode of communication, unless it is clearly not feasible to do so;
> (2) Have been validated for the specific purpose for which they are used;
> (3) Are administered by trained personnel in conformance with instructions from the producer;
> (b) Tests and other evaluation materials include those tailored to access specific areas of educational need and not merely those which are designed to provide a single general intelligence quotient;
> (c) Tests are selected and administered so as best to insure that when a test is administered to a child with impaired sensory, manual or speaking skills, the test results accurately reflect the child's aptitude or achievement level or whatever other factor the test purports to measure, rather than reflecting the child's impaired sensory, manual, or speaking skills (except where those skills are the factors which the test purports to measure);
> (d) No single procedure is used as the sole criterion for determining an appropriate educational program for a child and placement;
> (e) The evaluation is made by a multidisciplinary team or group of persons, including at least one teacher or other specialist with knowledge in the area of suspected disability;
> (f) The child is assessed in all areas related to the suspected disability, including, where appropriate, health, vision, hearing, social and emotional status, general intelligence, academic performance, communicative status, and motor abilities.

Section 300.531 requires that before a child is initially placed in a special education program, a complete and individual evaluation of his or her educational needs must be conducted in accordance with Section 300.532. Section .533 regulates placement procedures and the use of evaluation results. Public agencies must:

(1) Draw upon information from a variety of sources, including aptitude and achievement tests, teacher recommendations, physical condition, social or cultural background, and adaptive behavior;

(2) Insure that information obtained from all of these sources is documented and carefully considered;

(3) Insure that the placement decision is made by a group of persons, including persons knowledgeable about the child, the meaning of the evaluation data, and the placement options; and

(4) Insure that the placement decision is made in conformity with the least restrictive environment rules in Secs. 300.550-.554.

Reevaluation must occur at least every three years or more often if "conditions warrant" or the child's parent or teacher requests it [Sec. 300.534].

The regulations require parental consent for a preplacement evaluation only. In the event the parents withhold consent, a due process hearing may be held at the school's request. Federal law does not require parental consent for subsequent evaluations [Sec. 300.504 (b) (1) and (2)]. It does allow states to require consent.

The cases follow the IDEA's commands, almost without exception. There may be no placement until the child is evaluated according to the nondiscriminatory evaluation requirements. If those requirements are not met, the child's individualized education program (IEP—see chapter 5) may be rejected.[27]

This general rule—that there may be no program or placement in special education until evaluation occurs according to the nondiscriminatory evaluation requirements—also is the command of *Honig* (the "stay-put" case involving suspension) and of the long line of cases that followed *Turlington* (the suspension/exclusion cases). Both *Honig* and *Turlington* require nondiscriminatory evaluation before a school may suspend or expel (except for suspension for a period of less than ten days). As chapter 7 (due process) points out, a change of the child's placement in the sense of movement from one school to another does not trigger the nondiscriminatory evaluation requirement; only a change of program, which can occur simultaneously with a change of placement, does.

By the same token, it is well settled that the administration of standardized tests to an entire group of students does not constitute an individualized assessment that must comply with the nondiscriminatory evaluation requirements. Thus, a school may administer the Iowa or California achievement tests or minimum-competency tests to a student with a disability and not have to comply with the nondiscriminatory evaluation requirements. Those tests are not administered for the purpose of evaluating the child for special education services.

IDEA's second principle, "nondiscriminatory evaluation," is addressed by the 1990 amendments only indirectly. Section 1401(27) defines certain "underrepresented" populations (namely, "minorities, the poor, the limited English proficient, and individuals with disabilities") and requires state and local educational agencies to make special efforts to reach out to and provide services to these populations. Moreover, Section 1409 requires the Department of Education to conduct or fund special studies on the overrepresentation of minority students (principally, students of color) in special education. In these two provisions, IDEA implicitly acknowledges that a bias based on socioeconomic, racial, or ethnic characteristics may exist against these populations. The recognition of that bias in testing is the basis for the principle of "nondiscriminatory evaluation." It should go without saying that ADA (like Section 504 of the Rehabilitation Act, another antidiscrimination law protecting people with disabilities) does not distinguish between individuals on the basis of race, ethnicity, or socioeconomic status. It protects all equally.

Ceiling

Congress placed a ceiling on the number of children a state may count for the purpose of receiving federal funds under the IDEA [Sec.1411(a)(5)(A)(i) and (ii)]. The limit is 12% of the number of all children aged five through seventeen. The ceiling reflects Congress's concern that recipients might have counted children who were not in fact disabled in order to receive more federal funds. More than 12% of the school population may be classified as disabled, but federal funding will be available only for up to 12%.

Part H—Infants and Toddlers

The requirements for nondiscriminatory evaluation of infants and toddlers are set out in its regulations, not in the statute. In a nutshell, these regulations require that tests be given in the parent's native language or other mode of communication, that they not be racially or culturally discriminatory, that no single procedure be used, and that qualified personnel administer the tests. Evaluation is for the purpose of determining a child's eligibility for Part H. Assessment is for the purpose of identifying the child's needs, the family's strengths and needs, and the services necessary to meet the child's and family's needs.

There are special rules for evaluation and assessment of the child and of the family. Generally, with respect to the child's evaluation and assessment, appropriate personnel must administer nondiscriminatory procedures and use *informed clinical opinion*. With respect to the family's assessment, the purpose is to determine the family's strengths and needs related to enhancing the child's development. Thus, the family assessment must be voluntary on the family's part, and it must be based on information provided by the family through a personal interview and incorporate the family's description of its strengths and needs with respect to the enhancing the child's development.

As a general rule, child and family evaluation and assessment must be completed within forty-five days after the state lead agency is notified of the family's application for service.

As pointed out in chapter 3, the 1986 amendments to the IDEA created a new program—Part H, early intervention services for disabled infants and toddlers. Part H requires that the instruments and procedures for evaluating those children be "appropriate." It also provides that the children and their parents shall have certain procedural protections, including rights to a hearing on the child's evaluation.

Does the requirement of nondiscriminatory evaluation also apply to infants and toddlers? Yes. There are two reasons why this is so, despite the fact that Part H makes no explicit provision incorporating the nondiscriminatory requirements of Part B of the IDEA.

First, Part H itself is part of the IDEA and, for that reason, the provisions of the IDEA generally apply to infants and toddlers. Second, Section 504 and its regulations (which require nondiscriminatory evaluation) also apply to the programs that administer Part H. Those programs therefore must use nondiscriminatory evaluation methods.

"Learning Disability" Narrowly Defined

Congress carefully defined "children with specific learning disabilities" [Sec. 1401(15)] so that children who do not satisfy the definition will not be classified as disabled. In addition, the Department of Education has adopted regulations that specifically regulate the procedure for evaluating students to determine if they are learning disabled. The IDEA and DOE regulations set up specific requirements for evaluation of children thought to have specific learning disabilities. First, the general requirements of nondiscriminatory evaluation [Sec. 300.530-.534] must be followed. These are the same requirements that apply to all children thought to be disabled. Additional evaluations must be made if the child is thought to have a specific learning disability.

Second, the evaluation team must consist of either the child's regular education teacher, a regular education teacher if the child is not then in regular education, or an early education specialist if the child is younger than school age. In addition to one of those people, the evaluation team must include at least one person qualified to conduct an individual diagnostic examination (school psychologist, speech/language pathologist, or remedial reading teacher).

Third, the regulations allow the evaluation team to determine that the child has a specific learning disability if:

> (1) The child does not achieve commensurate with his or her age and ability levels in one or more of the areas listed . . . , when provided with learning experiences appropriate for the child's age and ability levels; and
> (2) The team finds that a child has a severe discrepancy between achievement and intellectual ability in one or more of the following areas:
> (i) Oral expression;
> (ii) Listening comprehension;
> (iii) Written expression;
> (iv) Basic reading skill;
> (v) Reading comprehension;
> (vi) Mathematics calculation; or
> (vii) Mathematic reasoning.

The team may not identify a child as having a specific learning disability if the severe discrepancy between ability and achievement is primarily the result of:

> (1) A visual, hearing, or motor disability;
> (2) Mental retardation;
> (3) Emotional disturbance; or
> (4) Environmental, cultural, or economic disadvantage.

The purposes of the regular and special evaluations in the area of specific learning disability are several. First, they seek to reduce the number of children classified as having a learning disability. They do this by erecting additional procedural hurdles to that classification.

Second, by seeking to limit the number of children so classified, they seek to hold down the costs of special education. Congress and the states realize that a very large number of children could be classified as learning disabled. After all, a large number of children simply do not perform well but do not have obvious other disabilities—and they are candidates for classification as having a learning disability. If all students were classified as having that disability, the costs of educating them appropriately would be enormous.

Third, the regular and additional evaluation requirements recognize that there is a stigma attached to having any disability. Accordingly, they seek to prevent that classification to prevent stigmatization of the child.

Yet the regular and special evaluation requirements for learning disabilities convey a strange message—that it is worse to have the stigma of sensory, physical, mental, or emotional disability than to have the stigma of learning disability. This message is inherent in the definition of learning disability: Children with a specific learning disability do not include those who have learning problems that are primarily the result of sensory (visual or hearing), physical (motor), mental (mental retardation), or emotional (emotional disturbance) disabilities [Sec. 1401(15) and Sec. 300.541].

Another message is inherent in the definitions of specific learning disability, and it is essentially culturally, racially, and socioeconomically biased. The Act [Sec. 1401(15)] and regulations [Sec. 300.541] make it clear that a child may not be classified as having a specific learning disability if the child's learning problems are primarily the result of environmental, cultural, or economic disadvantage. In the views of some, this limitation gives the message that specific learning disabilities are those that are primarily of white middle-class or upper-class children.

Service Priorities

Congress also established the service priorities. (See chapter 3 for a discussion of the priorities.) Like the ceiling, the service priorities are intended to stop an LEA from miscategorizing children as disabled in order to increase the amount of federal funds it may receive. Serving the *first-priority* (previously excluded) and *second-priority* (most severely disabled not receiving an appropriate education) children makes it unlikely that the LEAs will soon have federal funds free to spend on disabled children who do not fall in either category. There is little risk that LEAs will unnecessarily classify children as disabled, since many of them are still a long way from satisfying the needs of the first- and second-priority children.

Recoupment

Congress required the SEAs to adopt procedures for recouping funds from LEAs in order to furnish services for children who were erroneously classified and thus were not eligible for federal funds [Sec. 1416(a)(5)]. This requirement is intended to prevent misclassification. The desire for federal funding, after all, does make it tempting to count a child as disabled.

Accounting

Congress provided that SEAs and LEAs must report and account for the receipt and expenditure of IDEA money. It granted the secretary of education the power to audit those agencies and check the accuracy of their data with regard to the number of disabled children the state is actually educating [Secs. 1412 and 1416]. The secretary's power to trace federal dollars is intended to help enforce the service priorities and thereby prevent misclassification.

Due Process Hearing

Congress granted procedural safeguards—essentially a due-process-hearing right—to children who have been identified, evaluated, and placed in programs for the disabled [Sec. 1415]. These safeguards protect against misclassification by furnishing a forum for investigating whether a misclassification has occurred. (See chapter 7 for further discussion of due process.)

Sanctions

Congress provided that federal funds be withheld from any SEA that is alleged to be or found to be in violation of provisions of the IDEA [Sec. 1416]. These sanctions contain an element of overkill not evident in the other enforcement measures described in the preceding paragraphs. For that reason, the other measures should be used before invoking the sanction of withholding. The withholding sanction has an undoubtedly counterproductive element: It can penalize the disabled (by cutting off federal dollars) in the name of aiding them.

Section 504

Like the IDEA regulations, the regulations of Section 504 acknowledge that failure to provide disabled students with an appropriate education is usually the result of misclassification or incorrect placement. Accordingly, Section 104.35(a) requires an evaluation of any person who needs or is believed to need special education or related services because of a disability. The evaluation must be completed before a school takes any action (including denial or placement) with respect to *initial* placement in a regular or special education program or any subsequent significant change in placement. But a full reevaluation is not obligatory every time a lesser adjustment in the child's placement is made.

Section 104.35(b) and (c) sets out procedures to ensure that children are not misclassified, unnecessarily labeled as disabled, or incorrectly placed because of inappropriate selection, administration, or interpretation of evaluation materials. Section 104.35(b) requires schools to establish standards and procedures for evaluation and placement to ensure that tests and other evaluation materials are validated for the specific purpose for which they are used and are administered by trained personnel in conformance with the instructions of their producer. Tests and other evaluation materials are to include those tailored to assess specific areas of educational need and not merely those designed to provide a single general intelligence quotient.

In addition, tests are to be selected and administered to students with impaired sensory, manual, or speaking skills so that the test results accurately reflect the student's aptitude or achievement level—or whatever other factor the test purports to measure—rather than the student's impaired skills, except when those skills are the factors that the test seeks to measure. Section 300.35(b) drives home the point that tests should not be misinterpreted, that undue reliance on general intelligence tests is undesirable, and that tests should be administered in such a way that their results will not be distorted because of the student's disability.

Section 104.35(c) requires schools, when evaluating and placing students, to draw upon information from a variety of sources, including aptitude and achievement tests, teacher recommendations, physical conditions, social or cultural background, and adaptive behavior. Schools must establish procedures to ensure that information obtained from all such sources is documented and carefully considered, and the placement decision is to be made by a *group* of people, including those knowledgeable about the child. The meaning of the evaluation data and the placement options must be made clear to all concerned, and placement decisions are to conform with the doctrine of least restrictive (most integrated) setting.

Section 104.35(d) requires periodic (though not necessarily annual) reevaluation. It makes clear that reevaluation procedures consistent with the IDEA (which allows reevaluation at three-year intervals unless more frequent reevaluations are requested) are a means of meeting the requirement of reevaluation.

Section 104.36 requires schools to provide for due process in evaluation procedures. This includes notice, right of access to records, impartial hearing, right to counsel, and appeal procedures. Chapter 7 discusses due process in detail.

CASE LAW

As noted, a vital and hotly debated issue (in special education as well as in legal circles) is whether standardized intelligence tests discriminate against students from economically deprived or racial minority backgrounds by placing them in classes for mentally retarded or learning disabled children. The early decision in *Larry P. v. Riles* seemed to signal the death knell of these tests. But a later case, *PASE*, validates use of the tests when evaluation is accomplished by additional means and seems to mute the tune that *Larry P.* sang.

Larry P.

Larry P. v. Riles held that schools no longer may use standardized but unvalidated IQ tests for the purpose of identifying and placing black children into segregated special education classes for educable mentally retarded (EMR) children. The district court ruled that schools using such tests violate Title VI of the Civil Rights Act of 1964, Section 504 of the Rehabilitation Act of 1973, the IDEA, and the equal protection clause of the Fourteenth Amendment to the federal Constitution. The violation occurs because the tests are racially and culturally biased, have a discriminatory impact on black children, have not been validated for the purpose of essentially permanent placements into "educationally dead-end, isolated, and stigmatizing classes for the so-called educable mentally retarded," evidence the schools' discriminatory intentions (in violation of equal protection), and cannot be justified under the "compelling interest" standard applicable to racial discrimination cases.

The district court found that the Stanford-Binet, Wechsler, and Leiter IQ tests discriminate against blacks on several grounds: They measure achievement, not ability; they rest on the "plausible but unproven assumption that intelligence is distributed in the population in accordance with a normal statistical curve" and thus are "artificial tools to rank individuals according to certain skills, not to diagnose a medical condition (the presence of retardation)''; and they "necessarily" lead to placement of more blacks than whites in EMR classes. The court rejected two explanations for the disproportionate enrollment: the *genetic* argument ("natural selection has resulted in black persons having a 'gene pool' that dooms them as a group to less intelligence'') and the *socioeconomic* argument (poverty and inferior home and neighborhood environments explain why more blacks than whites are EMR). Instead, it explained the difference in IQ test scores by the *cultural bias* argument that IQ tests measure intelligence as manifested by white, middle-class children and therefore are racially and culturally biased against blacks.

The district court converted its 1972 temporary injunction into a permanent one and (1) enjoined the state from using any standardized IQ tests for identifying EMR children or placing them into EMR classes without prior court approval, which will be granted only if the defendants, by statistical evidence, can show that the tests are not racially or culturally discriminatory, will not be administered in a discriminatory manner, and have been validated for the determination of EMR status or placement in EMR classes; (2) required the state superintendent and board to compile statistics enabling them to monitor and eliminate disproportionate placement of blacks into EMR classes and required local school boards to prepare and adopt plans to correct the imbalance; and (3) required the state superintendent and board to direct each local school to reevaluate nondiscriminatorily every black student already identified as EMR.

On appeal, the Ninth Circuit Court of Appeals affirmed the district court's conclusions and remedies. Specifically, it rejected the state's argument that tests that are valid predictors of future performance can be used even if they have a discriminatory impact. The court of appeals stated that assignment of children to classes for EMR students means that they are denied an academic education and therefore experience a discriminatory impact because of the tests. In addition, the court of appeals found that the state could not sustain the burden of showing that the tests predict specifically that black elementary-school children who score in the EMR range (IQ of 70 or below) are mentally retarded and incapable of learning in the regular school curriculum. Finally, the state did not use other measures or criteria—such as the child's educational history, adaptive behavior, social and cultural background, or health history—for determining special education placement.

In language that suggests that discriminatory intent does not have to be proven, the court of appeals noted that improper placement in EMR classes has a demonstrable and negative impact, putting children into dead-end classes that do not teach academic skills but do stigmatize them, and that no nondiscriminatory factors, only the tests, are the cause of the adverse impact. Accordingly, it upheld the district court's remedy of suspending the use of the tests and requiring school districts with disproportionate racial balance in special education to devise three-year remedial plans and to report racial disparities to the district court.

Larry P. may be poor precedent for special education in light of *PASE* and, considering that it was, as much as anything, a race discrimination case that put the court in the unenviable position of choosing among three possible explanations for the overrepresentation of minority children in special education: (1) the tests and their invalidity, (2) the "gene pool" argument that minority children are inherently less intelligent than nonminority children, and (3) the socioeconomic explanation of low performance on standardized tests. Given that the court in *Larry P.* found minority overrepresentation in special education, the tests were the most likely candidates for the court. The court could hold them invalid and impose a remedy (no more testing, under most conditions), but it would have been at a loss to impose a remedy that spoke to the politically charged gene pool or socioeconomic arguments.

PASE

In *PASE*, however, the court did not face these choices as dramatically as in *Larry P.* and took care to consider the tests' validity. Far more than *Larry P.*, *PASE* is a special education decision that, in light of requirements of the IDEA for multifaceted, multidisciplinary evaluation, commands special educators' adherence.

By contrast, *PASE v. Hannon* upheld the same tests that *Larry P.* had held unlawful as racially discriminatory. Although *PASE* found that some items in the tests were discriminatory, it upheld the tests as generally nondiscriminatory. More important, it found that the tests were not the *sole* basis for classification and that the school district therefore was complying with the IDEA, which requires multifaceted testing. The minimal discrimination in tests and the adherence to classification safeguards were the decisive factors in this carefully reasoned opinion. To understand that *PASE* is an exceptionally appealing case, at least as it compares with *Larry P.*, it will be useful to examine the court's reasoning.

The Gene Pool Argument. With respect to the gene pool argument, the court recognized that since "the early days of standard intelligence tests, around the time of World War I, blacks as a group score about one standard deviation—15 points—lower than whites" on the tests. There is, however, "considerable disagreement" about the causes of that result.

Noting that the "genetic view never did take account of the fact that many blacks scored above the white mean," that "northern blacks scored higher on the average than southern blacks," that blacks who moved north "often experienced an increase in their IQ scores," and that black infants adopted by white families tended to achieve IQ scores in later years that correlated "highly" with the scores of the natural children of the adoptive parents, the court concluded that IQ tests measure something that is changeable rather than fixed for all time, something that can be increased and improved. It also noted that the parties to the case—both the students and the school officials—agreed on that much. Moreover, it stated that "there is no evidence to support a hypothesis that blacks have less innate mental capacities than whites." Accordingly, the court rejected the gene pool argument as an explanation for the disproportionate representation of blacks in special education.

Racial/Cultural Bias Arguments. The court also rejected the argument that the disproportion is caused by blacks' use of nonstandard English: "The evidence does not establish how the use of nonstandard English would interfere with performance on the Wechsler and Stanford-Binet tests. . . . What is unclear is how the use of such nonstandard English would handicap a child either in understanding the test items or in responding to them." In addition, a child's response in nonstandard English "should not affect a child's score on the (test) item, since the examiners are specifically instructed by the test manuals to disregard the form of the answer as long as the substance is correct."

In addition, the plaintiffs made no effort to show that any of the ninety-six words challenged as racially biased are peculiar to the culture of whites but not blacks. The vocabulary words are of "ordinary, common usage." Accordingly, the court also discounted the argument that the tests are "Anglocentric" rather than "Afrocentric" and therefore necessarily biased against blacks. Blacks' lack of exposure to white culture and the fact of a separate co-existing black culture, said the court, "has not been connected to the specific issue in this case," which was "whether the (three tests—WISC-R, WISC (Wechsler), and Stanford-Binet) are culturally biased against black children, so that it is unfair to use these tests in the determination of whether a black child is mentally retarded."

In determining that the tests are culturally neutral, the court examined carefully all items of the three tests, particularly the ones that the plaintiffs alleged were culturally biased. It found—after thirty-five pages of its opinion—that only eight items on the WISC-R and WISC are "either racially biased or so subject to suspicion of bias that they should not be used," and only one item on the Stanford-Binet falls into the same category.

As to the WISC-R and WISC, the suspect items are:

1. What is the color of rubies?
2. What does C.O.D. mean?
3. Why is it better to pay bills by check than by cash?
4. What would you do if you were sent to buy a loaf of bread and the grocer said that he did not have any more?
5. What does a stomach do?
6. Why is it generally better to give money to an organized charity than to a street beggar?

7. What are you supposed to do if you find someone's wallet or pocketbook in a store?
8. What is the thing to do if a boy (girl) much smaller than yourself starts to fight with you?

On the Stanford-Binet, the only item that the court found to be biased or racially suspect was on the "aesthetic comparison" test, in which four-and-a-half-year-old children are asked to identify which of two similarly colored persons is "prettier."

Having found that only 9 of 488 items on the three tests are racially biased or racially suspect, the court turned its attention to interpretation of the tests. It found that the importance of an individual item is lessened by the fact that "the child continues with the sub-test (in which the item appears) until he has a certain number of consecutive misses." In addition, as far as some items of the tests are concerned, they occur at a level of difficulty that children in their early school years (when EMR placement generally is made) are not expected to reach the item or answer it correctly. The tests thus are not interpreted in a way that indicates racial bias but, rather, in a way that reflects racially free educational assessment. In the Stanford-Binet, the consequences of racial bias are "negligible" since only 1 item of 104 is biased or racially suspect.

Moreover, the IQ score is "not the sole determinant" of whether a child is classified as EMR; "clinical judgment plays a large role in the interpretation of IQ test results." Indeed, "the examiner who knows the milieu of the child can correct for cultural bias by asking the questions in a sensitive and intelligent way."

Finally, "the likelihood of a black child being placed in an EMH [educably mentally handicapped] class without at least one black professional having participated in the evaluation is very slight." The court thus concluded that "the possibility of the few biased items on these tests causing an EMH placement that would not otherwise occur is practically nonexistent."

The Socioeconomic Argument. The court addressed the socioeconomic explanation for special education placement by acknowledging that, "[E]arly intellectual stimulation is essential. . . . Lack of opportunity for cognitive development is . . . often due to factors associated with economic poverty in the home." Moreover, it was "uncontradicted that most of the children in the EMH classes do in fact come from the poverty pockets" of Chicago. "This tends to suggest that what is involved is not simply race but something associated with poverty."

The Assessment Process. The court then addressed the assessment process, finding that it involves several levels of investigation (IQ testing, observation in the classroom, screening conferences by educators, individualized examinations by professionals, multidisciplinary staff conferences, and a potential veto of special education placement by the psychologist who has evaluated the child). In that process, the court observed, any "hypnotic effect" of an IQ score is substantially mitigated. Indeed, later reevaluation of the children involved in the case indicated that they were not mentally retarded and had normal intelligence but "suffer from learning disabilities which make it difficult for them to perform well in certain kinds of learning situations."

***Comparison with* Larry P.** Finally, the court addressed *Larry P.*, noting that, while the court there "largely" devoted its lengthy and scholarly opinion to the question of legal consequences resulting from a finding of racial bias in the tests, it engaged in "relatively little analysis of the threshold question of whether test bias in fact exists" and even noted that the cultural bias of the tests "is hardly disputed." Indeed, the *Larry P.* court made reference to specific test items on only one page and, then, only with respect to one item. Its inferences of bias from the one item, in a case that "hardly disputed" the cultural bias of the tests, were unpersuasive, lacking a more detailed examination of the test items.

Ability Grouping

Just as the first school classification case, *Hobson v. Hansen*, raised the issue of ability grouping and the disproportionate effect it has on racial minorities, so another, more recent case has charged that ability grouping is illegal because of its effects on minorities. In *Georgia State Conference of Branches of NAACP v. Georgia*, the use of ability or achievement grouping was challenged on the basis that the disproportionate racial impact violates the equal protection clause of the Fourteenth Amendment, Title VI of the Civil Rights Act (prohibiting discrimination on the basis of race), Section 504 (prohibiting discrimination on the basis of disability), and the IDEA.

The federal court of appeals found, however, that ability or achievement grouping violates none of those laws. The court ruled that ability or achievement grouping is a sound education practice that provides the benefit of significant educational and academic progress. It also noted that the plaintiff (NAACP) had failed to show the existence of equally beneficial education practices that would result in less racial disproportionality.

Larry P., PASE, and Ability Grouping Cases—Effects

Fundamentally, *Larry P.* and *PASE* were school desegregation cases that took the form of a challenge to special educational practices. *Georgia NAACP* was a school desegregation case that took the form of a challenge to a regular education practice that had special education impacts.

On their surface, *Larry P.* and *PASE* clearly sought to prevent the schools from classifying students as disabled and providing them with special education. Both cases challenged the use of IQ tests, which are the integral—some would argue, the principal—means for classifying students as disabled. If the tests could be held invalid because they discriminate against minority students and if their use were prohibited because of their invalidity, a major tool for classification would be outlawed.

One result of prohibiting use of IQ tests would be that schools would have to find other means for classifying students as disabled. But another, and probably more fundamental, result would occur: Classification of minority students into special education would be more difficult because the primary means for classification would be illegal. In turn, the number of minority students placed into special education would decrease. Finally, the number of minority students retained in regular education would increase, so the schools—that is, the regular education programs—would be more racially integrated.

Thus, *Larry P.* and *PASE* clearly were cases that sought racial desegregation of the schools; this was their basic purpose. Their secondary purpose was to reduce the number of minority students who—already having the factor of their race as a potential stigma—would be placed into special education and thereby acquire an additional stigma—that of being "disabled."

Likewise, the *Georgia NAACP* case sought to prevent the use of tracking systems that had racially disproportionate results: more minority students being placed into lower or "special" tracks than whites, as a proportion of their representation in the school population as a whole.

Whatever one might think of the results of the cases—and it seems clear that the court's reasoning and use of evidence in *Larry P.* is not as persuasive as in *PASE*—it is clear that several policy issues are being fought out and resolved. First, the issue of means of classification is being challenged. In *Larry P.* and *PASE*, the means were the IQ tests; in *Georgia NAACP*, the means were ability or achievement tracking systems.

Second, the means are challenged to prevent minorities from being classified as disabled and having to bear a double stigma of racial minorityship and disability. (This observation assumes that, for some, the stigma of racial minorityship is a reality. It does not condone that result: Race should not be stigmatizing. But it accepts as a fact that, for some people, both black and white, it may be. It also accepts as a fact that disability is stigmatizing. Again, it does not condone that fact.)

Third, the challenge seeks not simply to affect special education. At its heart, it seeks to reform the process of resegregation of regular education. It acknowledges that school desegregation by race is an elusive goal. It admits that the goal is imperfectly realized. And, to more fully realize the goal, it attacks the means by which segregation by race, allegedly under the guise of classification by disability, occurs.

Fourth, the challenge is less than fully successful. Although *Larry P.* outlawed the use of IQ tests, *PASE* did not, and *Georgia NAACP* sustained the use of ability or achievement grouping.

Do the results make good law? In *PASE* and *Georgia NAACP* the results seem defensible on the basis of the legal analysis. In *Larry P.*, the results are defensible but not as carefully reasoned. Do the results make good social policy? That is a question that the reader must answer. What is clear, however, is that the social policies of desegregation and of fairness in classification so that appropriate education can be provided (if necessary, in special education) may seem to be in conflict with each other.

What is also clear is that the issue of educational policy is only the surface issue. These cases—and indeed the entire history of special education and especially its recent history and the IDEA—essentially are social policy issues. The issue underlying them is this: What is the role of a government agency (the schools) and of the law in addressing the segregation of people by race and disability? Posed another way, the issue is this: What kind of society shall the schools and the law seek? Shall it be one that is more integrated than segregated? And posed still another way, the issue is this: How shall "we" (whether we are black or white, nondisabled or disabled) be with "them?" How shall people *be* with others, or shall they have the liberty not to *be* in the presence (and in the schools) with others who are different?

Other Cases

As noted earlier, classification concerns also affect the learning disabilities programs, not just MR programs. Thus, in *Riley v. Ambach*, New York's commissioner of education was enjoined from defining a learning disabled child as one who exhibits a discrepancy of 50% or more achievement (based on intellectual ability) and actual achievement. The court criticized the state's regulation for determining a learning disability on grounds that the standard is too inflexible, tends to underidentify LD children, and is not sufficiently individualized. The standard (50% discrepancy) was the same one previously adopted by the U.S. Office of Education but later rejected by it. On appeal, the decision was reversed, not on the merits of the lower court's decision but because the plaintiffs failed to exhaust their administrative remedies.

Another federal district court later approved a settlement in a class action that challenged the procedures in New York state regarding evaluation, classification, and placement of disabled children. The classification procedures were somewhat at issue in *Riley*. The settlement was approved in *J.G. v. Board of Education of Rochester City School District*.

With respect to parental consent for evaluation, the court in *Rettig v. Kent City School District* held that the school district is not required by the IDEA to obtain parental consent for testing a student with standardized tests when the test results are not used for evaluation, an appropriate education, or placement, but only to comply with funding legislation. This result was unchanged by the Sixth Circuit Court of Appeals, affirming in part and reversing in part. And when a school tests a disabled child as part of its reassessment (to assure an appropriate education, as required by the IDEA), it does not have to obtain parental consent to the reevaluation (*Carroll v. Capalbo*).

In *Mullen v. District of Columbia*, a federal court held that, in order to obtain reimbursement for the cost of an independent evaluation of their child, parents are not required to notify an LEA that they are obtaining the evaluation, and that the LEA must show that its evaluation was appropriate in order to avoid paying the cost of the independent evaluation.

OBSERVATIONS ABOUT CLASSIFICATION

As the early cases on nondiscriminatory evaluation recognized, as Congress acknowledged in the IDEA, and as various critics have pointed out, classification of a person as disabled can have important educational and adult-life consequences. At the worst, it can relegate the person to second-class citizenship and, as such, subject the individual to a *dual system* of law. That dual system allows some of us (the nondisabled) to treat others (the disabled) as less worthy than us because of their disabilities.

It may be helpful to show how a dual system occurs by discussing the "classification system" and its consequences at law. It is appropriate to start by describing society's perceptions of disabled people because those perceptions too often are reflected in law. Next is a discussion of who classifies. Then, how society uses professionals to classify and why professionals play pivotal roles is covered. This is followed by a discussion of the legal effects of and responses to classification.

But, first, it is important to recall that special education is not a new invention. It originated, according to Sarason and Doris (and as fully documented by them in their definitive text *Educational Handicap, Public Policy, and Social History*),[29] as a response to the inability of the schools to accommodate to the wave of immigration that began in the middle of the nineteenth century. As Irish, Italian, German, Russian, and other immigrants came to the United States, they were classified as "special" and segregated in their education from well-established Americans. (The fact that this classification had religious undertones and was done by native language, country of origin, or ethnicity should not pass unnoticed.)

For Sarason and Doris, classification of the new immigrants was a prelude to classification of other students who are different, in a different time. The separation of blacks, Chicanos, and Hispanics from other students during the remainder of the nineteenth century and into the twentieth century has its origin in the eighteenth century. And yet its reasons are the same, according to Sarason and Doris: Classification occurs to (1) preserve the social status quo and prevent disruption of the social structure, (2) put distance between people so that those who are different (read: subject to a negative stigma) are not in the presence of others, and (3) altruistically justify some ameliorative (read: special education) interventions.

Sarason and Doris direct their attention to a single disability—mental retardation—arguing that classification of a person as having mental retardation reflects social policy—that the disability itself is a social invention. To make this point, they argue that disability—unlike genetic make-up—is not a characteristic inherent in a person. Rather, disability is a consequence of how a person functions within a social context. It is a transactional phenomenon—something that results from the way a person relates to and transacts social relations with others.

If the person functions differently from others, the person is said to be disabled. And thus the person is said to be at fault; the disability is part and parcel of the person (it is inherent in the person). That being the case, special interventions—special education, for example—are warranted. The disability reflects a "broken" aspect of the person, and the person must be "repaired" or "fixed." Similarly, separation of those who are "different" or "broken" from those who are not "different" becomes justifiable. Those with disabilities need certain interventions that the others do not. The "abnormal" and the "normal" are not just different but should be maintained as different. The consequence of this "pathology focus," Sarason and Doris show, is that special education is justified. The person with a disability is provided something that is intended to change the person.

What that focus fails to acknowledge, however, is that changing the person is only one part of the solution to the "misfit" of the person in society—only one way of accommodating to the fact of difference. The other part of the solution is, of course, to change the society itself. Accommodation, after all, should be a two-way street.

The IDEA and Section 504 attempt to make mutual accommodations. They acknowledge that certain special intervention is warranted; the IDEA provides rights to special education. They also acknowledge that special adjustments in society are required, too. The IDEA's principles of zero reject and presumptions of integration (the doctrine of the least restrictive environment) and Section 504's prohibition of discrimination solely on the basis of disability requires adjustments by society to the person.

Given that mutual accommodations must be made and that the IDEA and Section 504 attempt to ensure those accommodations, the issue remains: How shall the law respond to the fact of classification? To answer that question, it is appropriate to make additional observations about classification and then to document the law's response.

Perceptions and the Bias in Classification

Consider the disabled person. The characteristic of the person on which intervention usually is predicated is "disabled," not "person." Disabled people are seen to be qualitatively different from other people in this important and debilitating sense: They are "deviant." For example, the retarded newborn is commonly called a "defective child." Because the defect is seen to inhere in the child itself rather than in the society into which the child is born,[29] it must be "treated" in the sense of being subjected to diagnosis, prescription, regimen, and "cure." The treatment is rendered by many "helping" professionals, not just physicians. But this kind of treatment frequently strips the disabled person of social being.[30]

Disabled persons then can be regarded as "perpetual patients" for whom a cure can never be found. They are defined by what they are *not*, not by what they are or may become. Regarded as "sick" (i.e., disabled) and not responsible for their own condition, they are obliged to "fulfill permanently the role obligations of the good patient." In this role, they learn to be helpless and inferior, to accept professionals' control over their lives.[31] Infrequent rebellion against professional dominance is itself treated as a symptom of sickness, and the person's parents or family also become "patients."[32]

The obedience of the person and family to professional dominance reinforces the original perception that the person is incapable and possibly incurable. "Treatment" of this sort essentially reflects the prevailing social mores.[33] Classifying a person as disabled enables "us" to use a convenient concept—one ostensibly rooted in science—to do unto others what we would abhor being done to us, all in the name of altruism. Incorrectly seeing disabled persons as sick and not responsible for their condition,[34] "we" can easily conclude, as "the law" traditionally did, that they are not responsible (competent) and must be dealt with in unusual ways.[35]

Thus, able-bodied and mentally competent people come to regard the disabled person's incapacity as a kind of failure of the person. Given that the person is a failure, there is a reduced duty, if any, of the professions and of society as a whole to act on the person's behalf. "We" are off the hook for any responsibility to "them."[36] "We" have, ultimately, no responsibility for their exclusion from normalcy and, with relatively clean consciences and legal impunity, we can assign them to lower echelons of life, to second-class citizenship at law.

Who Classifies

Every society needs its "operatives"—professionals who will do society's bidding by bringing their expertise to bear on difficult situations and resolving those difficulties through the use of special training, talents, and status.

Physicians. It is ironic in the extreme that physicans are agents for dealing with physically or mentally disabled people—ironic because, while they have great ability to help these people, they also have great ability to injure them. Thus, physicians' curative abilities (to prevent a disability, intervene early so that its effects are minimized, and be a sustaining force throughout a person's life) make them important resources for saying who is disabled. They do this through developmental testing of newborns, infants, and children. Since disabled children need treatment, the disability is the physician's province. Given the need of society and its lawgivers for professional operatives, it is little wonder that physicians also have become one of the law's group of agents for deciding what to do about disabilities. Exactly how the law has allowed them to discharge their agentry will be discussed later.

Educators. Educators are another of society's classifiers. Schools label more children as disabled than does any other governmental or social entity.[37] This classification has massive consequences—both positive and negative—for children, especially when the disability is questionable or mild. Educational classification as disabled can, among other things, determine the nature or effectiveness of the child's curriculum,[38] the characteristics of his or her peers and thereby the child's tendency to learn from peer interactions,[39] the extent of teacher demands and the type of teacher expectations of the child,[40] his or her self-image, the nature of educational resources made available, the child's mobility within or even out of special education, the nature of disciplinary proceedings, and the child's potential for higher educational opportunities, especially those of a vocational nature.

Some disabled children are spotted and classified well before they enter the public school system. Their disabilities are such that they are unmistakably disabled. Others, however, become known to us only when schools tell us they are different, special, exceptional, or otherwise regarded as atypical,[41] as not being easily subjected to the mass education of the masses. The reasons for and techniques of educational classification, and the procedures for challenging them, are not relevant here. The fact that schools classify children as disabled who frequently "become" nondisabled when they have exited from public education's jurisdiction should, however, give us pause.

Other Professionals and Agencies. Educators and physicians are not the only professional sorters, though they are the principal ones.[42] Any profession having contact, however tangential, with different people classifies, notwithstanding its limited competence to do so. Social workers, psychologists, and rehabilitation specialists classify. Institutions of higher education, particularly vocational, technical, and community colleges, do their own classification. Law enforcement and criminal justice agencies classify. Courts accept classification arguments in order to assess whether and, if so, to what extent persons are criminally or civilly liable for their actions or failures to act. The armed forces classify. Nearly every agency of government classifies. None comes to mind that does not.

Professional Organizations. Professional organizations classify. The American Association on Mental Retardation classifies by changing its definition of mental retardation (the lower the cut-off point of mentally subaverage, the more people are "cured" and classified by exclusion from being mentally retarded) and creating and altering its adaptive behavior scales. The American Psychiatric Association classifies when it changes the standards and definitions in its *Diagnostic Standards Manual*. Learning disabilities societies classify by defining a specific learning disability to exclude some types of children.

Families. Finally, families classify. It is not so much that families say that their child, brother or sister, or relative is disabled; others do that for them. It is more that they classify by determining how they will react to what others say. The decision to risk keeping a child in one's own home or securing placement in an institution, or to try a mainstream education instead of a more specialized one, is in the first (and sometimes the last) place a family decision. Among other things, it reflects a decision to classify a person more or less into or out of a disabled status. The option is less likely to be available if the person is severely or profoundly disabled than mildly retarded. For that reason, it is all the more important that the decision be made carefully.

Everyone. Everyone classifies. We all make choices to associate or not with certain other people. Human beings are discriminating in the neutral sense of the word. We make discriminations about ourselves and others. We also are discriminating in a different sense. We discriminate for invidious as well as altruistic purposes. We let defective newborns die because their existence horrifies us, but we say we do it because we are concerned about the quality of their and others' lives. Classification is not inherently wrong, merely natural.

How We Classify

By Resorting to Science. There is some magical quality in the concept of *science*. Call something scientific and it becomes less assailable. There is a presumption that science and its products are researched, reliable, validated, evaluated, and unbiased. But what we do—our policies—are not always based on good science, on defensible science. It is little wonder, then, that our policies are not always good.

The medical model's fallibility is well known.[43] After all, science taught that retarded people were a menace, so the eugenics movement spawned legalized compulsory institutionalization and sterilization.[44] Science teaches that intelligence can be measured, so classification as learning disabled or mentally retarded and categorization into special education receive the blessings of the law. It is no great matter that the basis for scientific facts is open to doubt as long as it is not clearly erroneous. There is far less debate about the fallibility of medical assessment for developmental delay (whether physical or mental), yet decisions by physicians, other service providers, and families, made on the basis of relatively acceptable assessment techniques, can still be highly debatable.

The case of Phillip Becker proves the point. There was no doubt about the fact that he was a young boy with Down syndrome and a heart defect that could be corrected surgically, with little risk to his life, as a means of substantially prolonging his life. Yet his family decided to refuse to authorize the surgery and, up to a point, so did the courts of California, because of debatable medical decision making.[45] Thus, we classify by using relatively fallible or infallible science or by acting in someone's interests on the basis of what that science tells us.

By Social Vulnerability. Classification is affected by other scientific means, and by nonscientific ones as well. Educators, for example, identify students as disabled who make life difficult for them. Boys are more subject to special education classification than are girls, aggressive students more than acquiescent ones, racial and ethnic minority students more than white students.[46] The "science" of these classifications is highly doubtful. Instead, some students' differential vulnerability to special education classification appears to be a factor of cultural, social, or economic differentness.

By Legal Proceedings. Likewise, classification as disabled occurs in a host of legal proceedings, often without a sufficient "scientific" basis. For example, if persons are aggressive, unable to care for themselves, or, because of mental disability, "in need of treatment," society's caretakers—family, mental health, public health, or social services agencies—may choose to intervene by involuntarily committing them, adjudicating them to be incompetent so the third-party consent to treatment or placement can be obtained, securing temporary social service custody for treatment of neglect or abuse, or obtaining criminal prosecution for alleged violation of a crime.

Any of those four responses is legally sanctioned and may be effective as a way of intervening appropriately. So, too, is doing nothing; inaction is a form of action. Whatever the choice—whether to intervene and, if so, how—classification results. In Alan Stone's typology,[47] the classified person becomes mad, sad, or bad—mad if committed involuntarily, sad if referred to special education, social services, mental retardation, or developmental disabilities agencies, or bad if convicted of a crime. The classifier, of course, is good.

By Reason of Serendipity. There is, moreover, no clear reason why a particular intervention prevails. So much depends on serendipity. Is the school's staff overloaded with disabled students? Is the state psychiatric hospital full? Are there enough beds in an MR center? What agency does the family of the person have the most contact with? Are private or third-party funds available to pay for services? Is the person an "interesting case" for the professional staff? How effectively does a lawyer represent the parties? Have political or social influences been brought to bear on the agencies or courts? Have community resources been tried unsuccessfully? These are some of the factors—all of them far removed from the allegedly precise scientific basis for classification that is supposed to be obtained in special education or mental health intervention, for example—that affect whether a person is classified and, if so, how, why, and with what effect.

Why We Classify

It may be impossible to avoid classification. We are, after all, discriminating, choosy, selective, and exclusive in almost every facet of our lives, whether the issue be so trivial as the choice of food at a carry-out restaurant or so momentous as the choice of a mate. In addition to our natural restrictions (age, gender, race, and ability), we restrict ourselves voluntarily,[48] such as by the jobs we choose. And in most cases the law recognizes our rights to be selective in the important matters of speech, religion, and personhood, as well as in less significant matters such as the types of clothes we wear ("symbolic speech").

Yet our natural instincts and legal rights to be selective, to classify ourselves and others, are not unbridled. Our rights of free speech do not extend to some aspects of pornography. Some consensual conduct is regulated and, of course, so is nonconsensual conduct (crimes against persons or property).

One reason for regulation is that the effects of absolute liberty for anyone are unacceptable to someone. Thus, the possession of pornography may be protected but its sale or distribution are not. The reasons for governmental classification must be examined; the due process and equal protection clauses of the federal Constitution forbid invidious, irrational, indefensible classifications (such as those made on the basis of race or, in some instances, disability, as discussed in chapter 3). It is legally relevant, therefore, to inquire into why people classify others as disabled.

Altruism. Sometimes classification is done for the most altruistic of purposes. When someone is classified as disabled, it enables him or her to be the recipient of services that the classifier (schools), and sometimes the classified, thinks will be helpful (special education). Classification also may prevent the person from being subject to disadvantaging conditions. Segregation of students by disability has been thought by some to protect them from nondisabled students and the ordinary conditions of regular schools.

There are, however, negative results of classification that is motivated by social beneficence. Lionel Trilling[49] has made the point that people who are the objects of our pity become the objects of our coercion, and Kai Erickson[50] has highlighted the paradox that deviance—differentness on account of disability—is nourished by the agencies that were designed to inhibit it, in proportion to society's ability to control it. Thus, the conditions of education, including special education, have been disadvantageous to children in some instances. Sarason and Doris[51] have cast doubt on the motives and efficacy of special education systems. Blatt[52] documented the horrible conditions to which disabled people have been subjected in institutions originally predicated on a medical model. And Gleidman and Roth[53] have produced strong evidence of the shortcomings of the medical model in a host of "helping" professions.

Negative Reactions. We also classify for reasons having to do with our instinctive negative reaction to disabilities. After all, the grossly macrocephalic child may not be easily or immediately lovable. Fecal smearers can be unpleasant to live or work with. Some severely emotionally disturbed children are aggressive, and some profoundly disabled people are slow to show affection. Many aspects of disabilities, such as severe self-injurious behavior, are not only especially intractable, but deeply disturbing to families and caretakers alike. Thus, when the decision is made to place a child in special education, to institutionalize a child or, more seriously, to withhold medical treatment of a "defective" newborn, it seems inevitable that our instincts for being with pleasant, attractive, able, and promising people are at work.

By the same token, our ability to "succeed" with a disabled person—if we are a physician, to "cure," or an educator, to "teach"—is threatened by some disabled people. Surely the emotional reactions of parents are not the only ones operating in a classification decision. Physicians report on the terribly difficult task of telling parents that their child is mentally retarded.[54] To place a child in an institution—to put him or her out of sight and sometimes out of mind—is partly a human condition. And the human condition is an imperfect one.

Riddance Motive. We also classify because we sometimes actively and admittedly wish to rid ourselves of the disabled person. The decision to abort a "defective" fetus, while constitutionally protected, may reflect the mother's wish to avoid life with a disabled child. Decisions to withhold life-sustaining medical treatment or to institutionalize a child may reflect similar reactions of parents to not be disabled by reason of having a disabled child.

Parents are not alone in their reaction to disabilities. Educators who refer a child to a special education program, community agency social workers who counsel for institutionalization, and institutional psychologists who recommend deinstitutionalization all may be motivated by a desire to rid themselves of a "problem" person.[55]

Agency Self-Interest. Another motive that explains classification is more related to agency interests than to personal interests. Educators and others test and thereby engage in classification decisions to absolve themselves of moral responsibility for decisions about what happens to disabled people, taking refuge in science. By resorting to science, they also gain credibility with parents.

Finally, agencies serve school interests in categorization and program efficiency. A well-organized school system has to have categories of children so that programs can be planned, financed, operated, and perpetuated.[56] By the same token, social services, health, and mental health agencies sometimes classify a person as disabled or as having a certain degree of disability (mild to profound) for self-serving purposes. They may want to include or exclude a person from a service category because it will increase their head count (number of people served) and thereby their budget or constituency base, or decrease it and thereby enable them to serve someone else. Resource allocation is a powerful motive.

Dual Diagnosis. One familiar but subtle issue in classification is that of double diagnosis. Some mentally retarded people display symptoms of emotional disturbance. And some mentally ill people (or people whose behavior can be characterized as a mental illness) may be mentally retarded. How should the person be classified—as mentally retarded or as mentally ill? Or can a person be classified as both mentally retarded and mentally ill? The same choice of classification applies to mental retardation and learning disabilities or to learning disabilities and emotional disturbance.

The choice of diagnosis is important. It may determine whether the person receives a label as MR or ED, whether he or she receives one type of special education service or another, whether confinement in a mental retardation center or a psychiatric hospital could occur, whether the person will be placed in one type of community-based residential or service system or another, and so on.

Many times service agencies are required by their regulations or operating procedures to classify a person as having a single disability. As a result, they report a single diagnosis even though a double diagnosis would be professionally feasible. The regulations or agency procedures may be valid in the sense that they seek to channel into the agency's service streams only those who can benefit by the services provided or who can be served effectively by agency personnel. But they also may have untoward consequences. They may prevent a person from obtaining services for a coexisting disability and, in the long run, make intervention less than maximally useful.

Agency regulations or procedures also may have the consequence of locking a person into the primary system and preventing him or her from transferring out of it and into another (or into none) when the system has outlived its usefulness or has become dysfunctional and harmful to the person.

The choice of diagnosis, therefore, is a critical one when there may be a choice to make a dual diagnosis. Special attention to the motivation of the classifier and to the effect of classification is warranted in these difficult cases. Since professionals cannot help but take into account parental or family wishes (e.g., the learning disabilities classification seems to be far less stigmatizing to families and client than the mental retardation classification), the motives of parents and family also are of concern.

Desire to Dominate. Finally, classification occurs because the classifier seeks to subject the person to a position of powerlessness. An intelligence test given in English to a Spanish-speaking student may, but is not likely to, test accurately the student's potential to be successful in school or in his or her inherent or acquired skills. Persuasive arguments have been made that classification, especially by public schools, is a means for subjecting ethnic or racial minorities to a second-class status, thereby perpetuating the political, economic, or social dominance of nonminority people.[57]

LEGAL RESPONSES TO CLASSIFICATION

Legal efforts to rescue disabled citizens from second-class citizenship through classification have addressed both the techniques for classification and action founded on the classification. They require both procedural safeguards and substantive protection.

Fair, Individualized Assessment

As an illustration of the techniques (procedures), the IDEA requires a multidisciplinary, multifaceted, nonbiased evaluation of a child before classification and before provision of special education. The evaluation prohibits sole reliance on "scientific" assessment measures, such as IQ tests, and provides instead that "soft" data, such as teacher observations, may be used to evaluate and then classify someone as disabled.

The requirement of a fair evaluation as a prerequisite to classification also is a requirement of individualization. Due process mandates nothing less.[58] If a person is not assessed individually when the result of that assessment could be a benefit (e.g., special education if needed) or a special burden (e.g., assignment to special education if the child is *not* disabled), the child's constitutional rights to due process—enjoyment of life, liberty, and property—may be violated. In this regard, the law has erected substantive protection.

Thus, legal requirements for fair assessments reflect constitutional concerns and traditional combinations of procedural and substantive safeguards. They also evidence an attempt to prevent people from being relegated to second-class citizenship. In addition, they reflect sound professional practice, assuring that service providers will deal appropriately with people whom they are trained to serve. This result inures to the benefit of the person and the provider alike.

Major Legal Restraints on Consequences of Classification

It is not legally sufficient that the techniques of classification be regulated. The use that one makes of the techniques is an important concern as well. The techniques may be entirely acceptable, but invidious classification and treatment of people could still obtain unless their uses were scrutinized. For example, simply being disabled is not a reason for being placed in special education; the person must need special instruction because of the disability (not in spite of it). Thus, the law limits the scientific basis for classification by a rigorous insistence that the techniques and effects of classification be mutually compatible. This approach is reflected in the cases involving students with AIDS (see chapter 3).

Just as the law seeks to minimize the potential for bias or error in educational or other scientific classifications, so it seeks to eliminate the "whimsy" factors in other classifying actions. It does so by four principle techniques: (1) It insists on knowable and measurable standards, (2) it requires procedural safeguards, (3) it sometimes provides affected parties access to professionals' records, and (4) it enables affected persons or their representatives to participate in decisions ordinarily made by professionals.

Standards. For example, a person may not be classified as disabled under the IDEA unless the person has one or more of the disabilities listed in the definition (see chapter 2) and "by reason thereof require(s) special education and related services" [Sec. 1400]. Similarly, a disabled child does not qualify for a related service unless it is "required to assist (the child) to benefit from special education" [Sec. 1400]. In both cases, classification (as disabled or as qualifying for related services) has a "but-for" element; the causal relationship between the service and the classification must exist.

Procedures. Procedural safeguards also tend to minimize the risk of error. Thus, under the IDEA the disabled student's parents are entitled to notice of the action that the school proposes to take, a hearing before an impartial tryer of fact and law, an opportunity to present and rebut evidence, and the right to appeal from the initial decision (see chapter 7).

Access to Records. A third technique is to grant affected persons or their representatives access to the professional records concerning them or service systems that may be brought to bear on them. Thus, the IDEA allows a student's parents to see the school records or records of school system special education programs. Some states also have enacted statutes that allow disabled people or their representatives access to social work, health, or mental health records.

Court and quasi-judicial proceedings or records (such as the impartial hearing guaranteed under the IDEA) normally can be accessed by disabled people or their representatives. And some courts have taken the innovative step of requiring service professionals to divulge their records or make known certain information to the affected person or interested others.

Participatory Decision Making. Finally, the IDEA and federal law governing vocational rehabilitation provide for the participation of disabled persons or their representatives with professionals in planning the goals and methods of professional services. Chapter 5 offers further discussion on this subject.

As already noted, the law's response to the reasons we classify a person as disabled or as having a certain degree of disability is to insist on knowable and precise standards (e.g., for mental retardation, subaverage intelligence, and inability in adaptive behavior), procedural safeguards (notice, hearing, counsel, and appeal), access to records, and student/parent participation in decision making.

Eligibility

More than that, the law has created eligibility standards (e.g., if a person is disabled, he or she becomes entitled to special education) and accompanying funding streams (federal special education funds may be spent only on disabled students or for administrative costs associated with their education). Sometimes the law selects certain kinds of disabled people for special benefits (and thereby denies others of those same benefits). For example, funds of the IDEA are earmarked for the more disabled person, not the mildly disabled person. This type of "bottom-up" legislation—attacking the problems of disability at their more severe level and working upward to the least disabled person—contrasts with the "creaming" legislation or executive-administrative action that furnishes services to the mildly disabled person in preference over the severely disabled one (e.g., deinstitutionalization by transfer to group homes affects mildly mentally retarded people more often than severely mentally retarded ones).

Prohibiting Discrimination

Another legal response is to prohibit governmental agencies or recipients of governmental aid from discriminating against otherwise qualified people solely because of their disabilities [Sec. 504]. For example, it is a violation of federal law for a school system to exclude disabled children solely because they are disabled (see chapter 3).

Effect and Motive

The law entitles an advocate to inquire into both the effects of classification and the intent of the classifier (see chapter 3). If a discriminatory (invidious) effect can be found (e.g., the child may not attend school because he or she is disabled and disruptive), the classifer's intent may be irrelevant. But if the classifier also has an invidious intent and seeks to discriminate against the person solely because he or she is mentally retarded, the law will provide a remedy. Fear alone—fear of a person with a disability—does not justify segregation. That rule of law is well settled by the United States Supreme Court in *Connor v. Donaldson, City of Cleburne v. Cleburne Living Center*, and *Board v. Arline*.

Advocacy

To challenge the discriminatory effect or intent of classification, a disabled person must have an advocate. For example, the IDEA requires state educational agencies to appoint *surrogate parents* for disabled children who have no parents or are wards of the state. Recent federal law (the Developmental Disabilities Act of 1975) also has established a "protection and advocacy" system to enable disabled people to challenge unwarranted classification. Under this law, states that receive federal funds for use in serving disabled people must create a system to advocate for them against state and local governmental agencies. Federally financed P & A offices have been extensively involved in special education lawsuits involving retarded children's classification and education. Another federal effort to provide advocates for disabled people has been by way of funding the Legal Services Corporation, which in turn allocates its money for local legal services for disabled and other disadvantaged citizens.

Personal Liability

A similar legal response has been the court's use of a provision of the Civil Rights Act of 1971 that holds a state or local official liable for depriving someone of his or her rights under the federal Constitution or federal statutes. If, for example, a public school agency expels all disabled children from school without cause, thereby violating the children's right to equal protection, a court may require the official to pay damages to the children (see chapters 9 and 10).

Least Restrictive Alternative

In its many responses to classification, the law recently has taken the posture that the government itself is the victimizer and the disabled person is the victim. The issue is how to govern the government, recognizing that government becomes involved in classification because it offers services (education) and responds in a variety of ways (by excluding an otherwise qualified person from services, by subjecting a person to improper or unconstitutional treatment in a service system, or by treating a nondisabled person as disabled) to a complex set of explanations for classification.

A major principle of constitutional law—the doctrine of the least restrictive (least drastic) alternative—has become a useful device for curbing governments that harm citizens (see chapter 6). The doctrine forbids a government from acting in a way that restricts a person's liberty any more than necessary to accomplish its legitimate purposes. If a government has a defensible reason for restricting someone and may accomplish that restriction in either of two ways—one that infringes individual liberty to a greater extent and another to a lesser extent—it must choose the lesser of the two ways.

For example, sometimes it is legitimate to place people in institutions against their will because they are dangerous to themselves or others. But the nature of confinement may not be excessive. Thus, under the doctrine of least restriction, courts have reformed the conditions in institutions by requiring programs of education and training for children in institutions and by preventing institutional placement when community-based education would be as effective to serve the state's purposes. (Chapter 6 discusses the doctrine of least restrictive environment in detail.)

Substitute Consent

Courts have even been able to address one of the most debilitating aspects of classification as mentally disabled—the loss of legal capacity to act for one's self. As a general rule of law, a person may not legally consent or withhold consent to educational, health, or mental health services if he or she is not mentally competent; mental capacity is an indispensable element of consent.[59] Moreover, children generally are presumed to be incompetent to act for themselves, especially in regard to special education services. And some disabled children have no parents alive or available and are wards of the state.

Thus, it has been necessary for legislatures and courts to provide for the appointment of a legal guardian for incompetent children and to authorize the guardian to consent to services on their behalf. In addition, the IDEA requires states to appoint surrogate parents for parentless children (see chapter 7).

Who Should Make Policy?

As chapters 5 and 6 indicate, Congress (in the IDEA) and the courts (in appropriate education and least restrictive cases) rely heavily on professionals to say who is disabled and needs special education. Certainly the court in *PASE v. Hannon* indicated that professional judgment—in establishing, administering, and interpreting intelligence tests and other measures of "disabled"—plays a powerful role in resolving important legal issues (e.g., about special education and racial segregation).

By contrast, the court in *Larry P. v. Riles* did not give much weight to the professionals' views concerning intelligence testing and classification. But *Larry P.* was an exception to the normal judicial response to disability-classification issues—which has been to defer to professional judgment. The courts usually rely mightily on the perceived expertise of professionals, although professionals' expertise is certainly unexceptional in informing anyone what to do about social policy and "different" people.

By turning to the professionals to help determine who is disabled enough to be treated differently, Congress and the courts can avoid coming to grips directly with the social, political, and moral dilemmas posed by disability. Thus, decisions about institutionalization are characterized as "medical" just as other types of decisions are called "educational" or otherwise dignified by being seen as "professional." The consequence is that the true nature of the decisions—what shall be done about disabilities, disabled people, and schools—is answered by letting professionals decide.

Classification, Professionals, and Policy

By the fiction that disabled people really are different and should be treated differently, largely by "professionals," the "law" has avoided the ultimate questions: Who should decide who should care for disabled people, where, how, at whose expense, and why? Even more fundamentally, who is different enough to be treated differently? And who has the sagacity to tell us the answer? These are the issues of classification.

The answer to the first and last questions has been: the professionals. Once policy makers know that professionals can give the answers, they tend to seek answers to other questions from them. (Is this psychological examination valid for the purpose it is used? Is the student's program appropriate?) Thus it is that our responsibility (or lack of it) for "other" people, for disabled people, is made manifest to us: Do as the professionals say.

Dual Systems

By avoiding some of the hard policy questions and by allowing disabled people to be devalued, the law can do an injustice not only to them but to itself. It condones a double standard, a dual system (see chapter 6). But when courts and legislatures insist on substantive and procedural changes in dealing with disabled people, the law not only reshapes itself but, it is hoped, our culture itself.

EFFECTS OF THE NONDISCRIMINATORY EVALUATION RULE

The requirements for nondiscriminatory evaluation have had multiple benefits and drawbacks. But they also have raised several important concerns.

Major Effects

Standard Intelligence Tests. First, the requirements for nondiscriminatory evaluation, as interpreted by the courts, clearly have both outlawed and legitimized standard intelligence tests and their use in classifying students. The *Larry P.* and *PASE* cases cannot be read consistently with each other insofar as intelligence tests are concerned. For more than a decade now, the California federal district court has taken an unchanging stand against the use of tests except under the most stringent conditions. On the other hand, the Illinois federal district court has found the tests to be culturally fair and has allowed their continued use, in conjunction with other measures for classifying students. One unanswered question, then, concerns the future use of such tests, under law.

Additional Measures for Classification. The limitation that other measures for classification also must be used is an important one and reflects another significant contribution of the requirements for nondiscriminatory evaluation. The requirements for multifaceted and multidisciplinary evaluation have created more equitable and more elaborate procedures for classification. In a sense, they have recognized that intelligence testing has a hypnotic effect, and they have tried to mitigate that effect by requiring that other procedures be brought to bear in classification.

Investments in Time. Of course, in creating these more equitable and elaborate procedures, the requirements have caused educators and their colleagues to spend a great deal more time in evaluation and classification. The benefit of this new investment is a more thorough, comprehensive picture of the student and, as a consequence, a greater ability to identify a student's strengths and build on them and a greater ability to identify a student's weaknesses and remediate them. The drawback of this new investment is that some school districts have long waiting lists of students to be evaluated and, some would say, increased frustration among educators, their colleagues, and parents concerning the delay between referral, evaluation, and service.

Careful Documentation. A fourth effect of the nondiscriminatory evaluation requirements is that educators, their colleagues, and parents have more carefully documented the child's abilities and disabilities and relevant educational decisions. The benefits of careful documentation are to establish more data-based and objective foundations, created by all affected persons, for educational decisions. Although subjective evaluation is still valid because the law recognizes the usefulness of teacher observation and professionals still recognize the legitimate role of clinical experience, this type of evaluation is less likely to prevail, especially as it is made by a single person.

The drawback of the new requirements is the increased emphasis on paper compliance—on meeting the letter of the law. It may be that in their quest to comply precisely with the procedures, educators, their colleagues, and parents have recorded the "trees" (the disparate parts of the child) but not the "forest." They may have failed to take a holistic view of the child, seeing only parts, particularly those that are problematic or pathological.

Who is Disabled and the Distribution of Disabilities. Fifth, and finally, the new requirements clearly have impacted policymakers' concerns about who is disabled and about their distribution of disabilities.

Behaviorally Disordered/Emotionally Disturbed. For example, Congress in 1984 required the secretary of education to review and evaluate the term *behaviorally disordered* and to submit a report of that review and evaluation within six months after the effective date of the amendment (P.L. 98-199). The report recommended against any change. There are several reasons for the result:

1. A change in definition or terminology probably would cause an increase in the number of students eligible for services. For example, the change in definition might include students who are "socially maladjusted."
2. A change would increase the number of students referred for evaluation. This is so because the change would decrease the stigma, thus reducing a barrier to referral.
3. A change would not affect the settings in which students are educated. Absent an effect on settings, there is no substantial benefit to students.
4. Although the stigma perceived by parents and teachers may be reduced if the special education label is abandoned, there would be no change among nondisabled students' attitudes because they judge their disabled peers by behavior, not labels.
5. A change would not affect professional training, and thus not produce any benefit there.

Learning Disabled. Another example of policymakers' and educators' concerns about who is disabled and the distribution of disabilities involves the classification of students as learning disabled. On the one hand, the category has been extraordinarily useful and popular. It is a way to classify a child who has problems with academics but is not mentally retarded or seriously emotionally disturbed. In addition, it is a relatively stigma-free classification. It certainly does not carry as much opprobrium and devaluation from the norm as mental retardation or serious emotional disturbance. Therefore, it has been acceptable to middle-class educators and parents.

But the rapid and large growth of the category (between 1976–77 and 1985–86 the LD population increased by 119%) has posed some problems.[60] Educators and policymakers are concerned about the definition of *learning disability*. They are worried about over-classification—placing too many children into the LD category because of its relatively low stigma and relatively high acceptability. They also are concerned because of the alleged lack of truly reliable conceptualizations of the term and the absence of highly dependable systems for classifying and educating students as learning disabled. And they are concerned about the increased cost of educating so many children who may not be truly disabled or are marginally disabled.

Mildly Mentally Retarded. In addition, the variable definition of *mild mental retardation* has posed similar problems. In 1973, the American Association on Mental Retardation (AAMR), the nation's oldest and largest professional organization concerned exclusively with mental retardation, reduced the IQ cut-off for classification as mentally retarded from 85 to 70. In 1979, the Council for Exceptional Children began to press for a modification of the cut-off at 70. And in 1983, the AAMR, on its own, defined "mild" mental retardation as having a cut-off at 70 but being particularly subject to clinical judgment and experience of the evaluators. Indeed, the AAMR recognizes a "zone of uncertainty" of between 62 and 78 IQ.[61] The 1992 restatement by the AAMR does not alter the IQ ranges (70–75 or less) but does focus much more on adaptive behavior and situational capacity.

New Concerns

Clinical Judgments. There is reason to believe that clinical judgments are not the only or even the major bases for classification of some minority children into special education. A study commissioned in 1979 by the Office of Special Education, U.S. Department of Education,[62] examined school practices for referring, assessing, and placing children in special education. The study attempted to determine whether those procedures were resulting in the erroneous classification of children.

Several findings are notable. One is that elementary-aged minority children were referred for special assistance (of any kind) at a rate proportionate to their incidence in the school-aged population. But secondary-aged minority students were referred at a higher rate than their incidence in the school-aged population. This result suggests that age is a critical variable.

A second finding is that school diagnosticians and teachers rated academic functioning to be the most important factor in determining disability classification and placement for both minority and nonminority students. They rated nonacademic factors as less important for both minority and nonminority children, but as somewhat more important for minority children. This finding suggests that adaptive behavior, aggression, or hallmarks of minority culture were at play in assessment.

A third finding was that approximately twice as many minority students as nonminority students were designated as "probably mentally retarded." But those students were not subsequently placed in special education programs in these larger percentages. Indeed, the greatest percentage (24%) of minority students was placed in educational programs for learning disabled. By comparison, only 21% of nonminority children were so classified. In addition, only about 4% of minority children were placed in programs for mentally retarded children; a similar percentage was placed in programs for seriously emotionally disturbed children. Thus, assessment and placement do not match perfectly.

Stigma. Several other conclusions are fairly inferable from known effects of the nondiscriminatory evaluation requirements. First, the stigma of mental retardation or serious emotional disturbance is powerful, and it acts to prevent classification in those categories. Second, clinical judgments are subverted by other judgments about how minority children should be classified and educated. Third, there are countervailing concerns about special education as a "dumping ground" for minority children. These concerns address the potential for using special education classification and placement as a disguise for resegregating the nation's schools by race. Finally, there is reason to believe that the science of classification is not precise, at least not at the edges between nondisabled and disabled. This inference is supported by the various redefinitions or attempts to redefine certain types of disabilities, particularly mild mental retardation, learning disabilities, and serious emotional disturbance.

Research and Practice. The fuzziness concerning who is disabled and the nature of the disabilities may reflect poorly on past special education practices, which have been predicated on the purported ability to measure and classify with precision. Moreover, the fuzziness justifies new questions about the validity of prior special education research (and practices based on it), which was conducted on ostensibly "known" disabled children—those whose classification was thought to be reliable and undoubted.

Other Influences. In addition, the ambiguity about classification and the reports concerning classification practices suggest that a student's age, race, socioeconomic status, or sex may influence classification practices as much as any test results. Further, the preferences of educators and parents, as well as their educational philosophies and objectives, may be influential.

Slow Learners/Underachievers. Finally, classification procedures and practices raise fundamental questions concerning the education of slow learners. On the one hand, children who are underachievers may be disabled. On the other hand, they may not—they may just be below "average" but still not classifiable as disabled. If they are disabled, they arguably have the right to be classified as such and given the benefits of special education. On the other hand, if a child is not disabled and in no way can be classified into special education but is still an underachiever or slow learner, there is an obvious need to provide the child with an appropriate education. Should that help come from special education?

Sharing Techniques and Resources. It is important for special education to share its techniques with regular education. Individualization and the related-service provisions are powerful tools for helping a child. But sharing techniques is not the same as sharing funds, personnel, and other resources. If the definition of disabled is expanded to include underachievers and slow learners, there will be new claims on federal, state, and local resources, particularly on funds and personnel.

With every new claim, there will be at least two responses. First, the special education profession and the parents of disabled children will seek to increase appropriations for special education. This will be problematic given the success, or lack thereof, of any education program in commanding new resources, and the current fiscal conditions of federal, state, and local governments. If the claims are successful, it is fair to assume that there will be an augmentation of resources sufficient to accommodate the new class of disabled children. If they are not successful, there will be a second response: to restructure the resources presently available to the traditional disabled children so as to provide some resources both to children whose classification and claim to special education is and always has been certain, and to children in the new class. That result is patently unacceptable to both slow learners and disabled children.

In sum, results of the nondiscriminatory evaluation rule have been generally positive. With respect to some school issues, however, it is still troubling and still unresolved.

NOTES

1. Brown v. Board of Education.

2. Larry P. v. Riles.

3. *Id.*

4. Larry P. v. Riles; Mattie T. v. Holladay; and Hobson v. Hansen.

5. Guadalupe Org., Inc. v. Tempe Elem. School Dist.; Diana v. State Bd. of Ed.; and Hernandez v. Porter.

6. LeBanks v. Spears; Larry P. v. Riles.

7. Larry P. v. Riles; Hobson v. Hansen.

8. Hernandez v. Porter; Diana v. State Bd. of Ed.; and Guadalupe Org. v. Tempe.

9. Larry P. v. Riles.

10. LeBanks v. Spears.

11. Carrington v. Rash.

12. Stell v. Savannah-Chatham County Bd. of Ed.; Miller v. School Dist. No. 2, Clarendon County.

13. Hobson v. Hansen.

14. Larry P. v. Riles; Diana v. State Bd. of Ed.; and Mattie T. v. Holladay.

15. Larry P. v. Riles; Diana v. State Bd. of Ed.

16. *Id.*

17. Diana v. State Bd. of Ed.; Guadalupe Org. v. Tempe; and Lau v. Nichols.

18. Larry P. v. Riles.

19. LeBanks v. Spears.

20. Larry P. v. Riles; *cf.* Carmichael v. Craven, on use of intelligence tests to screen jurors.

21. Larry P. v. Riles.

22. LeBanks v. Spears; Mills v. D.C. Bd. of Ed.; and Hernandez v. Porter.

23. Hobbs (Ed.), *Issues in the Classification of Children* (2 vols.) (San Francisco: Jossey-Bass, 1975, p. 100).

24. *Ibid.*, at p. 101.

25. *Id.*

26. U.S. Senate, Report No. 94-168, *Education for All Disabled Children Act*, June 2, 1975, pp. 26-29.

27. Bonadonna v. Cooperman,.

28. Sarason and Doris, *Educational Handicap, Public Policy, and Social History: A Broadened Perspective on Mental Retardation* (New York: Free Press, 1979).

29. *Ibid.*

30. Gleidman and Roth, *The Unexpected Minority: Disabled Children in America* (New York: Harcourt Brace Jovanovich, 1980).

31. *Id.*

32. Turnbull and Turnbull, *Parents Speak Out: Then and Now* (Columbus, Oh.: Charles E. Merrill, 1985).

33. Sarason and Doris, *supra* n. 28.

34. Gleidman and Roth, *supra* n. 30; Sarason and Doris, *supra* n. 28.

35. Morse, "Crazy Behavior," *Southern California Law Review* 51(1978):528.

36. Gleidman and Roth, *supra* n. 30.

37. Sorgen, "The Classification Process and Its Consequences," in *The Mentally Retarded Citizen and the Law*, edited by Kindred et al. (New York: Free Press, 1976).

38. *Id.*

39. Sorgen, *supra* n. 37; Gleidman and Roth, *supra* n. 30.

40. Kirp, "Schools as Sorters," *Pennsylvania Law Review* 121(1973):705; and Kirp, Buss, and Kuriloff, "Legal Reform of Special Education: Empirical Studies and Procedural Proposals," *California Law Review* 62(1974):40.

41. Hobbs (Ed.), *The Futures of Children* (San Francisco: Jossey-Bass, 1975).

42. Gleidman and Roth, *supra* n. 30; and Sarason and Doris, *supra* n. 28.

43. Gleidman and Roth, *supra* n. 30; Sarason and Doris, *supra* n. 28; Blatt and Kaplan, *Christmas in Purgatory* (Boston: Allyn and Bacon, 1966); Blatt, *Souls in Extremis* (Boston: Allyn and Bacon, 1973); and Blatt, McNally, and Ozolins, *The Family Papers* (Boston: Longman Press, 1979).

44. Wald, "Basic Personal and Civil Rights," in *The Mentally Retarded Citizen and the Law*, edited by Kindred et al. (New York: Free Press, 1976).

45. *In re* Phillip B.

46. Office of Civil Rights, U.S. Department of Education, 1987; Kirp, *supra* n. 40; Mercer, *Labeling the Mentally Retarded* (Berkeley: University of California Press, 1973); Larry P. v. Riles; and Hobbs, *supra* n. 23.

47. Stone, *Mental Health and Law: A System in Transition* (Washington, DC: National Institute of Mental Health, 1976).

48. Turnbull (Ed.), *The Least Restrictive Alternative: Principles and Practice* (Washington, DC: American Association on Mental Retardation, 1981).

49. Trilling, quoted in Rothman, ""Convenience and Conscience," *The Asylum and Its Alternatives in Progressive America* (Boston: Little, Brown, 1980).

50. Erickson, *Wayward Puritans: A Study in the Sociology of Deviance* (New York: John Wiley and Sons, 1966).

51. Sarason and Doris, *supra* n. 28.

52. Blatt, *supra* n. 43.

53. Gleidman and Roth, *supra* n. 30.

54. Sarason and Doris, *supra* n. 28.

55. Hobbs, *supra* n. 41.

56. Sorgen, *supra* n. 37; Kirp, *supra* n. 40.

57. Hobbs, *supra* n. 41; Mercer, *supra* n. 46; and Larry P. v. Riles.

58. Turnbull et al. (Eds.), *The Consent Handbook* (Washington, DC: American Association on Mental Retardation, 1978).

59. Turnbull, *supra* n. 48.

60. U.S. Dept. of Education, *Sixth Annual Report to Congress* (Washington, DC: Government Printing Office, 1984).

61. Grossman, *Classification in Mental Retardation* (Washington, DC: American Association on Mental Retardation, 1983).

62. U.S. Dept. of Education, *supra* n. 60.

For 1994 Update on Nondiscriminatory Evaluation please see page 397.

5
Individualized and Appropriate Education

CONSTITUTIONAL FOUNDATIONS

In its findings of facts in the IDEA, Congress zeroed in on individualized education, characterizing it in terms of "appropriate" education and stating in Sec. 1400(b) (2) and (3) that:

—the special educational needs of disabled children are not being fully met; and
—more than half of the disabled children in the United States do not receive appropriate educational services and are thus denied full equality of opportunity.

These claims are well grounded on the constitutional principles of substantive due process under the Fifth and Fourteenth Amendments and on equal protection under the Fourteenth. The common element of substantive due process and equal protection, in the context of individualized or appropriate education, is *exclusion*. Total exclusion from any type of educational opportunity arguably violates both constitutional principles (see chapter 3 on zero reject). Functional exclusion from a meaningful educational opportunity likewise arguably violates both principles, since education that lacks meaning or significance for the pupil is tantamount to no education at all.

Pre-IDEA Case Law

The courts early on realized the importance of *substantive due process* for opportunity. *Maryland Association for Retarded Children (MARC) v. Maryland*, for example, took the position that if all disabled children are to be furnished an education, the purpose of that education must be redefined, since many of them are inherently unable to master even a modified regular academic program. The goal of their education must be to develop their capabilities to the highest possible level of achievement for each child. *Mills* required a disabled child's education to be "suited to [his or her] needs," and *PARC* ordered that it be "appropriate to [his or her] learning capacities." *MARC*, *Mills*, and *PARC* addressed the substantive due process aspects of appropriate education (a meaningful education in order to prevent functional exclusion). *Lau v. Nichols* skirted the issue but arguably gave comfort to it (see chapter 3).

Equal protection is the other constitutional foundation for claims to an appropriate education for children with disabilities. A federal district court thus ruled that learning disabled children make a viable claim under the equal protection principles that they are victims of unconstitutional discrimination when they are not given instruction specially suited to their needs although nondisabled and mentally retarded children are being provided an *appropriate* free public education. The discrimination exists in learning disabled children being treated differently from nondisabled or mentally retarded children.[1] Another federal court denied a state's motion to dismiss a case alleging that multiply disabled persons were denied equal protection because the nature of the educational programs offered to the plaintiffs was such that no chance existed that the programs would be of benefit to them.[2] Both cases relied on equal protection concepts to argue discrimination in the provision of meaningful (i.e., appropriate or suitable) education.

Pre-IDEA Court Remedies

None of the courts in the early cases defined "appropriate" or "suitable." At the most, they discussed the special educational opportunities that should be made available. *Mills* and *LeBanks* required compensatory or adult education to overcome the effects of prior exclusion. Although early intervention (preschool training) for disabled children has not been ordered by the courts, legislatures often find, as a matter of state policy, that early education is desirable.[3] Congress made similar determinations in the IDEA.

Zero-reject policy did not mean that all children must be placed in regular classrooms within the public school system. "Suitable education" included homebound instruction for physically disabled children who were unable to attend school. In some instances, however, homebound or in-hospital instruction was held permissible only if the pupil was physically unable to attend school.[4] A child who could not benefit from a program of instruction within the public school system could be assigned to the state department that oversaw state institutions, but he or she was nevertheless entitled to an appropriate program of education and training.[5] *Mills*, *PARC*, and *MARC* all ordered that tuition grants be made available if suitable education must be obtained from a private school or institution. These cases also noted, however, that a state has not discharged its duty to provide education if it refers a child to a private facility where he or she is only placed on a waiting list. (See chapter 3 for a fuller discussion of the tuition cases.)

Clearly, alternatives to regular classroom education were recognized as sometimes being the most appropriate form of education for a child. Some courts, however, stated that regular classroom instruction (with auxiliary services if necessary) is preferable to separate special classes, which in turn are preferable to homebound instruction.[6] This preference for mainstream placement is based on the belief that children with special problems benefit from contact with nondisabled children and suffer less from the stigma of difference attached to children who are separated from the regular program.

FEDERAL LEGISLATION

Individualized Education

The requirement that a child's education be appropriate or suitable to his or her needs is simply a requirement that it be individually appropriate or suitable. In the language of the IDEA, the requirement of an appropriate education boils down to a requirement that the education be individualized to redress problems found by Congress [Sec. 1400(b)(2) and (3)].

The IEP

The policy of providing an appropriate education [Sec. 1400(c)] is achieved principally by the device of the individualized education program (IEP) [Sec. 1401(19)]:

> The term "individualized education program" means a written statement for each disabled child developed in any meeting by a representative of the local education agency or an intermediate educational unit who shall be qualified to provide, or supervise the provision of, specially designed instruction to meet the unique needs of disabled children, the teacher, the parents or guardian of such child, and whenever appropriate, such child, which statement shall include (A) a statement of the present levels of education performance of such child, (B) a statement of annual goals, including short-term instructional objectives, (C) a statement of the specific educational services to be provided to such child, and the extent to which such child will be able to participate in regular educational programs, (D) the projected date for initiation and anticipated duration of such services, and (E) appropriate objective criteria and evaluation procedures and schedules for determining, on at least an annual basis, whether instructional objectives are being achieved.

The SEA and the public agency must assume responsibility for implementing a child's IEP in a private or parochial school. This responsibility includes initiating a meeting to develop an IEP before the child is placed in the private or parochial school and ensuring that a representative of the school attends the meeting or that other methods, such as individual or conference telephone calls, are used to ensure participation.

Meetings must be held to review or revise the IEP after a child is placed in a private or parochial program. A representative of the public agency must be involved in any decisions made at these meetings and must agree to proposed IEP changes. The public agency also is responsible for ensuring that an IEP is developed and reviewed for each child placed in a private or parochial school by the agency [Sec. 300.341, .347, and .348].

Each LEA must establish, or revise, if appropriate, an IEP for each disabled child at the beginning of each school year. The provisions must be reviewed and, if appropriate, revised at regular intervals, but not less than annually [Sec. 1414(a)(5) and Sec. 300.343]. Similarly, each SEA is required to assure the U.S. Department of Education, Office of Special Education and Rehabilitative Services, through its Special Education Program unit, that each LEA will maintain records of the IEP for each disabled child and that the program will be established, reviewed, and revised as required in Section 1414 (a)(5) [Sec. 1412(4)].

The state plan must contain procedures for the SEA to evaluate—at least annually—the effectiveness of LEA programs in meeting the educational needs of disabled children. The evaluation is to include an evaluation of IEPs [Sec. 1413(a)(11)]. If a child is placed in a private program by the SEA or an LEA, he or she is still entitled to an IEP in the private school [Secs. 1413(a)(4)(B)(i) and (ii) and 300.341(b), .347, and .348].

Section 300.346 requires the IEP to include the following elements:

(a) A statement of the child's present levels of educational performance;

(b) A statement of annual goals, including short-term instructional objectives;

(c) A statement of the specific special education and related services to be provided to the child, and the extent to which the child will be able to participate in regular educational programs;

(d) The projected dates for initiation of services and the anticipated duration of the services; and

(e) Appropriate objective criteria and evaluation procedures and schedules for determining, on at least an annual basis, whether the short-term instructional objectives are being achieved.

The regulations make it clear that the IEP is not a legally binding contract and that no agency, teacher, or other person may be held accountable if the child does not achieve the projected progress based on the annual goals and objectives [Sec. 300.349]. This section does not prevent parents from using due process procedures for problems related to the IEP, the agencies, or the teachers.

Developing an IEP. The following people must be involved in developing the IEP: a representative of the public agency (other than the child's teacher) who is qualified to provide or supervise the child's special education, the teacher, one or both of the child's parents, the student, when appropriate, and other individuals at the discretion of the parents or agency. When a child is first evaluated, an IEP committee member must be a member of the team that evaluates him or her, or the public agency representative, the teacher, or some other person attending the IEP meeting who is knowledgeable about the evaluation procedures used and is able to interpret the results. Either the agency representative or the teacher should be "qualified" in the area of the child's suspected disability [Sec. 300.344].

Since parent participation in the child's education, and particularly in planning the IEP, is a high priority under the IDEA, public agencies are to take specified steps to ensure that one or both of the child's parents has a chance to attend the IEP conference. These steps include advance notice of the meeting, mutually convenient scheduling of the meeting, and arranging for interpreters for deaf or non-English speaking parents. If the parent(s) cannot attend the meeting, they may still participate through individual or conference telephone calls. The agency may have an IEP meeting without parent participation only when it can document that it unsuccessfully attempted to have the parents participate. The documentation should include detailed records of telephone calls, copies of letters to and from the parents, and the results of visits to the parents' homes or places of work. The agency must give the parents a copy of the IEP if they ask for it [Sec. 300.345].

Timing of the IEP. An IEP for each child must be established, or revised if appropriate, by the beginning of each school year. Exactly when must the conference be held? The regulations specify that the planning conferences for a disabled child who is already receiving special education and related services must be conducted early enough to ensure that the child's IEP is developed (or revised) by the beginning of the next school year. To meet this provision, a local education agency may conduct the meeting at the end of the school year or during the summer [Sec. 300.343]. If a disabled child is not receiving special education, an IEP committee meeting must be held within thirty days of the determination that the child needs special education and related services [Sec. 300.343(c)].

Rationale for the IEP. The IEP is justified on many grounds:

1. The IEP is, of course, a method for assessing the child and, based on the nondiscriminatory evaluation, for prescribing an appropriate program, with related services, and an appropriate placement in the least restrictive environment (thereby overcoming objections based on substantive due process or equal protection—claims of functional exclusion or discrimination).
2. The IEP enables the teacher and other educators to better help the child develop his or her potential (not *maximum* potential). It is one of the most important elements of the child's success in school.
3. It enables the school and the parents to monitor the child's progress in school, measure development, identify areas of weakness, and concentrate on remediating those weaknesses.
4. It recognizes that each child is unique and should be treated in light of his or her own needs.
5. It is a safeguard not only for the child but also for the parents, inasmuch as they are legitimately concerned about misclassification, inappropriate placements, and inadequate programs.
6. The requirement of parental involvement not only recognizes parents' legitimate concerns to have their child protected against potential wrongs, but also strengthens the child's educational program by linking the parents' views of his or her needs and their needs with the school's and parents' ability to train the child. Parents have a wealth of information about their child that can enhance the child's schoolroom training and be carried over into the child's family life if it is shared with school personnel and incorporated in the IEP. The "six-hour disabled child" (one who is seen as disabled only when at school) is too familiar, but parental involvement in the IEP has the potential of relegating this child to history. Quite simply, what happens to the child in school is relevant to his or her home life, and vice versa.

7. The IEP is a technique for sharing decisions and decision-making powers among school personnel and parents. It is another step along the line toward achieving participatory democracy in public education.

8. It is also a powerful device for assuring accountability. It makes the schools accountable to the child for what they do, by requiring an assessment of achievement, a statement of goals, services, and timetables, and procedures and criteria for determining if the goals are being met. It makes schools accountable to the parent as a taxpayer and as a participant in developing the individualized program. Parent involvement in curriculum decisions also promotes accountability on the part of the parents. As an outgrowth of IEP development, parents may come to assume specific responsibility for teaching or reinforcing particular skills and concepts at home.

9. By securing parent participation, the IEP also helps forestall the possibility of a due process protest and hearing under Section 1415. It is not a device of cooption, although some may see it that way. Rather, it is a positive force that assures parent/school decision sharing, contributing to a collaborative relationship instead of an adversarial confrontation between parents and school personnel.

10. IEPs are, of course, necessary to accomplish the zero-reject principles; they tend to assure that no child is overlooked once identified as disabled. They enable school authorities to plan services for disabled children and to provide those services. In addition, they furnish a basis for OSERS evaluation of school programs at the federal level. They are a way to focus the capacity of a school system on the child. Like procedural due process, the IEP is child-centered, not system-centered.

11. IEPs reflect the best current thinking of special educators.

12. Finally, the policy of the IFSP, IEP, and ITP—individualization—is reflected in the IDEA and in other federal laws affecting disabled students or adults, such as the Rehabilitation Act and the Developmental Disabilities Assistance and Bill of Rights Act. These laws require individualized programs for disabled persons.

Appropriate Education, Transition, ADA, and Outcome-Based Education

By far the greatest changes in IDEA occur with respect to the principle of an "appropriate education" and by far the greatest impact of ADA on students and other individuals with disabilities occurs in this context.

Two amendments were the catalysts. Section 1401(a)(20) adds a requirement to the IEP and now mandates the equivalent of an Individualized Transition Program (ITP)—"transition services"—for certain students. Section 1401(a)(19) defines "transition services." Each of these amendments warrants separate discussion.

Section 1401(a)(20) now requires a "statement of the needed transition services for students." This statement is to be added to the student's IEP "no later than age sixteen and annually thereafter (and, when determined appropriate for the individual, beginning at age fourteen or younger)." The services must be "needed," a word that should be read in the context of "appropriate education." Thus, a transition service that is necessary to ensure an appropriate education must be provided. Also, the law specifies ages fourteen or sixteen for the transition services to begin, but it allows them to be provided earlier. Given that transition is a process and given the outcomes that IDEA and ADA expect, it is entirely consistent to provide the services earlier than ages fourteen or sixteen.

As noted in chapter 6, Congress was not willing to make any amendments in IDEA's substantive provisions relating to the principle of the least restrictive environment. For Congress to have attempted to change those provisions would have involved it in one of the most heated battles in the field of disability and special education: What is the least restrictive environment, from whose perspective is the question to be answered, and is the meaning of the term the same for all persons with disabilities, whatever the nature or extent of their disabilities?

Yet, through the transition provisions requiring community-based instruction, Congress pushed the schools to deliver their instruction in the community, that is, in the environment that is most normal and therefore arguably the least restrictive.

Section 1401(a)(20) defines "transition services." The term has several components. First, it includes a "coordinated set of activities for the student." This language means that there must be more than one activity and that the activities must operate in sync with each other (be a "coordinated set").

This set of activities must be "designed within an outcome-oriented process." This language means that the activities must be rationally related ("designed") to each other and to the IDEA outcomes. It also means that the process definition from the IEP and *Rowley* applies to the ITP ("outcome-oriented process") and that the process must be focused on the IDEA outcomes—in short, that outcome and process alike are criteria for appropriate transition services.

This set of activities also must "promote" various outcomes—"movement from school to post-school activities, including post-secondary education, vocational training, integrated employment (including supported employment), continuing and adult education, adult services, independent living, or community participation." Note that the word "promote" implicates the concept of "benefit." If the transition services do not promote the outcomes (i.e., they are not effective or efficacious toward the outcomes), then the services do not confer any benefit on the student.

The ITP and transition amendments relate to the United States Supreme Court's decision in *Rowley*. In that case, the Court held (among other things) that a student is entitled to a reasonable opportunity for "educational benefit" and that the student's progress toward educational goals is evidence that the "benefit" test is being met. Thus, if a student's transition goals are not being met, it is likely that the student can successfully claim a violation of the "benefit" test and a denial of appropriate education under the Court's decision.

Note that Congress put parentheses around "including supported employment." By doing so, Congress intended supported employment (work with a job coach) to be only one work-related outcome, but not the only one. Indeed, it intended regular employment to be preferred over supported employment or else it would not have put parentheses around "including supported employment." In summary, Congress has specified the outcomes (or "results" or "ends") of special education in the ITP provisions.

The list of outcomes ("including postsecondary education, vocational training, . . .") presents a difficult problem of interpretation. On the one hand, the word "or" in that list may mean that it is legally defensible for a student's IEP/ITP to list only one of the outcomes. The argument would be that because the outcomes are listed in the alternatives (the word "or" creates the alternatives) only one is required, not more. On the other hand, the list follows the phrase "movement from school to post-school activities . . . ." The phrase "post-school activities" could be interpreted to mean that there must be more than one activity (the moving word is "activities") and thus that there must be at least two, and could be more than two, of the activities listed ("including . . ."). Happily the federal regulations do clarify the meaning of this provision of IDEA. Also, it is certain that the courts will have to do so.

Moreover, this set of activities "shall include instruction, community experiences, the development of employment and other post-school adult living objectives, and, when appropriate, acquisition of daily living skills and functional vocational evaluation." This requirement makes three commands. First, it tells local educational agencies to use specified means ("instruction, community experiences," etc.) in order to achieve the outcomes (results, ends) that the transition provisions specify. Thus, the law sets out both the ends and the means. Second, it tells local educational agencies that "acquisition of daily living skills and functional vocational evaluation" are appropriate in transition plans for some, but not all, students. Thus, the law sets a general rule in favor of "employment or other post-school adult living objectives" for most students. Third and finally, it tells local educational agencies that they should use community-referenced, community-based, and community-delivered instruction. Thus, it acknowledges the principles of generalization and durability (students learn best when they must actually use their skills), and it acknowledges that skill development should take place in the least restrictive, most normal settings.

The ITP and transition amendments represent a significant change in the IDEA. Until now, the Act generally was process-oriented; it told the LEAs and SEAs what processes to follow to educate children with disabilities. Now, however, the Act makes explicit that there shall be certain outcome-oriented education.

Accordingly, a student's IEP and certainly the ITP should contain goals that are consistent with these outcomes. The student's progress (or lack of progress) toward these outcomes may be evidence that the student is not receiving an appropriate education. And, the student's curriculum should be community-based/referenced (in order to produce the targeted outcomes) and delivered in the most integrated/normal setting (so that the skills will be learned in the natural setting, generalize to it, and thus tend to ensure that the student will learn the skills in the place the student will have to use them).

Congress further required [Sec. 1401 (a)(19) and (20) (D)] the ITP to include a statement of the interagency responsibilities or linkages (or both) that the student needs before he or she leaves school. Also, the local educational agency must reconvene the student's IEP team to identify alternative strategies for meeting transition objectives when an agency that has agreed to provide transition services fails to do so.

In the past, before the 1990 amendments, schools played the role of a "sending agency"—they prepared a student for the adult world and sent him or her off to it after graduation or when the student no longer was eligible for school services. After the 1990 amendments, schools will play the same role.

But there will be a big difference in the "receiving agencies," those to which schools sent students. Before the 1990 amendments, the receiving agencies too often were disability-provider agencies such as local mental health, mental retardation or developmental centers, independent living centers for people with physical disabilities, vocational rehabilitation agencies, or facilities such as group homes or sheltered workshops.

After the 1990 amendments, the receiving agencies no longer should be just these, because IDEA and ADA make it clear that special education outcomes should be those that nondisabled students expect, such as postsecondary education, continuing and adult education, adult services, and integrated employment. Given these expected outcomes, it seems that schools, as sending agencies, will have to begin to include nondisability agencies (so-called "generic" agencies, to distinguish them from disability-specific agencies that are "specialized") in the transition planning. It is also clear that many parents and students will want to plan for transition to generic agencies. Now that schools must associate with generic as well as specialized receiving agencies, it is also clear that Congress again opened a door, albeit a backdoor, for more integration, for greater power behind the principle of the least restrictive alternative.

Section 1401(a)(19) also requires the IEP/ITP process to take into account the student's choices with respect to post-school goals. This is an explicit affirmation that student participation in the IEP process (allowed before the 1990 amendments under Sec. 1401(a)(19)—"whenever appropriate") is appropriate when the IEP/ITP process begins. It also is an implicit recognition that special education should include decision-making and choice-making skills for the student as part of the student's progress toward "independence" as an outcome of special education.

Finally, with respect to "transition" issues generally, Section 1477 (providing for an individualized family service plan), Section 1425 (relating to transition planning for adolescents), and Section 1409(c) (relating to grants, contracts, and cooperative agreements awarded by the Department of Education and allowing the secretary to require recipients to address transition issues) acknowledge that transition-planning is a generic skill and appropriate at various life-stages of the student and family.

Sections 1401(a)(25) and (26) add two new definitions, "assistive technology device" and "assistive technology service," respectively. These definitions are the same as used in P.L. 100-407, Technology-Related Assistance for Individuals with Disabilities Act of 1988. (Under that Act, states are given federal funds in order to develop statewide systems of technology-related assistance for individuals with disabilities. The Act leaves it up to each state how it will develop that system and who will benefit from it.) Under IDEA, if a student with a disability needs technology-related assistance and the student's IEP calls for such assistance (either "devices" or "services"), the student may obtain them from the student's LEA or from the statewide system. Thus, assistive technology services or devices are part of the student's educational program, where appropriate. A student's IEP should call for these services and devices, where appropriate, in order to be regarded as legally sufficient. In a sense, the requirement concerning technology affirms the decision of the First Circuit Court of Appeals in *Timothy W. v. Rochester*, discussed in chapter 3, that (at least for students who have profound disabilities) "state of art" in special education includes the use of assistive technology and devices.

Section 1401(a)(16) affects "related services." These now clearly include therapeutic recreation, social work services, and rehabilitation counseling [Sec. 1401(a)(16)]. Again, this is not so much a change as a clarification. Before the amendments recreation was a listed related service. The amendments now clarify that recreation includes therapeutic recreation. Similarly, before the amendments "counseling services" were designated related services. The amendments indicate simply that "rehabilitation counseling" is a "counseling service" and thus emphasize that counseling for vocational rehabilitation is a related service (consistent with the Act's expectation for vocational outcomes as a result of special education).

And, in another sense, the requirement concerning assistive technology speaks to the national concern for containing the costs of health care. Students (and adults) with disabilities already need assistive technology devices and services. Moreover, the private sector no longer may discriminate against them and may have to accommodate them by providing assistive devices (a reasonable accommodation, required under ADA). Thus, there is a combination of (1) a need by persons with disabilities and (2) increased demand by special education agencies and entities that make reasonable accommodations under ADA. This combination of need and demand could very well stimulate a new market for more assistive technologies and for less expensive ones. Indeed, if the market is created, it is likely to be most viable if it supplies relatively inexpensive devices. This could happen if there is such a large demand that economies of scale in producing and distributing the devices occur. In turn, it is possible that the cost of the technologies will decrease and, as it does, the costs of health care may also decrease.

Section 1401(a)(19), requiring the local educational agency to reconvene the IEP/ITP when adult agencies do not carry out their agreement to provide transition services, and the amendments to the Social Security Act [42 U.S.C. Sec.1396(b), enacted in 1988], allowing the state Medicaid fund to pay for certain related services, together show that Congress does not want any gaps in services and indeed expects state and local educational and health-care agencies to work together to fill any gaps in service or funding for students with disabilities. This expectation in effect affirms the "appropriate education" rule by providing for services and allocating their costs across various agencies.

As suggested in the discussion of ADA in chapter 2, ADA's purpose and goals are consistent with IDEA's. ADA's purpose is to provide clear, strong, consistent, and enforceable standards prohibiting discrimination against individuals with disabilities, without respect to their age, nature of disability, or extent of disability. ADA recognizes that discrimination occurs in many ways, for many reasons, and in almost all sectors of society, and that the proper goals of the nation for individuals with disabilities are to assure equality of opportunity, full participation, independent living, and economic self-sufficiency.

In carrying out these goals and prohibiting discrimination in so many private and public sectors of society, ADA is consistent with IDEA in terms of the expected outcomes for individuals with disabilities. ADA assumes that individuals with disabilities will participate in society in a variety of ways. Similarly, IDEA now states that transition services must be geared toward that type of participation. Together, these two laws are a double-barreled statement of what life for people with disabilities should become: equal opportunity for a life of full participation, independent living, and economic self-sufficiency [ADA, Sec. 2(a)(8)]. Education is appropriate when it furnishes the training that helps the student develop the skills for this outcome, and nondiscrimination is necessary to ensure that, once the student has these skills, there will be no barriers to using them. Thus, IDEA focuses on the individual and attempts to remediate the student's disabilities, and ADA focuses on society and bans discrimination against the individual. This is the principle of "dual accommodation" or "mutuality": the student/individual and the society each must change and be changed to accommodate the other.

Finally, it is notable that the principle of "dual accommodation" or "mutuality" is not unlimited under either IDEA or ADA. With respect to IDEA, the courts have allowed local educational agencies to raise a "cost defense" against a claim that they are furnishing an inappropriate education. This defense essentially allows schools to escape providing certain services or settings/facilities if the cost of doing so is unreasonably high (see this chapter under subsection entitled "Related Services" and chapter 3 under the subsection entitled "Section 504's Requirements: Reasonableness, Cost, and Burden of Proof"). With respect to the ADA, Congress also allows costs to be a defense. When an accommodation to a person with a disability causes an undue hardship on an employer, public accommodation, state/local government, transportation or telecommunication service, the accommodation is not required.

Yet even the cost defense reflects the fundamental approach of the IDEA and ADA, which is individualization. IDEA requires an individualized education whose goals and strategies are set out in a student's IEP and IEP/ITP or in an IFSP for infants/toddlers and their families. Likewise, ADA requires individualized approaches, since "unreasonable accommodation" is based on the "burden" as it occurs in the context of one or more individuals with disabilities.

Outcome-Based Education. As just noted, IDEA has become an outcome-based law, with expectations that special education will produce certain results in students during their transition years. This approach, while complementing the "process" approach that the statute adopted before the 1990 amendments, is not altogether new.

In enacting P. L. 93-380 in 1974 (see chapter 2), Congress had at least four outcomes in mind when it first provided funds to the states for special education. First, it wanted to enforce the Fourteenth Amendment and the equal protection guarantees on behalf of students with disabilities. In this respect, it responded to the *PARC* and *Mills* cases (see chapters 2 and 3). Second, it wanted to help the states carry out their own self-imposed duties, reflected in their constitutions and statutes, to provide an education to all students, including especially students with disabilities. In this respect, it expected that the states would comply not just with the federal guarantee of equal protection but also with their own state laws. Third, it wanted to overcome the practices of total and functional exclusion (chapter 2). In this respect, too, it wanted to assist students with disabilities secure their legal rights and the benefits of an education. Finally, it wanted to initiate a "system change" process, reforming the school systems so that they would accommodate students with disabilities.

Having recognized that P.L. 93-380 was but a first step, Congress enacted P.L. 94-142, the Education of All Handicapped Children Act. Like its predecessor, this law had the same four expectations, but it added two others. First, it created an "in-put" into the education of students with disabilities, represented by the four principles of zero reject (chapter 3), nondiscriminatory evaluation (chapter 4), appropriate education (chapter 5), and least restrictive environment (chapter 6). It also created two accountability techniques, the principles of procedural due process (chapter 7) and parent participation (chapter 8).

Second, it declared its real interest in system change by providing for such techniques as coverage of students in private schools and institutions, the child census, service priorities, comprehensive system of personnel development, and single-agency responsibility (see chapter 3). Each of these was intended to have significant impacts on the school systems, and each did. The 1986 amendments that began to fund states for transition services and activities (P.L. 99-372, chapter 3) were intended to keep the implied promise of special education, namely that the student would "transition" from school to work (i.e., that special education would result in employment). However implicit or indirectly stated, these amendments were clearly outcome based in that they were aimed at (1) affecting students' curriculum and increasing their potential for independence, productivity, and integration into their communities, and (2) affecting schools and adult service provider systems (the so-called "receiving agencies").

The 1986 amendments clearly were the prelude to the 1990 amendments related to IDEA and transition-planning (the ITP), as pointed out in this chapter. More than that, they underscored Congress's concern for outcomes, since, in that very year, Congress had amended the Developmental Disabilities Assistance and Bill of Rights Act by making it clear that the results of developmental disabilities services are independence, productivity, and integration.

This direction also is reflected in Congress's 1986 amendments to the Rehabilitation Act, creating a special federal/state program for "supported employment" and designating new funds for that program (Part C of the Rehabilitation Act, created by P.L. 99-506).

Also in 1986, Congress emphasized its concern with outcomes in still other amendments to the IDEA. Part H (P. L. 99-457), providing federal funds for infant and toddler programs (ages birth through two), expects certain outcomes and is explicit about its expectations. These are that infant/toddler interventions and programs will help child development, assist families, prevent institutional placement, and reduce the number of children who receive special education services.

By its enactment in 1990 of the Americans with Disabilities Act and the transition amendments of IDEA, Congress makes explicit what it had only implied earlier: namely, that it expects schools to provide special education that ensures certain outcomes. Thus, the early outcome-based initiatives (P.L. 93-380, P.L. 94-142, P.L. 99-372, and P.L. 99-457) were just the predecessors of the clear, explicit, and strong outcome-based expectations set out in the IDEA's transition amendments and in the ADA.

Other Statutory Provisions for Appropriate Education

Although the IEP is the principal means in the IDEA for assuring an appropriate education, it is not the only one.

1. Procedures to assure nondiscriminatory testing serve as safeguards against inappropriate placement and resultant inappropriate education [Sec. 1412(1)].
2. The requirement of placement in the least restrictive appropriate program also protects against inappropriate placement and unsuitable programs [Sec. 1412(5)]. It advances the concept of appropriate education by ensuring appropriate placement.
3. The rights of parents to see and comment on LEA records enables them to hold the school accountable for providing an appropriate education [Sec. 1414(a)(4) and Sec. 1415(b)(1)(A)].
4. The due process hearing is yet another method for accountability and compliance with the requirements of appropriate education [Sec. 1415].
5. The infants/toddlers and the early childhood incentive grants are intended to make elementary education, especially in the least restrictive setting, appropriate for the child upon attaining elementary-school age.
6. The exclusion (not more than 12% of a state's children aged five through seventeen may be counted as disabled for the purpose of receiving federal funds under the Act) is also a device for appropriate education. It tends to prevent overcategorization and miscategorization of children as disabled, thereby preventing inappropriate identification, evaluation, placement, and unsuitable programs [Sec. 1411].
7. State education agencies must develop and implement a "comprehensive system of personnel development"; a means for disseminating to school personnel "significant information derived from educational research, demonstration, and similar projects" [Sec. 1413]; and, where appropriate, "promising educational practices and materials development through such projects" [Sec. 1413]. These requirements are intended to improve the schools so that they can provide appropriate education to disabled children. SEA evaluation, particularly for IEP compliance, also will help LEAs provide appropriate programs [Secs. 1418 and 1413].

Determining What Is Appropriate

There are few statutory definitions of "appropriate education" in the IDEA. One of them derives from an understanding of the IDEA as a whole. That definition seeks to define appropriate education by a *process*. The definition of appropriate education looks first to the child and second to the means by which an appropriate education is to be provided. It is child-centered and process-oriented, not system-centered or result-oriented. It takes account of educational "inputs," not educational "outputs."

For example, assume a nine-year-old child is moderately mentally retarded and school personnel (and the parents) are concerned about what kind of education, what kind of placement, is appropriate. How do they answer this question? They do it by (1) making a nondiscriminatory evaluation; (2) developing an individualized education program; (3) attempting to place the child in the least restrictive appropriate program; (4) seeing that the parents have access to the child's school records throughout this process; and (5) calling a due process hearing if the parents wish to protest the placement or any other action related to the child's right to a free appropriate education. The Act's technique for defining "appropriate," then, is to require that a process be followed in the belief that a fair process will produce an acceptable result—an appropriate education.

The regulations also define free appropriate education for special education and related services in terms of standards and conformity with IEPs [Sec. 300.4]. Thus, there are two techniques for determining what is appropriate. Specifically, Section 300.4 of the regulations defines free appropriate public education as one that (1) is provided at public expense, under public direction and supervision, without charge; (2) meets the standards of the SEA; (3) includes preschool, elementary school, and secondary school education; and (4) is provided in conformity with IEP requirements of the IDEA and its regulations.

Part H

Part H (infants and toddlers) requires a basically similar approach to individualization and appropriateness. We will describe the regulations in this chapter and discuss the major differences that affect professional practice in chapter 10. The major difference is that Part H requires an individualized family service plan (IFSP), not an IEP.

The regulations implementing Part H are very specific about the IFSP and deserve extended discussion here. The IFSP must:

- be developed by the family and appropriate qualified providers of early intervention services;
- be based on the multidisciplinary evaluation and assessment of the child and the assessment of the family;
- include the services that are necessary to enhance the child's development and the family's capacity to meet the child's special needs.

In addition, specific content of the IFSP must include:

- a statement of the child's present levels of physical, cognitive, language/speech, psychosocial, and self-help development;
- professionally acceptable objective criteria as a basis;
- a statement of major outcomes for the child and family and the criteria, procedures, and timelines used to determine the degree of progress and whether modifications or revisions of outcomes or services are necessary;

- a statement of specific early intervention services necessary to meet the child's and family's unique needs, including
  - the frequency, intensity, location, and method of delivering services;
  - the payment arrangements, if any;
  - to the extent appropriate, a statement of medical and other services that the child needs but that are not required to be provided under Part H;
  - if necessary, a statement of the steps to be taken to secure those services through public or private resources;
- a statement of the projected dates for beginning the services and of how long the services will be provided;
- the name of the case manager assigned to the family;
- a statement of steps to be taken to support the child's transition from early intervention services to preschool or other services, including discussions with and training of the child's parents regarding future placements and other matters relating to the child's transition.

There is an important note added to the regulations on the IFSP. It reminds you that family members play a variety of roles in enhancing the child's development. It also says that it is important that the degree to which the family's needs are addressed in the IFSP should be determined collaboratively with the full agreement and participation of the child's parents.

The participants in the initial and each annual IFSP meeting must include:

- the child's parent or parents;
- other family members as requested by the parent(s) if it is feasible to include them;
- the case manager;
- a person(s) directly involved in conducting the child and family evaluations and assessments;
- as appropriate, persons who will provide services to the child or family.

If a required person is not available to attend the meeting, other means for participation must be used, such as telephone conference calls, attendance by a knowledgeable representative, or making pertinent records available at the meeting.

The initial meeting for developing the IFSP must be within forty-five days after the child or family is referred to the state's lead agency. Thereafter, periodic review is available in two ways: (1) every six months the IFSP must be reviewed for progress and appropriate revision, by a meeting or other means agreeable to the parties; and (2) a meeting must be held annually to evaluate the IFSP and review it as appropriate.

The meetings must be at times and places convenient to the family. The family's native language or other mode of communication must be used. And the meetings must be scheduled so that the families have enough time to plan to attend.

There are special rules for providing services before the evaluation and assessment of the child and family are complete. Services may begin prior to evaluation and assessment if the parents agree; an interim IFSP is developed (naming the case manager and demonstrating that the services are needed immediately by the child and family); and the evaluation and assessment are in fact completed within the forty-five-day period.

Every agency or person having a direct role in providing early intervention services is responsible for making a good faith effort to assist each eligible child in achieving the IFSP outcomes. But no agency or person may be held accountable if the child does not achieve the growth projected by the IFSP.

There is one important difference between Part B (IEP) and Part H (IFSP) with respect to rights. The requirements for case management and transition planning do not appear at all in Part B.

But it is clear that the IFSP and Part H generally have potential for strengthening families by helping them:

1. Develop great expectations for their infant/toddler and themselves.
2. See the positive contributions that the infant/toddler can make to the family, its friends, and society.
3. Make choices about how they want to be involved in their infant/toddler's life.
4. Create relationships with professionals and with others who are not in the business of providing disability services.
5. Learn what their strengths and needs are.
6. Learn what new strengths can be developed.
7. Determine how they can cope with difficulties and learn new coping skills.
8. Improve or develop new techniques for communicating within the family and with professionals.
9. See the possibilities for the integration and independence of the infant/toddler and, indeed, of the whole family.
10. Secure and coordinate services from a variety of disciplines, service providers, and funding streams.
11. Learn how to take charge of their situation and become their own case manager if they wish to do so.
12. Be launched successfully as families affected by a disability.

Moreover, the IFSP recognizes that families play a crucial role in the infant/toddler's development and will always play an important role in child development. The IFSP really extends the notion of "parent participation" to that of "family participation," subject to the final decision by the parent(s). It recognizes that families are systems and that no one member of the family (the infant/toddler) truly can be helped unless all members of the family are strengthened and unless the whole family plays from a position of strength.

Section 504

The regulations under Section 504 [Sec. 104.33(b)] provide a third way to define appropriate education by requiring schools to furnish disabled children with special education and related aids and services designed to meet their educational needs as adequately as the needs of nondisabled children are met (an *equivalence* definition). The program must be based on least restrictive placement principles and include a full and individual preplacement evaluation, a nondiscriminatory test, an annual reevaluation of special education placement, and procedural due process.

Implementing an IEP is one way to provide an appropriate education, but Section 504 does not require an IEP, nor do its regulations. Like the IDEA, Section 504 addresses the requirement of appropriate or individualized education by requiring that schools follow a process and requires equivalency between those with and without disabilities. In commenting on the present Section 104.33, the Department of Health and Human Services said:[7]

> Section 84.33(b) [now, Sec. 104.33(b)] concerns the provision of appropriate educational services to disabled children. To be appropriate, such services must be designed to meet disabled children's individual educational needs to the same extent that those of nonhandicapped children are met. An appropriate education could consist of education in regular classes, education in regular classes with the use of supplementary services, or special education and related services. Special education may include specially designed instruction in classrooms, at home, or in private or public institutions and may be accompanied by such related services as developmental, corrective, and other supportive services (including psychological, counseling, and medical diagnostic services). The placement of the child must, however, be consistent with the requirements of Sec. 84.34 [100.34] and be suited to his or her educational needs.
>
> The quality of the educational services provided to disabled students must equal that of the services provided to nonhandicapped students; thus, disabled students' teachers must be trained in the instruction of persons with the disability in question and appropriate materials and equipment must be available. The Department is aware that the supply of adequately trained teachers may, at least at the outset of the imposition of this requirement, be insufficient to meet the demand of all recipients. This factor will be considered in determining the appropriateness of the remedy for noncompliance with this section. A new Sec. 84.33(b)(2) [100.33(b)(2)] has been added, which allows the full implementation of an individualized education program developed in accordance with the standards of the EHA [IDEA]. [Author's note: Section 504 regulation references have been updated, in brackets.]

POST-IDEA CASES

Given the IDEA's process definition of appropriate education, the IEP definition in the IDEA regulations, the comparability definition of the Section 504 regulations, and the requirement that an appropriate education must be in the least restrictive environment (LRE), it was clear at the outset that courts would be called on to define *appropriate education* and its relationship to the *least restriction* requirement. For the purpose of explaining the courts' interpretations, it will be helpful to consider separately the LRE cases and their impact on the meaning of appropriate education (see chapter 6). Here, it will be useful to consider how courts have interpreted the other definitions of appropriate education.

Appropriate Education and the Supreme Court

The Supreme Court defined appropriate education in its first special education case, *Board of Education v. Rowley*. The *Rowley* decision has become the touchstone for all subsequent appropriate education cases. It incorporated much of the reasoning and results of other appropriate education cases decided by other courts. Its history and principles, therefore, are worthy of close examination (see Appendix C for the Court's opinion).

In *Rowley*, a federal district court and the Second Circuit Court of Appeals both held that a school district must provide a sign language interpreter in the classroom as part of a deaf child's individualized education program in order to comply with requirements of the IDEA. The courts found that, as a matter of law, a disabled child's education must be comparable to that given nondisabled children, not the best education available. Under the facts in this case, they found that comparability would not be achieved without an interpreter.

The court of appeals noted that the decision was restricted to the facts of this case (the child's parents were also deaf, and evidence at the trial showed that, without an interpreter, only 59% of what transpired in the classroom was accessible to the child). One judge filed a lengthy dissent citing the extensive efforts the school district had already made on behalf of the child.

The U.S. Supreme Court reversed the court of appeals, holding that the IDEA does not require the school to provide the student with an interpreter in order to comply with the mandate of an appropriate education. The Court emphasized the IDEA legislative history. As the Court read that history, it concluded that Congress had not intended that the schools try to develop disabled children to their maximum. Instead, the IDEA's purpose was basically to open the schools' doors to disabled students, granting them access to educational opportunities. Accordingly, congressional intent is satisfied when the school provides the student a reasonable opportunity to learn.

Because the student in this case had progressed from grade to grade without an interpreter's help, there was evidence of the school's compliance with the "open doors" intent of Congress. In this aspect of the case, the Court essentially adopted the comparability standard (the Section 504 approach). If the open doors rule were not adopted—i.e., if comparable treatment were not required—the "maximum development" purpose would be appropriate. Because it is not, *the comparability test prevails*.

The Court also stressed the importance of the law's procedures for defining and providing an appropriate education. Specifically, it noted that all of the professionals involved in developing the child's IEP were of the opinion that the child could be educated appropriately without an interpreter. In addition, it pointed out the many ways in which the law allows the child's parents to be involved in the IEP process and otherwise.

The *Rowley* decision undoubtedly is quite limited by its facts as precedent for other cases. For example, because the student was mainstreamed, it is doubtful that the Court's emphasis on grade-to-grade promotion would apply to disabled children who do not or cannot progress from grade to grade or whose progress cannot be measured by that standard. It also is doubtful whether the decision would apply to disabled children who require related services in order to be educated in the mainsteam, such as the spina bifida children in *Tatro* and *Tokarcik*, two cases that are discussed later in this chapter under "Related Services." The Supreme Court's own *Tatro* decision confirmed that suspicion.

But *Rowley*'s impact—the principle of rough comparability in opportunity and the Court's reliance on professionalism and process—is great. Some of the cases summarized in the following paragraphs reflect *Rowley*'s fallout. Others were decided before *Rowley*.

Appropriate Education, Not Maximum Development

The first of *Rowley*'s principles is that the IDEA was designed only to provide to disabled children the same basic opportunities for an education that nondisabled children have. Opening the school doors so that disabled children have reasonable opportunities to learn, but not assuring them an opportunity to reach their maximum potential, was considered to be Congress's intent, nothing more. *Rowley* thus addressed the goal of an education, not just how that goal is to be reached (e.g., with or without an interpreter). Several other cases also addressed the goal of special education. The trend of the cases is to hold that the IDEA provides only *an* appropriate education, not the best one or one designed to help the child reach his or her maximum potential.

The principal case, *Springdale School District v. Grace*, held that the child is entitled to an appropriate education (in the public school, in this case), not the best (in a residential facility). On appeal, the Eighth Circuit Court of Appeals affirmed, applying *Rowley* and holding that the mainstreaming goal is served by education in a local school district, where instruction is reasonably calculated to provide the child with educational benefits. The best education available does not have to be offered. Note that the court does not consider cost of implementing a school district program if it provides an appropriate education. Other cases agree with this result.[8] Under these cases, the child's maximum development is not the goal of his or her education. In other cases, however, maximum development is the goal, and the "best" or "near best" education is the appropriate one.[9]

If a state by its own laws provides that a goal of the special education program is to develop a child's maximum potential, a court will enforce that requirement and command a program of education that is appropriate to developing a child's maximum potential. That is the rule of *David D. v. Dartmouth School Committee*, and it has been followed in subsequent cases.[10] Thus, a state may set a higher standard than the IDEA, and a court will enforce that standard.

The "maximum development" doctrine—namely, that a state may set a higher standard than IDEA and be required to provide more than just the "appropriate education" outlined under IDEA and *Rowley*—is involved in *Conklin v. Anne Arundel County Board of Education*. There, the Fourth Circuit Court of Appeals has asked a lower court to determine if the Maryland state law sets a higher standard than IDEA.

The reason for this result is simple. The IDEA is a national law, not one that sets standards, other than minimum ones, for each state. Moreover, its intention—as declared by Congress and interpreted by the Supreme Court in *Rowley*—is to open the doors to an appropriate education. This goal is essentially one of providing equal opportunity for education, commensurate with the student's capacities.

Thus, equal educational opportunities mean just that—equal, not exceptional in the sense that the maximum development is the goal. If maximum development were the goal, equal opportunity would not be the dominant theme of the IDEA. Indeed, the three ways of obtaining equal educational opportunity for students with disabilities require only that an appropriate education be provided, not that the maximum development be sought. Thus, equal treatment, equal treatment plus accommodations, and unequal but favorable treatment (see chapter 3 for a discussion of the concept of equality and equal treatment for students with disabilities) are the means for equal educational opportunity. If maximum development were the goal, these three means would have to be added to; another one would be "equal treatment plus favorable accommodations for extraordinary opportunity, not just ordinary opportunity."

Although this result may be desirable, it is not consistent with the IDEA's goals of equal educational opportunity. Thus, it is not part of the federal law. But because it is a desirable goal, a state may adopt it, and a court will enforce it. That result—state-set goals with judicial enforcement—also is consistent with the federalism principle. This principle (explained more in chapter 3) allows a state to have discretion in the education of its students, as long as it does not deny them equal protection of the laws (i.e., as long as the state does not violate the Fourteenth Amendment). Thus, a state may set a higher standard (maximum development), but if it does not, it is bound only to the IDEA standard of equal (not extraordinary) educational opportunity.

The courts have been consistent in holding—per *Rowley*—that federal law does not require the student's maximum development, only an opportunity to benefit from the education offered (*Burke County Board of Education v. Denton* and *Matta v. Board of Education, Indian Hill Exempted Village Schools*).

The Twelve-Month School Year

Another of *Rowley*'s tenets is that professionally developed, individualized education programs are deemed to be appropriate. That proposition flies squarely in the face of legislative judgments, usually based on fiscal policy, that a school year should be limited to a fixed number of days a year. Although fiscally and politically defensible, that decision does not satisfy the *Rowley* demand for individualization of education, based on professional judgment.

It was therefore predictable that inflexible school year limits would be tested. On twelve-month education, the leading case is *Armstrong v. Kline.* In that case, the district court held that the state's refusal to pay for more than 180 days' schooling each year for severely and profoundly retarded and severely emotionally disturbed children violated their rights to an appropriate education under the IDEA. An appropriate education is one that allows the children to become self-sufficient within the limits of their disabilities, not just one that allows them to share equally in programs provided to nondisabled students or to reach one of several other goals (the court relied on legislative intent to define appropriate education). The court also noted that some children will regress significantly during breaks in their education and recoup their losses more slowly, and thus are denied an appropriate education when they are not given year-round education. Other cases concur in this result.[11]

The *Rowley* Standard Interpreted

The essence of the *Rowley* standard is "educational benefit." A school district must ensure, through the student's IEP, that there is some educational benefit from the education provided.

Courts have interpreted this provision in several cases. For example, one court[12] held that the *Rowley* standard means that grade-to-grade advancement of a child classified as trainable mentally retarded is not valid. The "benefit" must be measured by some means other than such advancement. Otherwise, the student will be deprived of the opportunities for placement in the mainstream (regular education programs—see chapter 6). Likewise, the *Rowley* standard as applied to a child who has never attended regular classes means that the child must be given instruction that ensures some educational progress, not any regression or trivial educational advancement.[13] It is clear from these cases that the *Rowley* standard of educational benefit is interpreted on a case-by-case basis, and that the student's present placement, diagnosis, disability, and capability must be taken into account in measuring "educational benefit."

It should be no surprise that the courts have wrestled with the *Rowley* requirement that there be an opportunity for educational benefit in order to comply with the appropriate education law. By and large, they have ruled that there must be more than trivial progress in the student's performance for the schools to satisfy the *Rowley* standard (*Polk v. Susquehanna I.E.U. No. 16*). Thus, when a student has made no improvement in performance on standardized tests over a three-year period and continues to receive failing grades over the same time period, the student has not been provided an appropriate education, even though he or she has been in a mainstream program, and should therefore be transferred to a special education (learning disabilities) program (*Hall v. Vance County Board of Education*). Likewise, when a student has regressed in skills and increasingly manifests behavior problems, it is clear that an appropriate education has not been provided (*Board of Education of East Windsor Regional School District v. Diamond,* and *Doe v. Smith*).

Moreover, *Rowley* requires not only educational benefit, but an individualized approach to a student's education. Thus, it is a violation of the appropriate education rule for a school district to adopt a standard, blanket policy of refusing to provide direct physical therapy to any student and to insist instead that, for all students, there may only be a consulting physical therapist who will work with the students' teachers (*Polk v. Susquehanna I.E.U. No. 16*). A blanket policy covers all students and is not individualized, is not calculated to benefit a particular student, and therefore is invalid under the *Rowley* individualization and educational benefit standard. The requirement of individualized decision-making also was restated in the Supreme Court's decision in *Sullivan v. Zebley*, invalidating the regulations of the Department of Health and Human Services that denied certain Social

Security benefits (Supplemental Security Income) to children simply because they were children and without regard to whether they otherwise met the criteria for eligibility for SSI benefit.

Inevitably, the courts have had to chose between at least two proposed placements and programs in deciding which is appropriate or more appropriate than the other. They have tended to take into account the relative richness or insufficiency of programs (*Springdale v. Grace*) as well as the ability of one program (in contrast to another) to deal with a child's multiple disabilities, work with the student's parents, provide effective communication between staff and student, and be reasonably priced (*Matta v. Board of Education Indian Hill Exempted Village Schools*). In addition, it is not required that full-time, twenty-four-hour programs be provided, including in-home programs, if in-school programs are reasonably likely to benefit the student and also if the twenty-four-hour services consist of psychotherapy (*Burke County Board of Education v. Denton*). Nor is it required that the school provide a desirable related service if the student will benefit without it and through receiving only necessary related services (*Rettig v. Kent City School District*). If, however, the student requires twenty-four-hour services in order to benefit from other, more typical six-hour schooling, it violates the appropriate education rule to deny those services and therefore it is permissible to place the student in a residential school instead of a homebound program, since the former provides around-the-clock programming (*Chris D. v. Montgomery County Board of Education*).

The case *Angevine v. Jenkins* illustrates how courts approach the balancing test in assessing whether an appropriate education and educational benefits will occur. In determining whether a particular placement is consistent with the appropriate education principle and conforms to the *Rowley* benefit test, the court said, a school district must consider the student's capability to make educational progress. Its failure to do so constitutes a violation of the appropriate education rule. Thus, the appropriate education and educational benefit requirements are met where (1) a placement has higher expectations for the student than another proposed placement (as reflected in its IEP goals and objectives and in the classroom placement and curriculum), and (2) the program uses appropriate curricula to teach functional academics to a student with mental retardation, has identified and is using appropriate instructional and behavioral strategies to maximize the student's learning, has addressed the student's particular learning styles and has demonstrated progress in the student's rate of learning, has helped the student learn to pay attention and interact socially with staff and peers, and has demonstrated all this when the alternative placement has failed to demonstrate progress.

Likewise, in *Carter v. Florence County School District Four*, the court held that a student classified as learning disabled is entitled to a placement at a private school (although the school is not state-approved) where the facts indicate she will make educational progress there and benefit from its program to a greater degree than from the public school program. The public school's IEP resulted in her achieving only four months of progress in a nine-month year through only three periods of work with resource teachers per week. Its program basically resulted in her regression and failed to ensure her passing from grade to grade (in compliance with the *Rowley* standard as appropriately applied to this student, who has LD and thus is capable of grade-to-grade advancement during the high school years). The court of appeals affirmed and noted that reimbursement of tuition for placement in an unapproved school was permissible. To condition reimbursement on state approval of the private school would enable the state to avoid its duty to provide a free appropriate education, since by withholding its approval the state would foreclose the placement of the student and thereby require the student to have only the inappropriate program in the public school.

Some courts resist the "balancing of benefits" approach and tend to confirm whatever the school district proposes. These cases are in the minority and usually older. For example, *G.D. v. Westmoreland School District* discounts the "balancing of benefits" test. Also discounting the balancing approach are *Manuel R. v. Ambach*, *Bertolucci v. San Carlos Elementary School District*, and *Scituate School Committee v. Robert B.*

Some unusual techniques of assisting students with disabilities to benefit from school are developing. One is the use by people with disabilities of specially trained animals, such as the "guide dog" that people with visual impairments have used or the trained monkeys that individuals with cerebral palsy or other physical disabilities use. Recognizing that specially trained animals are helpful and that a ban on them in schools may impair students' abilities to obtain educational benefit, one court has ruled that it violates Sec. 504 of the Rehabilitation Act to prohibit a physically disabled student from bringing a service dog to school (*Sullivan v. Valejo City Unified School District*). This case obviously has implications for students who use guide dogs, other animals, or assistive technology, especially where (as in *Sullivan*) the animals do not pose any public health risks.

The Process Definition

The appropriate education cases lead to other conclusions. Clearly, the process definition of appropriate education is at work: Enroll the child, evaluate, do an IEP, and place him or her in the least restrictive environment. The cases, other than *Rowley*, are *New York Association for Retarded Children v. Carey, In the Matter of the "A" Family*, and *Harrell v. Wilson County Schools*.

The "process definition" as set out in the IDEA and in *Rowley* has been applied by several courts, with interesting results. The basic rule seems to be that the process of identification, evaluation, and program (IEP) must be followed. If it is not and if the noncompliance results in some actual harm or some likelihood of harm, the student's IEP is inappropriate. For example, if the IEP fails to address the diagnosed aspects of the child's education (that is, it does not pay attention to the nondiscriminatory evaluation), it is not appropriate because it cannot provide an education that is reasonably calculated to benefit the child.[14] Likewise, if a school district fails to comply with the procedures for nondiscriminatory evaluation and IEPs and fails to give notice to the parents concerning their rights (in violation of the due process safeguards, chapter 7), the IEP is inappropriate.[15] Similarly, the school district's failure to properly evaluate a student results in an inappropriate and invalid IEP.[16]

Rowley required the schools to follow a certain process to ensure that a student would have an appropriate education. If, however, the student's parents, not the school, interrupt or block the process from being carried out, they are not entitled later to claim that the process definition has not been satisfied (*Doe v. Defendant I* and *Burke County Board of Education v. Denton*). Moreover, if the process is only slightly flawed in that the IEP does not contain all of the relevant information required by the statute but the parents as well as the school are aware of the missing information, that defect in the IEP will not make it invalid or cause the courts to find that the process definition has not been met (*Doe v. Defendant I* and *Burke County Board of Education v. Denton*). (Procedural flaws, caused in part by parents and which do not impair the student's ability to benefit, are not fatal and do not cause a violation of the appropriate education rule.)

These cases do not stand for the proposition that any procedural error is excusable. The process definition still has teeth as evidenced by the holding that the failure of the IEP team to take into account the student's objectives, including general educational needs and services that will be required to ensure that the student receives an appropriate education, violates the student's right to an appropriate education (*Doe v. Smith* and *Spielberg v. Henrico County Public Schools*).

The courts seem reluctant to insist on strict compliance with the process definition if there is no demonstrable harm to the student as a result of noncompliance with process. Thus, failure to give notice to the parents does not result in harm when the parents attend the IEP meeting and know its purpose.[17] This is the "harmless error" exception to the general rule.

In summary: The process definition must be followed if there is actual or potential harm to the student if it is not followed. But there is an exception for "harmless error"—the situation in which error occurred (failure to follow process) but the error caused no harm.

Judicial Reliance on Expert Judgment

Rowley made it clear that the courts should defer to the experts in matters related to the child's right to an appropriate education. This rule—judicial deference to expert judgment—comes into play after the courts determine that the educational benefit test and the process definition have been met. Thus, if there is a dispute between parents and the school district about the appropriateness of a student's education and if there is some proof that the student is benefiting from the education offered and that the process for determining appropriateness has been met, the courts will not substitute their judgments for that of experts concerning the student's education.

For example, in *Rowley* the Court mentioned many times that the experts had determined that Amy Rowley did not need an interpreter, in large part because she was receiving an educational benefit from schooling without an interpreter; after all, benefit—progress from grade to grade—was clearly evident. Likewise, in *Lachman v. Illinois Board of Education*, a court found that if an LEA fulfills its procedural responsibilities in developing an IEP and experts differ on whether the student should be educated by one means or another (here, by one type of educational method for the deaf or another), the parents have no right to insist on the child's placement in a program that uses only cued speech instruction.

It bears mention that the rule of judicial deference to expert judgment is well settled. The Supreme Court has announced it in *Honig* and *Arline* (both of which are discussed in chapter 3), *Tatro* (discussed immediately below, see Appendix D), and other disability cases.[18] As pointed out in chapter 4, the rule allows the courts to make "correct" judgments on matters that are very technical and on which experts may disagree; the courts lack capacity to make their own independent judgments and must rely on experts. But the rule also allows the courts to duck the hard issues of social policy—deferring to experts instead, as in *PASE v. Hannon* (see chapter 4) and *Armstrong v. Kline* (discussed in this chapter).

Other Factors, Including Neighborhood Schools

An appropriate education also depends on the presence of developmental or age-appropriate peers;[19] on education with students of the same gender, where education with students of the opposite gender would be inappropriate because of the student's imitative tendencies;[20] on a healthful environment;[21] on instruction by certified teachers;[22] and on placement in residential facilities fairly near the child's home;[23] or with nonhandicapped children.[24]

The neighborhood school cases are a mixed lot. Where a student has a very severe disability and the school district has created a centralized program for her and others like her so that there is a critical mass of students and a cost-efficiency in providing services, then some courts have permitted placement in an appropriate program other than in the neighborhood school. This was the result in *Barrett v. Fairfax County School Board*, where the student had a severe hearing loss. Instruction of that student and others was in a school where nondisabled students also had been instructed in how to use the same methods of communication and where this particular student had been integrated academically and extracurricularly very successfully. Placement in the neighborhood school would have required the district to atomize the services and also would have required intensive training of nondisabled peers in the neighborhood school. Similar cases included *DeVries v. Fairfax County School Board* (student had autism), *Schuldt v. Mankato* (student was in a wheelchair and expert opinion was in favor of not integrating into the neighborhood school), and *Thomas v. Cincinnati Board of Education* (student was severely disabled).

In other cases, however, courts require the student to be placed at the neighborhood school, where the following factors enter into the court's decision:

- presence of certified teacher (*A.W. v. Northeast R-1 School District*)
- appropriate program available or can be created at neighborhood school (*Manchester School District v. Williamson, Kettle Moraine School District v. Gover,* and *Lachman v. Illinois State Board of Education*)
- age appropriateness exists in the neighborhood school (*Manchester School District*)
- "associational values," that is, the benefits of students with and without disabilities associating with each other are advanced (*Manchester School District*)

- the alternative placement is a state school (*Kettle Moraine*)
- placement at neighborhood school will not adversely affect student's educational benefit (*Kettle Moraine*)
- extracurriculars (recreational sports and adaptive physical education) are available at neighborhood school (*Kettle Moraine*)

Related Services

An appropriate education also depends on the availability of related services. These are transportation and such developmental, corrective, and other supportive services (including speech pathology and audiology, psychological services, physical and occupational therapy, recreation, early identification and assessment, counseling services, school health services, social work services in school, parent counseling and training, and medical and counseling services, except that such medical services shall be for diagnostic and evaluation purposes only) as are required to assist a disabled child to benefit from special education [Sec. 300.13].

Catheterization. The U.S. Supreme Court itself has clarified one important aspect of related services. The general issue was how to distinguish between a related service and a medical service. The specific issue was whether catheterization is a related service that schools must provide or a medical service that they are not required to provide except for diagnostic or evaluation purposes. Federal trial and appeals courts had held in *Irving Independent School District v. Tatro* that clean intermittent catheterization (CIC) is a related service. The Supreme Court affirmed, holding in a unanimous opinion that CIC is a related service that schools must provide.

In *Tatro*, the Supreme Court found as a matter of fact that CIC is a "simple procedure . . . that may be performed in a few minutes by a layperson with less than an hour's training." Indeed, the student herself soon would be able to perform the service, as her parents, babysitters, and teenage brother had been doing all along.

The Court was faced with the legal issue of whether CIC is a related service under the IDEA [Sec. 1401(17)]. To decide that, it had to determine whether CIC is a supportive service required to assist a disabled child in benefiting from special education and, next, whether CIC is excluded from the supportive service definition because it is a medical service serving purposes other than diagnosis or evaluation.

The Court held that CIC is a supportive service because without it the student could not attend school and thereby benefit from special education. Congress's intent, said the Court (relying on its earlier decision in *Rowley*), was to make a public education available to disabled children and to make their access to school meaningful. A service that makes it possible for the child to "remain at school during the day is an important means of providing the child with the meaningful access to education that Congress envisioned." It is clear that the Court was not about to allow any violation of the zero-reject principle by permitting schools to escape the obligation of this type of related service. It also is apparent that the

Court was concerned that disabled children have an opportunity for *meaningful* access. Its concern with prohibiting functional exclusion is apparent, too. And the Court may have been concerned with exclusion of the student from education with nondisabled students, although it did not refer to the LRE principle.

Next, the Court found that CIC is not a medical service that the school must provide for diagnosis or evaluation. There are two reasons for this conclusion. First, the Court deferred to the Department of Education regulations, which ruled CIC to be a related, not a medical, service. (This was its approach in *Arline*, too.) Second, the Court found that Congress plainly required schools to hire various specially trained personnel and that school nurses have long been a part of educational systems. It also noted that nurses have authority to dispense oral medication and administer emergency injections and that it is difficult to distinguish CIC from these services.

Note that *Tokarcik v. Forest Hills* also held that catheterization is a related service. Similarly, tracheotomy cleaning and reinsertion is a related service (school health service).[25]

Psychotherapy. Several of the dispositive facts in *Tatro* and its holding that CIC is a related service are not present in cases involving psychotherapy. For example, trained laypersons can perform CIC. Indeed, CIC can be self-administered. By contrast, psychotherapy can be performed lawfully and competently (it is presumed) only by licensed physicians with special training and qualifications in psychiatry. Rarely is it self-administered in the sense of the patient and psychiatrist being one and the same person.

In addition, the cost of CIC is relatively low, and its benefits to the child (enhanced opportunity for life and for education, particularly with nondisabled children) are great. The cost-benefit ratio favors CIC and disfavors schools' objections to providing it. On the other hand, psychotherapy is expensive and its benefits seem questionable in some cases. It is therefore no wonder that the courts have divided opinions on whether psychotherapy is a related service that school districts must either pay for (so others can provide it) or provide themselves.

In the Matter of the "A" Family held that out-of-state placement in a private residential facility for seriously emotionally disturbed children, at which the child would receive psychotherapy, is placement in the least restrictive alternative for the child and the tuition and the therapy must be paid by a local school district under the IDEA's provisions for related services. Psychotherapy is a related service, not a medical service, because it is a "treatment of mental or emotional disorders or of related bodily ills by psychological means," according to *Webster's New Collegiate Dictionary*. It thus comes within the definition of psychological services [Reg. Sec. 121a.13(b)(8)—"planning and managing a program of psychological services, including psychological counseling for children and parents"]. A case reaching a similar result is *T.G. v. Board of Education of Piscataway.*

By contrast, *McKenzie v. Jefferson* held that the residential component of a psychiatric hospital placement is medical, not educational, in nature and is not to be paid for by a school district because it is not a related service. A concurring case is *Darlene L. v. Illinois State Board of Education.*

Other cases tend to be expansive and liberal about psychotherapy, usually in the context of residential hospitalization (as contrasted with school-based special education and psychotherapy as a related service). Thus, *Gladys J. v. Pearland Independent School District* and *Kruelle v. New Castle County School District* both held that an appropriate education for severely emotionally disturbed children includes psychotherapy and twenty-four-hour, twelve-month residential placement. Other cases concur in this result,[26] holding that school nurses' and physicians' charges at a residential facility should be paid by the school district that placed the child there, but the physicians' charges are for evaluations and diagnostic and prescriptive services, not treatment.

Similarly, in *Gary B. v. Cronin*, the plaintiffs were emotionally disturbed children alleging that a state rule excludes counseling and therapeutic services from special education services. The court issued a preliminary injunction preventing implementation of the rule to deny money from counseling, therapy, and so forth, failure to pay the plaintiff for costs of therapy, counseling, and so forth, and denial of a free appropriate education to the plaintiff. (Note the opposite trend in *McKenzie* and in *Darlene L.*, mentioned earlier.)

What if a student with disabilities becomes a user of illegal drugs and is referred by a court to a drug-treatment program? Is that program a "related service" for which special education funds and a local school district must pay? The answer in the first case to consider the matter is "no." The drug treatment program is essentially a medical intervention, not a special education program (*Field v. Haddonfield Board of Education*).

Other Medical or Health-Related Services. Although the trend in the cases involving psychotherapy barely tilts toward holding that service to be a related service, there is a clear trend in the opposite direction in cases involving other medical or health-related services. The leading case is *Detsel v. Board of Education of the Auburn Enlarged City School District*. The student (Detsel) is an oxygen-dependent person who requires a constant supply of oxygen. The supply must be calibrated to provide a mixture of 40% oxygen. The means for providing that supply is a respirator. The respirator is operated by a trained nurse or other professional, who must be in attendance with the student and the respirator on a constant basis.

The issue in *Detsel* was whether the school district must pay for the nurse—that is, whether the provision of a nurse to constantly monitor and provide the necessary respirator-support and oxygen is a school-health service that meets the test of a related service. The federal courts held that the district does not have to provide the nurse and that the service is not a school-health or related service.

The reasons for this result have to do with the nature of the service and its relationship to the child's education. The person who must provide the service must be professionally licensed, and an aide for the principal professional usually is required. A registered nurse or licensed practical nurse is the only person professionally qualified to perform the procedure. A school nurse's duties have not included this service. The procedure itelf is complex, consisting of many separate but interrelated steps. The expense of providing the service is great. The service is life-sustaining, and the risk of a malfunction in the service—that the student experiences respiratory distress and, if not rescued, may die—is great. Provision of the service is supervised and prescribed by a physician. And the student, although clearly benefiting from the service, is not using the service directly to benefit from special education; the service is necessary, but not for the purposes of special education.

A similar result was reached in *Bevin H. v. Wright.* There the court ruled that the school district is not required to pay for nursing and related health services for a child who is severely and profoundly disabled. The services are respiratory support (breathing through a tracheotomy tube inserted into the student's throat) and nutritional support (being fed through a tube inserted into the student's stomach). Because the student's care is varied, intensive, must be provided by a nurse under a physician's supervision and prescription, cannot be provided by a layperson, is time-consuming and expensive, and involves life-threatening situations that require the constant vigilance of a professional, these health services are not related to the student's special education.

Air Conditioning. An unusual related service case, *Espino v. Besteiro*, held that a school district must provide an air-conditioned classroom for a child with multiple disabilities who was unable to regulate his body's temperature. Placing him in an air-conditioned Plexiglas™ cubicle restricted him from interacting with his peers.

Summary of Related-Services Cases. The *Detsel* case has had a prolonged history. After the federal court of appeals ruled earlier in the same case that the school is not required to pay the costs of nursing care for her during school hours (*Detsel v. Board of Education*), Congress amended the Medicaid law in 1986 to allow Medicaid funds to be used for health-related services of a student whose IEP calls for those services to be provided [P.L. 99-272, 42 U.S.C. Sec. 1396n(g)] so long as a state's Medicaid plan permits the funds to be used for those services and the child is Medicaid-eligible. (See chapter 3 for a discussion of the Medicaid Catastrophic Coverage Act and its impact on special education funding.) Following the unsuccessful attempt to have the nursing care provided as a related service and after Congress amended the Medicaid law, Detsel's parents sued to require the Department of Health and Human Services, which administers the Medicaid program, to provide a private duty nurse to the student during her time in school. The secretary of HHS declined to authorize payment for the private duty nurse but lost the case in court when the court ruled that the secretary's regulations (prohibiting payment) were unreasonable because they contravened congressional intent (*Detsel v. Sullivan*). The result is that some students, such as Melissa Detsel, may receive Medicaid funding for services that traditionally were denied as not being "related services."

Recently, the U.S. Department of Health and Human Services announced a new policy concerning private duty nursing services. Consistent with the *Detsel* decision, the Health Care Financing Administration (HCFA, which administers Medicaid under the auspices of the Department of Health and Human Services) will now pay for private duty nursing services (via the Medicaid program) when those services are provided during the hours when a student (who receives Medicaid benefits) is outside his home engaging in normal life activities such as attending school (*Pullen v. Cuomo*). Thus, a student whose IEP calls for him to have private duty nursing services during school hours and who has become entitled to Medicaid benefits now can charge the private duty nursing costs to Medicaid for the time he is in school and receiving those services. This result will encourage schools to help students qualify for Medicaid services, write IEPs that call for private duty nursing services, and charge the costs of those services to Medicaid.

The *Detsel* case, however, does not signal a general trend toward relaxing the meaning of "related services." Some courts still resist charging the schools with essentially psychotherapeutic services: *Burke County Board of Education v. Denton* (denial of twenty-four-hour, in-home, behavior-management training for student and family) and *Clovis v. California Office of Administrative Hearings* (LEA may not be charged with costs of placement and therapy at a psychiatric hospital that does not operate a full-time school and where physicians, not educators, determine what services the student will receive as a patient).

But it is not uniformly true that courts will interpret the "related services" provisions conservatively. The same court that decided the *Clovis* case, holding that psychotherapy is not a related service, also held that an LEA must pay for all of the services provided to a student with severe emotional disturbance who is placed in a rehabilitation facility for educational, not medical, reasons, and whose program is developed by educators and delivered in a school setting within the rehabilitation facility (*Clevenger v. Oak Ridge School Board, Jefferson County Board of Education v. Breen*, and *Taylor v. Honig*). Whether the state characterizes a facility as a psychiatric hospital or as an education-based rehabilitation facility makes a difference to the courts. Likewise, the nature of the program offered, the type of setting in which it is offered, the professional expertise of those who develop and carry out the program, and the necessity of the program to advance the student's education, not just his or her medical therapy, also make a difference to the courts. It is consistent with the courts' deference to administrative agencies, as required by *Rowley* (courts should defer to the judgment of experts and the state and local educational agencies), for them to accept and be bound by the reasonable characterization of a program that is developed by an agency (*Detsel* and *Sullivan v. Zebley*).

In addition, other courts are lenient in interpreting the related services provisions of the law. One held that a student is denied an educational benefit when deprived of related services provided by physicians and psychologists who develop and implement a behavior-modification program that is designed to improve the student's educational performance and is based on the student's classification as seriously emotionally disturbed (*Brown v. Wilson County School Board*). Others have invalidated LEA limitations on related services when the limitations have the effect of denying the student the necessary services for acquiring an educational benefit. For example, a blanket ban on direct physical therapy is invalid because some students may require direct physical therapy and because *Rowley* and the statute require individualized decision-making (*Polk v. Susquehanna I.E.U. No. 16*). Likewise, merely providing some related services but not ensuring that the services address all of the student's needs (as where occupational therapy addresses only one of the student's several needs) is out of compliance with the related services rule (*Rapid City School District 51-4 v. Vahle*).

Although the cases on psychotherapy are not fully consistent with each other, there are some clear criteria that determine whether a service is related or medical. These criteria are the complexity, constancy, costs, and ultimate value of the service. If the service is very complex (in *Tatro*, the service was simple and could be self-administered or performed by a layperson with only a little training and no back-up professional help; in *Detsel* and *Bevin H.*, the service was highly complex, requiring a licensed and specially trained professional working under the supervision and prescription of a physician), it is not apt to be a related service. If it is not required to be performed or monitored constantly (in *Tatro*, CIC was required only a few times a day; in *Detsel* and *Bevin H.*, the service had to be performed without interruption and required constant attention), it is apt to be a related service.

Further, if the service is low cost or has a high cost-benefit ratio (in *Tatro*, the service was inexpensive and very helpful to the student's inclusion in regular settings or regular programs; in *Detsel* and *Bevin H.*, the procedure was very expensive and did not ensure placement in schools but, more often, education at home), it is apt to be a related service. If it directly benefits a child to be educated or even placed in a school building or regular school program (as in *Tatro* but not *Detsel* and *Bevin H.*), it is apt to be a related service.

In addition, if the service is a traditional function of a school nurse or a modest extension of the nurse's function (in *Tatro*, CIC is not unlike other school nurse functions, whereas in *Detsel* and *Bevin H.* the service is far more like a hospital-based service), it is apt to be a related service. Clearly, the courts are concerned about the function of the school nurse because, fundamentally, they are concerned about converting the role of the schools from education to all-purpose service agencies (including health services).

Also, the courts are concerned, it seems, about the expense of a service not just because educational dollars are limited and should be spent for traditional educational purposes (that is, for roles that are consistent with the usual or slightly expanded duties of a school nurse), but also because the expenditure of huge amounts of money for one child for essentially health-related reasons may deprive other disabled students of funds in the special education budget. The issue is a classic competing-equities issue (explained fully in chapter 3): To what extent shall one person be given an advantage at the expense of another?

Finally, the courts may well be concerned about the liability that schools would incur if the medical services were to malfunction or be improperly provided. Medical malpractice or health-care negligence issues are a very real concern in the public policy debates of the 1990s. There is a great deal of debate about cost containment and health-care expenses, along with concern about the impact of huge liability judgments on physicians' willingness to provide certain kinds of service. It may be that the courts are (silently) sensitive about these issues in the related-services cases and, taking them into account, tend to rule against the student when the service is of the type that can create medical malpractice or health-care negligence claims by the student against the schools.

GOVERNMENTAL PROBLEMS ARISING FROM THE RELATED-SERVICES REQUIREMENTS

New policies, such as the requirement that schools must educate disabled children appropriately and provide them with related services, rarely are executed perfectly. Those who analyze problems (such as the total and functional exclusion of disabled children from schools) and propose solutions to them (such as requiring the provision of related services) must be on guard to anticipate barriers to the appropriate education of disabled children and plan ways of overcoming these barriers. No matter how thoroughly the obstacles are anticipated and prepared for, they will inevitably pose greater problems than anticipated.

Related services are a case in point. Besides the problems in interpreting what these services shall be, difficulties arise in providing them. Essentially these are intergovernmental; they go to the heart of the functions of governmental agencies involved with disabled children.

Intergovernmental Coordination

One major problem is intergovernmental coordination. The immediate task has been to assure that the federal, state, and local agencies that can offer special education and related services will provide those services in the least restrictive setting. Because there are so many service providers and because they often are operated by separate federal agencies (each with its own state and local counterpart), it is important, though difficult, to coordinate these agencies' activities and thereby assure that their collective resources can be brought to bear on the educational problems of disabled children.

But federal interagency agreements are not always translated into action at the point where federal services are delivered, and state and local counterparts do not necessarily enter into interagency agreements or carry out these agreements. When these fairly typical bureaucratic problems are added to the interpretation problems, the results are either a failure to deliver services or its opposite—duplication of services (with a resulting competition for funding and a waste of professional time and effort and increased cost of service).

The Single-Agency Provision

Another major problem has been caused by the section of the IDEA that makes the state-level education agency ultimately responsible for assuring that each disabled child is given special education and related services. The single-agency provision has caused some public agencies (such as those that furnish occupational and physical therapy, and mental health and mental retardation services) to withdraw their services from school-aged disabled children on the ground that the state education agency is responsible for furnishing those services. Their refusal usually occurs when the child is difficult or expensive to serve or does not fit neatly into already existing programs.

On the other hand, some agencies tend to compete to serve disabled children. Schools try to increase their social work or psychological services; social services and mental health agencies try to retain their clients and even offer educational programs for them. Competition to serve a disabled child typically occurs when the child is easy or inexpensive to serve or fits into already existing programs.

Thus, there exists both a symbiotic and a competitive relationship between educational and other agencies. The relationship is symbiotic because schools use the other agencies as "safety valves" or outlets, placing in them children who are particularly problematic for the schools. The relationship is competitive because, for other, easier-to-serve children, educational agencies compete with other agencies to serve the children. When they provide service, they usually can draw down "outside" money (from federal or other entitlement programs), justify the maintenance or expansion of services, and retain or increase their staffs.

Several additional factors aggravate the problems caused by the single-agency requirement:

1. The state education agency does not control the funds of many providers of related services. It has the ultimate responsibility but not adequate authority and resources to discharge its duty.
2. State and local governments usually have been designed so that the single-agency provision cannot work well. Social services, mental health, and education agencies receive funds from different sources and for different purposes, are governed by independent elected or appointed boards, and have always operated with relative independence from each other.
3. Children with disabilities placed in private schools by local schools still retain their rights to related services, even at the usually higher cost incurred in private education.
4. Some regions of a state lack services, even when all state and local resources are mobilized and coordinated.
5. Although transportation is a related service in federal and state law, lack of transportation remains a barrier to providing other related services. This is especially true in rural areas.
6. Schools are reluctant to have their limited funds used for related services that they believe other agencies should provide and that do not fit within the traditional functions of education. This response reflects a misunderstanding concerning the role of related services: They are provided when necessary to enable a child to benefit from special education, and they are intended to prevent functional exclusion. This reluctance also reflects the need to stretch limited public school resources by requiring other agencies to put the "first dollar" into a related service that they traditionally furnish. (The first-dollar requirement assures that one agency will pay for services up to a set level before another agency is required to pay for them.)

   It reflects still another problem concerning governmental financing: Many disabled children are eligible for health, mental health, or social services (and thus for certain related services) only if they or their families are income-eligible (poor). After the income-eligible children are served, there still may be related-services costs to be borne by the schools or other agencies. And, of course, some disabled children who are not income-eligible are entitled to related services. Thus, an income-eligible child might receive Early

Periodic Screening, Diagnosis, and Treatment (EPSDT) screening, but children who are not income-eligible may have to qualify for screening by the Crippled Children's Program.
7. A final problem is that there are few legal restraints on the demand for related services. If a child's individualized education program calls for the schools to provide related services and a due process hearing officer or court sustains the child's right to these services (ruling on the child's claim to an "appropriate education"), the schools have no choice but to provide them.

INTERESTS OF CHILDREN WITH DISABILITIES AND FUNCTIONS OF GOVERNMENTS

Notwithstanding the progress made at federal, state, and local levels of government to overcome intergovernmental problems by adopting interagency agreements, a fundamental problem remains with the agreements and the related services provisions. This flaw is that there is massive disagreement among service providers and policy makers concerning the nature of public education for disabled children.

Traditional Roles of Education
Traditionally, public education had been mass education. The purpose and techniques of public education were remarkably stable until a quarter of a century ago. Gradually, however, the schools have become the battleground for beginning and carrying forward substantial changes in American life: racial desegregation, extension of public services into historically private areas of family life (health and sex education, counseling, social services, and other activities that tend to supplement or even supplant, in the eyes of some, the family's role), integration of disabled children and adults into the mainstream of life, and individualized services to disabled people (not the provision of mass-produced and mass-consumed services).

Education was nearly as inevitable as death and taxes. Second only to the tax collector, the school cast the largest net thrown by government. Thus, schools have been asked to bear the brunt of social reform. But in making schools the focal point of social reform and new government services for disabled children, policymakers have undertaken to transform the school and probably change its function from one of education alone to one of education plus physical health, mental health, and social services. Can the schools carry this burden? Should they be asked to? If so, how can they be helped? If not, who should be active in this area? These are the questions that thoughtful observers raise.

New Functions of Education
Children with disabilities have a very real and defensible interest in obtaining an appropriate education and related services. The schools have an equally real and defensible interest and responsibility to satisfy those needs. In light of the present difficulties in providing related

services, however, some people think that it is only proper to ask whether schools *alone* should be required to meet every educational need of a disabled child and, if so, how they can best carry out this responsibility and with what funds (federal, state, or local).

In this matter, the function of one agency of government (schools) is being balanced against the functions of other agencies (health, mental health, and social services) and against the interests of disabled children and the various agencies. It is increasingly clear that this issue—the issue of government functions and whether the school alone should bear the brunt of efforts to educate (in its fullest sense, by providing related services) disabled children— has not been addressed adequately in the context not only of disabled children but of education as a whole. The infants/toddlers law (P.L. 99-457), the Medicare amendments (P.L. 100-350), and the Technology Related Assistance Act of 1988 (P.L. 100-407) prove this point: Schools are asked to do more functions. Until the issue is adequately addressed, the present problems will continue and proposed solutions will fall short because they will not reach the underlying issue of how public agencies are to respond (or fail to respond) to the presence of disabled persons in society. This is an issue not only of behavior and function but of values and principles as well.

Values and Principles

In my judgment, the Supreme Court's *Tatro* decision (concerning clean intermittent catheterization) was correctly decided and its principles are sound, both with regard to the behavior and functions of schools and with regard to values and principles. The same is true, I believe, of the twelve-month-school-year cases and *Rowley*. All of these cases seem to emphasize the need for integration of disabled students with nondisabled students. *Tatro* required catheterization so that the student could continue her education at school (instead of home). The twelve-month-school-year cases seem to say that the extended school year is required so some children can continue to receive school services. In the absence of summer schooling, they may regress so much that it would be pointless to require schools to educate them at all. And *Rowley* made much of the fact that the student was integrated with disabled students and passing from grade to grade.

In these cases, the principle that schools must provide certain services is associated with the value of integration. The cases thus require a new *behavior* of schools—appropriate education (i.e., the opposite of functional exclusion). And the cases require a new *function* of schools—to take on some of the responsibilities of other agencies. The value is integration. The objective is to prevent exclusion.

Just how far the courts will pursue these behavior-shaping and function-changing principles and values remains to be seen. The decisive tests were in *Detsel*, involving technology-supported children, and *Timothy W. v. Rochester*, involving the issue of educability. Thus, the courts may consider the costs of school-provided therapy, the drastic change of role from providing education to practicing medicine, the length of time required for successful intervention, the professional qualifications required of the provider, and the comparability requirements of the IDEA (as interpreted in *Rowley* and as seen under the "reasonable accommodations" test of *Davis*).

In considering any one of these factors, and especially in considering a combination of them, the courts may decide that the integration principle should yield to practical considerations of cost, time, and professionalism and should be modified because the child could receive more effective individualized services in other service systems. In this event, the child arguably would not be denied an appropriate education (since the psychiatric and possibly educational services would still be provided by other agencies) but would receive them in a less integrated setting (e.g., in a psychiatric hospital).

Indeed, that result—exclusion from school-based services and inclusion in other service providers' systems for receipt of special education and related services—is a major issue of the IDEA's requirements for least restrictive alternatives or environments (LRA/LRE). It is therefore timely to consider the LRA/LRE rules next, in chapter 6.

NOTES

1. Frederick L. v. Thomas.

2. Fialkowski v. Shapp.

3. *See* Education Commission of the States, *Final Report, Special Education in the States: Legislative Progress Report, Handicapped Children's Education Project* (Denver: Author, 1974).

4. PARC.

5. MARC.

6. PARC; LeBanks v. Spears.

7. *Federal Register*, May 4, 1977, pp. 22690-91.

8. Concur: Rettig v. Kent City School Dist.; Bales v. Clark; Hines v. Pitt County Bd. of Ed.; Isgur v. School Bd. of Newton; Gladys J. v. Pearland I.S.D.; Campbell v. Grissett; Buchholtz v. Iowa Dept. of Public Instruction; Riley v. Ambach.

9. Age v. Bullitt.

10. *Concur*: Georgia ARC v. McDaniel; Crawford v. Pittman (limited to the particular plaintiffs only); Yaris v. Special School Dist.; Lee v. Thompson (in which the court appointed a master to oversee implementation of the twelve-month school year, the court finding the district to be in contempt for failure to carry out the order filed two years before); Birmingham and Lampere School Dists. v. Supt.; Stacey G. v. Pasadena I.S.D. For cases denying twelve-month education, *see* Rettig v. Kent City School Dist. and Bales v. Clark.

11. Geis v. Bd. of Ed. of Parsnippany-Troy Hills.

12. Thornock v. Boise Ind. School Dist.

13. Bd. of Ed. of East Windsor Regional School Dist. v. Diamond.

14. Russell v. Jefferson School Dist.

15. Jackson v. Franklin County School Bd.

16. Bonadonna v. Cooperman.

17. Scituate School Committee v. Robert B.

18. Board v. Rowley; Youngberg v. Romeo; O'Connor v. Donaldson; Honig v. Doe; PASE v. Hannon; Board v. Arline, Florida; Southeastern Community College v. Davis; S-1 v. Turlington; Roncker v. Walters; Timothy W. v. Rochester School Dist.; Tatro v. State of Texas; and Parham v. J.R.

19. Age v. Bullitt.

20. County School Bd. of Loudon County v. Lower.

21. Espino v. Besteiro.

22. Rowley v. Bd.; Age v. Bullitt; Springdale v. Grace; Monahan v. Nebraska.

23. Erdman v. State of Connecticut; Hines v. Pitt County Bd. of Ed.; and Manchester Bd. v. Connecticut State Bd.

24. Campbell v. Grissett.

25. Dept. of Ed. v. Katherine D.

26. *Concur*: Papacoda v. State of Connecticut; Harris v. D.C. Bd. of Ed.; and Woods v. Pittman.

For 1994 Update on Appropriate Education please see page 398.

6

Least Restrictive Appropriate Educational Placement

THE DEBATE

No requirement of the right-to-education movement and the federal law that codified the cases was as likely at the outset to generate as much heat as light as the requirement that children with disabilities be educated in the least restrictive placement. Given the inaccurate code name "mainstreaming," this requirement had the potential for encountering the same levels of opposition, misunderstanding, and ill will as the earlier constitutional and legislative/judicial requirements for racial desegregation of the public schools. This book will largely use the term *least restrictive alternative* (LRA). It has also been called the *least restrictive environment* (LRE).

This requirement also had the potential for significantly improving the education of children with disabilities, redressing some of the wrongs that schools had imposed on them and their families, and contributing to the education of all pupils, training of all educators, and enlightenment of the public at large. Interestingly, the potential for not-so-good and good results has been realized, and the debate concerning the desirability, meaning, and implementation of the requirement that children with disabilities be educated in the least restrictive setting appropriate to their needs continues even now.

It will be useful to examine the LRA requirement along several dimensions, paying attention to (1) the constitutional basis (foundations) for the requirement, (2) the case law that preceded the IDEA, (3) requirements of the IDEA and Section 504, (4) reasons for the LRA requirement, (5) the nature of the requirement as a rebuttable presumption and the role of presumptions in law, (6) the public policy values that the LRA requirement seeks to achieve, (7) the relationship of the policy to the requirement for an appropriate education (the third of the six principles of the IDEA), (8) the role of professional and judicial interpretation of the LRA and appropriate education requirements, and (9) an evaluation of the efficacy of the LRA doctrine—its power to accomplish its stated purposes.

The debate concerning integration has been raised to a new level by the "regular education initiative" (REI), proposed by the Department of Education's Office of Special Education during 1988 and 1989. Under the REI, additional resources for integration of students with disabilities into programs for students without disabilities would be provided by discretionary programs of the Office of Special Education and by state and local educational agencies. The REI is similar to another reformulation of the integration movement, namely, the "supported education" doctrine, which, like REI, seeks to integrate students with disabilities by providing them more support for participating in regular education programs.

CONSTITUTIONAL FOUNDATIONS

LRA as a balancing mechanism in the education of disabled children is derived from the constitutionally based legal doctrine of the least restrictive alternative. This doctrine states that even if the legislative purpose of a government action is legitimate (e.g., promoting public health, regulating commerce, or providing education), the purpose may not be pursued by means that broadly stifle personal liberties if it can be achieved by less oppressive restrictive means. Legislative and administrative intervention must take the form of the least drastic means for achieving the same basic purpose.[1] In Chambers's[2] memorable metaphor, LRA forbids a state from using a bazooka to kill a fly on a citizen's back if a fly swatter would do as well. LRA, then, is a constitutional principle that accommodates individual and state interests to each other. It enables government to act but does not permit it to take just any action that it might want to take.

The LRA Principle

The LRA principle generally has been applied in areas affecting state regulations of interstate commerce,[3] personal liberties,[4] and procedural rights.[5] An example of one of the earliest LRA cases involved South Carolina's purported effort to conserve natural resources off its shoreline.[6] To do this, the state imposed a $25 licensing fee on residents shellfishing off the South Carolina coast and a $2,500 licensing fee on nonresidents, in an obvious attempt to discourage out-of-state fishermen. The Supreme Court invalidated the statute, ruling that South Carolina could use a less restrictive means of accomplishing its legitimate goal of conservation (e.g., by imposing a tax on the shellfish catch by weight) while minimizing the impact upon the private right of nonresidents to earn a living.

The LRA doctrine also has been applied in cases involving disabled citizens in public institutions. A long line of cases addresses this issue.[7] In one notable case, *Wyatt v. Stickney*, the court stated that residents shall have a right to the least restrictive conditions necessary to achieve the purpose of habilitation. This phraseology is significant because it highlights the point that achievement of the purpose of commitment (treatment) is primary, and elimination of infringement on rights (in this case, deprivation of liberty) is secondary.[8] In legal terminology this means that the LRA doctrine is a *rebuttable presumption*.[9] That is to say, when it is not possible to grant total liberty and at the same time provide effective treatment, the doctrine allows the state to deprive the citizen of his or her liberty but only to the extent necessary to provide the treatment. The presumption in favor of liberty, thus, is rebutted by the action of commitment. Rebuttable presumption is discussed in detail later in this chapter.

The LRA Doctrine in Education

The same point applies to the principle of LRA in education. The right to placement in an integrated or "regular" educational environment is not an absolute right but is secondary to the primary purpose of education in the public schools—namely, an appropriate education. Thus, under federal law, educational services are to be provided "so that all handicapped children have available to them a free appropriate public education."[10]

LRA's power is derived from three important constitutional principles: *procedural due process*, *substantive due process*, and *equal protection*.[11]

1. Procedural due process requires that a state must grant citizens an adjudication procedure, allowing them to challenge an action before it may infringe upon their private, individual rights. The state must prove that the proposed action is warranted, and the individual is given the opportunity to point out less restrictive or less drastic means of accomplishing the state's goal.

   In special education matters, due process guarantees a hearing at which the disabled child (or his or her representative) can try to show why the rebuttable presumption against deprivation of liberty—as by exclusion from public schools or placement in an arguably stigmatizing special education program—should be overcome. The hearing requires individualized decision making and imposes an accountability device on government, all to the end of protecting the child's interest in education and against classification as disabled.

2. Substantive due process (a doctrine now rarely used) places an outer limit on what a state may do, independent of the level of procedural protections provided. It protects certain individual rights from all forms of government intrusion and requires that the government use the least intrusive means to accomplish its goals.[12] LRA is a progeny of substantive due process in that it prohibits the state from using more restrictive means than are necessary to accomplish its purpose. In special education affairs, LRA and substantive due process regard unwarranted, inappropriate special education classification and placement as too restrictive.

3. The third and last principle, equal protection, requires that a state deal with similarly situated individuals in an even-handed manner. If a state discriminates, the equal protection clause places the burden of proof on the state to show a compelling, important, or rational reason for its discrimination. The level of justification depends on the nature of the

rights being limited and the political insularity of the affected individuals. Recent equal protection developments indicate that the Supreme Court rejects a "middle tier" form of judicial review for disabled individuals, not requiring the state to demonstrate an "important" reason for its discriminatory practices.

Equal protection was the basis for the right-to-education cases that challenged exclusion of disabled children from public schools in the early 1970s. The courts' attitude toward educational segregation can be summarized in the following comment from PARC: "[A]mong the alternative programs of education and training required by statute to be available, placement in a regular public school class is preferable to placement in . . . any other type of education and training."[13] Other court decisions have continued to expand these basic rights.[14]

A Mississippi case, *Mattie T. v. Holladay*, serves as a good example of educational uses of the LRA doctrine. The case focused on the provision of inadequate educational services to disabled children who were placed in self-contained special education classes that separated them from nondisabled children. The court ruled that the state goal of providing an appropriate education for these children could be met in a more *integrated* setting, thus maximizing the disabled students' right to associate with nondisabled students.

Thus, the LRA doctrine is a constitutionally derived way of balancing the values surrounding provision of an appropriate education (the student's right to and need for an appropriate education) with the values of individual rights of association. It is supported by, and implemented through, the constitutional principles of procedural due process, substantive due process, and equal protection. Whether premised on substantive or procedural due process or on equal protection, LRA has been a powerful doctrine for accommodating legitimate state interests (in educating all students appropriately, not just those with disabilities) and individual interests (in an appropriate education in settings and associations with nondisabled and disabled students). Its application to involuntary commitment,[15] to conditions in institutions,[16] and to less clearly analogous areas of state–individual conflict has made it a useful doctrine for courts that were determined to correct schools' discrimination against disabled children.[17] At the same time, it established a firm judicial mind-set against institutions—firm, but not unshakable, and clearly vulnerable in right-to-education cases.

PRE-IDEA CASE LAW

Preference for the LRA

In *PARC* and *LeBanks*, there was ample evidence of, among other things, functional exclusion, misclassification resulting in inappropriate placement, and general inadequacy of special education programs (in terms of financing, programs, and personnel). There was additional evidence of the indisputable denial of equal educational opportunities for disabled children in violation of equal protection and procedural due process principles (see chapters 3 and 7). Like Hamlet, a court faced with such overwhelming evidence might have been inclined to say, "There is something rotten in the State of _____; oh, cursed spite that I was born to set things right."

Court Remedies

Given the facts, the courts had to fashion remedies. One remedy, particularly appropriate for the practice of functional exclusion, was stated as follows (in *PARC*):

> It is the Commonwealth's obligation to place each mentally retarded child in a free, public program of education and training appropriate to the child's capacity, within the context of the general educational policy that, among the alternative programs of education and training required by statute to be available, placement in a regular public school class is preferable to placement in a special public school class and placement in a special public school class is preferable to placement in any other type of program of education and training.

As far as the case law initially was concerned, least restrictive placement reflected a judicial preference for students to be placed or tracked in a "normal" track rather than in a special education track and for students to be educated in the regular school environment rather than in the confines of a special school. LRA was no more than a *preference* in favor of regular educational placement; it was not an inflexible rule. It was a guide for conduct, not a rule of conduct. As a guide, it did not prohibit alternatives to regular class and regular school placement. When children with disabilities are educated with nondisabled students, usually in the same classes, their integration is sometimes called *mainstreaming*.

Reasons for the LRA Preference

Why was LRA a judicial preference? The reasons were many. The preference was a reaction to the exclusion of children with special needs from both the *opportunity* for education (placement in a school system) and the opportunity for a *meaningful* education (placement in an appropriate program). It addressed total and functional exclusion, with an emphasis on the latter.

LRA also was a reaction to the view traditionally accepted by many educators (and institutionalized in school practices) that children with special needs are different from, and therefore should be excluded from education with, nondisabled children. LRA was an attempt to protect exceptional children from the stereotype that they are different and deficient. It spoke to the stigmatizing effects of special educational placement—the effects that such placement has on a child's self-image and on the school's and peers' image of the child.

Further, LRA was a method for individualizing an exceptional pupil's education because it prevented a child from being placed in special programs without first determining that the child could not profit from regular educational placement. It simultaneously addressed the requirements of an appropriate education—an individualized education—and nondiscriminatory classification. It promoted the concept that curriculum adaptations and instructional strategies tailored to the needs of exceptional children could occur in regular classrooms as well as in special classrooms.

LRA was preferred because the existence of separate, self-contained special education programs and schools was found to be equivalent to the establishment of separate but unequal systems of education. Separate generally meant unequal, and special education was not equated with equal educational opportunities. Some commentators argued that the pattern and practice of some schools was to assign the "worst" children, typically those with special needs, to the least capable teachers, putting them in the most inferior facilities, with less than adequate educational materials. Often, special education programs were funded less generously than normal mainstream programs. In the face of such biased treatment, LRA adopted some of the strategies used to bring about racial integration of the schools.

One strategy for racial integration was to integrate a racial minority into the racial mainstream. The hope behind the strategy was that the racial majority would not neglect its children's education in integrated schools, and continued attention of the white majority to "quality education" would assure the black minority of the same quality education as the white majority. Similar hopes undergirded the preference for LRA.

LRA has more than a civil rights aspect, however; it was imbued with a sense of desperation. A court wishing to redress the manifold wrongs of functional exclusion, misclassification, and inadequate special education programs could (and we suspect did) easily contrast regular education with special education, see that nondisabled children were not excluded, misclassified, or shortchanged, and reach the conclusion that the quickest remedy was to order placement, to the maximum extent appropriate, with the nondisabled. The remedy was sure. The regular programs were already in existence and could accommodate some disabled children without extensive revision. Extensive revision of special education programs was hardly certain to be achieved satisfactorily despite court orders for revision. The courts fired with buckshot, not single rounds, and revision undoubtedly would not be quick. LRA, then, gained popularity as an easy and readily available remedy.

Moreover, LRA was a reaction to the terminal aspects of special education. Placement of an exceptional child in a self-contained special education program usually was the last step in a child's development; it often was the terminal placement. The preference for LRA rested on the hope that the self-fulfilling prophecies and the self-limiting characteristics of special educational placement would not be the end result for children with special needs.

LRA also was preferred because it was widely and forcefully advocated by many educators. They argued that the disabled child would learn more, and more easily, by being educated with the nondisabled child. They contended that there were serious doubts about the educational efficacy of special (separate) programs, and they said that disabled children needed the educational and experiential benefits of coming into contact with nondisabled children.

Finally, placement in the least restrictive appropriate school program cannot be divorced from two related legal developments: (1) application of the least restrictive principle to at least two other areas of state action—(a) criminal law and placement in the least restrictive environment, and (b) civil commitment of persons dangerous to themselves or others; and (2) the trend toward deinstitutionalization—preventing mentally disabled persons from being placed in institutions except as a final resort, and discharging as many as possible from institutions.

In one sense, the deinstitutionalization movement was part of a more generalized application of the least restrictive doctrine. But it was different because of its implications for the public schools. Deinstitutionalization prevented many disabled children from being placed in institutions. Instead, they remained in the community. By requiring that all children be given a free appropriate public education, the court cases and the IDEA put pressure on the public schools, particularly in terms of the zero-reject principle. In responding to this pressure, the schools had to begin training the more severely disabled children, who were, after all, the most apt candidates for institutionalization and were traditionally most excluded from school. Schools could choose not only to create new (or more extensive) programs for severely disabled children but also to broaden the range of nondisabled children by placing the mildly disabled children in the mainstream. Thus, although the least restrictive placement doctrine was born in nonschool contexts as part of the constitutional requirement of substantive due process, it has had significant implications for the public schools, as will be discussed hereinafter.

FEDERAL LEGISLATION

The IDEA

It is not surprising that many of Congress's findings reflected in the IDEA are identical to conclusions of the courts and the reasons the courts required children to be placed in least restrictive educational settings. These findings include the following:

1. Children with disabilities have been inappropriately educated [Sec. 1400(b)(3)].
2. They have been denied the opportunity "to go through the educational process with their peers" [Sec. 1400(b)(4)].
3. There is a lack of adequate services available to them within the schools [Sec. 1400(b)(6)].
4. Educators have the ability to provide effective special education and related services, including, presumably, education and services in the regular program [Sec. 1400(b)(7)].

Legislative requirements will be examined in regard to (1) least restrictive appropriate placement and (2) other statutory provisions.

Least Restrictive Appropriate Placement. It was predictable that Congress would require SEAs [Sec. 1412(5)(B)] and LEAs [Sec. 1414(a)(1)(C)(iv)] to follow a policy of least restrictive placement [Sec. 300.550]. They must develop procedures to assure that, to the maximum extent appropriate, disabled children—including children in public agencies, private institutions, or other care facilities—will be educated with children who are not disabled. Further, the requirements stipulate that special classes, separate schooling, or other removal of disabled children from the regular educational environment will occur only when the nature or severity of a child's disability is such that education in regular classes with the use of supplementary aids and services cannot be achieved satisfactorily.

The regulations prohibit placement outside the mainstream program except under limited circumstances. The regulations thus create a presumption in favor of integration; integration of disabled children into the mainstream should occur "to the maximum extent appropriate." It is clear from the legislative history and a proper interpretation of the Act that "appropriate" is to be defined in terms of what is appropriate for the disabled child, not whether the school system can conveniently absorb that child into the mainstream or whether the child will have beneficial or detrimental effects on nondisabled peers. It is inescapable, in light of IDEA policy, to provide disabled children with an appropriate education. This much is clear from the IDEA and regulations. But, as will be shown, the courts are not strictly adhering to the focus on only the student with a disability.

The presumption in favor of integration can be overcome (rebutted). The regulations provide that a disabled child may not be removed from the regular educational environment unless the nature or severity of the disability is such that education in regular classes, even with supplementary aids and services, cannot be achieved satisfactorily. This condition, too, focuses on the nature or severity of the child's disability as opposed to the convenience for the school or the consequences for nondisabled children. Conditions for a particular placement are inexorably linked to the concept of appropriate education and are to be child-centered, not system-centered. Again, this approach is not followed consistently by the courts.

The regulations [Secs. 300.550–556] speak to one of the most potentially troublesome aspects of placement in the least restrictive environment: placing disabled children into regular programs without regard for their individual needs. Section 300.552 of the regulations makes it clear that each disabled child's educational placement must be determined at least annually, be based on his or her individualized education program, and unless the IEP requires special alternative arrangements, the child must receive an education in the same school he or she would attend were it not for the disability. In selecting the least restrictive environment, any potentially harmful effect on the child or on the quality of services received is to be taken into consideration [Sec. 300.552]. This is a focus on the child's needs for an appropriate education. Comments on the regulation make it clear that if the child disrupts nondisabled students in the regular classroom to the degree that their education is significantly impaired, the child's needs cannot be met in that classroom and placement there is inappropriate. This is the approach used in the expulsion cases and in those involving students with AIDs.

Section 300.551 puts pressure on public agencies to develop appropriate alternative placements by requiring that the options include instruction in regular classes, in special classes, in special schools, home instruction, and instruction in hospitals and institutions. This is a policy judgment favoring a continuum of services. The LRE doctrine permits this policy choice. The agency also must provide supplementary services such as resource rooms and itinerant teachers in conjunction with regular class placement.

Children with disabilities must be given a chance to participate in nonacademic and ex-

tracurricular services and activities. They are to have access to meals, recess periods, counseling services, athletics, transportation, health services, recreational activities, special interest groups, and clubs. They should be referred to agencies that give assistance to disabled
persons and be employed in and outside of the public agency [Secs. 300.553 and .306].

SEAs must make suitable arrangements with public and private agencies to ensure that
the least restrictive placement rules are effectively carried out [Sec. 300.554]. They are to provide technical assistance to the other agencies to help them implement the rules [Sec.
300.555], and must monitor programs and assist public and private agencies in correcting
noncompliance with the rules [Sec. 300.556].

The 1990 amendments address the "least restrictive environment" principle in several ways.

- Section 1401(a)(16)(A) restates the "continuum" of allowable settings for special education, including regular education classroom on one end and the home, hospitals, institutions, and other settings, on the other. In short, Congress declined to narrow the continuum and thus reaffirmed that separate, segregated education is permissible.
- Section 1424(a)(3), however, provides special grants to state and local educational agencies to help them with their integration efforts.
- Section 1424(b) likewise requires extended-school-year programs to make special efforts
  to integrate children with and without disabilities.
- Section 1426(a)(3) and (4) places special emphasis on the integration of students with
  severe emotional disturbances.
- Section 1431(b) provides for special grants for in-service education of regular educators
  so that they might become more able to accommodate special education students in their
  programs.
- Section 1401(a)(17) clarifies that therapeutic recreation is a related service and thus emphasizes that students in special education will have opportunities to learn skills that help
  them participate in community park-and-recreation programs, which under ADA no
  longer may discriminate against otherwise qualified individuals with disabilities.

ADA seems far more clearly dedicated to the integration principle than IDEA. Section
2(a)(8) sets the goals of equal opportunity, full participation (presumably in the mainstream),
independent living, and economic self-sufficiency for individuals, including students, with
disabilities. It also declares goals of independent living and economic self-sufficiency for
individuals with disabilities. To carry out these goals and desired outcomes, it bans discrimination in a broad range of public and private sectors of society. In short, ADA looks to
integration more forcefully than IDEA. It does not set up a rebuttable presumption of integration, but rather it requires accommodations for people with disabilities so that they will
have the opportunities to live in an integrated society.

Other Statutory Provisions. The policy of least restrictive appropriate placement is in-
divisible from other policies. It is a method for assuring an appropriate education, a technique of individualized education, a way of preventing misclassification, and, ultimately, a
trigger for a due process hearing. Its success will depend, in part, on personnel development

[Sec. 1413(a)(3)], and it is advanced by the requirement that schools spend IDEA funds, first, for the education of disabled children who are not receiving an education, and, second, for the most severely disabled children within each disability who are receiving an inadequate education [Sec. 1412(3)]. Since federal funds may not be spent on mainstream (regular) programs until the other priorities have been met, schools are required to spend their own funds (state or local funds, or federal funds from other sources) for mainstream purposes.

The "ceiling" on the number of disabled children has the same effect. No more than 12% of all children may be counted as disabled. If there are, in fact, more disabled children than an LEA can accommodate within the ceiling, the LEA may tend to count as disabled only those who fit the two service priorities, and count the less disabled children as nondisabled. As a result, the less disabled children are served in the mainstream or served (outside the mainstream, in some cases) in state or locally funded programs.

Part H. The regulations under Part H clearly create a strong preference for community-based services, to the extent appropriate for the child. Thus, to the extent appropriate, services must be provided in the types of settings in which infants and toddlers without disabilities would participate. Also, early intervention centers, hospitals and clinics, and other settings appropriate to the child's age and needs are permissible. And the Department of Education recommends that services be community-based and not isolate a child or family from settings or activities in which children without disabilities would participate.

The purpose of Part H is to enhance infants' and toddlers' development by maximizing their potential for independent living in society, minimizing their potential for a developmental delay, and assisting states to provide quality early intervention programs [42 U.S.C. Sec. 1471(a)]. Accordingly, states must put into effect a statewide system of "appropriate early intervention services" [42 U.S.C. Sec. 1476(a)]. Under this system, early intervention services "must" be provided in the types of settings in which infants and toddlers without disabilities would participate "to the extent appropriate" for infants and toddlers with disabilities [34 C.F.R. Sec. 303.12(b)]. The word "must" is strong and leaves no doubt about the preference for integration.

Part H's regulations, however, make it clear that separate settings are permitted, such as hospital settings when infants and toddlers require extensive medical intervention [34 C.F.R. Sec. 303.12(b)]. But this exception is narrow and depends on the necessity of medical services (the infant "requires" them) and the nature of the services as determined by the extent of need and disability ("extensive medical intervention"). The Department of Education acknowledges the narrowness of the exception and the strong integration presumption in its comments on the regulations, urging providers to take efforts to provide services in "settings and facilities that do not remove the children from natural environments (e.g., the home day-care centers, or other community settings)" and recommending against isolating an eligible child or family from settings or activities in which nondisabled infants and toddlers will participate.[18]

Section 504

Section 504 regulations are substantially similar to those of the IDEA. Section 104.34 requires schools to provide each qualified disabled student in their jurisdiction with regular or mainstream education to the maximum extent appropriate to the disabled person's needs. The school must place disabled students in the regular educational environment operated by the school unless the school can demonstrate that a student's education in the regular environment with the use of supplementary aids and services cannot be achieved satisfactorily. Although the disabled student's *needs* determine what is a proper placement, the department's comments on regulation Section 104.34 make it clear that if a disabled student is so *disruptive* in a regular classroom that other students' education is significantly impaired, the disabled student's needs cannot be met in that placement and regular setting placement is not appropriate or required.[19]

Children with disabilities also are to be provided with nonacademic services in as integrated a setting as possible. This requirement is especially important for children whose educational needs require them to be solely with other disabled children during most of each day. To the maximum extent appropriate, children in residential settings are to be provided with opportunities for participation with other children. In providing or arranging for the provision of extracurricular services and activities, including meals, recess periods, and nonacademic services and activities as set forth in Section 104.37(a)(2), a school must ensure that each disabled student participate with nondisabled students to the maximum extent appropriate for the student in question.

If a school operates a facility for disabled students, the school must ensure that the facility and the services and activities it provides are comparable to its other facilities, services, and activities. This is not intended to encourage the creation and maintenance of such facilities. A separate facility violates Section 504 unless it is necessary for providing an appropriate education to certain disabled students. When special facilities are necessary, this provision requires that the educational services provided be comparable to those provided in the recipient's regular facilities.

Among the factors to be considered is the need to place a child as close to home as possible. Under Section 104.34, schools must take this factor into account. The parents' right to challenge their child's placement extends not only to placement in special classes or a separate school but also to placement in a distant school and, in particular, to residential placement. If an equally appropriate educational program exists closer to home, the parent or guardian may raise the issue under the least restrictive placement doctrine through a procedural due process hearing.

The Federal Agency Position. Commenting on the proposed Section 504 regulations (which are comparable to the ones adopted as final regulations), the Department of Health and Human Services (HHS) took the position that, within the requirements of the regulation, schools must show that the *needs* of the individual disabled child would, on balance, be furthered by placement outside the regular educational environment. According to HHS, for many disabled children "the most normal setting feasible is that which combines the use of special and regular classes." Education of disabled children, including those in public and private institutions and other care facilities, in the most normal setting feasible means educating them with nondisabled persons "to the maximum extent appropriate." It also means educating them as close to home as possible.

Thus, as HHS conceived it, the requirement for placement in the most normal setting feasible was intended to encompass the same concept as placement in the least restrictive alternative setting. HHS chose to use the "most normal" rather than the "least restrictive" terminology because placement alternatives "cannot, in many instances, be compared on the basis of relative restrictiveness: i.e., while institutional education is indeed more restrictive than noninstitutional instruction, placement in special education is not necessarily more restrictive than instruction in regular classes." Despite a change in language, it does not appear that the final regulation represents a change in policy from the proposed regulations.

As HHS's comment on the proposed regulations indicated, what is restrictive or inappropriate for one person may not be restrictive or inappropriate for another. The principle of "most normal" or "least restrictive" placement rests on the policy of individualized or appropriate education. However it is phrased, the principle is a technique for individually appropriate instruction and should be viewed in that context. This view is consistent with the case law history and with proper interpretation of the IDEA, as later discussion of court cases indicates.

The Department of HHS also said that an orthopedically disabled child may not be placed in a classroom or school that is "primarily" for disabled children, since that placement would violate the "most normal" principle. A school district is not, however, required to make every classroom and school building barrier-free. Hence, an orthopedically impaired child may be placed away from the neighborhood school, but not in a class primarily for the disabled. This is not true for other disabled children; their placement must be in the "most normal" setting possible. This appears to have been followed in the final regulation, which requires the school to take into account the proximity of the alternative setting.

A separate regulation [Sec. 104.37] requires schools to provide nonacademic and extracurricular services and activities in such a manner "as is necessary to afford disabled students an equal opportunity for participation." Because these services are part of a school's education program, they must be provided in the most integrated setting appropriate. Nonacademic and extracurricular services and activities include, without limitation, counseling services, recreational athletics, transportation, health services, recreational activities, special interest groups or clubs, referrals to agencies providing assistance to the disabled, and employment of students by the school or other employers. In giving personal, academic, or vocational counseling and placement services to disabled students, a school may not discriminate because of disability and must make sure that students are not counseled toward more restrictive career objectives than nondisabled students who have similar interests and abilities.

Physical Education. In providing physical education courses, athletics, and similar programs to any of its students, a school may not discriminate on the basis of disability and must provide qualified disabled students with an equal opportunity to participate in interscholastic, club, or intramural athletics. These activities may be separate or different from those offered to nondisabled students only if separation or differentiation is consistent with the least restrictive principle [Sec. 104.35] and only if no qualified disabled student is denied the chance to compete for teams or to participate in courses that are not separate or different. Commenting on the physical education and athletics portion of the regulation, HHS noted that "most disabled students are able to participate in one or more regular physical education and athletics activities. For example, a student in a wheelchair can participate in regular archery courses, as can a deaf student in a wrestling course." (See chapter 3 for recent cases of alleged discrimination in athletics brought under Section 504.)

REASONS FOR THE LRA REQUIREMENT

Dual Systems in Society and Education

The very existence of an LRA policy means that there is more than one environment in which disabled children may be educated and disabled people served. These multiple environments are the result of the evolution of a system for legal, social, and educational treatment of disabled people that is separate from and external to the more general society. In effect, it is a dual system—one for people with disabilities and another for people without disabilities.

In Society. The legal status of disabled people is subject to procedural and substantive rules that are, generally speaking, different from those applied to nondisabled citizens. Historically, these rules were shaped by the presumption that the state acts in the interest of the disabled person rather than in a role that is potentially or actually adverse to the disabled person's interests. Thus, the doctrine of *parens patriae* established the power of the state to intervene in the lives of disabled people, in order to provide care and treatment.[20]

Although the doctrine of *parens patriae* justified the state's protective intervention, it also curtailed the legal rights of those who came under its ambit. In contrast to their concern about autonomy when considering the civil and criminal rights of nondisabled people, courts and legislatures tended to rely on the judgments of professional caretakers of the disabled.[21] For example, courts have given special attention to the LRA principle and its application to mentally disabled persons and the state's protective role when they have reviewed decisions regarding commitment and institutional care and treatment.[22]

In short, the parens patriae doctrine led to creation of a separate legal system for disabled people, in which less rigorous procedures to protect legal rights applied. This dual system has come under vigorous attack in the last decade, resulting in a plethora of lawsuits and legislation to correct perceived wrongs. Although progress has been made, disabled people still face a dual legal system firmly in place.

People with disabilities also have fallen outside the mainstream of the nondisabled community. In the late nineteenth and early twentieth centuries, theories of biological evolution gave rise to noxious social theories (particularly Social Darwinism), which held that "genetically inferior" human beings should be segregated from the general populace lest they "contaminate" the race. Despite a growing awareness of the role of environment on human development, traces of Social Darwinism linger. Perceptions of disabled people as different still lead to their exclusion from the educational, recreational, residential, and vocational services available to most nondisabled citizens. This exclusion heightens public perceptions of disabled people's differentness and further stigmatizes them.

The principle of *normalization*[23] has helped to reduce the perception of the differentness of disabled people and has encouraged their greater integration into society. As with the legal system, however, integration and the dissolution of a dual social system have been only partially realized.

In Education. The dual-system approach of the legal and social status of disabled individuals predictably has been reflected in the nation's public school system. Children with disabilities were routinely placed in separate programs or educational facilities because of their unalterable traits,[24] in much the same manner as minority children had been subjected to separate facilities on the basis of race.[25] The practice of excluding disabled children from the public school system has been supported by the erroneous rationale that these children lack the capacity to learn at a rate similar to that of their nondisabled counterparts.[26]

Prior to 1800, few states had health or educational programs for disabled children.[27] During the early nineteenth century, however, social changes in America were reflected in the establishment of state-supported free public school systems for nearly all children. Advocates for free public education saw the schools as a tool that would enable democratic government to continue and expand while assimilating newcomers to the dominant "American way of life."[28]

Not coincidentally, the educational reforms and "common schools" established in the nineteenth century also provided the impetus for state-supported special education programs. Educational leaders such as Horace Mann, Samuel Gridley Howe, Dorothea Dix, and Thomas Hopkins Gallaudet gave impetus to the establishment of the first American residential schools for blind, deaf, epileptic, retarded, and orphaned children. These schools offered training and a protective environment. But placement within them was often permanent. Despite the achievements and innovations of these early educational and political reformers, state-supported special education efforts began to dwindle.

It was not until the passage of compulsory education laws in the late nineteenth and early twentieth centuries that the questions of what to do with children who were "different" became more urgent. The "special" public school classes that evolved during this era became a dumping ground for truants, non-English speaking immigrants, and disabled students—all of whom were outcasts of the public school system.[29] A few school districts established separate facilities to educate their disabled students, but most excluded them entirely. The practice of exclusion persisted until the mid-1960s, when special educational programs became less rare. Nonetheless, the programs usually were separate from, and sometimes their quality was unequal to, educational opportunities offered to nondisabled students.

The dual system of education for disabled children was similar in many important ways to the segregated programs for black students. In *Brown v. Board of Education*, the Supreme Court identified the effects of segregation on blacks:

> To separate them . . . generates a feeling of inferiority . . . that may affect their hearts and minds in a way unlikely ever to be undone.
>
> Segregation . . . has a detrimental effect upon the . . . children. . . . [T]he policy of separating [them] is usually interpreted as denoting . . . inferiority. . . . [I]n the field of public education, the doctrine of "separate but equal" has no place.

It is not difficult to argue convincingly that segregation of disabled children results in similar detrimental effects. The stigma of being labeled disabled is thus underscored by the additional stigma of separation. Despite current federal and legislative guidelines, the stigma imposed on disabled children as a result of being relegated to separate educational facilities continues to have important externalities. This stigma has been perpetuated in part in the attitudes of nondisabled students, parents, teachers, and special educators toward disabled students, as well as in the attitudes of disabled students themselves.[30]

In summary, the dual system of law and social status is echoed in the public school system. Segregation of disabled children from regular classes has been the norm since the turn of the century and, until passage of the IDEA, was the accepted policy among teachers, school administrators, and other educational policymakers.

Effects of the Dual System in Education

LRA requirements of the IDEA responded to a multiplicity of problems in the education of disabled children, not the least of which was the refusal of state and local education and other agencies to educate disabled children with nondisabled children. But that practice was merely symptomatic of more generalized and widespread discrimination by those agencies against disabled children.

The dual system in education has had a variety of effects, but the overall result has been a denial of educational opportunities for disabled children. In its early findings of fact leading to enactment of the IDEA, Congress found that special education needs of the more than eight million disabled children in the United States were not being fully met. Specifically, more than half of these disabled children were in educational programs that were inappropriate for their needs, and an estimated one million disabled children were excluded entirely from the public school system.[31]

A variety of administrative and educational practices contributed to these results. These practices fall into four basic categories: exclusion, misclassification, inappropriate education, and restrictive placements. Parents and advocates of disabled children were unable to correct these practices because they lacked two important safeguards: procedural due process and a systematic method of parent involvement.

Exclusion. As indicated in chapter 2, a variety of educational practices resulted in the exclusion of many disabled children from educational services. These included placing them on long waiting lists, using disciplinary procedures to remove disabled children with behavior problems from classrooms, initiating limited (if any) child census programs to identify children, failing to provide educational programs to some institutionalized children, choosing to educate one group of disabled children but not another, and denying all education to some children.[32]

Children with disabilities who were not denied total access to education were often functionally excluded from an appropriate education because school systems tended to group all disabled children together, ignoring their individual strengths and weaknesses.[33] Even when school systems recognized the individual needs of disabled children, they frequently did not provide related services, as discussed in chapters 3 and 5.

Misclassification. Historically, testing and classification procedures have been (and remain) powerful political tools, capable of regulating people, degrading them, denying them access to educational opportunity, and excluding them as undesirables, as discussed in chapter 4. Children with disabilities often have been misplaced or wrongfully tracked in the educational system, primarily because of the misuse of testing and classification procedures. Many school evaluation procedures were racially and culturally biased, based on a single criterion rather than being multifactored, administered by untrained personnel, rarely based on multidisciplinary assessment, and focused on only one area of disability.[34]

Inappropriate Education. Many factors have caused disabled children to receive an inappropriate education. In addition to misclassification practices, classroom teachers often had no method for organizing disabled children's educational needs and the services required to meet them. Special educational programs themselves seldom received periodic review, and placements typically were made without regard for the unique needs of the affected children. Teachers of disabled students were often not only uncertified in special education but were the least skilled teachers in the system as well.[35]

By classifying a child as disabled and referring him or her to a separately financed and organized school bureaucracy,[36] schools had established and legitimized a dual system of education:[37] "regular" education for nondisabled children and "special education" for disabled or minority ones. The former was substantially better financed and staffed than the latter, which became a classroom of last resort.[38]

Restrictive Placements. Educational opportunities for disabled children were restricted because a full range of services often was not available. Typically, the only placement available was in separate classrooms or schools. These classrooms generally were the oldest and most poorly equipped, and their location often presented many architectural barriers. Often, the physical layout of schools limited disabled children's access to libraries, gymnasiums, and cafeterias, and therefore curtailed any opportunity to participate in extracurricular activities. In general, disabled children were given few opportunities to interact with age-equivalent, nondisabled students in the school environment.[39]

Not infrequently, children who were assigned to the special education system experienced permanent segregation[40] from nondisabled children or, what seemed worse, placement in institutions for mentally ill, mentally retarded, deaf, or blind children and adults.[41] The sad irony of this segregated system was that it satisfied the interests of so many agencies[42]—public schools, public institutions, private schools, and regular and special educators—while depriving so many children of an opportunity to be educated appropriately,[43] to attend school with their age peers,[44] to avoid the indisputably adverse effects of institutionalization,[45] and to remain with their families,[46] by attending the schools they would attend if they were not disabled.

Lack of Procedural Due Process. Educational practices resulting in exclusion from or reduction of educational opportunities for disabled children were perpetuated by a system that contained no safeguards to assure correction of inappropriate action (or inaction) on the part of school officials. Educational placement and evaluation of disabled children typically were implemented without their parents' knowledge or consent. Parents generally had neither access to their child's school records[47] nor a formal protest mechanism to appeal educational decisions concerning their child. Any children who were legal wards of the state usually were not represented by advocates, guardians, or surrogate parents.

Lack of Parental Involvement. In addition to the absence of procedures for review and appeal of educational decisions, there were few mechanisms for involving parents in their child's education. As a general rule, school systems had not encouraged parental involvement. Besides being denied legally enforceable access to their child's records, parents received little information about available programs for disabled children,[48] had no meaningful way of participating in the process of planning the education of their child, and frequently were not represented on local or state school advisory panels.[49]

During the late 1960s and early 1970s, an increasing number of parents and special educators became committed to solving the problems caused by dual educational systems. Although more and more parents began to demand a voice in the education of their disabled children, they were frustrated by the school system's failure to provide channels through which their voices could be heard. In their frustration they turned for solutions to the state legislature and the courts. As the decade of the 1970s began, parents turned to the federal government, particularly the courts.

THE NATURE OF LRA: REBUTTABLE PRESUMPTION

The LRA principle disguises a complex debate concerning the educational rights of disabled children. The reasons for the complexity are twofold. One is that the principle (as set out in the IDEA and the regulations under it and Section 504) is a rebuttable presumption: It sets forth a general rule of conduct (integration of disabled and nondisabled children), but it allows it to be rebutted when integration is not appropriate for the disabled child.[50] In what cases should the presumption be rebutted? The other reason for complexity is that the principle takes into account the "appropriate" education to which the child is entitled by other legal principles and policy considerations. LRA is inextricably tied to the notion of appropriateness, which makes it all the more complex because appropriate education itself is difficult to define (as chapter 5 demonstrates).

The LRA principle is examined here in the context of appropriate education and, by closely analyzing major judicial decisions involving both appropriate education and least restrictive placements, the common law of an appropriate, least restrictive education for a disabled child.[51] More than that, the question of whether LRA is interpreted according to a "rights" to and need for an appropriate education, or a rights to integration model, is addressed. Do the courts blindly follow a traditional continuum of services or a stereotypical image of more and less restriction,[52] requiring disabled children to receive regular, or mainstream, education even when it will have little, if any, benefit for them? Or do they infuse LRA with a sense of appropriateness so that appropriate education sometimes means more, rather than less, separation from normal or regular education? Do they recognize that the right to an appropriate education, to satisfy the child's educational or other developmental needs, is as compelling an interest as the right against unnecessarily restrictive, unprofitable placements? The answer is *yes*.

It will be helpful to consider one point of this chapter—that needs sometimes do prevail over the presumptive right to regular education placement and programming—by recognizing that the LRA principle was certain to generate as much heat as light concerning the educational rights of disabled children. Even in 1978, just a year after the federal regulations implementing the 1975 Act became effective, it seemed

> clear that the broad-based challenges to self-contained special education (i.e., programs that are not in the mainstream or do not meet every aspect of least restrictive placement) inevitably will have to answer those parents and educators who remain unconvinced of the educational value of the principle, who can adduce research and expert testimony to indicate that placement in the least restrictive program is not an automatic assurance of an appropriate education, and who assert that the least restrictive placement principle hinges on what is most enhancing or most habilitating for the disabled person, not what is close to "normal."
>
> The risk is great that judicial and administrative interpretations of the principle will not depend on two indispensable factors: 1) The principle has its recent history in the massive denial of an adequate education for the many disabled children who were placed in self-contained and separate programs (a history that is not necessarily doomed to be re-

peated, given the other rights and access to resources that disabled children have under case and statutory law); and 2) the principle is best understood and applied in terms of what is appropriate for the child himself where "appropriate" is defined not only by the IEP content but also by concepts of enhancement: What is enhancing is sometimes necessarily more restrictive than "normal" (e.g., a classroom for seriously emotionally disturbed children or severely retarded children may be highly "restrictive" and separated from "regular" programs but also highly enhancing of their abilities to learn). The future issue, then, is whether courts and agencies will apply the least restrictive principle by taking into account the relative "richness" or "poverty" of educational services in separate programs and the likelihood that such programs will be more enhancing for the disabled child than not.[53]

But more is at issue concerning LRA and its judicial interpretation than balancing the relative needs and rights of disabled children (given the policy choice, made in the IDEA, in favor of a full continuum of services). A fundamental policy issue is inherent in LRA. It is one thing to concede that, when a government has a legitimate interest in restricting a citizen's liberty, it may act only in the way that is least restrictive of his or her liberty. The "least drastic means" standard thus serves to restrict governments from unnecessarily restricting citizens. But it is another thing altogether to answer the question: What is an unwarranted or unnecessary restriction of a disabled child when the state is required to educate him or her appropriately? Any constitutional limitation on the ability of the state to act also is a limitation on the ability of its agents—educators—to act and, in turn, on the ability of the child's parents or guardians to act, and, finally, on the rights of the child.

Taking this chain of events as a focal point for discussion of LRA as it applies to persons with mental retardation, a publication of the American Association on Mental Retardation set forth the argument (in language that applies to all disabled children) that LRA should not be interpreted as an absolute restriction on placement of disabled people in unusual, atypical, or less "normal" settings, where those settings have been chosen by Congress, SEAs, or state legislatures as legitimate options on a continuum.

> One concern in analyzing the [LRA] doctrine is with the lives of persons who are subject to these natural limitations imposed by retardation. Another concern centers on limitations that lawmakers either impose on professionals or that professionals impose on themselves, which in turn are imposed on mentally retarded persons. In a nutshell, do these presumptions and assumptions, part and parcel of the [LRA] concept, overly restrict mentally retarded persons? Do governments and professionals misunderstand and misapply the [LRA] doctrine so that it becomes a force for further limitation? . . . The editors' preference is to increase the range of choice for retarded people and mental retardation professionals by infusing the [LRA] doctrine with a sense of liberation, not a sense of restriction.[54]

Have the courts given that prediction and argument a hospitable reception? By and large, they have. Close analysis of the reported decisions shows that LRA does not prevent courts from authorizing the placement of a disabled child into more restrictive settings that also are more or equally enhancing as presumptively less restrictive (more "normal") ones. Indeed, LRA as a function of appropriate education sometimes requires such placement into a setting along a continuum away from the regular school or program. The child's rights to and need for an appropriate education prevail over his or her integration rights where appropriate, and enhancing *placement* (the need) conflicts with the presumption in favor of *integration* (the presumptive right). Were it not for the deplorable restrictiveness of most public residential institutions, and, indeed, the limitations in programming and associations in many special education programs, and if it were not for the unimaginative use of the LRA doctrine by the courts in right-to-education cases, this result might be acceptable.

LRA as a Presumption

As noted, LRA is a presumption in that it requires disabled children to be placed in educational programs with nondisabled children to the maximum extent appropriate for the individual and allows removal from such settings and placement in special classes, separate schools, or other separate activities only if the nature or severity of the disability is such that education in regular classes, even with the use of supplementary aids and services, cannot be achieved satisfactorily.

Rebuttable presumptions set forth a rule of conduct that must be followed in every case unless, in a particular case, it can be demonstrated that the general rule will have unacceptable consequences for the affected individual.[55] Thus, LRA favors integration but allows separation. One reason for presumptions and for LRA specifically is that choices about appropriate placements should be made available within reason. LRA does this by being a presumption, not an iron-clad rule.

There is another reason to prefer rebuttable presumptions such as LRA. They occupy a middle ground between irrebuttable presumptions at one extreme and unguided case-by-case decision making at the other, and have several advantages over either of the other approaches. They tend to assure more consistency of behavior and thus are useful for predicting what will be legally tolerable in like cases.

In addition to *consistency* and *predictability*, rebuttable presumptions tend to prevent people from being subjected to the perceived harm they might experience if they were not governed by a presumption. Rebuttable presumptions allow policymakers the opportunity to avoid alternatives that are perceived to be harmful. Yet, because they are rebuttable, these presumptions allow greater *freedom of choice* than irrebuttable presumptions. Iron-clad rules may not, after all, be good policy decisions for everyone. Presumptively, institutional or other segregating placement is more harmful than regular school placement.[56] Only when it is shown that such a placement is necessary for appropriate education purposes in order to satisfy the individual's interests or valid state purposes is the presumption overcome.

The federal statutes and the regulations implementing them, along with the applicable judicial decisions, make it clear that LRA is a rebuttable presumption.[57] But the statutes and regulations also demonstrate that LRA depends on and must be interpreted and applied in the context of *appropriate* education for the disabled child. Under the applicable statutes and regulations, the child's placement is determined by his or her rights to and needs for special education, related services, or both, and by the individualized education program (IEP) developed for the child. And the IEP—the document that reflects educators', parents', and sometimes the child's determination of an appropriate education—cannot be accomplished until and unless the child has been evaluated nondiscriminatorily and, even prior to evaluation, accepted for enrollment into a publicly supported school system.

Thus, at least three other principles precede LRA and affect its interpretation: the *zero-reject* principle (which requires that the child must be given a free and appropriate public education—a rule against "pure exclusion"), the *nondiscriminatory evaluation* principle (which requires fair assessment so that the child's strengths can be improved and weaknesses remediated), and the *appropriate education* rule (which requires that the child be given an education that potentially benefits him or her—a rule against functional exclusion from education).

Precisely because LRA is entwined with these other principles, its interpretation and application have been the subject of many lawsuits and much controversy. Before trying to untie the knot, however, it will be useful to consider the values that underlie the LRA requirement.

LRA and Values

LRA is especially value laden because it promotes three sets of public policy values. One is the value of an *appropriate education* for disabled children. LRA promotes this value because it creates an impetus toward integration of disabled children with regular education, where their education arguably is enhanced.

The second is the value of *conservation of political and fiscal capital*. Equal access of disabled children to regular education also decreases the likelihood that unequal services (special education) will be thought to be politically untenable and fiscally unfeasible. Duplication of resources in times of economic retrenchment sometimes is neither politically astute nor economical.

Third, LRA may promote an important constitutional value—the right of disabled people to associate with nondisabled people. LRA's legal history clearly is related to the First Amendment and particularly relevant to disabled people. The right of association is more than a constitutional imperative. It is also a positive force in broadening individual and cultural dimensions of the citizenry and in dispelling stigmatizing and discriminatory attitudes of nondisabled people concerning disabled people. As stigma is less attributable to disability and as *de jure* and *de facto* discrimination accordingly recede, persons with disability acquire greater opportunity to pursue the constitutional values of liberty and choice in association.

Two points, however, cannot escape mention. One is that the public policy value of appropriate education for disabled children can conflict with a similar value—the appropriate education of nondisabled children. The other is that the families of disabled children do not always choose integration and association with nondisabled children. Evidence and implementation of these facts are explored later in this chapter. For now, it is well to note that many commentators have provided explicit or implicit goals for the LRA principle.[58] A synthesis of these with the previous analysis of values, constitutional bases, and interests can be illustrated by a matrix in which the three basic levels of the policy interact with the two major value assumptions concerning appropriate education and the right of association to produce six dimensions of the LRA policy.

Dimensions of the LRA Policy

Value Assumptions

Value Assumptions	A. That individuals and societies benefit when all are educated to our fullest potential	B. That individuals and society benefit when all its members are free to associate with each other
Produce: Legal Principles *and*	1. Right to Education	4. Right to Association
Educational Strategies *Resulting in:*	2. Appropriate Education	5. Integration
Social Effects	3. Enhanced Individual Potential	6. Decreased Stigma

LRA is both a legal principle and an educational strategy that circularly produces social effects. The legal principle assures a disabled student's appropriate education and thereby the right to associate with nondisabled students and other citizens. As an educational strategy, LRA enhances individual potential through appropriate education. Education, in turn, is thought to mitigate the effects of disability by decreasing stigma and thereby increasing associational rights, individual opportunity, and potential.

These six dimensions provide a framework to organize stated goals of the IDEA and the LRA principle. The following list summarizes the goals of the IDEA and its LRA component:

1. *Right to Education*: To provide education to all disabled children.
2. *Appropriate Education*: To provide an education that is appropriate to the unique strengths and weaknesses of each disabled child.
3. *Enhanced Individual Potential:* To provide the opportunity for disabled children to develop to their potential.[59]
4. *Right to Association*: To provide education in an environment that promotes association with nondisabled peers.[60]
5. *Integration:* To provide the opportunity for nondisabled peers to develop sensitivity to individual differences, and to prepare the disabled child for future integration into regular education as well as integration into society in general.[61]
6. *Decreased Stigma:* To enhance the social status of the disabled child.[62]

Given this understanding of the goals of LRA, the final question to be determined is how these goals are to be implemented and how the value conflicts embedded in the goals can be resolved in practice. To resolve these questions, it is necessary to return to the legal concept of LRA as a rebuttable presumption and to translate that principle into an educational strategy.

The relative restrictiveness of an educational environment should be judged only in light of the individual educational need (right to an appropriate education) of each disabled child. In light of that need, the most "normal" environment may not always be the least restrictive of the child's right to an appropriate program of education.[63] To determine the least restrictive environment for a given child, two decisions must be made. The first involves choosing the range of available programs or environments to satisfy the child's requirements for an appropriate education. Conceivably, this might include more than one possible environment. Second, decision makers, such as the individualized education planning committee, must identify the particular programs or environment, from among the range of satisfactory ones, that can contribute most substantially to the child's freedom to interact with students who are not disabled. Thus, when making a placement decision, priority is given to providing an appropriate education and to a consideration of provision for appropriate education in an environment that minimizes infringement on the liberty to associate with nondisabled peers.

The principle is illustrated below. Circle A represents the set of all appropriate educational programs or environments available for a given disabled child. Circle B represents the set of all environments that allow the same child to interact with nondisabled peers. In an ideal case, circles A and B overlay one another perfectly or nearly perfectly (1a). More likely, they will marginally overlap, providing decision makers with relatively fewer choices for placement (1b). Or they may not meet at all, forcing decision makers to choose environments entirely on the basis of what is available within circle A (1c). In actuality, the problem is much more complex because the interests and needs of others (e.g., parents) enter the decision process (1d). Moreover, the decision of Congress and state legislatures to have a continuum of services further complicates the choice because the continuum supports placement in segregated or special programs and thus reduces the likelihood that appropriate programs will be developed within more, rather than less, integrated environments.

A = All possible educational environments capable of providing an education for an individual disabled child

B = All possible environments capable of maximizing freedom to associate with nondisabled peers

C = Needs of other interested parties

1a. Ideal case: Numerous choices available to satisfy both A and B

1b. Few choices available to A and B

1c. No available alternatives to satisfy needs of both A and B

1d. Complex decision process considering needs of A and B as well as other interested
     parties

THE JUDICIAL INTERPRETATION

LRA and Appropriate Education

The threshold inquiry would appear to be: What does the law mean when it requires that a
disabled child must be educated with nondisabled children to the maximum extent appropriate? What is the "maximum extent?" Even before that can be answered, one must ask:
What is "appropriate?" This value-laden term promised to provoke spirited litigation. As
the cases discussed here show, the promise has been more than fulfilled. For present purposes, it is necessary to analyze only those cases in which both LRA and appropriate education requirements are involved. (Much of what follows also was presented in chapter 5.)

In nearly all of the appropriate education/LRA cases, parents and educators of disabled
children have disagreed with each other over the meaning of appropriate education. Parents
and educators alike have sought both nonregular (non-LRA) and regular school (LRA) placements for disabled children. In trying to obtain nonregular (non-LRA) institutional or residential placement for a disabled child, they have desired the child's placement *out* of the
least restrictive setting. ("Least restriction" is defined by the image of a continuum on which
the most restrictive setting is usually homebound or residential placement and the least restrictive placement is in the mainstream with nondisabled children for the entire or majority of the disabled child's time in school.)

This was the situation as of 1985 in twelve of the reported cases.[64] In nine of them, the
courts ordered institutional or other "more restrictive" placement.[65] In those nine, the children were either severely or profoundly disabled. In four instances,[66] they were emotionally
disturbed; in four others,[67] mentally retarded; and in one,[68] learning disabled. In the three
cases in which parents were unsuccessful in seeking institutional or residential placement,
one child was severely multiply disabled[69] (retardation and autism), and two were mildly
learning disabled.[70] It seems difficult to harmonize the first with the seven cases ordering
residential placement. The latter clearly are distinguishable on the basis of the degree of
disability.

Conversely, each group also has sought least restrictive or more "normal" placement for disabled children. Thus, of seven cases reported by 1985, school officials were successful in five[71]—two children with severe multiple disabilities and one "trainable mentally retarded" (i.e., moderately retarded, not mildly or severely retarded), one severely to moderately retarded, and one learning disabled—and unsuccessful in two others[72] (profoundly deaf and severely and profoundly mentally retarded). In a fifth case, the child's parents did not contest institutional placement.[73]

Where parents and educators have not been able to agree on the proper placement for a particular child, courts have been required to define an appropriate education and LRA. In cases in which parents have sought institutional or other "more restrictive" placement, but schools have opposed such placement, courts, as of 1985, have decided in favor of the parents in a clear majority of the cases.[74] By the same token, where schools have sought institutional placement contrary to parents' desires, courts, as of 1985, ordered such placement in a majority of the cases.[75] Clearly the courts were disposed toward institutional placement. This trend in the cases did not change between 1985 and mid-1992. Several cases are particularly good illustrations of the trend (discussed later in this chapter).

Two initial and partial conclusions emerge from these cases. The first reflects a concern that the perspectives of the disabled person should be taken into account. Interestingly, the children's perspectives—their self-declared interests in placement—have not been reflected in the LRA cases. Indeed, all of special education law insufficiently allows for the child's self-declared interests to be advanced. The locus of control—the power to make decisions—is never placed with the disabled child.[76] The paradox is that, in the name of removing a restriction, the LRA rule, as practiced in schools, by parents, or both, tends to disregard the choices (and thereby restrict the autonomy) of the person who is ultimately restricted by any placement. The second conclusion is that, given a choice between more or less restriction, parents and educators more often choose the former—greater restriction—than the latter, and the courts are now prone to affirm that choice.

On its face, this latter conclusion might seem surprising for two reasons. First, it suggests that the LRA principle either is unacceptable to a majority of parents, educators, and courts and is therefore a shaky basis for law simply because of its low potential to command the assent of the governed. (Some reasons for this result are suggested in chapter 4, on nondiscriminatory education, in the portions on why and how we classify.) Second, it appears that the LRA rule is being interpreted in ways not anticipated by many who thought it would result in substantial inclusion of disabled children in traditional public school settings.[77]

But another explanation exists. If one studies the nature[78] and extent[79] of the disabilities of the children around whom the cases have been litigated and the nature of the choices presented—the choice between a public school and a residential program—it becomes clear that courts are concerned primarily about appropriate education and its provision, not about lock-step adherence to a hard-and-fast rule of integration. Alternatively stated, the exception has become the rule in these cases. More often than not, the presumption is rebutted because of a mismatch between the child's needs for an appropriate education, through the continuum of services, and the right to least restrictive (more integrated) placement.

In a sense, these cases instruct us that presumptively least restrictive placements (where that means more, not less, movement of disabled children into regular educational settings and programs) can be functionally more restrictive where the continuum of services is allowed a legitimate policy choice. The paradox—less restriction is more—can be resolved only if the child's needs (right to an appropriate or enhancing education) are held paramount over his or her rights to integration.

Appropriate Education

Disagreement over placement clearly begins as a disagreement concerning "appropriate" education. That this is so should not be unanticipated. As chapter 5 showed, it is conceptually difficult to define appropriate education and even more danger-fraught to apply the definition to a particular child.

Process Definition. In the process definition, the disabled child will receive an appropriate education if he or she is "processed" properly. The child is not subject to "pure exclusion" (a zero-reject approach) and is evaluated nondiscriminatorily, furnished an IEP, and placed in the least restrictive appropriate setting. Several cases demonstrate the validity of this definition, but none so well as *Rowley*.

In *Rowley*, the school district had evaluated the child, placed her in regular class programs, and developed an IEP as required by law. The IEP did not call for an interpreter. The parents of the child, however, believed a sign language interpreter was necessary to ensure the child's maximum achievement. The school resisted, arguing that the child was making satisfactory progress without an interpreter. A due process hearing officer agreed with the parents. So did the district and circuit courts. The lower courts looked to the exceptional ability of the child and said that although her education was adequate, it could not be considered appropriate until an interpreter was provided.

The Supreme Court reversed and interpreted the IDEA to require individualized educational services, developed through the IEP process by educators and parents, that are individually designed to benefit the child. It laid great emphasis on professional judgments, parent–professional collaboration through the IEP process, compliance with other procedural safeguards, and a "legislative conviction that adequate compliance with the procedures (of the Act) would in most cases assure much, if not all, of what Congress wished in the way of substantive content in an IEP."

IEP Definition. A second way to define appropriate education has been to assure that the child is given the special education and related services called for by his or her IEP. This definition clearly is the statutorily accepted one. It also has received the sanction of all of the appropriate education/LRE cases, including *Rowley*, in which the Court noted that the child's IEP did not require an interpreter.

In *Laura M. v. Special School District No. 1*,[80] for example, the court not only acknowledged this definition but also set out in its order the components of a judicially acceptable IEP. By the same token, when a federal court ordered a school district to educate a severely retarded boy in the same building in which it was educating nondisabled children, it also specified the major contents of the child's education program.[81]

Comparability Definition. A third definition of appropriate education derives from the Section 504 regulations.[82] These require schools to provide disabled children with special education and related aids and services designed to meet their educational needs as adequately as the needs of nondisabled children are met. The comparability definition has strong equal protection overtones and, as the cases demonstrate, has been a draconian sword for disabled children. It has enabled them to obtain some, but not all, of what some believed was due them.

The court in *Springdale v. Grace*, relying on the district court's *Rowley* opinion, concluded that, when residential and "less restrictive" educational placements are comparable and even when the residential one is preferable because it is "better" for the child, the comparability standard, coupled with the LRA presumption, requires the regular school placement. A similar result was obtained in *Isgur v. School Board of Newton*,[83] in which a state court held that the LRA principle modifies a state law provision requiring that the child be placed in the program that would benefit him to the maximum extent feasible; an appropriate education is not tantamount to maximum development, only adequate development of the disabled child.

In adopting a process definition and requiring *some* educational benefit, the Supreme Court's *Rowley* opinion explicitly turned its back on a definition that has the purpose of maximizing a disabled child's development. Beyond these rather traditional definitions, however, the meaning of "appropriate" has become increasingly protean. As suggested, some courts view an appropriate education as that which gives reasonable assurance that a disabled child will be developed to the full potential. Thus, *Age v. Bullitt*[84] characterized the purpose of the IDEA as being to provide for the child's maximum development. To that end, the court required the most effective instruction of the child. Other courts seem to reject the maximum development concept without simultaneously holding that the child is entitled only to a barely adequate education. This is the *Rowley* standard, now adopted by several other courts as well.[85] From the cases decided after *Rowley*, clearly the substantive right to an appropriate education, required by the IDEA, is to an education that is intended to provide, and indeed does in fact provide, some educational benefit. (See chapter 5 for a discussion of these cases.)

Related Services. It also is now clear that the availability of related services is a critical factor in determining whether a child's education and educational placement will be appropriate and in the least restrictive setting. These cases are discussed in chapter 3.

Costs as a Standard. To what degree, if any, may courts weigh the costs of an appropriate special education in determining the LEA's duty to a disabled child? There are mixed answers to this issue. But it is important to recognize that the IDEA and its regulations, and

Section 504 and its regulations, are absolutely silent on the issue of whether costs are legitimate considerations in defining an appropriate education in the least restrictive (most integrated) setting. Thus, any considerations relating to costs are created by the courts and SEAs or LEAs that seek to minimize the cost to themselves.

There are two sets of cases involving costs, appropriateness, and the LRA doctrine. The first set relates to this issue: When a residential program (i.e., a relatively nonintegrated one) is appropriate, are the SEAs or LEAs ultimately responsible for the full costs? The answer is yes, but usually the costs are shared between the SEA and LEA, on the one hand, and the state agencies providing the programs in the residential setting, on the other.

Concerning this issue, courts have not usually regarded the relatively high cost of appropriate residential placement as a factor that should mitigate against the child's right to placement in residential facilities. The cost factor usually comes into play when the child is so disabled that residential placement is acknowledged by all the parties to be the appropriate placement and the issue is whether educational agencies will bear the full cost of residential placement or other agencies (typically mental health or social service agencies) will contribute to the cost.[86] The decisions unanimously assess the cost to educational agencies on the grounds that the IDEA imposes single-agency responsibility on the state and that the one agency solely responsible to implement the IDEA is the state education agency, together with its local counterparts.

Two exceptions to this general rule appear to be developing, however. One seems to be a "reasonableness" rule. If the school has made good faith efforts to provide the disabled child an appropriate education in the least restrictive environment, the school will not be charged residential school tuition.[87] Conversely, the cost of residential school tuition will be assessed to the public school, not the child's parents, unless "reasonable alternatives" to the residential placement are available.[88]

The other exception arises from the "current-status" regulations. [89] If the parents of a disabled child remove him or her from a public school and place the child in a private school and subsequently seek to recover the tuition from the public school, some courts[90] refuse to award them tuition on the grounds that, under federal regulations (1) the child's current educational status may not be changed during the pendency of any administrative or judicial proceedings concerning placement,[91] and (2) school-initiated private placement is free of cost to parents but parent-initiated placement is not.[92]

The second set of cases explicitly takes into account the costs of an appropriate education. These cases usually address this issue: Does the student have a right to an appropriate education in more integrated settings or in more segregated settings, and may the costs of providing the appropriate education in integrated settings legitimately be weighed against the costs of the education in less integrated settings? The trend of the cases answering the question is "yes."

The Davis Standard—Costs. Although it dealt with an unrelated legal issue involving disabled people, *Southeast Community College v. Davis*, holding that a hearing impaired applicant for admission to a school of nursing is not "otherwise qualified" for admission under Section 504 regulations, and that the regulations do not require the nursing school to make extensive, professionally indefensible adjustments in its program to accommodate the applicant, seems to provide a final layer of judicial gloss on "appropriate education." Taking a cue from the Supreme Court's decision in *Davis* that Section 504 does not mandate certain accommodations, several courts seem to conclude that, when the child's disability is so great that his or her successful placement in a regular education program is impractical or improbable without substantial modifications in the school's facilities or regular or special education programs, the LRA principle does not require such modifications.[93]

An appropriate education, these courts reason, lawfully may be provided under the federal Act and its regulations (without violation of the LRA prescription) by special programs if the cost of modifying regular programs is too great. In a sense, this is a "competing equities" approach, wherein, unlike the harmful effects test, the issue is balancing the child's interests against school system interests. In this posture, the *Davis* accommodations criteria modify the integration principle and justify the inference that courts conclude it is more appropriate for severely disabled children to be educated in separate programs or schools.

Several cases illustrate the new "cost-consideration" approach. *Roncker v. Walters*, decided in 1983 by the Sixth Circuit Court of Appeals, involved the Ohio system of separate schools for students with moderate to severe disabilities. The immediate issue was whether a student classified as trainable mentally retarded should be educated in the school system that serves nondisabled and mildly disabled students or in the system that serves those with more severe disabilities. The court of appeals set aside the lower court's order that the student be placed in the separate system and ordered the lower court to make a new determination of the student's placement.

A basic (rather than immediate) issue in *Roncker* was the meaning of the LRA provisions of the IDEA. The court of appeals observed that the very strong congressional preference for mainstreaming was found in the Act's requirement that the student with a disability be educated with nondisabled students "to the maximum extent appropriate." It then said:

> The proper inquiry is whether a proposed placement is appropriate under the Act. In some cases, a placement which may be considered better for academic reasons may not be appropriate because of the failure to provide for mainstreaming. The perception that a segregated institution is academically superior for a handicapped child may reflect no more than a basic disagreement with the mainstreaming concept. Such a disagreement is not, of course, any basis for not following the Act's mandate. *Campbell v. Talladega City Bd. of Education*, 518 F. Supp. 47, 55 (N.D. Ala. 1981). In a case where the segregated facility is considered superior, the court should determine whether the services which make that placement superior could be feasibly provided in a nonsegregated setting. If they can, the placement in the segregated school would be inappropriate under the Act. Framing the issue in this manner accords the proper respect for the strong preference in favor of mainstreaming while still realizing the possibility that some handicapped children simply must be educated in segregated facilities either because the handicapped child would not benefit from mainstreaming, because any marginal benefits received from mainstreaming are far outweighed by the benefits gained from services which could not feasibly be provided in the non-segregated setting, or because the hand-

icapped child is a disruptive force in the nonsegregated setting. Cost is a proper factor
to consider since excessive spending on one handicapped child deprives other handicapped children. *See Age v. Bullitt County Schools*, 673 F.2d 141, 145 (6th Cir. 1982).
Cost is no defense, however, if the school district has failed to use its funds to provide
a proper continuum of alternative placements for handicapped children. The provision
of such alternative placements benefits all handicapped children.

This statement develops a new standard by which to judge "the maximum extent appropriate" requirement of the IDEA. Under the Roncker standard, "the maximum extent appropriate" depends on the feasibility of providing, in a nonsegregated setting, those services
that make a segregated facility "superior." If it is feasible to duplicate those services, placement in the segregated setting is inappropriate. Thus, courts must determine what is and is
not feasible in each case where the segregated and nonsegregated programs are the only two
options presented.

This approach seems valid for two reasons, at least. First, it forces courts to make a decision based on the student's rights to an appropriate education and to an integrated setting
for that education. Alternatively stated, this approach is a student-centered, individualized
determination, consistent with the IDEA's overall approach.

Second, this approach forces the courts to look into what can be done ("feasible") to
modify the otherwise inappropriate integrated setting. Alternatively stated, it forces the courts
to require the schools to show why an integrated setting cannot be modified or accommodated
to the student. Under this approach, the schools bear the burden of proof that an integrated
setting (that is, the student's right to an integrated, least restrictive education) cannot possibly satisfy the "educational benefit" standard of *Rowley* (the student's right to an appropriate education). The *Roncker* approach is an excellent illustration of the LRA principle at
work. The principle requires that state's interests in providing an appropriate education be
balanced with and, if possible (feasible), merged with and, at least, balanced with the individual student's interest in associating with nondisabled students.

But what does "feasible" mean? *Roncker* defines the term by stating three exceptions
to the appropriateness/integration requirement: "(S)ome handicapped children simply must
be educated in segregated facilities either because the handicapped child would not benefit
from mainstreaming, because any marginal benefits received from mainstreaming are far
outweighed by the benefits gained from services which could not feasibly be provided in
the nonsegregated setting, or because the handicapped child is a disruptive force in the nonsegregated setting."

The three exceptions, then, are:

1. No benefit to the child;
2. Greater benefits in segregated settings even after the feasibility standard is applied (that
   is, after the courts determine what segregated-setting services can be created in nonsegregated settings);
3. Disruption in a nonsegregated setting.

The court then said:

> Cost is a proper factor to consider since excessive spending on one handicapped child deprives other handicapped children. . . . Cost is no defense, however, if a school district has failed to use its funds to provide a proper continuum of alternative placements for handicapped children. The provision of such alternative placements benefits all handicapped children.

Here, the court clearly uses a "competing equities" approach. As explained in chapters 3 and 5, competing equities issues always raise this question: At whose expense, and at how much expense, is one person to be given an advantage? Or, to what extent will one or more people be burdened to give an advantage to another? The court's use of the competing equities approach is apparent when it says that "excessive spending on one handicapped child deprives other handicapped children." That is, the "equity" of one child can be too expensive to require other children to pay for.

As appealing as this approach might be (in light of the fact that school districts have limited local, state, and federal funds in special education and must educate all disabled children appropriately), there is something wrong about it. Namely, the court assumes that a benefit for one student is not or cannot be a benefit for others as well.

In fact, what may seem to be excessive expenditures for one student may create benefits for others. If a school facility, program, curriculum, or faculty/staff is modified to accommodate one student's right to an appropriate education, the modification also may create benefits for others. There is no necessary or unavoidable connection between spending for one student and not having adequate funds for another. True, there may be such cases, but they are apt to be infrequent, as when a child whose accommodations are very expensive is the only one for whom the accommodations are, or most likely will be, beneficial and the school district is relatively poor. But the usual case will be the opposite: An accommodation for one will be an accommodation for others, if not immediately, then within a relatively short time.

The court said more than that excessive expenditures on one student may cause a disadvantage to others. It also pointed out that cost is "no defense" if the district has not provided a "proper continuum" of alternative placements. Thus, if a district does not provide an alternative to an integrated appropriate program, it may not complain about the cost of modifying the integrated one. This is true because the "marginal benefit" exception to integrated education requires the courts to compare segregated and nonsegregated programs. When there is no segregated program to compare to an integrated program, the school district can hardly complain that it must provide integrated education, since it must, under the IDEA, provide not only an appropriate education but also, if feasible, one that is integrated. The "cost-is-a-consideration" approach does have its limitations after all: It does not apply when a court can make no choice at all between one program and another.

One other case shows that cost is a consideration in balancing the student's right to an appropriate education against the right to an integrated education. In *A.W. v. Northwest R-1 School District,* decided by the Eighth Circuit Court of Appeals in 1987, the court of appeals upheld a lower court decision to place a child with severe mental retardation into a segregated program. The district court had concluded that no certified teacher is available for the student in an integrated program, and that the addition of a teacher is not an acceptable solution because "the funds available are limited so that placing a [certified] teacher [in the integrated setting] for the benefit of a few students at best, and possibly only one child, [A.W.], would directly reduce the educational benefits provided to other handicapped students by increasing the number of students taught by a single teacher [in the segregated setting]." To educate the one child in an integrated setting creates a benefit for that child, but the benefit is "insufficient to justify a reduction in unquestionable benefits to other handicapped children which would result from an inequitable expenditure of the finite funds available."

The court of appeals upheld the district court. In doing so, it relied on *Roncker* as allowing a court to consider cost to the district and benefit to the child (as cost-benefit approach). It also relied on *Rowley*'s observation that available financial resources must be equitably distributed among all disabled children.

Reasons for the Cost-Consideration Approach. It is clear that the courts are applying an economic analysis to the IDEA requirement that appropriate education be provided in the integrated setting to the maximum extent appropriate. Why are the courts taking this approach? The obvious reason is that they are very reluctant to become involved in issues of school financing. This is a familiar posture for the courts.

The Political Thicket and Separation of Powers. The Supreme Court's decision in *San Antonio Independent School District v. Rodriquez* in 1973 clearly is the basis for this reluctance to get involved in school financing. In that case, the issue before the Court was whether the state's system of supporting local school districts discriminated against the poorer districts in favor of the wealthier ones. The Court refused to rule on the matter, holding that there is no federal constitutional right under the equal protection doctrine to equal subsidies in school financing.

In *Rodriquez*, the Court made it very clear that it wanted to avoid the "political thicket" that would entangle it if it were to hold that such a right exists. Holding that such a right exists would require it to determine whether the states have violated such a right. That decision, in turn, would require it to create remedies to correct a violation. To create remedies, however, is to become involved in the most fundamental of all legislative decisions—namely, how a state and its political subdivisions should raise and spend money to apportion equally among its school districts. Thus, the Court's concern about the separation of powers doctrine—that legislatures enact laws and appropriate funds to carry them out, and courts interpret and apply the laws in disputes—impelled the Court to steer clear of the fiscal allocation and legislative determinations involved in school financing.

That is one political thicket that the Court earlier learned to avoid. After all, it had been embroiled in school governance and legislative matters as a result of its school desegregation decision in *Brown*. And it had been equally involved in state legislative matters as a result of its decisions in the legislative reapportionment cases that began with *Baker v. Carr* and *Reynolds v. Sims*. Clearly, it was not going to become involved in another such thicket, and thus it ducked the school financing issue in *Rodriquez* and continued to avoid it in *Rowley*.

Thus, the doctrine of separation of powers justified the courts in avoiding these matters that are fundamentally legislative, not judicial, dispute resolutions.

Congressional Intent and Majoritarian Decision Making. But there is another reason for the courts' reluctance to become involved as a superordinary school board, or even as a supervisor of state legislative decisions. It is, as the Supreme Court pointed out in *Rowley*, that "(t)he primary responsibility for formulating the education to be accorded to a handicapped child, and for choosing the educational method most suitable to the child's needs, was left by the [Education of the Handicapped] Act to state and local educational agencies in cooperation with the parents or guardian of the child."

Alternatively stated, the Congress has chosen to limit the courts' role in making educational decisions. For the courts to make any incursion into educational policy matters, therefore, would be opposite congressional intent. That is to say, it would violate the decisions made by the elected representatives of the people. It would be "undemocratic" in the very basic sense that it would violate the will of the people. It would be "anti-majoritarian." As long as the Constitution itself does not prohibit a certain legislative result, there is no reason, the Court in *Rowley* is saying, for courts to substitute their judgments for those of the representatives of the people.

This principle of majoritarian democracy—that the will of the people is expressed in laws enacted by their representatives—is the foundation for judicial restraint, or for judicial conservatism. It also is the principle that allows the courts to escape from making educational—that is, "professional" or "scientific"—decisions and for deferring to the judgment of experts in those fields.

State/Local Government, Federal Government, and Federalism. There is a third reason for the courts' reluctance to become too closely involved in matters of school governance and educational policy-making. It is based on the principle of federalism. Federalism (as explained in chapters 1 and 2) is a principle of government that allocates responsibility and power between the federal government, on the one hand, and among the states, on the other. It rests on the premise that shared responsibility and power are means for checking and balancing powers of all governments, and checks and balances are necessary and desirable to advance the interest of the people in liberty and the pursuit of their interests (including the pursuit of "happiness" and property) by various means.

Federalism also rests on the assumption that the pursuit of people's interests requires a great deal of flexibility and variability in the ways chosen by the federal, state, and local governments. Because people are so different and have so many different interests, no single government and certainly no single response ("answer") to their needs and interests will do the whole job.

The IDEA takes the federalism principle into account by allowing states to create a continuum of services and to satisfy students' rights to an appropriate education in the least restrictive setting/program by choosing not only from the continuum but also from various means of delivering services (such as curriculum, methodology, teacher certification, staff-student ratios) within the continuum.

As the Supreme Court said in *Rowley*, the IDEA leaves the primary responsibility on these matters to the state and local education agencies and to parents. Thus, the principle of federalism is another reason explaining the courts' reluctance to become the superordinary school boards.

Parental and Professional Decision Making and Judicial Deference. Finally, the rights and interests of parents and educators constitute a reason for the courts to avoid becoming too involved in matters of education. If the courts begin to become heavily involved, they will begin to displace parents' rights and natural instincts to rear their children in ways suitable to or chosen by the parents, consistent with parents' duties to act in ways that do not hurt their children. The Supreme Court itself has recognized the important and valuable role that parents have in their children's education and care in the *Parham* decision, involving the parents' right to place their children in state psychiatric or mental retardation institutions.

In addition, if the courts become heavily involved in educational decision making, they will displace the experts, substituting judicial opinion for that of educators. The Supreme Court is clearly reluctant to do this, as its decisions in *Davis* (see chapter 3) and *Rowley* (see chapter 3, also) point out. And courts as a whole have reasons not to substitute their judgment of professionals, as the discussion on classification (see chapter 4) indicates.

REBUTTING THE PRESUMPTION

It should be fairly evident by now that the LRA presumption has been overcome more often than many "integrationists" wanted or expected. Some of the justifications for rebuttal clearly emanate from the appropriate education principle, as construed and applied. And there are additional reasons why LRA has not compelled integration.

The Harmful Effects Issue

Is the harmful effect of institutional placement a standard for defining appropriate education? Curiously, none of the courts, save one,[94] appear to have been faced with an argument that placement in institutional or residential settings would have a harmful effect on the disabled child and therefore not be appropriate, despite the well-known data and cases indicating that such placement can cause the disabled child to regress.[95] Indeed, one court explicitly adopted the contrary view, saying that the child would regress if he were excluded from an institution for emotionally disturbed children. [96] Another court ordered residential placement of a schizophrenic child because evidence showed that she had made no meaningful progress in a regular school environment and was experiencing some intellectual regression there.[97] The only court that did consider the institutional regression factor could not have failed to do so, for the parties had entered into a prior consent decree requiring the defendants to de-institutionalize the plaintiff-class children.[98]

Statutory and regulatory language excuses the LRA from being applied to a child who cannot be educated satisfactorily in regular programs or schools even with the use of supplementary aids and services. This is the harmful effects standard. The harmful effect of integrating the disabled child is a legitimate concern. Likewise, departmental comments about regulations under Section 504 entitle schools to place the disabled child outside of regular education if placement in a regular classroom would significantly impair the education of nondisabled children. The harmful effect of integration on nondisabled children, thus, is another legitimate concern.

As chapter 3 demonstrates, this is precisely the approach adopted in *Honig* and the other expulsion cases and in the AIDS cases. Both of these harmful effects criteria reflect a more general "competing equities" concern: To what extent should children (disabled or not) be disadvantaged (by LRA integration) at the expense of others or at their own expense?

The harmful effects application of the competing equities doctrine (essentially, a familiar "balancing" test) is at work in several cases. For example, in *Tatro v. Texas*, the court was faced with deciding whether clean intermittent catheterization is a related service that a school must furnish to a spina bifida child with normal intelligence. The school sought to avoid that responsibility and assigned the student to homebound status, effectively blocking her presence in any programs at school sites. The court weighed the catheterization "burden" the schools would face with the exclusion the child would face and ruled in her favor. Similar balancing occurred in *Cox v. Brown*,[99] where the competing interests were those of the Department of Defense in avoiding the cost of residential placement of two learning disabled youths and the certainty that they would experience the humiliation of failure in DOD programs.

It appears, then, that the harmful effects test is solidly entrenched as a factor in determining whether a disabled child will be educated appropriately. Its effect, however, is far from singular: It does not always prevent residential or institutional placement (more restrictive placement, in the stereotypic view); nor does it always command regular education placement. It is an important factor and requires careful attention to individualized, child-specific considerations.

The harmful effects issue is especially important because of its direct relationship to one of the values that LRA seeks to advance—the *appropriate* education of disabled children. But the states' responsibilities extend to nondisabled children, too. If placing a disabled child in a program with nondisabled children negatively affects the education of the latter, the states' responsibilities to them are compromised. And if it does no good for the disabled child either, the states' responsibilities to all students are jeopardized.

Some courts recently have not been disposed to integration. They have held that students with disabilities legally may be placed in separate schools, in separate programs, outside of their local or neighborhood school district, or in similar "restrictive" or "atypical" settings when (a) the extent of the student's disability is such that appropriate education cannot be achieved satisfactorily in integrated or neighborhood school settings and programs, (b) the student is receiving an appropriate education or greater benefit in the separate program, (c) the costs of accommodation in the regular programs would deprive *other* students of some educational benefits, (d) the student's mainstream placement in some academic subjects will detract from the education of other, nondisabled students in the same class, (e) teachers are not readily available, (f) experts in the LEA determine that an appropriate education can be provided in separate settings or programs, or (g) when the student receives some separate academic education and some integrated academic or extracurricular programs. In addition, these courts support their separate-placement results on the grounds that the LRA doctrine is rebuttable, not an iron-clad rule of integration, and that the student's maximum development—which would be more likely in integrated settings than in separate ones—is not required under the statute.[100]

To the contrary, other courts resist the trend away from integration. For example, in *Hendricks v. Gilhool*, the court ruled that separate placement violates the LRE rule when (a) the separate schools and programs are not comparable to those in the regular education programs, (b) relocations of students with disabilities in order to accommodate an unexpected influx of nondisabled students were disruptive to the students' education, (c) restrictive special settings were the only ones offered to children with mild and moderate disabilities (but were legal when offered to students with severe disabilities), and (d) the LEA failed to create new classrooms to accommodate special education students. Here, the court seemed most concerned that disparate and unfavorable treatment was the order of the day for children with disabilities.

In two other cases, *Liscio v. Woodland Hills School District* and *Gillette v. Fairland Board of Education*, a court allowed a separate special program for academic purposes but also required an integrated program for other academic and/or nonacademic (mainly, extracurricular) purposes, stating that the LRE rule seeks not only appropriate education but also integration and association between disabled and nondisabled students.

Finally, given a choice between an appropriate program in a separate, full-time residential school on the one hand and an appropriate program in a homebound program on the other, the courts split on the outcome. In one case, the court held that the residential program is preferable under the LRE doctrine because it offers a greater educational benefit than a homebound program, given the severity of the student's behavior (*Chris D. v. Montgomery County Board of Education*). In another, *Hulme v. Dellmuth*, the local school district wanted to change the placement of a fourteen-year-old student with low-mild, high-moderate mental retardation and cerebral palsy from the school for orthopedically impaired (where his parents wanted him to be retained) to a regular-education high school. The student was not orthopedically impaired, and the district acknowledged that the special school was its most restrictive placement. His progress there had made it possible for him, in the judgment of the district's experts, to function in a school setting with nondisabled students, with age-appropriate peers, and with necessary support services (speech, OT, and transportation). In agreeing with the school district and ordering the student's removal from the special school, the court placed a great deal of weight on the "associational rights" approach: "In a mainstream environment, (the student) will be able to interact with nondisabled peers and thus enhance his life support and social interaction skills."

Two other cases illustrate the pro-integration reasoning that supports the "more mainstream type" placement. In *Greer v. Rome City School District* a child with Down syndrome was originally placed in a self-contained class, over parental objections. In reversing that placement and agreeing with the parents, the court determined that the student remains capable of benefiting from a regular education placement with the assistance of appropriate supplemental devices. The self-contained classroom, though perhaps better for academic reasons, does not comply with the requirement for adequate mainstreaming and therefore is not appropriate for a student with Down syndrome, moderate to severe speech deficit, and a language impairment. The court of appeals affirmed, concluding that the school district failed to fully consider whether the student could be educated successfully in a regular education environment, with supplementary aids and services.

Likewise, in *Harmon v. Mead School District No. 354,* a fourteen year old with fragile x syndrome and accompanying moderate mental retardation was placed by the school district in a self-contained classroom for all six periods of the school day. Upon appeal by the parents, the court ruled for the parents and ordered a less restrictive placement. The district, said the court, failed to prove by preponderance of the evidence that the student "required" placement in a self-contained classroom and that he could not receive an educational benefit in a less restrictive setting with the use of supplementary aids and services. The court required the district to prepare an IEP that calls for a minimum of two class periods per day in integrated settings. The court cited *Wilson v. Marana United School District* for proposition that the school has burden of proof that the student cannot succeed in a less restrictive placement, even with supplemental aids and services. It also cited *Daniel R. v. State Board of Education* for the proposition that an appropriate education is secured through an IEP that calls for four periods in the resource room and two in regular classrooms. Increasingly, *Daniel R. v. State Board of Education* is a leading case followed by other courts. For example, it influenced the court in *Greer v. Rome City School District,* as well as in *Harmon v. Mead School District No. 354.* In *Daniel R.,* the Fifth Circuit Court of Appeals developed the following two-pronged test to determine whether a placement is appropriate and consistent with the LRE rule: (1) whether placement in the regular classroom, with the use of supplementary aids and services, can be achieved satisfactorily [the statutory approach, Sec. 1412(5)(B)]; and (2) if not and the school intends to remove the student from regular education and provide special education, whether the school has placed the student in the least restrictive setting ("has mainstreamed") the student to the maximum extent appropriate [again, this is the statutory approach, Sec. 1412(5)(B)].

In applying these two tests, the court must consider a series of factors in an individualized, fact-specific inquiry. These factors are: (1) the nature and severity of the student's disabling condition; (2) the student's needs and abilities; and (3) the school's response to those needs and abilities.

Adhering to the *Daniel* tests, the court in *Greer v. Rome City School District* then applied other standards and procedures to determine the appropriate but least restrictive placement. Since these standards and procedures are consistent with those in prior cases (as explained in chapters 5 and 6), they are worth repeating in full:

> First, the school district may compare the educational benefits that the disabled children
> will receive in a regular classroom, supplemented by appropriate aids and services, with

the benefits he or she will receive in a self-contained special education environment. We caution, however, that "academic achievement is not the only purpose of mainstreaming. Integrating a disabled child into a nondisabled environment may be beneficial in and of itself." Accordingly, a determination by the school district that a disabled child will make academic progress more quickly in a self-contained special education environment may not justify educating the child in that environment if the child would receive considerable nonacademic benefit, such as language and role modeling, from association with his or her nondisabled peers. If, however, the school board determines that the disabled child will make significantly more progress in a self-contained special education environment and that education in a regular classroom may cause the child to fall behind his or her disabled peers who are being educated in the self-contained environment, mainstreaming may not be appropriate. In such a case, mainstreaming may actually be detrimental to the child and, therefore, would not provide the child with a free appropriate public education as mandated by the Act.

Second, the school district may consider what effect the presence of the disabled child in a regular classroom would have on the education of other children in that classroom. The comments to the regulations promulgated pursuant to the Act provided:

[W]here a disabled child is so disruptive in a regular classroom that the education of other students is significantly impaired, the needs of the disabled child cannot be met in that environment. Therefore regular placement would not be appropriate to his or her needs.

A disabled child who merely requires more teacher attention than most other children is not likely to be so disruptive as to significantly impair the education of other children. In weighing this factor, the school district must keep in mind its obligation to consider supplemental aids and services that could accommodate a disabled child's need for additional attention.

Third, the school district may consider the cost of the supplemental aids and services that will be necessary to achieve a satisfactory education for the disabled child in a regular classroom. As the Supreme Court noted in *Rowley*, Congress did not intend for school districts to furnish "every special service necessary to maximize each disabled child's potential . . ." This is not to say that a school district may decline to educate a disabled child in a regular classroom because the cost of doing so, with the appropriate supplemental aids and services, would be incrementally more expensive than educating the child in a self-contained special education classroom. On the other hand, a school district cannot be required to provide a disabled child with his or her own full-time teacher, even if this would permit the child to be satisfactorily educated in a regular classroom. The school district must balance the needs of each disabled child against the needs of other children in the district. If the cost of educating a disabled child in a regular classroom is so great that it would significantly impact upon the education of other children in the district, then education in a regular classroom is not appropriate.

Prediction and Placement

Most of the cases relying on the harmful effects exception have involved children whose education in less restrictive programs has been demonstrably unsatisfactory. Evidence of failure was so compelling as to require the children to be placed in a more restrictive (less integrated) program or school. It is not beyond the pale of fair inference to suggest that the more normal placements or programs would have been more restrictive because they were less beneficial for these children.

But these cases raise a disturbing question: Must the child always be subjected to experiences (placements or programs) in which he or she predictably will not be educated satisfactorily before he or she can be placed in more restrictive programs? Or will educators, related services personnel, and parents be able to place the child in the less integrated placements or programs on the basis of reasonable, professionally defensible expectations, projections, or predictions that the child will benefit from less restrictive programs as much as from more restrictive ones? In one case,[101] the clear answer is that professionally defensible predictions are permissible foundations for placements; the risk of unsatisfactory integration does not have to be undertaken.

Besides legitimizing a common practice, this decision seems to venture into the morass of uncertainty raised by the involuntary commitment cases—the quagmire of prediction of dangerousness.[102] Upon closer analysis, however, it is not so easy to make the analogy stick. The prediction of dangerousness is bogged down in the muddy soil of psychiatry, whereas the prediction of unsatisfactory school experiences seems to be on firmer soil—namely, the ability of educators to assess school programs and placements, fairly accurately measure disabled children's potential, and make a not unhappy match between the two.

How a person will behave in future environments that are not clearly foreseeable is a different matter than how a child will function in well-known educational settings or programs. On the whole, prediction of future educational success or failure seems acceptable, albeit unenviable for courts, particularly in light of the procedural safeguards afforded by special education law, IEPs, periodic review of the child's placement or classification as a disabled child, and parent participation in the child's education. There are, moreover, critical differences between the deprivation of liberty through involuntary commitment and concomitant institutionalization and special education placement.

None of this is meant to suggest that prediction of failure in integrated settings should be made lightly (the evidence should be clear and convincing) or that the pressure on public education to accommodate all disabled children, regardless of the nature or extent of their disabilities, in community-based programs should be diminished. It *is* acceptable to predict; it is not acceptable to subject disabled children (and their parents) to the probable effects of failure.

As indicated previously, an exception to the LRA presumption is permissible under the Section 504 regulations (as interpreted by the enforcing agency) when the disabled child poses (a prediction issue again) or is a danger to nondisabled children or educators. Although courts have applied this exception to permit the LRA presumption to be rebutted, they also seem to graft two other conditions onto this exception: If the child is dangerous to self[103] or to property,[104] the presumption can be overcome. In these cases, there was concurrent evidence of dangerousness to others and the children were severely disabled. If there were isolated evidence of dangerousness to self only or to property only, it remains to be seen if the exception would obtain.

Educability

Courts seem to weigh other competing equities considerations in deciding whether to apply the harmful effects exemption. As indicated by *Timothy W. v. Rochester* (discussed in chapter 3), the child's educability—or ineducability—is a dispositive factor in whether the zero-reject rule will prevent a profoundly retarded child from being excluded from *any* educational programs, much less those that are comparably more or less restrictive. Until that case, the issue had yet to be decided.

Competing Equities (Other than Costs)

Competing equities problems arise in other troublesome guises in the appropriate education/LRA cases. Thus, the risk that an interpreter for a hearing impaired child might distract nondisabled children was discounted by the *Rowley* district court as essentially a *de minimus* (minimal) concern. And in *New York ARC v. Carey*, the hazard of infection from retarded carriers of hepatitis B likewise was found inconsequential. The very fact, however, that distraction and contagion were considered to be competing equities factors suggests that, in a different case (where the interests of nondisabled children are more substantial, as in the danger-to-others cases such as the expulsion or AIDS cases), the exception might apply and a sort of reverse discrimination judgment could be entered—the harmful effects standard being the ostensible justification but the realignment of competing interests being the real one.

Expulsion: Not an LRA Option

Unlike the harmful effects cases, which are statutorily grounded in appropriate education/LRA concepts, cases involving the attempted expulsion of disabled children rely instead on statutory zero-reject[105] principles. These cases appear to have only an indirect relevance to LRA, but the fact of the matter is that they are well positioned within an LRA ambit. The most restrictive educational placement, after all, is outside any educational program—total exclusion of the purest kind. Courts recognize this when they prohibit a disabled child from being expelled when the cause of the disruptive behavior is the disability. The harmful effect of the behavior on self and others is the bedrock factual issue in these cases. Instead, courts allow only a change of placement from a more regular/normal program to a more restrictive/special one, pursuant to a modification in the child's IEP.

The courts thus silently recognize not only that expulsion would be the greatest harm the disabled child might experience but also that the LRA presumption is properly rebutted when the justification is keeping the child in *some* educational program. Yet the courts have not articulated this rationale for their decisions. Instead, they rely on congressional intent and statutory zero-reject rules.

There can be no doubt, however, concerning the effect of these decisions: They bring the disabled child's interests into sharp relief by preventing expulsion—the most harmful effect of all and the most restrictive placement of all. The zero-reject principle thus limits the power of schools to expel some disabled children, and simultaneously it limits the LRA continuum: The most restrictive placement is necessarily one within the continuum (i.e., within a free appropriate education, wherever furnished), not outside it. Exclusion is not an option. It is, by definition, too restrictive.

Conclusion

What defensible conclusions can be drawn from the cases and the foregoing analysis of them? Surely, one is that the courts are capable of tremendous sensitivity toward disabled children and their parents. This is particularly encouraging in light of the Supreme Court's *Parham* decision, which was hardly a paradigm for the expression of concern for mentally disabled children, and *Davis*, a decision that reeked of paternalism.

Beyond this sensitivity lies a sense that there are so many complexities in the nature and degree of disabling conditions that marching lock-step down a stereotypical least restrictive continuum is bound to result in inappropriate education for some children. The child's needs—his or her rights to and interest in appropriate education, even when furnished in residential or institutional settings—seem to prevail when the extent of the disability is more severe or profound than mild or moderate. The contrary seems to exist when the disability is less disabling: The right to an appropriate education is more likely to be satisfied when the child is placed in regular settings or programs. In some cases, rights to appropriateness (to satisfy the need) and to integration occur simultaneously, leading to the same recommendations for placement. In others, courts are applying LRA by taking into account the relative "richness" or "poverty" of educational services in separate, nonintegrated programs and the likelihood that such programs will be more enhancing for a disabled child than not.

Still another conclusion emerges. Judicial interpretation and application of LRA rest on a sense of *appropriate education*, a concept that, by using a continuum approach, does not exclude separate and segregated placements or programs. It appears, then, that courts do not so misunderstand and misapply the LRA principle in the context of the continuum options that it becomes a force for limiting disabled children by denying them an appropriate education or for limiting educators by restricting their ability to educate disabled people appropriately.

One concern expressed in the AAMR publication on LRA—namely, that LRA should become infused with a sense of liberation, not of restriction[106]—seems to be shared by many courts. The courts seem to construe LRA as a tool for making sure that disabled children, their parents, and their educators have available to them choices that restrict their freedom to the minimum extent necessary. In a sense, then, the child's needs do prevail over his or her rights, where appropriate, and enhancing placement (the need) conflicts with a presumption in favor of integration (the presumptive right to LRA).

The risk of complacently accepting and sanctioning this result is that judicial legitimization of separate (segregating) or institutional placement is tantamount to judicial approval of the separate schools, programs, and institutions themselves. This is both paradoxical and unfortunate.

The paradox comes about because many courts have condemned institutional conditions on constitutional (Eighth Amendment) and other (*quid pro quo*) grounds.[107] It is odd that other courts, not squarely facing the institutional reform case, would bless institutional placement in right-to-education cases.

The misfortune arises because there are unacceptable consequences of institutionalization.[108] At the least, the child is put at risk of regression;[109] public school systems are relieved of the pressure to accommodate severely disabled children in their own programs (but not of the enormous cost of institutionalization); family ties can be attenuated (but family stress can be reduced); and "throw-away" children are put out of sight and out of mind.

In all of this, there is special irony. One of the values that LRA explicitly seeks to advance is that of the right of association. If disabled children are free to associate with nondisabled children in the public schools, the argument goes, the stigma and discrimination visited upon them *de facto* or *de jure* will dissipate and disabled people will be less restricted, more liberated. Yet, parents also share the stigma that attends their disabled children. Some have sought to (or thought they could) escape their child's and their own stigmatization by institutionalizing their children or having them educated only with other disabled children (in special classes, special schools, or special school districts). Thus, some parents seem to contribute to the very stigma they seek to avoid.

To the extent that the LRA doctrine creates educationally enhancing programs for disabled children in the public schools, it may be a technique for reducing public opinion that less able people are less worthy and increasing public acceptance of different (disabled) children and their families. But if some parents, some educators, and some courts continue to rely on institutional, residential placements, LRA will not be as useful as it might be in achieving either the values of an appropriate education or the right of (stigma-free) association.

LRA as a constitutional principle seeks to curtail overreaching by government. It was not intended, and should not be used, to restrict reasonable choices by courts, families, professionals, or disabled people. But, as used by the courts upon the initiative of some parents and educators in the LRA education cases, it does not realize one of its greatest potentials: It does not compel the creation of more acceptable, more enhancing, less harmful placement options that are noninstitutional. In implementing LRA in these cases, the courts have not focused on the *creation* of appropriate educational placements, only on the selection of one of two available choices, both apparently reasonable in the context of education of a disabled child and given the continuum approach to educational services.

The legally and educationally defensible placement is the one that is least restrictive of rights of education and association among those available that would adequately serve the child. The courts, however, are myopic and unimaginative because they have failed to use LRA, as it has been used in other disability cases, to create acceptable alternatives to institutions.[110] True, they recognize the disabled child's needs and decline to restrict those charged with his or her care.

But that posture, though necessary, is hardly sufficient. To refuse to eliminate or limit restrictive alternatives may inhibit the creation of less liberty-restrictive ones that can serve a person's interests equally well. Until the courts use LRA as an affirmative, rights-creating tool, their decisions will merit only qualified approval. In the words of the AAMR book, "The focus of LRE implementation must remain in the creation of less restrictive alternatives, rather than on the reduction of unduly restrictive choices."[111]

It is true that the courts have failed on the whole to require SEAs or LEAs to create programs of appropriate education within integrated settings. Even *Roncker*'s test of feasibility (of modifying the integrated setting) does not seem to be forceful enough. Instead, they have been content to defer to expert judgment about the student's educational needs and, depending on the extent of the child's disability and the experts' opinions, have chosen between the existing alternatives.

Those who favor judicial restraint (judicial conservatism) will argue that such an approach is proper. Those who favor judicial creativity (judicial activism) will object to this approach.

Yet it is clear that the forced choice—between one type of program and setting and another—is one that the IDEA and state law creates. That is, Congress and state legislatures have decided to rely on a continuum-of-services approach. Given this policy choice, courts themselves are reluctant to undo the policy by forcing one program and setting (e.g., an "integrated" one) to become more appropriate for the student's education. Of course, they could use their remedial powers to change the policies, and perhaps they should.

Is it only the courts' fault that the LRA doctrine still allows, indeed encourages, segregated placements? The answer has to be no. Institutions and other segregated special education are the creation of some policymakers in Congress and in state legislatures; of some educators, psychologists, physicians, and other professionals; and of some parents. As chapter 4 pointed out, the reasons for classification, and thus for segregation, are powerful, long-standing, and not always correctable by laws made by judges.

The "fault" that there is a continuum from which courts may choose thus is attributable to those who created the continuum in the first place. It is entirely defensible to criticize the courts for allowing the presumption in favor of integration (the LRA doctrine in education) to be rebutted (in my judgment, too often). But it also is worth remembering: Reducing the continuum so that certain placements are no longer possible, and concurrently expanding appropriate programs in integrated settings, is a choice for policymakers in legislatures and executive agencies, and for professionals and parents alike.

As pointed out earlier in this chapter (under the discussion about why costs are a consideration), there are reasons why courts are reluctant to be more active in prescribing remedies that exceed the policy choices made by legislatures. Whether these reasons are satisfactory is for the reader to determine.

NOTES

1. *See, e.g.,* Covington v. Harris, Lake v. Cameron, Shelton v. Tucker; Ellis, Boggs, Brooks, and Biklen, *The Least Restrictive Alternative: Principles and Practices*, edited by Turnbull (Washington,

D.C.: American Association on Mental Retardation, 1981) (hereafter called Least Restrictive Alternative). *See also* Chambers, "Alternatives to Civil Commitment of the Mentally Ill: Practical Guides and Constitutional Imperatives," *Michigan Law Review* 70(1972):1108 (least restrictive alternative in context of civil commitment).

2. Chambers, *supra* n. 1, at pp. 1108, 1150.

3. *See, e.g.*, Pike v. Bruce Church, Dean Milk v. City of Madison. *See also* Wormuth and Mirkin, "The Doctrine of the Reasonable Alternative," *Utah Law Review* 9(1964):254 (application of LRA to commerce clause, police power, and due process, first amendment, and procedural rights).

4. *See, e.g.*, Dunn v. Blumstein (voting rights); U.S. v. Robel, *citing* NAACP v. Button (freedom of association); Griswold v. Connecticut (right of privacy); Aptheker v. Sec'y. of State (right to travel); and Talley v. California (freedom of speech).

5. *See, e.g.*, Brenneman v. Madigan. *See generally*, "Constitutional Limitations on the Conditions of Pretrial Detention," *Yale Law Journal* 79(1970):941 (use of LRA in context of pretrial detention); and Wormuth and Mirkin, *supra* n. 3, at pp. 293-96.

6. Toomer v. Witsell, 334 U.S. 385 (1948).

7. *See, e.g.*, Covington v. Harris; Lake v. Cameron (*en banc*) ("Deprivation of liberty solely because of dangers to the ill persons themselves should not go beyond what is necessary for their protection"); Halderman v. Pennhurst State School and Hosp.; Dixon v. Weinberger; Lessard v. Schmidt; Wyatt v. Stickney. *See also* Least Restrictive Alternative, *supra* n. 1, at pp. 21-22.

8. *See* Least Restrictive Alternative, *supra* n. 1, at p. 28. *See also* Youngberg v. Romeo ("The state is under a duty to provide respondent with such training as an appropriate professional would consider reasonable to ensure his safety and to facilitate his ability to function free from bodily restraints").

9. Yarbrough, "The Burger Court and Unspecified Rights," *Duke Law Journal* 143, 154 (1977).

10. 20 U.S.C. Sec. 1413(a)(1976).

11. *See* Least Restrictive Alternative, *supra* n. 1, at pp. 21-25.

12. *E.g.*, the right to an abortion within the first 3 months of pregnancy. *See* Doe v. Bolton and Roe v. Wade. *See also* Bellotti v. Baird and Planned Parenthood of Central Missouri v. Danforth, both on the right to contraception; and O'Connor v. Donaldson, on right to liberty.

13. PARC, at p. 307 (amended consent agreement).

14. *See, e.g.*, LeBanks v. Spears, Panitch v. Wisconsin, and State of Wisconsin *ex rel.* Warren v. Nusbaum.

15. *See* O'Connor v. Donaldson, Jackson v. Indiana, Shelton v. Tucker, Covington v. Harris, Dixon v. Attorney General, and Lake v. Cameron.

16. *See* Pennhurst v. Halderman, Wyatt v. Stickney, Welsch v. Likins, New York ARC v. Rockefeller, Wouri v. Zitnay, and Evans v. D.C. Bd. of Ed. *See also* Stone, "Overview: The Right to Treatment—Comment on the Law and Its Impact," *American Journal of Psychology* 132(1975):1125.

17. An explicit origin of the minimum intrusion principle is found in Dean Milk v. Madison, at pp. 354–56, where the court found a city ordinance unconstitutional under the commerce clause. The ordinance prohibited the sale of milk within the city that had been processed more than 25 miles outside of the city. The court found that less drastic measures could protect the citizens from bad milk without banning the sale of nonlocally processed milk. For an earlier case in which LRA minimum intrusion is applied, *see* Toomer v. Witsell. The minimum intrusion principle has also been used in other cases that necessitated the balancing of individual interests against governmental needs: Dunn v. Blumstein (right to vote); U.S. v. Robel and NAACP v. Button (right to associate); Griswold v. Connecticut (right to privacy); Aptheker v. Sec'y. of State and Kent v. Dulles (right to travel); Sherbert v. Verner

(freedom of religion); and Talley v. California (right to free speech). In all of these cases, government activity and infringement of a constitutional right both triggered the minimum intrusion LRE/LRA principle. For a discusion of LRA, *see* Struve, "The Less-Restrictive Alternative Principle and Economic Due Process," *Harvard Law Review* 80(1967):1463 and Note, "Less Drastic Means and the First Amendment," *Yale Law Review* 78(1969):464.

18. *Federal Register*, 54(11a), p. 26313. For a full explanation of the LRE doctrine and Part H, see Turnbull, H. R. and Turrnbull, A. P. (1990), The Unfulfilled Promise of Integration: Does Part H Ensure Different Rights and Results than Part B of the Education of the Handicapped Act?, *Topics in Early Childhood Special Education*, 10(2):18–32.

19. *Federal Register*, May 4, 1977, p. 22691.

20. *See* Lessard v. Schmidt (discussed right of state to deprive an individual of liberty due to mental disability); Cohen, Oosterhout, and Leviton, "Tailoring Guardianship to the Needs of Mentally Handicapped Citizens," *Maryland Legal Forum* 6(1976):91; and Horstman, "Protective Services for the Elderly: The Limits of Parens Patriae," *Missouri Law Review* 40(1975):215 (discusses *parens patriae* as applied to the elderly).

21. *See* Youngberg v. Romeo: "[T]here certainly is no reason to think judges or juries are better qualified than appropriate professionals in making such decisions [about what is a reasonable restraint on a retarded individual's liberty interest consistent with his safety]. . . . For these reasons, the decision, if made by a professional, is presumptively valid; [42 U.S.C. Sec. 1983 (1976)] liability may be imposed only when the decision by the professional is such a substantial departure from accepted professional judgment, practice or standards as to demonstrate that the person responsible actually did not base the decision on such a judgment." *See also* Parham v. J.R. (commitment of children under age 18 is largely a medical and parental decision).

22. *See, e.g.*, Halderman v. Pennhurst State School and Hosp., Wyatt v. Stickney, and Covington v. Harris. *Cf.* Heryford v. Parker ("likelihood of involuntary incarceration . . . commands observance of the constitutional safeguards of due process"). For informative analyses of this problem, *see* Wexler, *Mental Health Law: Major Issues* (New York: Plenum Press, 1981), pp. 11–59; Morse, "Crazy Behavior," *Southern California Law Review* 51(1978):527; Cohn, "Standards for Civil Commitment and the Right to Liberty," in *Legal Rights of Mentally Disabled Persons* 1, edited by Friedman et al. (New York: Practicing Law Institute, 1979); Burt, "The Constitution of the Family," in *Supreme Court Review*, edited by Kurland and Casper (Chicago: University of Chicago Press, 1979), pp. 329–95; Teitelbaum and Ellis, "The Liberty Interest of Children: Due Process Rights and Their Application," *Family Law Quarterly* 12(1978):153; Ennis and Litwack, "Psychiatry and the Presumption of Expertise: Flipping Coins in the Courtroom," *California Law Review* 62(1974):693.

23. *See generally* Wolfensberger, *The Principle of Normalization in Human Services* (Toronto: National Institute of Mental Retardation, 1972); and Kugel and Wolfensberger, editors, *Changing Patterns in Residential Services for the Mentally Retarded* (Washington, D.C.: President's Committee on Mental Retardation, 1969).

24. *See, e.g.*, Mills and PARC.

25. *See, e.g.*, Brown v. Bd. of Ed. (abolished "separate but equal" doctrine; ordered desegregation of public schools); Gong Lum v. Rice (natural citizen, child of Chinese extraction, not denied equal protection when assigned to "separate but equal" school); Cumming v. Bd. of Ed. (federal government should not interfere with state economic reasons for closing school for blacks while leaving open school for whites); Plessy v. Ferguson (doctrine that "separate but equal" facilities satisfies equal protection).

26. *See* Watson v. City of Cambridge.

27. *See generally* Kanner, *A History of the Care and Study of the Mentally Retarded* (Springfield, Ill.: Charles Thomas, 1964); and Kauffman, "Nineteenth Century Views of Children's Behavior Disorders: Historical Contributions and Continuing Issues," *Journal of Special Education* 10(1976):335.

28. Sarason and Doris, *Educational Handicap, Public Policy, and Social History: A Broadened Perspective on Mental Retardation* (New York: Free Press, 1979), pp. 179–80.

29. *Ibid.*, pp. 282–95.

30. *See generally* Gleidman and Roth, *The Unexpected Minority: Handicapped Children in America* (New York: Harcourt Brace Jovanovich, 1981).

31. *See* P.L. 94-142, Sec. 3(b), (3) and (4) [commentary to 20 U.S.C. Sec. 1401 (1982)]; *Congressional Record* 25,526 (statement of findings and purpose), 25,537–38 (daily ed. July 29, 1975) (statement of Rep. Ford).

32. *See generally* Levine and Wexler, *PL 94-142: An Act of Congress* (New York: Macmillan, 1981); Comment, "The Least Restrictive Environment Section of the Education for All Handicapped Children Act of 1975: A Legislative History and An Analysis," *Gonzaga Law Review* 13(1978):717.

33. For a good recent illustration of functional exclusion, *see* Campbell v. Talladega County Bd. of Ed. *See also* Mattie T. v. Holladay, LeBanks v. Spears, PARC, and MARC v. Maryland.

34. *See* Gleidman and Roth, *supra* n. 29, at pp. 178–82, 204–8. *See also* Nazzarro, "Comprehensive Assessment for Educational Planning," in *Public Policy and the Education of Exceptional Children*, edited by Weintraub, Abeson, Ballard, and LaVor (Reston, Va.: Council for Exceptional Children, 1976) (hereafter called Public Policy); and Miller and Miller, "The Education for the Handicapped Act: How Well Does It Accomplish Its Goal of Promoting the Least Restrictive Environment for Education?" *DePaul Law Review* 28(1979):321, 339.

35. *See* Sarason and Doris, *supra* n. 27, at pp. 321–54; Miller and Miller, *supra* n. 33, at pp. 339–40.

36. Milofsky, "Why Special Education Isn't Special," *Harvard Educational Review* 44(1974): 437.

37. *See* Kirp, Buss, and Kuriloff, "Legal Reform of Special Education: Empirical Studies and Procedural Proposals," *California Law Review* 62:40; Kirp, "Schools as Sorters," *Pennsylvania Law Review* 121(1973):705; and Children's Defense Fund, *Children Out of School in America* (Cambridge, MA: Author, 1974).

38. *See* New York State Commission, *Report on the Quality, Cost and Financing of Elementary and Secondary Education*, 9 B. 2 (1972), *cited* in Kirp et al., *supra* n. 36; Hobbs, *The Futures of Children* (San Francisco: Jossey-Bass, 1975); Education Commission of the States, *States with Comprehensive Legislation and Education Services for Handicapped Children* (Denver: Author, 1974); Marinelli, "Financing the Education of Exceptional Children," in Public Policy, *supra* n. 33; Dunn, "Special Education for the Mildly Retarded—Is Much of Is Justifiable?" *Exceptional Children* 35(1968):5; Mercer, *Labeling the Mentally Retarded* (Berkeley: University of California Press, 1973); Budoff, "Providing Special Education without Special Classes," *Journal of School Psychology* 10 (1972):199; and Lilly, "Special Education: A Tempest in a Teapot," *Exceptional Children* 37(1970): 43.

39. Education of the Handicapped Act, P.L. 94-142 [commentary to 20 U.S.C. Sec. 1401 (1982) Sec. 3(b)(4), (6), (7)].

40. *See* Mills and PARC.

41. *See* Pennhurst v. Halderman and Wyatt v. Stickney.

42. *See* Turnbull, "Two Legal Analysis Techniques and Public Policy Analysis," in *Models for Analysis of Social Policy: An Introduction*, edited by Haskins and Gallagher (Norwood, N.J.: Ablex, 1981).

43. Over half of the more than eight million disabled children in the United States did not receive an appropriate education. *See* P.L. 94-142, Sec. 601(b)(1), (3).

44. One million disabled children in the United States received no public education and were not educated with their peers. *See* P.L. 94-142, Sec. 601(b)(7).

45. If appropriately funded, state and local educational agencies could provide for the educational needs of disabled children. *See* P.L. 94-142, Sec. 601(b)(7).

46. Because public education was not serving the needs of disabled children, many were educated away from their families. *See* P.L. 94-142, Sec. 601(b)(6).

47. *See generally* Abeson, "Confidentiality and Record Keeping," in Public Policy, *supra* n. 33.

48. Gorham, Des Jardins, Page, Pettis, and Scheiber, "Effect on Parents," in *Issues in the Classification of Children* (vol. 2), edited by Hobbs (San Francisco: Jossey-Bass, 1975), p. 154.

49. *See* Nazzaro, *supra* n. 33, at pp. 33–47; Turnbull, Turnbull, and Wheat, "Assumptions About Parental Participation: A Legislative History," *Exceptional Education Quarterly* 3(1982):2.

50. 20 U.S.C. Secs. 1412(5)(B) and 1414(a)(1)(C)(iv)(1976).

51. *See* Note: "Enforcing the Right to an 'Appropriate' Education: The Education for All Handicapped Children Act of 1975," *Harvard Law Review* 92(1979):1103.

52. Deno, "Special Education as Developmental Capital," *Exceptional Children* 37(1970):229.

53. Turnbull, "The Past and Future Impact on Court Decisions in Special Education," *Phi Delta Kappan* 523 (Apr. 1978).

54. *See* Least Restrictive Alternative, *supra* n. 1.

55. *See* Tribe, "Childhood: Suspect Classifications and Conclusive Presumptions: 3 Linked Riddles," *Law and Contemporary Problems* 38(1975):8.

56. *See* Pennhurst v. Halderman, Welsch v. Likins, Wyatt v. Stickney, and Covington v. Harris.

57. 20 U.S.C. Secs. 1412(5)(B) and 1414(a)(1)(C)(iv) and 34 C.F.R. Secs. 300.550 *et seq.* (1980); Bd. v. Rowley; and Roncker v. Walters.

58. *See generally* Turnbull, *Preschool Mainstreaming: A Policy and Implementation Analysis* (paper presented at Annual Meeting of American Educational Research Assn., April 1980; on file with author, Univ. of Kansas, Dept. of Sp. Ed.).

59. *See* Karnes and Lee, "Mainstreaming in the Preschool," in *Current Topics in Early Childhood* 13(1979); Cooke, Appolloni, and Cooke, "Normal Preschool Children as Behavior Models for Retarded Peers," *Exceptional Children* 43(1977):531; Neisworth and Madle, "Normalized Day Care: A Philosophy and Approach to Integrating Exceptional and Normal Children," *Child Care Quarterly* 4(1975):163; Devoney, Guralnick, and Rubin, "Integrating Handicapped and Nonhandicapped Preschool Children: Effects on Social Play," *Childhood Education* 50(1974):360.

60. *See* Hobbs, *supra* n. 37, at p. 180.

61. *See* Oversight of Public Law 94-142, the Education for All Handicapped Children Act Hearings before the Subcommittee on Select Education of the Committee on Education and Labor, Part I, 96th Congress, 1st Session (1979) (prepared statement of Deborah Olson, Sp. Ed. teacher, Laconia, N.H.); Wynne, Brown, Dakof, and Ulfelder, *Mainstreaming and Early Childhood Education for Handicapped Children: A Guide for Teachers and Parents* (1975) (on file with author, Univ. of Kansas, Dept. of Sp. Ed.).

62. *See* 1979 Hearings, *supra* n. 60, at pp. 75–77. *See generally* Hobbs, *supra* n. 37.

63. *See* Least Restrictive Alternative, *supra* n. 1.

64. *See* Abrahamson v. Hershman, Erdman v. Connecticut, Kruelle v. Biggs, Cox v. Brown, North v. D.C. Bd. of Ed., Matthews v. Campbell, Isgur v. School Bd. of Newton, In the Matter of the "A" Family, Manchester Bd. v. Connecticut Bd., Gladys J. v. Pearland I.S.D., Harris v. D.C. Bd. of Ed.,

and Zvi D. v. Ambach.

65. Erdman v. Connecticut, Kruelle v. New Castle, Cox v. Brown, North v. D.C. Bd. of Ed., Matthews v. Campbell, Manchester Bd. v. Connecticut Bd., In the Matter of the "A" Family, Gladys J. v. Pearland I.S.D., and Harris v. D.C. Bd. of Ed.

66. Erdman v. Connecticut, North v. D.C. Bd. of Ed., In the Matter of the "A" Family, and Gladys J. v. Pearland I.S.D.

67. Kruelle v. New Castle, Matthews v. Campbell, Manchester Bd. v. Connecticut Bd., and Harris v. D.C. Bd. of Ed.

68. Cox v. Brown.

69. Abrahamson v. Hershman.

70. Isgur v. School Bd. of Newton and Zvi D. v. Ambach.

71. DeWalt v. Burkholder, Victoria L. v. Dist. School Bd. of Lee County, Roncker v. Walters, Campbell v. Talladega, and Town of Burlington v. Dept. of Ed.

72. New York ARC v. Carey and Springdale School Dist. v. Grace.

73. Hines v. Pitt County Bd. of Ed.

74. *Supra* n. 64.

75. DeWalt v. Burkholder, Hines v. Pitt County Bd. of Ed., and Victoria L. v. Dist. School Bd. of Lee County.

76. The statute allows the child to participate where appropriate and the regulations allow the child to attend the IEP meetings, if appropriate. 20 U.S.C. Sec. 1401(19)(1976) and 34 C.F.R. Sec. 300.344(a)(4)(1980).

77. *See* Gilhool, "The Right to Community Services," *The Mentally Retarded Citizen and the Law* 173(1976).

78. Of the cases that have been analyzed here (all that have been reported through Dec. 1984): Roughly 14% involved children who were deaf (Age v. Bullitt, DeWalt v. Burkholder, Bd. v. Rowley, and Springdale School Dist. v. Grace).

79. The cases also can be categorized by the extent or degree of the child's disability. Thus: Five children were mildly disabled (Isgur v. School Bd. of Newton, Tatro v. Texas, Tokarcik v. Forest Hills, Espino v. Besteiro, and Zvi D. v. Ambach); two were mildly to moderately disabled (Laura M. v. Sp. School Dist. and Town of Burlington v. Dept. of Ed.); one was moderately disabled (Gary B. v. Cronin); fourteen were severely disabled (Abrahamson v. Hershman, Age v. Bullitt, Cox v. Brown, DeWalt v. Burkholder, Erdman v. Connecticut, Hines v. Pitt County Bd. of Ed., Victoria L. v. Dist. School Bd. of Lee County, North v. D.C. Bd. of Ed., Manchester Bd. v. Connecticut Bd., In the Matter of the "A" Family, Campbell v. Talladega, Gladys J. v. Pearland I.S.D., Harris v. D.C. Bd. of Ed., and *In re* Claudia K.); two were severely to profoundly disabled (New York ARC v. Carey and Kruelle v. New Castle); two were profoundly disabled (Springdale School Dist. v. Grace and Matthews v. Campbell).

80. *See also* Age v. Bullitt and Cox v. Brown.

81. Campbell v. Talladega.

82. 29 U.S.C. Sec. 706, 34 C.F.R. Secs. 300.1 *et seq.* (1980).

83. *See also* Gladys J. v. Pearland I.S.D.

84. *See also* Town of Burlington v. Dept. of Ed.

85. *See* Hines v. Pitt County Bd. of Ed., Springdale School Dist. v. Grace, Isgur v. School Bd. of Newton, Gladys J. v. Pearland I.S.D., Campbell v. Grissett, and Bales v. Clark.

86. Erdman v. Connecticut, Matthews v. Campbell, North v. D.C. Bd. of Ed., Manchester Bd. v. Connecticut Bd., and In the Matter of the "A" Family.

87. *See* Laura M. v. Sp. School Dist.; *contra*, Matthews v. Campbell.

88. Cox v. Brown.

89. 34 C.F.R. Secs. 300.500 *et seq.* (1980). *See* Honig v. Doe.

90. *See* Adams Central School Dist. v. Deist, Zvi D. v. Ambach, Abrahamson v. Hershman, Monahan v. Nebraska, and Victoria L. v. Dist. School Bd. of Lee County; *contra*, Cox v. Brown.

91. 34 C.F.R. Sec. 300.513 (1980).

92. 34 C.F.R. Sec. 300.403 (1980).

93. *See* New York ARC v. Carey, Kruelle v. Biggs, and Espino v. Besteiro.

94. New York ARC v. Carey.

95. *See* Halderman v. Pennhurst.

96. Gary B. v. Cronin.

97. Gladys J. v. Pearland I.S.D.

98. New York ARC v. Carey.

99. *See also* Kruelle v. New Castle and Espino v. Besteiro.

100. See, for example, A.W. v. Northwest R-1 School District; Barnett v. Fairfax County School Board, DeVries v. Fairfax County School Board; Schuldt v. Mankato Independent School District No. 77, Roland M. v. Concord School Committee, Thomas v. Cincinnati Board of Education; French v. Omaha Public Schools, Gillette v. Fairland Board of Education, Community Consolidated School District No. 21 Board of Education v. Illinois State Board of Education (also holds that court may take into account the parents' hostility to neighborhood school placement and school district and, with the hostility in mind, order placement in nearby private school, at district expense), Ewing Township Board of Education v. P.S.V., and Ash v. Lake Oswego School District No. 7J.

101. DeWalt v. Burkholder.

102. Stone, *Mental Health and Law: A System in Transition* (published in conjunction with the Center for Studies of Crime and Delinquency, National Institute of Mental Health, Dept. of HEW, Washington, DC, 1976).

103. In the Matter of the "A" Family.

104. Hines v. Pitt County Bd. of Ed.

105. *See* Blue v. N. Haven Bd. of Ed., Stanley v. School Admin. Unit, S-1 v. Turlington, and Stuart v. Nappi.

106. *See* Least Restrictive Alternative, *supra* n. 1.

107. The Supreme Court's decision in Youngberg v. Romeo established only a liberty-based interest in treatment for involuntarily committed profoundly retarded people and left in doubt the Eighth Amendment and substantive due process rationale.

108. *Id.*

109. *See* Halderman v. Pennhurst.

110. *See* Dixon v. Weinberger.

111. *See* Least Restrictive Alternative, *supra* n. 1, at pp. 43, 46, 52.

For 1994 Update on Least Restrictive Environment please see page 400.

7

Procedural Due Process

CONSTITUTIONAL FOUNDATIONS

The legal expression of fairness is procedural due process—the right of a citizen to protest before a government takes action with respect to him or her. In the case of the disabled child, that means having the right to protest actions of the state education agency (SEA) or the local education agency (LEA). For those who pioneered the right-to-education doctrine, the procedures for implementing the right were as crucial as the right itself. Procedural due process is a means of challenging the multitude of discriminatory practices that the schools had habitually followed. It also is a way of enforcing the first four principles of the IDEA and of putting them to work. Without due process, the children would have found that their right to be included in an educational program and to be treated nondiscriminatorily (to receive a free appropriate education) would have a hollow ring. Procedural due process—the right to protest—is a necessary educational ingredient in enforcing every phase of the disabled child's right to an education.

Procedural due process also is a constitutional requisite under the requirements of the Fifth and Fourteenth Amendments that no person shall be deprived of life, liberty, or property without due process of law. In terms of the education of disabled children, this means that no disabled child can be deprived of an education without the opportunity of exercising the right to protest what happens to him or her.

The success of the right-to-education movement reaffirmed a belief widely held by lawyers—namely, that fair procedures tend to produce acceptable, correct, and fair results. Due process took many forms in the right-to-education cases decided before Congress enacted IDEA.

PRE-IDEA COURT DECISION

Notification

A person who is adversely affected by the action or inaction of an SEA or LEA is helpless to protect himself or herself from the agency or to protest the decision unless he or she has adequate prior notice of what the agency proposes to do and for what reasons. The notion of *prior notice* clearly applies when a disabled child is actually involved with an agency—when he or she has applied for admission to a program, has been placed or refused placement, has or has not been identified as disabled, or has or has not been evaluated as disabled. All of these actions can occur only after the child comes to the school's attention.

Many disabled children, however, had been totally excluded from the schools, and often parents (or guardians) had been unaware of their child's right to an education. In the earliest right-to-education cases, *Pennsylvania Association for Retarded Children (PARC) v. Commonwealth of Pennsylvania* and *Mills v. D.C. Board of Education*, an initial issue for due process consideration was parental ignorance of a child's right to an education. In response, *PARC* ordered local school boards to conduct door-to-door canvasses and directed the department of public education and other state agencies serving children to comb their records for names of disabled school-aged persons. *Mills* ordered the D.C. Board of Education to locate all disabled children and advise them of their right to an education. In addition, *Mills* required that a notice be published in District of Columbia newspapers stating that all children, regardless of their disability, have a right to publicly supported, appropriate education. The notice informed parents of procedures for enrolling children in appropriate educational programs. *Mills* also required the school board to arrange for presentation of information on local radio and television stations.

Notice of the right to an education is related not only to the notion of fairness but also to the principle of *zero reject*—the idea that all disabled children have the right to a free appropriate public education, *without regard to the nature or severity of their disabilities* (see chapter 3). It is one thing to notify a child or his parents of legal rights. It is quite another to deal fairly with the child once he or she is enrolled in the public schools. Procedural due process speaks to both issues.

Evaluation and Placement

After disabled children are located, schools are required to evaluate them and place them in appropriate educational programs. *PARC* provided the first detailed set of requirements for placing a child or changing the placement, but these requirements applied only to the evaluation and placement of mentally retarded children. *Mills* extended basically the same procedure to *all* disabled children. Later cases included the same procedural requirements.[1] The cases were unanimous in requiring three basic procedural safeguards.

First, the child's parents or guardians must be notified in writing. There are special provisions, not specified in the orders, for parents who cannot read English or who cannot read at all. The notice must describe the action the school proposes to take, the reasons for it (including references to results of any test or reports on which the action is based), and available alternative educational opportunities.[2] The right to a hearing prior to educational evaluation or placement includes the right to a conference before the school evaluates or places a child.[3] It is logical for a conference to precede formal notice of proposed action or inaction because the development of a child's individualized education program in the requisite conference also becomes, at the least, the basis for the child's placement.

In a natural extension of the principle of notice prior to placement, notice must be given prior to reassignment as well[4] since both the initial placement and any subsequent placement affect the child's right to an appropriate education. The notice must inform the parents of the reasons for the proposed action and of their rights to object to the proposed action, to receive a hearing on his objection, and to obtain free medical, psychological, and educational evaluations.[5]

One of the purposes of written notice is to give actual notice—to inform the parents of the proposed action—and it is doubtful that actual notice can be conveyed without a detailed explanation of what the school proposes to do and why. A statement of proposed action is meaningless unless the *action* is fairly described, the details of the action clearly set forth. Likewise, a statement of proposed action is meaningless unless the *reasons* for the proposed action are fully described. The formality of notification is constitutionally insufficient; it is the reality of the notice—the *details of proposed action and the reasons* therefor—that is constitutionally required.

Second, if the parents request a hearing, it must be conducted by a hearing officer independent of the local school authorities, at a time and place convenient to the parent. The hearing must be held within a specified period after the parents request it, and is generally closed to the public unless they request otherwise.[6]

Procedural due process not only allows a potentially adversely affected person to protest proposed governmental action but it also furnishes him or her with a forum to present the objections and have them heard and ruled on by a disinterested party. The parents are not just entitled to a hearing; they have a *meaningful* right to have the hearing before an impartial tribunal and at a time and place convenient to them.

Justice delayed is justice denied, and the right to a reasonably prompt hearing is a prerequisite to any procedural safeguard. And because the hearing may involve evidence that divulges highly personal aspects of a child's or family's life (e.g., whether the child is emotionally disturbed or why he or she is physically disabled), the notion of a *right to privacy* permits hearings to be closed to the public unless the parents do not object to open hearings.

Third, the hearing must be conducted according to due process procedures. The parents must be informed of the right to be represented by counsel at the hearing, to present evidence and testimony, to confront and cross-examine witnesses, to examine school records before the hearing, to be furnished with a transcript of the hearing if they wish to appeal the hearing officer's decision, and to receive a written statement of the findings of fact and conclusions of law.[7] The parents also have the right to be assured that the evidence they present will come before the hearing officer,[8] that it will be considered by the officer, and that no evidence *not* offered by the parents or the school will be considered.

The results of a hearing significantly affect a child's right to an appropriate education and thereby affect the explicitly guaranteed constitutional rights of liberty and property as well. Sometimes (although not necessarily), due process hearings take on aspects of an adversarial hearing. The hearing, however, is governed by rules of procedure that offer each party in the hearing equal opportunity to present his or her "case." In a proceeding of such importance, an absence of legal counsel makes a mockery of the concept of fairness and due process. Parents must be made aware of their right to counsel.

The right to present evidence and examine and cross-examine witnesses is the foundation of the right to be heard. Moreover, the right to call expert witnesses speaks directly to the issue that is often the very reason for the hearing—namely, evaluation and placement of the disabled child. Access to school records is part and parcel of the right to examine and cross-examine witnesses. The right to appeal, to a record of the hearing, and to a statement of the hearing officer's decisions and reasons are indispensable in assuring parents that arbitrariness will not govern the hearing and its results—that the hearing will have both the appearance *and* the reality of fairness.

Periodic Reevaluation

Another important requirement of the cases was that student assignments must be reevaluated periodically. *PARC* required automatic biennial reevaluation of any educational assignment other than to regular class; annual reevaluation was available at the request of the child's parents. Prior to each reevaluation, there was to be full notice and opportunity for a due process hearing. *Mills* also required periodic reevaluation of the child's status.

Without mandatory periodic reevaluation and notice thereof to the child's parents, the opportunity for protest (i.e., the opportunity for due process) might be effectively lost, since schools would not likely encourage parents to exercise their due process rights. Some parents, having been put off by their first hearing—not having achieved a decision they wanted, or having learned not to challenge the professionals—would not continue to assert their child's rights without the enforced reevaluation.

Misuse of Disciplinary Procedures

In the past, some disciplinary procedures were misused to exclude disabled children from the public school. *Mills* directly addressed the problem of misused disciplinary procedures by setting out in detail the procedural safeguards to be used in any disciplinary proceeding.

Mills required that the D.C. schools "shall not suspend a child from the public schools for disciplinary reasons for any period in excess of two days without affording him a hearing pursuant to the [due process] provision ... and without providing for his education during the period of any such suspension." The provisions for notice and hearing in disciplinary cases were much like those that apply to placement, transfer, and exclusion. The essential elements were *notice* to the parents of the action to be taken and the *reasons* for it, and the procedural *rights* of the parents, including the right to an evaluation and to examine the school records.

Classification Criteria

A different type of concern for the procedures used in placing children within the school system was shown in the cases challenging use of various evaluation and testing materials and procedures for purposes of determining intelligence and student tracking. At issue was the validity of the criteria used in evaluation and placement—the alleged linguistic and cultural bias of the materials. In the leading cases in which classification was an issue, procedural due process became an essential element to safeguard the child against discriminatory classification.[9]

Expunction or Correction of Records

Mills provided for the expunction from or correction of records of any disabled children with regard to past expulsions, suspensions, or exclusions, through either academic classifications or disciplinary actions, that violated their rights. If a child is incorrectly placed in a program for the mentally retarded, his or her records can be examined and, if found in error, they must be corrected. Only then can the effects of an incorrect record be ameliorated.

It is not surprising that the case law requirements of due process are reflected, almost in perfect mirror image, in the applicable federal statutes.

FEDERAL LEGISLATION

To receive the formula grant authorized by Part B of the IDEA for the education of disabled children, the SEA and each public agency must give assurances to the federal Office of Special Education that they have adopted appropriate due process procedures [Sec. 1412(5)(A) applicable to the SEA; Sec. 1414(a) (7) applicable to the LEA and IEU; and Sec. 1415, applicable to all three]. The requirement of *procedural safeguards* is consistent with the IDEA intent to assure that the rights of disabled children and their parents and guardians are protected [Sec. 1400(c)]. The differences between Part H and Part B are set out in the following paragraphs.

As members of Congress made clear when they were introducing P.L. 99-457, the legislation is a "pro-family" bill. Thus, the focus of P.L. 99-457's Part H, infants and toddlers, is on the person with a disability and the person's family. This is very different from the other major provisions of IDEA—namely those in Part B that provide for the free appropriate public education of children with disabilities, because Part B focuses on the person and then on the parents, not the family.

Access to Records

Under Part B, a child's parents or guardians must have an opportunity to examine all relevant records relating to the child's identification, evaluation, or placement and the provision of a free appropriate public education for the child. Under Part H there is a specific right to confidentiality of personally identifiable information, and the general requirements of the Family Educational Rights and Privacy Act also apply to Part H programs.

Evaluation

Under Part B, the parents are entitled to an independent (nonagency) educational evaluation of their child. Section 300.500 defines evaluation as "procedures used to determine whether a child is handicapped and the nature and extent of the special education and related services that the child needs." This refers to procedures used selectively with an individual child and does not include basic tests administered to or procedures used with all children in a school, grade, or class. Section 300.503 defines who may make an independent evaluation—namely, a qualified examiner not employed by the public agency responsible for educating the child. A qualified person is one who has met certification, licensing, registration, or other such requirements of the SEA in the area in which he or she provides special education or related services [Sec. 300.12].

Section 300.503 also provides that public agencies must, upon request, give parents information about where they may have independent educational evaluations made. Under some circumstances, the independent evaluation must be made at public expense. The public agency either pays for the full cost of the evaluation or ensures that the evaluation is otherwise provided to the parent without cost to him or her.

Parents have the right to an independent evaluation at public expense if the hearing officer requests one for use in a due process hearing or if the parents disagree with the evaluation made by the public agency. But if, in a due process hearing that it initiates, the agency can prove that its evaluation was appropriate, the parents may be required to pay for the new evaluation. When parents obtain an independent evaluation at their own expense, the agency must take it into consideration as a basis for providing the child an appropriate education, or as evidence in a due process hearing, or both [Sec. 300.503].

Parental consent must be obtained for preplacement evaluation and for the child's initial placement in a special education program [Sec. 504(b)]. Consent, in this context and all others, means that (1) the parents have been fully informed in their native language, or in another suitable manner of communication, of all information relevant to the activity (e.g., evaluation) for which consent was sought; (2) the parents understand and agree in writing that the activity may be carried out; (3) the consent describes the activity and lists the records (if any) that will be released and to whom; and (4) the parents understand that they give their consent voluntarily and may revoke it at any time [Sec. 300.500]. The Department of Education's comments on Section 300.504 make it clear that any changes in a child's special education program, after the initial placement, are not subject to the parental consent rule but are subject only to the requirement of notice and opportunity for changes in the IEP.

If parents refuse to consent when consent is required, the parties must first attempt to resolve the conflict by complying with any applicable state law. If there is none, the agency may initiate a due process hearing. Should the hearing officer rule in favor of the agency, the parents' refusal will be overruled and the agency may evaluate or place the child, notifying the parents of its actions so that they may appeal [Secs. 300.504 and .510 through .513].

Part H (infants and toddlers) has its own rules about consent. Early intervention service providers must obtain parental consent before (1) conducting the initial evaluation and assessment of the child and (2) initiating the provision of early intervention services for the first time. If the parents do not give consent, the providers must make reasonable efforts to ensure that the parents (1) are fully aware of the nature of the evaluation and assessment or the services that would be available and (2) understand that the child will not be able to receive the evaluation and assessment or services unless consent is given. Also, if the parents do not give consent, the provider may initiate a due process hearing or other procedures to override the parents' refusal to consent to the initial evaluation of the child.

Surrogate Parents

Under Part B, Section 1415 and Section 300.514 require the SEA to ensure that the child's rights are protected if his or her parents are unknown or unavailable or if the child is a ward of the state. (The child's rights are not the responsibility of the SEA when the parents are simply uncooperative or unresponsive.) The SEA may comply with this requirement by assigning a surrogate parent. There are other ways, but Sections 1415 and 300.514 mention only this one.

If the SEA goes the route of parental surrogate, it must devise methods for determining whether a child needs a surrogate and then for assigning one. The regulations give no guidance on the methods. They do, however, set out the criteria for selecting a surrogate—primarily, there should be no conflict of interest and the individual should have the skill to represent the child. A superintendent or other employee of an institution in which a child resides may not serve as a surrogate. If there is disagreement about who the surrogate will be, the conflict may be resolved by a due process hearing. The regulations also make clear that a person paid by a public agency solely for the purpose of being a surrogate does not thereby become an agency employee. The surrogate may represent the child in matters affecting his or her identification, evaluation, and placement, and right to a free appropriate public education.

Under Part H, the rights of infants and toddlers whose parents are unknown or absent or who are wards of the state also are protected by procedures similar to Part B, including surrogacy.

Notice

Under Part B, the agency must give prior written notice to parents, guardians, or surrogates whenever it proposes to initiate or change, or refuses to initiate or change, a child's identification, evaluation, or placement and the provision of a free appropriate public education [Sec. 1415(b)(1)(C) and (D)]. Section 300.505 requires the notice to contain:

(1) A full explanation of all the procedural safeguards available to the parents . . . ;

(2) A description of the action proposed or refused by the agency, an explanation of why the agency proposes or refuses to take the action, and a description of any options the agency considered and the reasons why those options were rejected;

(3) A description of each evaluation procedure, test, record, or report the agency uses as a basis for the proposal or refusal; and

(4) A description of any other factors which are relevant to the agency's proposal or refusal.

It also requires that the notice be:

(1) Written in language understandable to the general public; and

(2) Provided in the native language of the parent or other mode of communication used by the parent, unless it is clearly not feasible to do so.

If the parents' native language or other mode of communication is not a written language, the SEA or LEA must take steps to ensure:

(1) That the notice is translated orally or by other means to the parent in his or her native language or other mode of communication;

(2) That the parent understands the content of the notice; and

(3) That there is written evidence that the requirements (of oral translation and parent understanding) have been met.

Under Part H there are similar requirements for notice in the family's native language when there is a proposed change or refusal to change the identification, evaluation, placement, or provision of early intervention services to the infant or toddler.

Complaints and Due Process Hearings

Under Part B, the agency must give the parents, guardians, or surrogates an opportunity to present complaints relating to any matter concerning the child's identification, evaluation, or placement, or right to a free appropriate public education [Sec. 1415(b)(1)(E)]. If the parents (or guardians) file a complaint with an agency, they are entitled to an opportunity for an impartial hearing conducted by the agency, as determined by state law or the SEA. The agency must inform the parents about any low-cost or free legal aid in the geographical area [Sec. 300.506].

The right to a due process hearing is not limited to consumers. Under Sections 300.504 and 300.506, an agency also may initiate a due process hearing on its proposal or refusal to initiate or change the identification, evaluation, or placement of a disabled child, or the free appropriate public education provided to the child.

Unless the parties agree to an extension, the hearing must be held and a final decision reached within forty-five days after the hearing is requested, and a copy of the decision must be mailed to the parties. (The hearing officer may extend this deadline.) The time and place of the hearing and each review involving oral argument must be reasonably convenient to the parents and child.

The Department of Education's comments on Section 300.506 make it clear that a state may use mediation prior to a due process hearing. In fact, many states now require mediation. But the Department also makes it clear that mediation may not be used to deny or delay a parent's rights to procedural due process. It is not clear when mediation will deny or delay rights, but if mediation takes a long time (perhaps more than the forty-five days in which the parent has a right to a hearing after requesting one), the parent may argue successfully that mediation has delayed the rights to procedural due process.

Each agency must keep a list of the hearing officers and their qualifications. The hearing may not be conducted by an employee of the agency involved in education or caring for the child [Sec. 1415(b)(2)]. Section 300.507 prohibits a due process hearing from being conducted by any person having a personal or professional interest that might conflict with objectivity in the hearing. A person who otherwise qualifies to conduct a hearing is *not* considered an employee of the agency solely because he or she is paid by the agency to serve as a hearing officer.

At the initial hearing and on appeal, each party has the right to be accompanied and advised by an attorney and by other experts (persons with special knowledge or training with respect to the problems of disabled children); to present evidence and confront, examine, cross-examine and compel the attendance of witnesses; to make written and oral argument; to receive a written or electronic verbatim record of the hearing; and to receive a written account of findings of fact. No evidence may be introduced by any party unless it was disclosed at least five days before the hearing. The parents must have the opportunity to have their child present and to have the hearing open to the public [Secs. 1415(d) and 300.508]. The decision must be sent to the state advisory panel established under Section 1413(a)(12).

Unless a party appeals from the initial hearing or begins a court action after the appeal, the decision of the initial hearing is final [Sec. 1415(e)]. If the hearing is conducted by an LEA, an aggrieved party may appeal to the SEA, which is required to conduct an impartial review of the hearing, reach a decision, and send a copy of the decision to the parties within thirty days. On appeal the hearing officer must make an independent decision after reviewing the matter [Sec. 1415(c)].

Persons who are aggrieved by the findings and decision in the initial hearing but who do not have the right to appeal to the SEA (the Act and regulations do not say who these people may be) and persons who are aggrieved by the findings and decision on appeal (that is, any party in the appeal) may file a civil action in either a state court or federal district court. (For purposes of the federal suit, the jurisdictional rules about dollar amounts in controversy do not apply.) The court, whether state or federal, is to receive the records of the administrative proceedings, hear additional evidence if offered, and, on the basis of the preponderance of the evidence, grant appropriate relief [Secs. 1415(e)(2) and (4)].

During the initial hearing or appeal, the child remains in his or her current educational placement unless the SEA or LEA and the parents or guardians agree otherwise. If applying for initial admission to school, the child will be placed in the public school program, if the parents and guardians agree, until all hearings (including appeals) have been completed [Sec. 1415(e)(3)]. The agency may, of course, use its normal procedures for dealing with children who are endangering themselves or others.

The Supreme Court's decision in *Honig*, discussed in chapter 3, makes it clear that the stay-put rule prohibits the LEA from making a unilateral placement of the child—that is, from placing the child outside of the child's present placement without parental consent—while a due process dispute is ongoing. But the Court also gave the LEA the right to seek appropriate judicial relief if the stay-put rule was creating an intolerable situation (as in preventing a placement that would reduce danger to the child, other students, or staff).

In another stay-put case, *Corbett v. Regional Center for the East Bay, Inc.*, a federal district court ruled that the LEA, not the parent, has the burden of overcoming the presumption that the child will remain in the present placement. The burden is overcome, the court said, if the child's present placement is "substantially likely to cause injury to himself or herself, or to others."[10] This decision allocates the burden of proof to the school to justify the change in placement—that is, to create an exception to the stay-put rule. That result follows the settled law that, where the stay-put rule is at issue, the burden is with the schools, as announced in *Doe v. Brookline School Committee*, a 1983 decision of the First Circuit Court of Appeals.[11]

Under Part H (infants and toddlers), the state must provide for the timely administrative resolution of complaints by parents. States have two options: (1) to adopt the Part B due process procedures; or (2) to develop new impartial procedures for resolving individual child complaints. The procedures, whether under either option, require that an impartial decision-maker resolve the dispute. The service provider is bound by that decision and must implement it unless it is reversed on appeal.

In addition, a state that does not use the Part B procedures must nonetheless ensure that its procedures result in speedy resolution of individual child complaints. A state may offer mediation as an intervening step before implementing due process procedures, but it may not require parents to use mediation. All disputes must be resolved within thirty days after the lead agency receives a complaint. All hearings must be in places and at times convenient to the parents. Parents have the rights to be accompanied and advised by counsel or other people with special knowledge or training in early intervention; present evidence and cross-examine witnesses; prohibit the use of evidence not disclosed to them at least five days before the hearing; obtain a transcript; and obtain written findings of fact and decisions. A provider or parent who is aggrieved by a decision may appeal it to a state or federal court.

As in the case of Part B, the infant/toddler also is protected by a specific stay-put rule under Part H. The rule is this: If a complaint is pending at any administrative level or on appeal to a federal or state court, then, unless the state agency and parents or guardians agree otherwise, the infant/toddler is entitled to continue to receive the appropriate early intervention services currently being provided, or, if applying for initial services, is entitled to receive those services that are not in dispute.

These rules under Part H deal only with complaints about individual children. Part

H's regulations also require the state lead agency to establish procedures to resolve complaints about how the state itself—so-called systemic complaints—implements Part H and its site plan.

Section 504

The Section 504 regulation [Sec. 104.36] provides that an SEA or LEA may satisfy Section 504 due process requirements by complying with the procedural safeguards of Section 1415 of IDEA. The alternative, and minimum, requirement for the SEA and LEA is to furnish notice, to make the child's records accessible, to guarantee an impartial hearing, to afford the right to counsel, and to assure an impartial review.

POST-IDEA CASES

Lawyers love procedures. They have a continuing *affair d'amour* with procedures for many reasons. Two are especially relevant here. First, they believe (and with good justification) that fair procedures will provide fair results. This fundamental premise undergirds the IDEA, which is ripe with procedural requirements (e.g., nondiscriminatory evaluation, IEPs, procedural due process). Second, they often successfully use procedural requirements to establish or to circumvent the substantive rights of their clients. Out of these two reasons have grown a plethora of judicial decisions.

Exhaustion of Remedies

The most vexsome issue is whether disabled children or their representatives (typically, their parents) must exhaust their administrative remedies (fully use up their IDEA procedural safeguard rights) before they may file a lawsuit in a federal or state court. By and large, the courts agree that they must exhaust their remedies, but as is their wont, courts create exceptions to the general rule. Usually the "futility" exception will allow some courts to hear the lawsuit before the administrative proceedings have been completed. The other exceptions involve cases in which the school district does not insist on exhaustion or the lawsuit is not one that deals with students' procedural rights under the IDEA.

Establishing the general rule, *Sessions v. Livingston Parish* held that parents must exhaust their administrative remedies before filing a federal court lawsuit. [12] A similar result is well explained in *Davis v. Maine Endwell Central School District*. Joining a Section 504 claim with an IDEA claim does not mean that the requirement of exhaustion will be avoided; the plaintiff still must exhaust the IDEA remedies.[13] Simply because administrative due process under the IDEA is protracted does not excuse failure to use administrative due process.[14] Moreover, exhaustion is not excused in a case involving many plaintiffs where factual questions concern needs particular of a child, where exhaustion does not result in duplication of effort, and where any resulting delay will flow from prior failure to exhaust.[15]

Although the general rule is that the parties must exhaust their administrative remedies before suing in court, there are instances when that rule will not apply. Generally, plaintiffs are excused from exhaustion of remedies when the exhaustion is apt to be "futile"—that is, when it will accomplish little to nothing in resolving the parties' dispute.[16] For example, if the LEA or the SEA does not argue that the plaintiff disabled child must exhaust administrative remedies and if there already has been an adjudication of part of the case, exhaustion will not be required.[17]

Plaintiffs also need not exhaust their administrative remedies under state law before filing a class action lawsuit in federal court because, first, the city board of education had failed in the past to carry out its obligations to disabled children (and a court had so found), and, second, the defendant's attorney conceded that exhaustion in each case in the class action "could not be expeditiously processed."[18] Similarly, *New Mexico Association for Retarded Citizens v. State of New Mexico* held that exhaustion of administrative remedies under Section 504 is not required where the only remedy is cut-off of federal funds upon petition by the Office of Civil Rights because, in that case, pursuing a cut-off would be futile since the plaintiffs sought a restructuring of the state's entire system of special education.

By the same token, a nonprofit organization (UCP) and individual students filing a class action suit against the New York City school board and officials did not have to exhaust their administrative remedies under Section 504 or the IDEA for the following reasons: (1) Two different federal agencies and offices were responsible for enforcing compliance with the IDEA and Section 504 (the commissioner of education in the former case, the secretary of the Department of Health and Human Services in the latter); (2) the sole means available to them to enforce the statutes was to cut off federal funds, and that alternative would be far more disruptive of the legislative scheme under the IDEA than a private lawsuit; and (3) the administrative remedies themselves were meaningless (because there were too many plaintiffs with common complaints).[19]

When there is proof that school officials have made extensive efforts to provide a disabled child with an appropriate education, the plaintiff must exhaust his or her administrative remedies. Exhaustion is not required, however, when there are undisputed facts conclusively showing that the child was receiving no education at all and that school officials would take no action to provide an appropriate education.[20] Moreover, residents of a state institution for people who are mentally retarded, for whom the state failed to appoint surrogate parents as required, are not compelled to exhaust their administrative remedies before suing under the IDEA, Section 504, the federal Developmental Disabilities Act, and the federal Constitution. The state's failure to appoint surrogates cannot benefit the state; children without parents have had no access to procedural remedies so they may bring their lawsuit without exhausting remedies.[21] Finally, exhaustion is not required because it would be futile where there were challenges to SEA regulations, to the state commissioner's performance of his duties under federal law, and to an alleged violation of due process (expulsion without hearing).[22]

In addition, a plaintiff claiming damages under the IDEA is not required to exhaust the state's administrative remedies because the state procedures are designed only to handle challenges to evaluation or placement, or both, not a claim of whether there is private remedy for damages implicit in the IDEA; there is no such remedy.[23] Also, a plaintiff who has exhausted administrative remedies under the IDEA need not also exhaust them under Section 504 because the legislative history of the IDEA indicates Congress's intent that compensatory damages are available under the law. A federal court may award damages.[24]

The general rule still is that a party must exhaust the administrative remedies before filing a suit in federal or state court (*Harper v. School Administrative District, Buffalino v. Board of Education, Howell v. Waterford Public Schools, Sullivan v. Vallejo City U.S.D.,* and *Kerr Parents Center Association v. Charles*). The purpose of the exhaustion-of-remedies rule is to ensure accuracy in the findings of fact, efficiency in the administration of the law, autonomy of the schools in administering the law, and economy of judicial resources by preventing some cases from coming to the courts if they are resolvable at administrative hearings.

The "futility" exception also remains alive and has been more clearly articulated in some of the recent cases. There seem to be several major exceptions, all falling within the futility exception: (1) the LEA absolutely denies an administrative hearing (*Ezratty v. Commonwealth of Puerto Rico, Quackenbush v. Johnson City School District, Mrs. A.W. v. Tirozzi, Christopher W. v. Portsmouth School Committee,* and *Kerr Center Parents Association v. Charles*); (2) severe harm will result to the student, which is not of the student's own making, as a result of having to exhaust the administrative remedies (*Phipps v. New Hanover County Board of Education, Crocker v. Tennessee Secondary School Athletic Association, J. G. v. Rochester City,* and *VanderMalle v. Ambach*); and (3) there will be inadequate relief from the administrative hearing, as where the hearing officer lacks any authority to grant the relief sought (*J. G. v. Rochester City, Quackenbush v. Johnson City School District,* and *Kerr Center Parents Association v. Charles*).

Burden of Proof

When one party brings a lawsuit against another, the law typically requires the party bringing the suit to prove his or her claim. Another way of stating this is to say that the *burden of proof* falls on the party bringing the suit. Since the IDEA does not assign the burden of proof to any potential party, the courts have relied on state law to determine which party has the burden of proof. Generally, the courts have held that the party bringing the case has the burden of proof. In most cases, the party bringing the case is the disabled child or the parents, so they have the responsibility of proving that their claim is worthy of judicial protection.

For example, they must prove that education in the LEA is inappropriate or that private school placement is appropriate and the state residential school or institution is not[25] or that the child is entitled to a vocational program, not an academic one, and that the LEA is unable to provide such a program.[26] Moreover, the burden of overturning a decision of a state due process hearing officer by a court falls on the party appealing the LEA-level decision, and that party must show that the SEA-level decision was not supported by substantial evidence, was arbitrary or capricious, or is clearly erroneous under law.[27]

Retroactive Application of the IDEA

Normally an Act of Congress speaks only to the future: It is "prospective" in its application. Sometimes, however, courts have found the IDEA to be "retrospective"—to apply to children who were discriminated against, in violation of the Act or other law, before the Act became effective. The cases—*Stemple v. Board of Education of Prince George's County* and *Frankel v. Commissioner of Education of New York*—reached opposite results. The general rule, however, is that laws are prospective.

In *Stemple*, parents of a multiply disabled child had placed her in a private residential school before the IDEA became effective. After it became effective, they sought reimbursement in due process hearings called by them. The district court held that it was not entitled to review the hearings because the IDEA's procedural guarantees were not in effect when the child was placed.

A similar result was reached in *Alexopulos v. Riles*,[28] which disallowed retroactive application of the IDEA in a case that claimed compensatory education. The court relied on congressional intent for the law to apply prospectively and noted that if the law applied retroactively to a claim for denial of appropriate education in the 1973 school year (two years before it was enacted), compensatory damages would have to be awarded. Because such damages are so much like monetary damages and because Congress did not authorize monetary damages to be awarded, retroactive application of the law clearly would violate congressional intent.

A different result was obtained in another case. The plaintiff's parents, in *Frankel*, sought to recover tuition costs they had paid for their disabled child's out-of-state private tuition, claiming that the school had failed to timely classify him and provide him with an appropriate education. The state commissioner of education denied their request, and they filed a civil action in federal court. The state and local schools filed motions to dismiss, arguing that the IDEA should not be applied retroactively.

The court denied the motion to dismiss, holding that, since the Act and its legislative history are silent on the issue of retroactivity, the U.S. Supreme Court's decision in *Bradley v. Richmond School Board* controls. The *Bradley* test is whether retroactive application would work an injustice in light of the nature and identity of the parties, the nature of their rights, and the nature of the impact of the change in law. Here, the court held that the IDEA may be applied retroactively.

Due Process Hearing Officer

The impartiality of due process hearing officers has come under scrutiny in several cases. Each of these demonstrates that the courts are meticulous about ensuring the officers' impartiality.

Robert M. v. Benton held that the state superintendent of schools was not an impartial hearing officer because he was an employee of an agency involved in the education of disabled children.[29] But *Vermont Association for Children with Learning Disabilities v. Kaagan* held that the state board of education members were not employees because they were appointed for fixed terms by the governor with the advice and consent of the state senate.[30] Also, *Smith v. Cumberland School Committee* held that employees of the state education agency may serve as due process hearing officers at the appeals (state-level hearings).[31]

Silvio v. Commonwealth of Pennsylvania held that the use of a state college professor as a due process hearing officer does not violate the IDEA. Simply because the professor was being paid by the state did not make him a partial person. Notwithstanding this early decision, later cases have held that university personnel who help formulate state special education policies are not impartial and may not serve as hearing officers.[32]

Helms v. McDaniel held that under the IDEA a state may continue to use a procedure in which the local school board treats the findings of a local due process hearing officer as a report that it can accept as final or automatically appeal. The process (automatic appeal if not accepted) is merely a "decision to appeal" and does not mean that the board itself is hearing the case. But the state violated the IDEA by treating the findings of the state-level hearing officer as the findings of a "special master" and not as a final decision. The law requires a final decision at the SEA level.

Likewise, *Cothern v. Mallory* upheld the state's procedures for selecting the due process hearing panel (the procedure calls for three panelists—one selected by the state, one by the parents, and another by both of the two previously designated members). But the IDEA allows a single panelist.[33]

When a Hearing Is Not Available

Although the IDEA grants a due process hearing as a matter of right to any party (typically, parents of a disabled child or the LEA charged with educating the child) in matters involving the child's identification, classification, or services, there are limitations on the right to obtain a hearing. The cases described in the following paragraphs show that the courts are unwilling to grant a hearing in every instance of an educational dispute.

The reasons for the court's reluctance to grant a hearing in every case of any minor change in a student's placement or program are fairly well grounded. First, Congress intended a hearing to be available when there is a change in placement (the child is moved from one type of program, such as a residential one, to another, such as an integrated one; or from one type of setting, such as a resource room, to another, such as a fully integrated program). Unless the change in placement or program substantially affects the student's rights to an appropriate education, there is no reason to create a due process right.

Second, allowing a due process hearing in all changes of placement or program, even those that are minor and not likely to affect the student's rights to an educational benefit, would open up the floodgates for many insubstantial claims. The administrative and judicial hearing process could become clogged with essentially frivolous cases.

Third, allowing a due process hearing in all changes of placement and program would involve the courts in oversight of school district decisions that are based on administrative grounds. To function effectively and efficiently, school authorities have to redraw school boundaries, open or close schools, move students from one building to another, and so on. If every such administrative decision can be challenged, the courts will become superordinary school boards and the administrative efficacy of the schools will be impaired.

The courts' reluctance to interfere with administrative and fiscal policy decisions of state or local educational agencies is reflected in a case that ruled that a private school does not have standing to challenge a state's decision to freeze the rates it pays to the school to educate students with disabilities (*Behavior Research Institute, Inc. v. Secretary of Administration*). Although this is the general rule, at least one state court has permitted private schools to challenge a reimbursement rate when the state educational agency set the rate arbitrarily (*Long Island Association for Children with Learning Disabilities v. Sobol*).

Finally, allowing a due process hearing in all such changes may put the courts in the position of having the opportunity to substitute their educational policy decisions or their administrative policy decision for those of the elected or appointed school boards and their professional staff. As has been argued throughout this book, courts are reluctant to take on that kind of authority, preferring to defer to the experts in those matters.

Thus, there is a line of cases that disallow hearings when parents seek to prevent SEAs or LEAs from carrying out administrative or organizational decisions affecting more than one child or school. For example, parents of disabled children placed by an LEA or their parents in a private school lack standing under the IDEA to use due process procedures to challenge a state-level decision to terminate funding for a private school.[34]

A case reaching a similar result is *Concerned Parents and Citizens for Continuing Education at Malcolm X (P.S. 79) v. New York City Board of Education*. The Second Circuit Court of Appeals concluded that prior notice and a hearing are not required when a disabled child is transferred from a special class at one school to a substantially similar class at another school within the same school district because there has been no official change of placement under the IDEA.

In that case, the plaintiffs filed suit in federal court to prevent the closing of an experimental school in New York City that employed innovative techniques to integrate and educate disabled and nondisabled students. The school was closed, and the children were transferred to other schools in the district in a very secretive way. Many parents learned of the decision after their disabled child had been reassigned to a different school in the fall. The lower court ruled that this transfer constituted a change of placement and under federal law there should have been notice and a hearing. Since the school was already closed, however, the court did not reopen the school. Instead, it ordered remedial improvements in the new programs.

The Second Circuit reversed the lower court, concluding that the transfer of students from one program to another in the same district was not a change in placement as contemplated under the IDEA, even though it noted that the transfer was "poorly planned" and the new placements did not duplicate the innovative program at the old school. The court was persuaded by several factors: (1) Under Section 1415(b)(1)(C) of the IDEA, placement seemed to be "limited to certain fundamental decisions regarding the existence and classification of the disability, and the most appropriate type of educational programs for assisting a child with such a disability"; (2) the regulations implementing the IDEA also interpret the term "placement" to refer only to the general educational placement. A broad interpretation would "cripple the Board's ability to implement even minor discretionary changes." The court emphasized, however, that the decision did not leave parents without a remedy. They still could file a complaint, request a full administrative hearing, and appeal any adverse decision to the courts.

Likewise, a due process hearing is not available when children placed in one school are transferred to another and there is no change in their educational instruction. But if the transfer involves a change in their IEPs, if only to incorporate additional supportive services, a hearing is available.[35]

Dima v. Macchiarola held that the wholesale transfer of students from a private school to alternative placements because the school district terminated contact with the private school after auditing it, was not a change of placement that triggers a due process hearing. Likewise, a state decision to reduce its tuition reimbursement rate to a private school does not trigger a due process hearing.[36] This New York decision has been followed consistently in that state, with *Lowell School, Inc. v. Ambach* holding that a private school for children with disabilities has no right to challenge (under due process safeguards) the decision of the state education commissioner to reduce future tuition payments to the school, and *Language Development Program of Western New York, Inc. v. Ambach* holding that a private school has no right to a hearing before the state modifies the scope of disabling conditions the school may serve at public expense. These cases, as well as the *Tilton* case, digested below, indicate that the courts will not tolerate use of the federal special education law to obstruct or modify state fiscal decisions.

Tilton v. Jefferson County Board of Education held that the stay-put provision of the IDEA (requiring that a disabled child's placement not be changed while administrative or legal remedies are being exhausted) does not prohibit a state from closing, for financial reasons, a regional mental retardation facility in which disabled children had been given special education. To apply the due process protections of the IDEA to school closings, even when the children receive substantially different programs as a result, would thwart the state's fiscal policies, a situation that Congress did not intend.

In a result slightly different from the New York cases and *Tilton*, a federal district court has held that the state of Oregon violated its duties under the IDEA and state law by discontinuing funding of a private education program.[37] In that case, the private residential center was certified by the federal government as an intermediate care facility for the mentally retarded and by the state as a residential training center. The center's students participated in a local school district's special education program, which received federal and state special education funds. When the state declined to fund the students' education adequately, the school district proposed to reduce the amount of services it provided and refused to grant the students any procedural safeguard (due process) opportunities to challenge its decision, and the state denied that it had any further responsibility to the students.

The court concluded that the students were participating in a state-operated program (the ICF-MR program), not a school district program, and, because the IDEA, its regulations, and state law all impose a responsibility on the state to provide an appropriate education to those students, the state would be required to provide such an education and to fund it. The students' failure to exhaust administrative remedies, further, does not prohibit the federal court from acting to prevent the state from discontinuing the students' funding. The school district had refused to allow due process hearings, and thus there could be no exhaustion of remedies. This result is distinguishable from the New York cases and *Tilton* on the basis that the New York cases and *Tilton* did not result in the denial of an appropriate education, only a change in funding patterns or opportunities.

The courts' reluctance to interfere with administrative and fiscal policy decisions of state or local educational agencies is reflected in a case that ruled that a private school does not have standing to challenge a state's decision to freeze the rates it pays to the school to educate students with disabilities, *Behavior Research Institute, Inc. v. Secretary of Administration*. Although this is the general rule, at least one state court has permitted private schools to challenge a reimbursement rate when the state educational agency set the rate arbitrarily (*Long Island Association for Children with Learning Disabilities v. Sobol*).

Statute of Limitations

General law is that a lawsuit or administrative action (such as a due process hearing) must be begun within a certain period of time. This rule ensures that disputes are heard when evidence is relatively fresh—when the witnesses are only recently removed from the time during which the facts arose. The rule also prompts parties to resolve their disputes sooner or later so that they may get on with their lives without the inevitable uncertainty and burdens that come with a lawsuit.

The means by which the rule for prompt litigation is enforced is called the *statute of limitations*. It is a law (statute enacted by a legislature) that places a limitation on the period of time beyond which a lawsuit may be filed. The IDEA contains no statute of limitation, and the courts have been compelled to create one. In every case, they have borrowed the statute of limitations that applies to administrative actions (a due process hearing) as enacted by the state legislature in which the hearing is heard.[38]

Although most courts have borrowed the state's administrative procedures act statute of limitations,[39] at least one court has rejected the state administrative procedures act limitation of thirty days and allowed a year for filing the case, reasoning that the longer time-frame is analogous to other federal and state education law and will permit the parties enough time to prepare for and argue the merits of a case (*York County School Board v. Nicely*).

Where a lawyer competently represents his client (student with disabilities) in all respects except that he files his case after the statute of limitations has barred him from doing so, a court will not overlook that mistake and will bar the student from proceeding against the school district, thus teaching the lesson that lawyers and students must be careful about statutes of limitations and suggesting that the student should sue the lawyer for malpractice (*I.D. v. Westmoreland*).

Standard of Review.   Under the Supreme Court's *Rowley* decision [458 U.S. 176, 206], a court that reviews an administrative hearing decision may undertake a de novo review of the dispute between the school and a student (that is, the court may hold a hearing that admits all of the evidence from the administrative hearing and any new evidence that the parties offer) and base its decision on the "preponderance of the evidence." This requirement does not allow a court simply to substitute its judgment for the hearing officer's but instead requires the court to give "due weight" to the hearing officer's decision (*Roncker v. Walter, Doe v. Smith, School Board of Prince William County v. Malone, Burke County Board of Education v. Denton, Gillette v. Fairland Board of Education*, and *Matta v. Indian Hill Exempted Village Schools*).

The judicial review consists of two inquiries: first, whether the state or local school district has complied with the procedural requirements of the statute; and, second, whether the student's IEP and placement are reasonably calculated to provide an educational benefit. Once the court determines that the law's procedural requirements have been met, then questions about methodology of instruction are for the state and local school district to determine (*Rowley, Roncker, Gillette*, and *Matta*). Thus, the reviewing court is required to be bound by the administrative record and additional evidence, but yet it is also independent in the sense that it must base its decision on the preponderance of the evidence before it (*Burlington School Committee v. Massachusetts Department of Education*). Thus, the court has discretion to give the administrative findings proper weight, but it also has an obligation to consider carefully and respond to the administrative resolution of those issues (*Burlington* and *Burke County Board of Education v. Denton*).

Open Hearings.   In order to protect the privacy of parents and students where there are sensitive matters involved in due process hearings (such as a student's mental health), a parent may require a due process hearing to be closed to the public, especially to newspapers or other media (*Webster Groves School District v. Pulitzer Publishing Co.*).

Involuntary Dismissal.   If a parent refuses to participate in any part of an administrative or judicial hearing (for example, the parent refuses to participate in pretrial discovery proceedings), the court may dismiss the parent's complaint against the parent's objection (involuntary dismissal) (*Nathaniel L. v. Exeter School District*).

THE REALITY

The reality of due process in the IDEA is fairly stark. It helps one to realize at the outset that parents or an LEA may pull at least thirty-six "triggers," or grounds for either party to seek a due process hearing.[40] This alone makes due process a provision that can be wielded in good faith or in bad, for the legitimate purpose of correcting deficits in a disabled child's educational rights or for purposes of harassment.

It also helps to realize that implementation of due process requirements early on was a matter of some concern. The requirements in the IDEA and its implementing regulations were hardly self-explanatory or self-executing.[41] Much of the ambiguity of the IDEA and its regulations has been eliminated by judicial interpretation, state-agency regulations and guidelines, and common practice (the so-called common law on conducting hearings). For example, early on the likelihood of due process hearing officers being not totally impartial or even well trained was great,[42] but by the mid-1980s most states had provided for a careful selection and training process.

Nonetheless, problems remain. The largest one seems to be the cost of due process. Cost consists of three elements: (1) the actual *financial cost* of the hearings—preparing for them, hiring attorneys and expert witnesses, paying for the documents required for evidence, and pursuing an appeal; (2) the *emotional or psychic cost*—the enormous energy and stress involved in a hearing and its appeal; and (3) the cost that consists of *time spent*, and perhaps lost, when the child may (or may not) be receiving an appropriate education.

A good measure of the actual costs involved in due process is the dramatic increase in the number of due process hearings since the IDEA was enacted and due process was made available under the IDEA.[43] Another measure of the actual cost is the increased use of *mediation* as a way of preventing due process. Mediation involves the use of less formal, less adversarial, more negotiated-settlement meetings for resolving disputes.[44]

It is increasingly evident that the psychic costs—the exacerbation of ill will that parents and educators already feel about each other—are the more serious ones, from the viewpoint of both the parents and the educators involved in due process.[45] That is not to minimize the huge financial costs, which are increasingly affordable only by the middle and upper classes and by schools.

Moreover, there is evidence that due process hearings do not satisfactorily resolve the disputes between parents and school systems.[46] There is a perception on the part of some parents that schools have the "home-court advantage" in due process and that parent-initiated due process will not be particularly helpful even if the parents gain the legal victory they seek. That is why many parents, especially those whose income level is upper-middle class and upper-class, can afford to withdraw their children from public education if they fail, in a due process hearing, to obtain the private school placement or other expensive service they sought for their child.[47]

For all of its problems, however, due process remains an important—indeed, an indispensable—element of the IDEA and the right to education. Like many other aspects of the legal process, it is flawed because it requires extraordinary amounts of energy, time, and money. The fault lies mainly with the system of dispute resolution in our society and with an inadequate understanding of the causes of due process in special education (an understanding that would help prevent due process). The necessity of due process, however, is beyond dispute.

NOTES

1. *See, e.g.*, LeBanks v. Spears, Guadalupe Org. v. Tempe Elem. School Dist., and Larry P. v. Riles.

2. Doe v. Kenny.

3. Cuyahoga ARC v. Essex.

4. Doe v. Kenny.

5. Mills, Cuyahoga ARC v. Essex, and Doe v. Kenny.

6. LeBanks v. Spears, and Mills; *contra*, PARC.

7. Cuyahoga ARC v. Essex.

8. *Id.*

9. Diana v. State Bd. of Ed., LeBanks v. Spears, and Larry P. v. Riles.

10. ____ F. Supp. ____ EHLR 559:373 N.D. Cal. 1988.

11. 722 F. 2nd 910.

12. *See also* Riley v. Ambach, Dima v. Macchiarola, Harris v. Campbell, Armstrong v. Kline, Monahan v. Nebraska, Timms v. Metro. School Dist., Doe v. Koger, Ezratty v. Puerto Rico, Akers v. Bolton, Greg B. v. Bd. of Ed., McGovern v. Sullins, Mitchell v. Walter, San Francisco Unified School Dist. v. California, Lombardi v. Ambach, Smith v. Ambach, and Davis v. Maine Endwell Cent. School Dist.

13. Smith v. Ambach, and Shannon v. Ambach.

14. Cluff v. Johnson City Cent. School Dist., and Kresse v. Johnson City Cent. School Dist.

15. Phipps v. New Hanover County Bd. of Ed., Riley v. Ambach, and Calhoun v. Illinois State Bd.

16. Christopher T. v. San Francisco U.S.D., Monahan v. Nebraska, Howard S. v. Friendswood I.S.D., ARC in Colorado v. Frazier, and Miener v. Missouri.

17. North v. D.C. Bd. of Ed., a case in which the parties were bound by the prior order of the same court in Mills.

18. Jose P. v. Ambach; but normally exhaustion is required: Riley v. Ambach, Lombardi v. Ambach, Vermont ACLD v. Kaagan (ruling on constitutional and statutory challenges to redefinition of "learning disabilities"), and Darlene L. v. Illinois State Bd. of Ed.

19. United Cerebral Palsy of NYC v. Bd. of Ed. of City of N.Y.

20. Harris v. Campbell.

21. Garrity v. Gallen, and (Ruth Anne) M. v. Alvin I.S.D.

22. J.G. v. Bd. (suit designed to correct alleged system-wide violation of IDEA's procedures).

23. Loughran v. Flanders.

24. Boxall v. Sequoia Union H.S. Dist.

25. Bales v. Clark.

26. Fitz v. Intermediate Unit #29, and Savka v. Pennsylvania Dept. of Ed.

27. Levy v. Pennsylvania Dept. of Ed.

28. ____ F. 2d EHLR 557:296 (9th Cir. 1986).

29. *Concur*: Vogel v. School Bd., involving deputy state superintendent; Monahan v. Nebraska, where the state commissioner had authority to overrule the decision of the state-level hearing officer; East Brunswick Bd. of Ed. v. New Jersey State Bd. of Ed., holding that an SEA employee is not an impartial hearing officer.

30. *See also* Timms v. Metro. School Dist.

31. *Contra*: Compochiaro v. Califano.

32. Mayson v. Teague; Kotowicz v. Mississippi State Bd. of Ed.

33. Nevada County Office of Ed. v. Supt.

34. Windward School v. State.

35. Brown v. D.C. Bd. of Ed.

36. *Concur*: Fallis v. Ambach.

37. Kerr Center Parents Ass'n. v. Charles.

38. *Supra* n. 32.

39. *Supra* n. 32; Manchester City School District v. Jason N.

40. Turnbull, Turnbull, and Strickland, "Procedural Due Process: The Two-Edged Sword that the Untrained Should Not Unsheath," *Boston University Journal of Education* (Summer, 1979):40-59 .

41. *Id*.

42. Turnbull, Strickland, and Turnbull, "Due Process Hearing Officers: Characteristics, Needs, and Appointment Criteria," *Exceptional Children* 48(1981):48-54.

43. U.S. Dept. of Education, Annual Reports to Congress on the Implementation of Public Law 94-142: The Education for All Handicapped Children Act (Washington, DC: U.S. Government Printing Office).

44. U.S. Dept. of Education, *Sixth Annual Report to Congress* (Washington, DC: U.S. Government Printing Office, 1984).

45. Budoff, "Special Education Appeals Hearings: Are They Fair and Are They Helping?" *Exceptional Education Quarterly* (Aug. 1981):37-48.

46. *Id*.

47. *Id*.

For 1994 Update on Procedural Due Process please see page 402.

8
Parent Participation and Shared Decision Making

CONSTITUTIONAL FOUNDATIONS

Participatory democracy is a term that describes shared decision making in the schools or in other public agencies. It refers to the legal right or political opportunity of those affected by a public agency's decisions to participate in making those decisions. It is a longstanding tenet of government in this country, but it has not always been in good standing. Too often it has been given little more than lip-service. But, as this chapter will show, the IDEA—like the cases—has started to make inroads on unilateral decision making in the schools.

Although the constitutional foundations for parent participation in the education of disabled children are not well articulated by the courts—probably because they involve the children's rights instead of the parents'—they nevertheless exist and can be identified and explained. At the core of the constitutional principles is the common law doctrine that parents have a duty to support their children and a corollary right to their children's services and earnings for as long as the children have the legal status of minors. Under common law and even by today's statutes, these rights and interests mean that parents may control their children in various ways.

For example, parents are empowered to consent (on the minor's behalf) to medical treatment for the minor and, more recently, to educational diagnosis and evaluation. The compulsory school attendance laws usually make the parents criminally liable if they do not require their child to attend the public schools. Also, state statutes make parents criminally liable for failing to support their minor children. The reason for these and similar laws is that a minor is presumed incapable, because of age, of acting on his or her own behalf except in limited ways, as granted by statute or as recently recognized under the constitutional "privacy interest" by the courts (for example, the rights to abortion, contraception, or treatment for substance abuse). Parents, then, have rights that they exercise on behalf of their child, and in many instances the child's right to have an education is exercised by the parents.

Children's rights to procedural due process, to a proper evaluation and appropriate classification, and to be included in school can be enforced by their parents acting in their representative capacity (acting on the child's behalf).

The cases have made an indirect but nevertheless damning criticism of the schools by recognizing that children have rights of their own and their parents have rights in a representative capacity. They have said that schools have been making unilateral decisions about disabled children's education but that, in the future, those decisions must be shared with the parents and other representatives of disabled children.

FEDERAL LEGISLATION

The IDEA declares that the Act is intended to assure that the rights of disabled children and their parents or guardians are protected [Sec. 1400(c)]. It carries out its policy in the following ways (in addition to those already mentioned in conjunction with classification, evaluation, individualized education programs, least restrictive placement, and procedural due process).

Notice, Consultation, and Hearings

The IDEA requires SEAs to give assurances to the U.S. Department of Education that, in carrying out the Act's requirements to provide a free appropriate public education, the state will establish procedures for consultation with persons involved in or concerned with the education of disabled children, including the disabled individuals and their parents or guardians [Sec. 1412 (7) and Sec. 300.137]. The IDEA also requires SEAs to establish procedures for making the state plan available to the public and to the parents [Sec. 300.284]; for having public hearings [Sec. 300.280] and for giving adequate notice of those hearings; and for allowing the general public to comment on proposed policies, programs, and procedures required by the IDEA before they are adopted [Sec. 1412(7) and Sec. 300.282].

As is more fully discussed later in this chapter, the regulations require SEAs to give public notice of policy hearings, to provide an opportunity for public participation and public comment, to review public comments before adopting the annual plan, and to publish and make the plan generally available [Secs. 300.280-.284]. In addition, the Act requires LEAs to give assurances that, in offering full educational opportunities to all disabled children, they will provide for the participation and consultation of the parents or guardians of the children [Sec. 1414(a)(1)(C)(iii) and Sec. 300.226].

Advisory Panels

The Act requires SEAs to create an advisory panel whose members are to be appointed by the governor or other official authorized to make such appointments. The panel should be composed of individuals involved in or concerned with the education of disabled children, including at least one representative of disabled individuals, teachers of disabled children, parents of such children, state and local education officials, and administrators of programs for disabled children [Sec. 1413(a)(12) and Sec. 300.651]. The panel is to advise the SEAs on the unmet needs of disabled students, make public comment on the annual plan and on pertinent state rules or regulations to be issued by the SEA, and assist the state in developing and reporting whatever data and evaluations the secretary might require.

Access to System Records

The Act requires that certain information about school programs for disabled children and about the children themselves be treated as public information, available to all, including parents of the disabled children. An LEA must give assurances that its application for federal funds and all documents related to the application are available to parents, or guardians, and other members of the general public. This includes information that is necessary for an SEA to perform its evaluation duties and information relating to the educational achievement of disabled children in programs financed under the Act [Sec. 1414(a)(3) and (4)]. Likewise, before submitting an amendment to the state plan, an SEA must give to parents, or guardians, and other members of the general public at least thirty days' prior notice of the amendment [Sec. 1412(2)(E)].

Protection of Student Records

The IDEA also provides for the confidentiality of student records and access to those records by parents or guardians [Secs. 1417(c) and 1412(2)(D)]. Both the SEAs and LEAs are subject to action by the secretary, in accordance with the Family Educational Rights and Privacy Act (FERPA), codified at 20 U.S.C. Sec. 1232g, and regulations, 34 C.F.R. Parts A-E.

FERPA requires recipients of federal education grants to give parents, or guardians, and in some cases, pupils, access to their own public school records. Parents must be given an opportunity for a hearing to challenge the content of the records, and certain parts of the records cannot be released without parental consent. The IDEA confidentiality regulations [Sec. 300.560-.576] conform to FERPA.

IDEA and the 1990 Amendments

Although the 1990 IDEA does not change the parent participation principle significantly, it does expand its utility. Section 1415(a)(17)) clarifies that related services include those that may benefit parents. Rehabilitation counseling can include parents, especially when the student is receiving (at least by age sixteen) an IEP/ITP. Social work as a related service can include work with the student's family. Finally, the early childhood education provisions [Sec. 1423] make it clear that parent education should be included as part of the student's early education, that transition planning should occur (and necessarily will involve the families of preschool children), and that the early education programs should address the needs of preschoolers exposed prenatally to maternal substance abuse (potentially including social work, school health, and parent-training services delivered to the mothers).

SIGNIFICANCE OF ADA AND IDEA FOR FAMILIES

It is far too early to predict clearly or confidently the significance of ADA and IDEA for families. But glimmerings of significance are on the horizon.

On a macropolitical level, there are many more political and legal battles to fight. They will involve some families directly, but most only indirectly, and will be waged by the families' advocacy organizations, such as the Association for Retarded Citizens or United Cerebral Palsy.

Politically, the exclusion of the insurance industry from ADA's coverage is highly problematic. Insurance is a major fringe benefit in many jobs and is essential in ensuring access to affordable and appropriate health care. The frankly political compromise—exclude the insurance industry or lose the votes necessary to pass ADA—may be addressed on three levels: in the state legislatures, in Congress again as part of an amendment of the ADA, or as part of comprehensive health-care legislation. The latter is clearly the likely route. The insurance industry is too powerful in head-to-head legislative fights. For families, then, the goal has to be to complement the ADA with comprehensive health-care legislation, enacted in Congress.

Also politically, the power of public opinion is problematic. For many years, now, it has been clear that incrementalism in law reform is the pattern and is not only effective (after all, ADA is a product of the Civil Rights Act of 1964 and the Rehabilitation Act antidiscrimination provisions of 1975) but also politically adept (to lose the sympathetic imagination of the dominant, nondisabled majority would be politically disastrous). For families, then, the future requires the skillful courting of public opinion.

Legally, families still must be involved in the regulation-making phases. They need to ensure effective advocacy to enforce the laws and create factual defenses (a so-called "Brandeis brief" chocked full of economic rationale) to the "reasonable accommodations/undue burden" defenses.

On a more personal and immediate level, individual families face the future with optimism and more arrows in their quivers than ever before. IDEA now creates a new equal access doctrine: Students with disabilities have access to the same and different resources of the education system, for the same and different purposes as children without disabilities. This is a major boon, expressed in the ITP provisions and the orientation of IDEA from a process-oriented law to an outcome-oriented law. It is a boon because it teaches families that appropriate education is assured principally by a community-based, community-referenced curriculum that helps a student develop the skills needed to participate in those sectors of society now affected by ADA. It also is a boon because, even though Congress did not frontally amend the least-restrictive-education provisions of the IDEA, Congress did, in a few small but telling ways, send the signal that it intends the curriculum to be delivered in integrated settings.

ADA expands the equal access doctrine from education to other domains of the person's and family's life. They now are entitled to access to the same resources as other individuals, for the same purposes. They have access to the same resources: opportunities in employment, transportation, public accommodations, state/local government services, and telecommunications.

And the access is for the same purposes: to participate in the mainstream [Senator Harkin, 136 Cong. Rec. S. 9684, 9689; President Bush, statement, July 26, 1990] and to have "equality of opportunity, full participation, independent living, and economic self-sufficiency" [Sec. 2(a)(8)].

This is clear from the parallels between IDEA and ADA. IDEA's "zero reject" principle, with its tenet of "educability" and purpose of inclusion, has become ADA's zero-reject principle for all of life, with a tenet of "employability" and "ability" and thus of inclusion. IDEA's "appropriate education" principle has become ADA's "reasonable accommodation" rule. IDEA's "least restrictive environment" principle has become ADA's ban against physical and attitudinal barriers in adult life—its promise of inclusion and "full participation." ADA's due process principle has been incorporated into ADA's enforcement provisions. And IDEA's "parent participation" principle has become ADA's participation rule: that the person with a disability (and thus the person's family, under the family-systems approach) will participate in deciding whether, how, and how much to exercise the new equality of opportunity that ADA creates.

But more than mere legal parallelism is involved, more than a continuation of the promises of education. Just as IDEA began to shape the views and values of families and students, so too does ADA affect them. ADA (together with IDEA) gives families reasons for great expectations, for realizing the positive contributions their members can make, for being able to act on their choices and play from their strengths, and for attaining full citizenship.

It is not beyond argument that IDEA and ADA together create a contract of lifetime support and access for individuals with disabilities and their families. IDEA's rights to free appropriate public education are the basis for ADA's rights to nondiscrimination and participation in not just the public sectors but in the private sectors as well. IDEA's Part H rights to early intervention become, in due course, Part B rights to early childhood education and then, also in due course, to appropriate education and transition services. Simultaneously, ADA's rights to nondiscrimination and participation are available to the infant/toddler, preschooler, and student as well. The social contract envisioned by Rousseau and the Enlightenment philosophers has, at last, been realized (at least as a matter of the formal law, if not yet fully as a matter of reality) for individuals with disabilities.

Accordingly, as rights to education and participation are enforced, and as individuals with disabilities, their families, and the nondisabled majority see each other in new ways (as educable/employable/able and entitled to and benefiting from education and participation), it is likely that the "norms" of society will change. The "norm" in the schools has become one of inclusion of students with disabilities and their families' participation. The norm in the world outside school will mirror that school norm as ADA is implemented.

The consequence will be that the "forms" of society will change, too. The physical, attitudinal, economic, and other barriers that excluded students with disabilities from education have been steadily disappearing. It is not unreasonable to expect that they will begin to disappear in the rest of America as well. That certainly is ADA's intent. It is likely, based on IDEA's (imperfect) results, that the result will be consistent with the intent.

What can be said in summary of ADA, IDEA, and families? It is this:

- These two laws affect families, not just their members with disabilities.
- These laws change the laws, the slogans, and the results by which families can live.
- These laws extend the Supreme Court's decision in *Brown v. Board* [347 U.S. 483 (1954)]. That decision, like these laws, had a singular, albeit vital, purpose: to ensure by law that the rights of citizenship apply to all alike, not just to a few.
- These two laws reflect the "social construct" or "transactional" nature of disability: disability may be an unchangeable trait of the person, but disability is that which the world creates by failing to accommodate to that difference. These laws affect the individual and make it possible for the person and the family to overcome the effects of disability. But they equally affect the world in which the person and family live and require it to adapt and accommodate.
- The underlying motives of federal law at last have been confirmed and applied to all sectors of American life. These motives are altruism (a concern to help those with disabilities), rebalancing power (eliminating the disadvantage that individuals with disabilities have experienced), anti-institutionalization (ensuring participation in the mainstream and barring segregation in institutions), and equal opportunity (creating a level playing field on which all may participate).[1]

In the last analysis, families of individuals with disabilities—while still facing macro-level and individual-level obstacles—have a different life before them. Not since Congress (one-and-a-half decades ago) enacted the Education of All Handicapped Children Act (P.L. 94-142, amending the Education of the Handicapped Act, now IDEA) and the antidiscrimination provisions of the Rehabilitation Act [Sec. 504] has there been such a confluence of opportunity: the opportunity to apply and benefit from new laws that have complementary purposes and provisions; to adopt and live by new creeds and slogans; and to establish—through laws and creeds—new norms and forms.

Part H

Part H defines "parent(s)" to be a parent, guardian, person acting as a parent, or surrogate parent. A person acting as a parent may be a grandparent or stepparent with whom the child lives or a person legally responsible for the child's welfare.

There are other Part H rules for parent participation. The law establishes a State Interagency Coordinating Council and requires that family members be on the council. In addition, all of the parent rights available under Part B relating to access to and confidentiality of information apply to Part H programs.

Parents and other members of the public may have access to information about state and local early intervention programs. Also, not all information about every student is accessible, but generally parents and other members of the public may obtain all information concerning the *programs* that the state or local agency runs. (This is different from the rights of parents to have access to their child's education records. That type of access does not belong to the public.)

Parents have the right to consent or object to the release of personally identifying information about their children. This protects family privacy. In addition to the right to assure confidentiality, parents also have the right of access to their own children's educational records. This assures the basis for a long-term and constructive relationship.

The state also must publish its proposed plan, give notice of when hearings will be held, allow for public opportunity to comment on the plan, hold public hearings, and review and comment on the public comments. It also must establish a public awareness program, comprehensive child find system, and a central directory of information.

Section 504

There is only one requirement under Section 504 regulations. That is that LEAs must annually try to identify and locate every qualified disabled person in the school district who is not receiving a public education and notify those persons and their parents or guardians of the school's duty to provide them with a free education [Sec. 104.32].

Sometimes parent participation can actually disrupt the legal process and jeopardize a child's rights under IDEA. That was the situation when a parent was so abusive of the legal process that she willingly disobeyed court orders in a case that she brought on her own behalf and on her child's behalf. To secure the judicial process and punish her, the court fined her five hundred dollars for contempt of court and dismissed the lawsuit that she filed on her own behalf. Recognizing, however, that her child, the student, should not be penalized because of the mother's behavior, the court did not dismiss the child's case (*Mylo v. Baltimore County Board of Education*).

JUDICIAL INTERPRETATIONS

Perhaps reflecting the fact that "family" nowadays includes more than just parents, incorporating brothers, sisters, grandparents, other blood or by-marriage relatives, and even "extended family" who are not related by blood or marriage, the term "parent" includes more than simply the natural (biological) parent of a child with a disability. Thus, permanent foster parents, appointed by the state welfare agency to be the student's "parents," are entitled to exercise all of the rights that the LEA gives to natural parents, and the foster parents, not the state agency, are entitled to make decisions about enforcing rights under the IDEA. Likewise, the state may not appoint surrogate parents for the student who has permanent foster parents.[2]

Even when a surrogate parent has been appointed for the student, the natural parents may still sue an LEA to enforce their—if not their child's—rights under the IDEA. This is true even if the child has attained the age of majority. The reason for this result is that the appointment of a surrogate is for the purpose of enforcing the child's rights. The appointment does not displace the natural parents' own rights.[3] Moreover, even after the child reaches the age of majority, the natural, adoptive, or foster parents retain the right to enforce their rights—if not their child's—under the IDEA.[4]

When a child's natural parents have separated or divorced, the general practice has been for the LEA to deal only with the parent to whom the child's custody has been awarded. This has proven to be sound practice and probably should not be modified except in one situation. That situation is one in which the noncustodial parent is responsible for the child's educational expenses. In that case, the LEA must seek to involve the noncustodial parent in all parent-rights matters and must accede to that parent's wishes to be involved as fully as the custodial parent, such as in the IEP development.[5]

A natural parent can lose the rights of participation, however, by his or her own action. Thus, when a parent, in order to obtain the child's admission to a state psychiatric institution, arranges for the county department of human services to be appointed as the child's conservator (guardian) and for a lawyer to be appointed as the guardian *ad litem* (a guardian for the purpose of a lawsuit only), and when the same parent fails to obtain a court appointment as the child's "next of friend" (a legal term designating the continuing parent-child relationship), the parent loses his or her right to sue on the child's behalf.[6] A foster child, whose natural parents have moved out of state but who lives with foster parents, is a resident of the state in which the foster parents live and is entitled to obtain a free appropriate education at that state's expense. To prohibit that result would apply residency requirements barring the children in foster homes from having or enforcing rights under the IDEA.[7]

It is becoming settled law that parents have a right to tape record an IEP conference when they have a hearing or physical disability that prevents them from fully participating in the conference and the recording does not violate any rights to privacy of teachers or the LEA, since the IDEA and its regulations seek to ensure full participation of parents in the IEP process (*E.H. v. Tirozzi* and *V.W. and R.W. v. Favolise*).

RIGHTS TO INFORMATION

A major implication of the parent participation regulations is that both LEAs and SEAs have new responsibilities for providing educational information to consumers. For example, an SEA must provide notice to parents of disabled students (in the parents' native language) that personally identifiable information (including the name of the child, parents, and other family members, address, any personal identifier such as a social security number or student number, or any list of personal characteristics or other information that would make it possible to identify the child [Sec. 300.500]) is on file. Further, it must explain the type of information it plans to collect and how it plans to use the information. An SEA might, for example, collect information on the number of children with a particular disabling condition, or it might seek data for a description of the educational achievement of a group of disabled children.

In addition, parents must be provided with a summary of policies and procedures to be used by "participating agencies" (*any* agency or institution that collects, maintains, and uses or provides information) for storing information, releasing it to third parties, or destroying it, as well as the agency's plan for protecting personally identifiable information. An SEA must publicly announce, through the newspapers or some other appropriate media, any child identification and evaluation activities it plans [Sec. 300.561]. Thus, the SEA has responsibility for developing policies for access to system records and protection of student records, to be followed by all participating agencies. Representatives from LEAs may wish to request an opportunity to participate in the SEA's development of these policies.

Parents and their representatives have the right to inspect personally identifiable information in their child's records within forty-five days, maximum, after requesting to inspect the records. If the record includes information on more than one child, parents are entitled to see or be informed about only the portion relating to their child [Sec. 300.564]. The agency may presume that the parent has access rights unless it is advised otherwise in cases of guardianship, separation, or divorce. Parents may request an explanation or interpretation of the information and must be provided with copies if failure to provide copies would result in their being unable to inspect or review the information [Sec. 300.562]. A fee for copies may be charged, unless the fee would prevent a parent from having access to the record [Sec. 300.566]. Upon request, parents also must be provided with a list of the types and locations of information collected and used by the agency [Sec. 300.565]. The school must keep a record of access [Sec. 300.563].

There are further requirements for the protection of student records. After reading the records and having them appropriately interpreted, parents may request that the participating agency amend the information. The agency must consider the request and give an affirmative or negative response within a reasonable time. If the agency disagrees with the request, it must inform the parents of their right to a hearing to protest this decision [Secs. 300.567-.570]. Thus, parents not only have rights of access to student records, but they also have rights to informally or formally challenge the contents of student records. This underscores the necessity for educators to recognize the importance of their responsibilities in maintaining accurate student records and developing skills in documenting educational progress.

The regulations safeguarding the confidentiality of student information set forth clear implementation guidelines for public schools. First, one official must be appointed at each participating agency to assume overall responsibility for ensuring that personally identifiable information remains confidential [Sec. 300.572(b)]. This person might be the director of special education, the director of special services, or some other administrator who has concomitant responsibility for implementation of the IDEA and Section 504. All persons who participate in the collection or use of confidential information must receive training related to the state's policies and procedures on confidentiality of personally identifiable information [Sec. 300.572(c)]. The participating agency also must maintain an updated roster of persons (and their positions) employed by the agency who have access to personally identifiable information. This list is to be available for public inspection [Sec. 300.572(d)].

Public agencies must obtain parental consent before releasing personally identifiable information to anyone other than the agency officials authorized to collect and use this information, unless otherwise authorized to do so under the Buckley-Pell Amendment in the federal Family Educational Rights and Privacy Act. The SEA must establish policies and procedures to be followed when a parent refuses to give consent [Sec. 300.571].

Public agencies must notify parents when personally identifiable information that had been collected and maintained is no longer needed for educational services. Upon the parent's request, the information must be destroyed. Permanent information that can be kept without regard to time limitations includes a student's name, address, phone number, grades, attendance record, classes attended, grade level completed, and year completed [Sec. 300.573]. Public agency officials should advise parents that their child's records may be needed for purposes such as securing social security benefits or qualifying for certain income tax deductions. In addition, the safeguards for maintaining confidentiality of records should be fully explained to parents before they make a decision about having the records destroyed.

In their annual program plans, SEAs are required to specify policies and procedures to assure the rights of children as well as the rights of their parents. Consideration should be given to the child's age and the type or severity of disability [Sec. 300.574]. The Family Educational Rights and Privacy Act requires the rights of parents pertaining to educational records to be transferred to the student at age eighteen. This requirement has major implications for schools serving disabled students in the eighteen to twenty-one age range.

NOTES

1. Turnbull, H. R., and Barber, P. A., 1985.
2. Criswell v. State Dept. of Ed.
3. John H. v. McDonald.
4. *Id.*
5. Doe v. Anrig.
6. Susan R.M. v. Northwest I.S.D.
7. Catlin v. Ambach.

For 1994 Update on Parent Participation please see page 404.

SECTION III
Enforcing the Law

9

Case Law Techniques

COMPLIANCE

Litigation has been a major—and, indeed, was the original—source for establishing the educational rights of disabled children. Were it not for the landmark decisions (e.g., *PARC, Mills, LeBanks, Larry P.,* and *Diana*), it is doubtful if subsequent litigation would have had such widespread success. It is also doubtful if the "second-generation" litigation (defining appropriate education) would have had any useful precedents or if state and federal legislation would have been enacted, much less mirror the case law so closely.

Court decisions and orders are not self-executing. They demand compliance by the parties involved, but they cannot assure or guarantee it. Court orders in the right-to-education movement are effective only if the defendants (school authorities) are willing or able to carry them out. When, as sometimes happens, the defendants are neither willing nor able, the plaintiffs are compelled to return to court and seek additional relief. The alternative types of relief they usually seek are described in the sections that follow.

PRE-IDEA COMPLIANCE TECHNIQUES

These sections describe only the compliance cases that were decided before the IDEA was enacted. They illustrate various techniques for compliance. The cases that have been decided after the IDEA was enacted are described in the latter part of this chapter.

Contempt Citations

In *Mills*, the court required the defendants to provide disabled children with an appropriate or suitable education. Three years later, their "victory" having proven shallow because the defendants were unwilling or unable to comply, the plaintiffs filed a motion to enforce the court's earlier order. The court granted the motion and found the superintendent, the board of education, and the director of the department of human resources to be in contempt of court for failing to make appropriate placements and to notify the court of problems that prevented them from complying with the court's order. The court chose not to impose any penalities because funds had been made available to appropriately place some of the disabled children.

A similar contempt citation was issued in *Rainey v. Tennessee*. In 1974, a consent decree was entered obligating the defendants to provide appropriate programs for disabled children. Two years later, the plaintiffs petitioned the court for a contempt citation, alleging that the defendants had not complied with the consent decree and were in continuing violation of the state's 1972 Mandatory Education Law for Disabled Children and Youth. Two years after the plaintiffs filed the petition, the court found the defendants to be in violation of the consent decree and issued a contempt order, rejecting the defense that they should not be held in contempt because they did not have sufficient funds to comply with the order. The defendants were ordered to submit an implementation plan by March 1977 and to put the plan into effect by July 1977.

The New York City School Board was held in contempt in *ASPIRA of New York, Inc. v. Board* for failing steadily and repeatedly to exercise its power and authority to make the board's employees proceed promptly and in good faith to accomplish the tasks commanded by a consent decree (to provide a broad program of bilingual education in New York City schools). The court found that there had been clear and convincing proof that the board, though not willfully flaunting the consent decree, had not been reasonably diligent and energetic in attempting to accomplish what the decree had ordered.

The board had failed to marshal its own resources, assert its "high" authority, and demand the results needed from subordinate agencies in order to accomplish the terms of the decree. It had allowed deadlines to pass without volunteering explanations and had tolerated long periods of nonperformance, inadequate performance, and outright defiance from community school boards. Furthermore, it had tolerated slipshod procedures, failed to enlist or order the placement of needed and available personnel, and had displayed a sense of nonurgency that bordered on indifference.

Court-Appointed Masters

Although a contempt order is an indication of the failure or unwillingness (or both) of the defendants to comply with court orders, its initial effect in both *Mills* and *Rainey* was to hold the individual defendants and the school systems potentially liable to the court through imposition of a fine. It is not intended to assure that the court's orders will be carried out— it only holds out the threat of punishment to those who fail to carry them out. Thus, it is of limited value for accomplishing the education of disabled children.

In both *Mills* and *Rainey*, however, the contempt order was accompanied by orders that the defendants must report to the court on the identification of other children needing services and how the defendants will provide those services, and file with the court a plan for implementing its orders. Like the original orders, the ones accompanying the contempt order in *Mills* required the defendants to make extensive changes in the way they provided special education services. And, as perhaps could have been predicted from the defendants' reaction to the 1972 orders, the defendants once again failed to adequately comply. Thus, a scant two months after finding the defendants in contempt, the court appointed a special master to oversee implementation of its order that the defendants furnish a suitable education to disabled children. A *master* is an agent of the court, appointed to accomplish certain court-assigned tasks to ensure that the defendants carry out the court's orders.

In *Mills*, the court assigned the master extensive duties: (1) to investigate and evaluate the appropriateness of special education programs in the public schools, institutions operated by the D.C. department of human resources, and alternative educational services furnished outside the school system; (2) to review the defendants' child-census and tuition-subsidy programs to determine if they were adequate; (3) to report on the status of procedures and programs formulated to carry out the court's order by the school board, the department of human resources, and the D.C. government; (4) to review the defendants' procedures for estimating the budgets, justifying special education needs, identifying budgetary shortages, and obtaining supplemental funding to make up deficits; (5) to help the defendants prepare a plan to implement the court's orders; and (6) to file periodic interim reports, file a final report with the court, and make recommendations to the court. The court did not grant the master power to give directions or orders to the school board or to supervise its operations. It did, however, order the board to pay the master for his services.

Other Judicial Remedies

There are judicial remedies other than contempt citations and masters. Indeed, courts have extensive power to enforce their decrees. For example, they may order a defendant school to regularly file with the court its plans for implementing a court decree or state statute.[1] They may retain jurisdiction over a case in order to monitor the school's implementation of the court's order,[2] and set dates by which certain of the orders must be carried out.[3]

Financial Reallocation and Withholding of Funds

One of the earliest defenses in right-to-education suits, which has fared least well in the courts, is the defendants' contention that they do not have sufficient funds to provide an appropriate education to all disabled children. In *Mills*, the court made short shrift of this argument, stating (in now well-known dicta) that absence of funds is no defense of a failure to provide constitutional rights (equal educational opportunities) to disabled students and that the burden of inadequate funds may not fall more heavily on disabled pupils than on nondisabled ones. In *MARC*, the Maryland Circuit Court also gave little heed to the defense claims of financial difficulty when it ordered the defendants to take appropriate action to request additional funds from the state legislature.

It is one thing to say that defendants must be equitable in the use of funds or that they should request more from their funding sources. It is altogether another to step into the budget process. Throughout the right-to-education cases, the courts have been extremely reluctant to interfere in any way with the financing of public education.[4]

The *Mills* court hesitated to appoint a master because it recognized that compensation to the master would drain off funds that would otherwise be available to educate disabled children. When it finally did appoint a master, it ordered only that he review the school board's budget process. Further evidence of judicial reluctance to interfere with the traditional legislative function of taxation and appropriation is shown in *Rainey*, where, in response to the defendants' claim that they could not comply with the consent decree because they had insufficient funds, the court ordered them to submit an implementation plan by March 1977 and to put it into effect by July. Voicing a threat it had the power to enforce, the court said, "From and after that date, the defendants shall be enjoined from expending money for the operation of a public school system in this state unless the plan to be submitted is incorporated into the operation of the department of education and fully pursued to implement the consent decree." The appeals court reversed the trial court's enjoining the state from spending any money for the education of any children in the state if children with disabilities were not receiving special education by July 1, 1977. The court of appeals held that the trial court's remedy was excessive and would cause more damage than it would yield benefits.

Federal Abstention, Mootness, Dormancy, and Voluntary Dismissals

Not every case reaches the stage at which judicial remedies become necessary. Indeed, there are several avenues "out" of litigation and enforcement of court orders. One way out is through use of the doctrine of *federal abstention*. When a right-to-education suit is filed in a federal court (on the grounds that the defendants are violating the equal protection and due process guarantees of the Fifth and Fourteenth Amendments), this doctrine permits the court to rule that the case, although involving federal claims, should be tried first in state courts because it also involves state issues that may dispose of the case and make it unnecessary for the federal constitutional issues to be tried. It is not uncommon for federal courts to dodge right-to-education cases on this ground[5] and to remit the plaintiffs to state courts. Defendants favor the abstention doctrine because it enables them to try their cases in forums traditionally less hostile to school systems and less inclined to find constitutional violations.

The federal trial court's power to abstain is discretionary. It may choose to abstain or not, and if its order of abstention or nonabstention is appealed, the appellate court will inquire only whether the trial court abused its discretion. In *Frederick L. v. Thomas*, the plaintiffs alleged that the Philadelphia school district did not provide learning disabled students with a minimally appropriate education, did not test all students in order to identify those with learning disabilities, and instead placed primary reliance on teacher referrals to school psychologists. The trial court held that the referral method was inadequate for identifying learning disabled students and ordered the district to submit a plan for identifying all learning disabled students in the district.

Responding to the defendants' claim that the trial court should have abstained because the case raised a constitutional claim of functional exclusion (see chapters 3 and 5) and an accompanying claim based on state law—which the defendants argued was ambiguous and should have been resolved by a state court before the federal court ruled on it—the appellate court found that the trial court had not abused its discretion and was not required to abstain. It said that: (1) the state statutes were not wholly ambiguous, (2) the defendant's abstention motion was not filed until more than a year after the plaintiffs had filed their complaint, and (3) ordering abstention now would mean that many members of the plaintiff's "class" (the case was a class action suit) would go through school without obtaining the education they claim they are entitled to under state law and the federal constitution.

If a federal court does not wiggle out on abstention grounds, it sometimes may avoid the issues on the ground of *mootness*. State courts, too, may defer or escape trying a case on that ground. Typically, a case is moot (and thus need not be tried) if state legislation or state agency regulations provide a sufficient answer to the claims that the plaintiffs have raised in their lawsuit. For example, a classic right-to-education case was brought in Michigan in a federal district court in 1972. After the case was filed, the state legislature enacted a right-to-education law, and, after that law was enacted, the defendant school officials successfully persuaded the court to dismiss the case because it was moot. The legislation ostensibly satisfied the plaintiffs' requests for relief.[6]

Some cases do not become moot. They simply become dormant or inactive. For example, in both North Carolina[7] and North Dakota,[8] federal right-to-education cases filed in 1972 were still awaiting a final disposition nearly a decade later, largely because the state legislatures enacted mandatory legislation and the plaintiffs and court were waiting to determine what effect, if any, the legislation would have on the plaintiffs' claims. In both cases, the legislation set a future date for full implementation. *Dormancy* gives plaintiffs the opportunity to resist any motion the defendants might make to dismiss the case, but it also gives the defendants temporary freedom from judicial intervention.

It is possible for plaintiffs to dismiss their cases voluntarily—on their own motion. Apparently the only case in which they have taken a *voluntary dismissal*, however, is the Colorado right-to-education suit.[9]

Access to Student Records in Class Action Suits

In *Mattie T. v. Holladay*, a class action suit that challenged classification practices, exclusion from mainstream programs, inadequacy of special education programs (functional exclusion), and absence of compliance with due process safeguards, the plaintiffs sought access to the records of individual members of the class bringing the suit. Although the plaintiffs stipulated that names and other information that would allow the students to be personally identified could be deleted, the defendant school districts declined to release the records, claiming that they were to be treated confidentially under provisions of the Family Educational Rights and Privacy Act of 1972[10] (see chapters 7 and 8).

The court granted the plaintiffs' request, holding that their request allowed personally identifying information to be deleted and that the plaintiffs did not have the burden of notifying the students or their parents that the records were being subpoenaed. The decision opens up wide avenues of discovery for plaintiffs in class action suits.

POST-IDEA COMPLIANCE TECHNIQUES IN COURT

As the pre-IDEA cases illustrate, it has never been easy to enforce court decisions in right-to-education cases. This is particularly evident in cases involving the racial desegregation of public schools, and it is now apparent in cases involving the education of disabled children. In an effort to enforce the IDEA, advocates for disabled children have resorted to an imaginative array of lawsuits.

Damages—Malpractice

Students have sought to hold school districts liable in monetary damages for failing to comply with the IDEA. These new *educational malpractice* cases until very recently had generally been unsuccessful. The majority of the courts have held that the IDEA does not authorize a suit for monetary damages.

In one of the earliest cases, *Loughran v. Flanders*, a plaintiff who claimed he was entitled to damages under the IDEA was held not entitled to damages. In another ruling in the case, he was not required to exhaust his state administrative remedies because the state procedures were designed only to handle challenges to evaluation or placement, or both, not a claim of whether there is a private remedy for damages implicit in the IDEA; there is no such remedy.

In the leading case, *Miener v. Missouri*,[11] a federal district court in Missouri dismissed that portion of the suit, filed by a seventeen-year-old resident of a state mental hospital, which sought *compensatory education* under the IDEA and Section 504 of the Rehabilitation Act. The court viewed the compensation as *damages*, which are barred by the Eleventh Amendment. The district court held that the patient could bring suit for injunctive relief under Section 504 and the IDEA, but not one for monetary relief. The context in which the claim was raised suggested that there was no difference ("Damages . . . are meant to compensate a party for a past violation of some duty"). Therefore, *Edelman v. Jordan* is controlling. In that case, the lower courts had awarded plaintiffs a retroactive award of monetary relief as equitable restitution, but the Supreme Court found that the Eleventh Amendment barred such an award, even though phrased in equitable terms.

On appeal of *Miener*, the Eighth Circuit Court of Appeals affirmed in part and reversed in part. The court held that the plaintiffs had a private cause of action under Section 504. Where administrative remedies were inadequate, a private action for damages was allowable for violations of Section 504 and may be instituted before administrative remedies are exhausted. The IDEA does *not* provide for damages, only for injunctive relief. The Eleventh Amendment, the appeals court ruled, does not preclude damages against a local education agency, only against the state. The IDEA does not abrogate the state's immunity under the Eleventh Amendment, nor does state participation in P.L. 94-142, and the Eleventh Amendment precludes an award of compensatory education.

The trend to deny damages for "educational malpractice" is evidenced in several recent cases. In *DeRosa v. The City of New York* and *Agostine v. School District of Philadelphia*, for example, the courts refused to award damages to students placed in special education programs where the students complained that they were improperly classified as disabled.

In summary, lower courts prohibit plaintiffs from recovering money damages for alleged violation of the IDEA for several reasons:

1. Congress has not expressly granted a right to sue for damages, so courts are reluctant to imply one. The exclusive remedy is due process hearings; damages are therefore not allowed.
2. To imply a right to sue for damages would involve the courts in the thicket of deciding what constitutes "good" or "bad" educational practice. Such a determination is necessary if a court is to find that malpractice exists.
3. If courts become involved in determining damages, they also will become involved in the daily governance of schools. Traditionally, the governance and curriculum of schools are matters courts have preferred to avoid.
4. Malpractice suits are apt to discourage implementation of the law by educators, who, because of the threat of litigation, will be more concerned about their liability than about the education of disabled children.
5. Malpractice suits will usurp the Act's present remedies (which are largely procedural, not substantive, in nature). Provision of an appropriate education is achieved by complying with certain procedural safeguards (nondiscriminatory evaluation, IEPs, LRE, and parent participation).
6. Moreover, courts are concerned whether the Eleventh Amendment to the federal Constitution (granting states immunity from suit unless they expressly consent to be sued) prohibits a child from suing the state. Their concern is that a state's participation in the IDEA does not amount to consent to be sued. Ordinarily, courts duck constitutional issues when they can.

For reasons set out in the following discussion, it is very likely that the U.S. Supreme Court will agree with the majority trend and disallow monetary damages in suits brought by disabled children against local or state education agencies. Its 1984 decision in *Smith v. Robinson* specifically side-stepped the damages question but contained language suggesting that the Court will rule consistent with the majority trend.

The major issue in *Smith* was whether a student who successfully sues a school district for violating his or her educational rights may recover attorneys' fees from the district. The

Court held that the student could not (as more fully explained later in this chapter under "Attorney Fees, Private Right of Action, and Exclusive Remedy").

In reaching that result, however, the Court was required to discuss the relationship of the IDEA to Section 504 of the Rehabilitation Act and Section 1983 of the Civil Rights Act. Under Section 504, a recipient of federal aid (including programs of public education) may not discriminate solely on the basis of a disability against any otherwise qualified person. Under Section 1983, anyone who, acting under "color of law" (i.e., in an official capacity, not a personal one), deprives another of federal constitutional or statutory rights may be held liable in monetary damages to the aggrieved person. Since both of these laws seek to prohibit discrimination and illegal conduct and both are civil rights protections, Congress also has permitted the plaintiffs (i.e., students who are disabled) to recover their attorneys' fees from the school officials or districts. Section 505 implements Section 504 and allows the recovery of attorneys' fees, and Section 1988 implements Section 1983 and allows the recovery of attorneys' fees.

The issue in *Smith* was whether a student may sue under the IDEA, Section 504, and Section 1983 where the alleged discrimination is prohibited under IDEA. That is, may the student use Section 504 and Section 1983 to enforce a right already granted by the IDEA and, if successful, recover attorneys' fees under Section 505 and Section 1988, although the IDEA does not allow attorneys' fees? The Court held that the student could not do that, since the IDEA provides the "exclusive remedy" and comprehensive scheme to correct violations of its provisions.

First, the Court observed that Congress intended the IDEA to be the exclusive remedy for asserting certain types of claims to educational discrimination based on disability. In addition, Congress intended children with constitutional claims to pursue them through the "carefully tailored administrative and judicial remedies" set out in the IDEA. Further, the IDEA is a "comprehensive scheme" to aid the states in complying with their constitutional obligations to educate children with disabilities. In light of Congress's intent and the nature of the IDEA, the Court concluded, it would be inconsistent with Congress's "carefully tailored . . . scheme" to allow a student to circumvent the IDEA's administrative remedies. Moreover, Congress itself perceived the IDEA as the "most effective vehicle" for protecting a student's constitutional rights. That was the reason that it made the IDEA the "exclusive avenue" for pursuing a claim.

It is easy to use this same reasoning—which resulted in the IDEA being the only method for redress and the disallowance of Sections 504 and 505, as well as Sections 1983 and 1988, as additional remedies in the attorneys' fee situation—to infer that the Court would follow the same approach in a damages case and hold that the IDEA is the sole remedy. And, since Congress did not specifically grant a remedy of monetary damages in the IDEA (but did in Section 1983 and arguably did in Section 504), no such remedy exists for a violation of the IDEA.

Another aspect of *Smith* seems to support that inference. In addressing the attorneys' fees issue, the Court resolved the conflict between the IDEA (which does not expressly allow recovery) and Sections 504 and 505 (which do) in favor of the IDEA. In addition, the

Court noted that if the IDEA is not available for redress of educational discrimination or Section 504 guarantees substantive rights that are greater than the IDEA's, then there is a different situation: The statutes do not grant equal rights, and the IDEA would not be the controlling one. That is, the IDEA will not prevent a party from recovering attorneys' fees under Section 504 because the IDEA simply does not apply. Again, the inference is that the IDEA will prevail when there is conflict between them. Since the IDEA does not grant a right to monetary damages but Section 504 arguably does, the result would be that a student cannot obtain such damages in an IDEA lawsuit and cannot use Section 504 (or Section 1983, for that matter) to bootstrap himself or herself into a position to obtain such damages.

To conclude, in *Smith* the Court expressly avoided the damages issue of the IDEA, Section 504, or Section 1983. But there is enough language and reasoning in *Smith* to support an inference that, when the Supreme Court must deal with that issue, it will rule that the IDEA is the exclusive remedy and that, because it does not expressly grant monetary damages, none are available.

Some courts, however, seem so upset with school districts' actions that they award compensatory education to plaintiffs, often using the compensatory education award as a substitute for a damages award. For example, in *White v. State of California*, the state court determined that it may not award monetary damages, as that would be against public policy (for the reasons stated earlier in this section of this chapter). But it did hold that the plaintiffs, who had been illegally excluded from special education in violation of the IDEA, are entitled to compensatory special education services to remedy any past denial of services for which they were eligible. The court reasoned that the award of compensatory education is preferable to the award of monetary damages because the IDEA entitles individuals to services, not money.

Other cases (clearly a minority) also allow whole or partial recovery of damages under the IDEA or Section 504. They include *Monahan v. Nebraska* and *Boxall v. Sequoia*.

A recent award of money was made in *Allen v. School Committee of Boston*, decided by a state court. There, the LEA had contracted with a private company for the busing of children to special education programs. When the private company's drivers went on strike, the students were unable to attend school for twelve days. The court awarded damages to the students for the time they missed, reasoning that the school district could have decided not to have a private company provide transportation and thereby could have retained control over transportation. In "abdicating" its responsibilities by entering into the private-company contract, the district is held liable for the company's drivers' action. Because the daily cost of educating each student was twenty dollars, the award of that daily amount times the number of days missed was a proper remedy under the theory of a *compensatory fine*. The difference between compensatory damages and a compensatory fine is not great in their effect; the students still obtain compensation. In theory, the difference is that the "damages" are for malpractice whereas the fine is for contempt of court. The court itself had previously held the school district in contempt (as explained earlier in this chapter) for failing to comply with its duties to educate children with disabilities.

The lesson of the damages cases seems to be this: An LEA will be free of damages if it does something for the children, however poorly it does that job, because an award of damages for malpractice is almost never granted, but not if it does nothing, for in that case, compensatory education rights will be granted.

Clearly, the trend of the cases is to deny monetary damages in actions brought under IDEA. The reason is that IDEA itself does not authorize damages (*Valerie J. v. Derry Cooperative School District*). But where there is a separate violation of Section 1983 (the Civil Rights Act) over and above the violation of IDEA, then courts may award monetary damages (*Valerie J. v. Derry Cooperative School District*).

Another case reiterated the general rule ("no damages under IDEA") when the court refused to award damages to a thirty-year-old woman who is blind and who sued the school district for failing to appropriately educate her and thus for causing her a loss of earning potential as an adult (*Hall v. Knott County Board of Education*). In this case, there were clearly at least two factors at work that prevented the plaintiff from recovering damages. One was the fact that IDEA and Section 504 do not explicitly permit damages to be awarded. The second was the fact that the statute of limitations began when the plaintiff was twenty-one and thus barred her lawsuit, filed nine years later.

Although it is not likely that the student or parents may recover damages when combining an IDEA claim with a Section 504 claim where both claims arise from and have identical facts (*Burke County Board of Education v. Denton*), there are situations where the student or parents will file an IDEA and a Section 504 claim and be entitled to injunctive relief (a court order to a school district to cease discriminating) or to damages for the Section 504 violation. The cases are *Begay v. Hodel* (denial of student's right of access to barrier-free schools denies the student's Section 504 rights), *Howell v. Waterford Public Schools* (denial of sufficient amount of physical therapy), *Sullivan v. Vallejo City Unified School District* (denial of use of a service dog), and *Reid v. Lincolnshire-Prairie View School District 103*. (Although IDEA does not allow parents to compel a school district to obey the order of an administrative hearing officer, they may sue the district under Section 1983 of the Civil Rights Act to require the district to obey the hearing officer's order and may obtain an injunction from a court to compel the district to obey that order.)

The courts that reach this result read the IDEA, as amended by the Handicapped Children's Protection Act (HCPA), to mean that a plaintiff may file both an IDEA and Section 504 lawsuit and get remedies under both statutes, since in enacting the HCPA Congress intended to permit the student to sue for attorneys' fees and also to proceed under all other federal laws, including Section 504.

Accordingly, a student or parent also may sue for a violation of the federal Constitution's equal protection or due process rights as declared by the Fourteenth Amendment (see chapters 3 and 7 for a discussion of the equal protection and due process rights, respectively). That lawsuit would be brought to enforce the Constitution and to recover damages or obtain an injunction in a claim filed under Section 1983 of the Civil Rights Act (*Begay*, *Howell*, and *Sullivan*).

When a student or parent prevails in a lawsuit filed under the IDEA, there is a right to recover attorneys' fees under HCPA. Likewise, when a student or parent prevails in a lawsuit filed under Section 504, there is a right to recover attorneys' fees under Section 505. Also, when a student or parent prevails in a lawsuit filed under Section 1983, there is a right to recover attorneys' fees under Section 1988 of the Civil Rights Act.

Thus, there is a real incentive for the student or parents to file a lawsuit with multiple claimed violations—under IDEA, Section 504, and Section 1983—and to recover not only attorneys' fees (under HCPA, Section 505, and Section 1988, respectively), but also damages under Section 504 and Section 1983. The fact of the matter is, however, that courts do not encourage these multiple-claims lawsuits and still attempt to limit the ability of students and parents to obtain damages under Section 504 and Section 1983 when the lawsuit is essentially an IDEA one.

The background to this result is important. Before 1985, plaintiffs in IDEA cases sued under the IDEA, Section 504, the federal Constitution (for equal protection and due process), and Section 1983. In their lawsuits, they sought damages (under Section 504 and Section 1983), an injunction (under both of those laws), attorneys' fees (under Section 505 and Section 1988), and their remedies under the IDEA, all in one lawsuit.

When the Supreme Court decided *Smith v. Robinson* and *Atascadero State Hospital v. Scanlon*, both in 1985 (discussed later in the chapter), it essentially made it impossible for the plaintiff to use both statutes—the IDEA and Section 504—for the same violation. By implication, it also barred plaintiffs from using Section 1983 as well.

In response to these rulings from the Supreme Court, however, Congress overturned *Smith* by the HCPA and *Atascadero* by an amendment to the Rehabilitation Act (P.L. 99-506).

Potentially, Congress's action meant that students or parents could obtain the relief available under the IDEA (for example, compensatory education, extended school year, tuition reimbursement, reevaluation, new IEPs, new placements, direct services from the state educational agency, and even the withholding of funds from a state or local school district) as well as the relief available under Section 504 (such as monetary damages and injunctive relief). It also meant that the plaintiff could get attorneys' fees under HCPA and Section 505 if successful in the lawsuit. Likewise, it meant that the plaintiff could sue under Section 1983 for a constitutional violation of equal protection or due process, seek damages, an injunction, and attorneys' fees under Section 1988.

Thus, every IDEA lawsuit could become a Section 504, Section 1983, and constitutional cause of action. That, however, would be undesirable because as a rule courts seek to avoid passing judgment on constitutional claims if they can instead decide a case on statutory grounds. It also would be undesirable because the IDEA generally sets out all of the student's federal educational rights. Section 504 essentially supplements the IDEA and provides similar but different rights and remedies.

Recognizing that it would be undesirable for plaintiffs to still file IDEA suits and combine them with Section 504, Section 1983, and constitutional claims, courts in IDEA cases have begun to limit plaintiffs from filing IDEA, Section 504, Section 983, and constitutional claims simultaneously. They have done this by using a previously obscure ruling of the Supreme Court, issued in the early 1980s. Here is the background to that clever use of the law.

In 1971, the Court held that a person whose constitutional right against unreasonable searches and seizures had been violated by federal law enforcement agents could recover monetary damages against the agents "if there are no special factors counseling hesitation (about the award of damages) in the absence of affirmative action by Congress" (*Bivens v. Six Unknown Narcotics Agents*). Eight years later, the Court restated the recovery-of-damages rule in a case where the plaintiff's rights to equal protection under the Fifth Amendment had been violated (*Passman v. Davis*). By that time, the rule had been made clear: the plaintiff can recover damages if there has been a violation of constitutional rights. Beginning in 1983, however, the Supreme Court began to limit the right to damages in constitutional-violation cases, using the "special circumstances" exception stated in *Bivens*.

In *Bush v. Lucas*, the Supreme Court ruled that a federal civil servant whose rights under the free-speech guarantee of the First Amendment had been violated could not recover damages, even though his administrative remedies (reinstatement in the job from which he had been dismissed) were inadequate and even though damages would be a more adequate remedy. The Court relied on the "special circumstances" exception in *Bivens* and said that the special circumstance there was the plaintiff's status as a civil servant. If the Court were to allow damages, the Court in effect would interfere with federal personnel policy, which it is reluctant to do because Congress, not the Court, is in a better position to determine federal personnel policy and whether there should be damages and administrative remedies or only administrative remedies.

The trend started by *Bush v. Lucas* continued, five years later, in *Schweicker v. Chilicky*. There, the plaintiff claimed that he had been illegally denied Social Security disability benefits because the Social Security Administration had illegally adopted quota systems that limit the number of disability awards without regard to an individual claimant's eligibility. In short, the plaintiff claimed a violation of due process under the Fifth Amendment. The Court declined to award damages to the plaintiff, again using the *Bivens* "special circumstances" exception, namely that the award of damages would substitute the Court's judgment about remedies for the Congress's judgment about remedies. The Court found that Congress's judgment not to award remedies had not been "inadvertent." That is, where Congress enacts a certain program (disability benefits under the Social Security Act) and that program carries its own remedies, then the Court will not create any new remedies.

This result is clearly consistent with the Court's approach to remedies under the disability cases, discussed later in the chapter. Congress, says the Court in its conservative reading of the law, must clearly express itself about a remedy or other right because the Court will not imply or create remedies or rights. Thus, under the *Bivens* line of cases and especially under the *Bush v. Lucas* and *Schweicker v. Chilicky* cases, a court must decline to award damages under Section 1983 or Section 504 unless Congress clearly expresses itself, in the IDEA and other statutes, that damages should be awarded.

This line of cases became relevant to the IDEA when Congress enacted the HCPA. In enacting that law, Congress made it clear that Section 1983 and Section 504 remedies were available for plaintiffs in IDEA cases. Thus, courts interpreting the HCPA have held that a plaintiff may sue under the IDEA, Section 504, and Section 1983 and seek appropriate relief under all three statutes.[12]

There is, however, a significant limitation to the plaintiffs' ability to recover under Section 1983 when suing under the IDEA. When the plaintiffs bring both an IDEA and Section 1983 lawsuit, the plaintiffs must show that the defendant's (school district's or state's) conduct constituted a constitutional violation beyond an IDEA violation. In other words, the plaintiffs must show not only that the defendants violated the IDEA but that they also violated Section 1983 over and beyond their IDEA violation. The cases are *Doe v. Maher, Edward B. v. Paul, Begay v. Hodel* (the expulsion case, see chapter 3), and *Doe v. Honig.*

In *Doe v. Maher*, the school district failed to redo the student's nondiscriminatory evaluation and IEP in an expulsion case, in violation of the stay-put rule. In *Edward B. v. Paul*, the defendant failed to furnish written transcripts of a due process hearing to the plaintiff, in violation of the IDEA's procedural safeguards. In both cases, however, the plaintiff was limited to the IDEA remedies for an IDEA violation and was not entitled to Section 1983 remedies, as there were no violations of the federal constitution or other federal laws (that is, other than the IDEA) over and above the IDEA violations.

In *Bagay v. Hodel*, however, the result, although not the legal doctrine, was different. There, the student was denied both her IDEA rights (the school district failed to notify her about her due process rights and later refused to convene a due process hearing at her request) and her Section 504 rights (to a barrier-free school). In addition, she experienced physical damage as a result of having to commute to an accessible school that was not in her school district. Thus, the student experienced two IDEA violations, a single Section 504 violation, and physical injury as a result of the Section 504 violation. Under these circumstances, she was entitled to bring a lawsuit based on IDEA, Section 504, and Section 1983.

A related question is whether the plaintiff in a Section 504 or Section 1983 lawsuit must prove that the defendant acted intentionally to deny rights under Section 504 or other federal law. In *Alexander v. Choate*, the Supreme Court held that a plaintiff in a Section 504 case need not prove intention to discriminate, only that the defendant's action had a disparate impact or effect on the plaintiff that is not the result of benign neglect but rather approaches or implies some amount of intent to discriminate. For example, benign neglect might occur where architectural barriers, which contravene Section 504, were not erected with the aim or intent of excluding people with disabilities. By contrast, intent to discriminate might occur where there are repeated denials of rights under Section 504 by the same defendant against the same plaintiff or people with disabilities who are in the same position as each other (that is, similar plaintiffs in different cases). Moreover, recovery under Section 1983 will not be possible if the defendant has engaged in "mere negligence" (*Daniels v. Williams*), such as mere lack of due care to the plaintiff.

So, some proof less than deliberate or intentional discrimination is required, but also some proof more than mere negligence or mere disparate impact is also required. Alternatively stated, the plaintiff need not prove intent to discriminate but must prove more than mere lack of due care (simple negligence) and more than disparate impact or effect.

This standard lacks real content, for the Supreme Court in the *Daniels* case did not define what is "more than mere negligence"—whether, for example, intent, recklessness, or gross negligence is required. And there are no subsequent cases filling in the definition.

In addition to these damage-granting approaches, there are other ways for courts to award damages, sometimes, but not always, against the school district. These are the new special education malpractice cases.

In *Tinkham v. Groveport Madison Local School District*, for example, a state court in Ohio held that a taxicab company is liable to a special education student who was sexually molested by a driver (the liability attaches under state tort law affecting common carriers). But the court did not impose liability on the school district because, under state law, it was exercising a discretionary function, not a mandatory one, when it contracted with the taxicab company to transport the student. The alternative to its entering into that contract would have been to provide transportation by its own personnel, as a regular school district function and in order to carry out federal and state special education law. By entering into the contract, it exercised discretion about transportation. The term "discretionary function" refers to a decision by a local government agency to adopt and carry out a policy that requires it to exercise certain judgment, discretion, and decision-making capacity (such as, whether to run its own transportation system or to contract with a private taxicab company to do so). If the school district, however, were exercising "mandatory function" and had no opportunity to make any kind of judgment but simply had to carry out law under a statutory mandate, then the district could be liable. Thus, the usual distinction between "discretionary" and "mandatory" functions made the school district immune from liability.

Just the opposite result was obtained in *Kansas State Bank & Trust Company v. Specialized Transportation Services, Inc.* There, the state supreme court held that a bus company and a local school district that contracted with it to transport special education students are both liable for the driver's sexual molestation of a student. Again, the issue was whether the school district exercised a "discretionary function" in contracting with the company. The court held that it did not because the district had a statutory duty to supervise the bus driver (imposed under state regulations governing common carriers such as the bus company) and especially to oversee whether the driver was carrying out his duties properly. (There had been several reports that he was sexually abusing the special education students whom he transported and these reports should have resulted in charges brought against him for child abuse and neglect or for failure to perform his duties properly.) Where a legal duty is imposed, there is no discretion. The district simply has no choice but to comply with the duty. By failing to comply with the legal duties to supervise and especially to follow up reports of abuse, the district subjected itself to liability.

The distinction between the Ohio and Kansas cases lies in the fact that the Ohio court found no legal duty and thus determined that there is a discretionary function, whereas the Kansas court found that there is a legal duty and thus no discretionary duty. The cases encourage students to sue and to attempt to prove that a school district has no discretion but instead must comply with a legal duty (mandatory function), with the district's failure being the cause of the injury and thus the ground for recovery by the student.

Another malpractice case recently was unfavorable to the school district's employees. Maryland's highest court has interpreted state law to mean that a school counselor has a legal duty to try to prevent a student's suicide when the counselor has notice of the student's suicidal intent. (*Eisel v. Board of Education of Montgomery County*). The decision, in a case of first impression in Maryland, rests on these bases: (1) first, there is a special relationship between the student and a counselor; (2) the special relationship consists of two components, a counselor's special duty to exercise care to protect a pupil from harm and the counselor's therapeutic relationship to the student; (3) general tort law imposes a duty to act to prevent harm when the harm is reasonably foreseeable and certain; (4) the state's education statutes impose an obligation on schools to prevent youth suicide; (5) there is a close connection between the counselor's conduct in not informing the student's parents or otherwise acting to prevent the suicide and the suicide itself; and (6) finally, the sum of these five factors results in liability against the counselor.

In the Maryland case, the student was not enrolled in special education, but for that reason the case is all the more important. This is so because some special education students may be more at risk than other students (whether in general or special education). Where there are special relationships between staff and a special education student (such as counselor or provider of health-related services such as some of the related services), a court may be all the more willing to use that special relationship, coupled with the usual fact that a special education student by definition is less competent than other students to protect him/herself against harm or is especially needy of supervision, to impose liability.

Still another type of malpractice issue arises if a school district fails to evaluate a student for a disability (specific learning disability). In *Bean v. Conway School District*, a high school graduate sued a school district, alleging that the district failed to evaluate her for special education eligibility while she was still in school and claiming that the district therefore owed her postsecondary remedial education (a form of compensatory education but not in the school district—the postsecondary education would be provided by an institution of higher education). The federal district court ruled against the student, reasoning that state law (New Hampshire) does not impose a common law duty on schools to evaluate and that IDEA does not provide the student with a remedy because she is no longer eligible for its benefits. In addition, she has not incurred any out-of-pocket expenses relating to her postsecondary education, compensatory education is not available because she has already graduated from school, her parents never requested an IEP while she was in school, and any of the district's procedural violations (under the process definition of appropriate education) had been minor (the harmless error exception).

Finally, a federal district court in Michigan has ruled that the parents of a special education student may recover monetary damages from a school district and its employees who disciplined a student and thereby caused his death (*Waechter v. School District No. 14-030*). The case turns on facts that distinguish it from a recent United States Supreme Court decision denying damages against a government agency whose behavior allegedly caused a child's death. To understand these cases, it is best to start with the United States Supreme Court decision.

In that case, *DeShaney v. Winnebago County Department of Social Services* [489 U.S. 189 (1989)], the Supreme Court ruled that a parent of a child cannot recover damages from a county department of social services for its failure to investigate and intervene in a family situation of abuse and neglect. (The child's parents were estranged and the one who sued did not have custody of the child, but the one who did have custody was the subject of the department's investigation.) The parent alleged that the department violated the child's substantive due process right—a right to not be denied life—when it failed to intervene and take the child away from the other parent. The Supreme Court acknowledged that the child had a right to substantive due process (life), but it ruled that the department was not liable for denying that right. It reasoned that the department did not have an affirmative duty under the due process clause to intervene in the family's situation. It also reasoned that, although the department did investigate, it did not violate the child's rights because, despite the investigation, it did not have custody of the child. If it had investigated, taken the child from the parent, and kept the child in its legal and actual custody (here, it took the child temporarily and then returned it to the abusing parent), then it would have denied the child's substantive due process right to life and would have been liable to the parents for that denial.

The factor of "custody" came into play in the recent case, *Waechter v. School District No. 14-030 of Cassopolis, Michigan*. There, a special education student died when he was required to do a "gut run" because he was speaking while "in line" waiting for recess to end. The student was thirteen years old, a fifth grader, and his special needs were well known to the school. They included a congenital heart defect that had required surgery twice and left him with symptoms of dizziness, fainting, chest pain, exhaustion, and rapid heart palpitations. He also had orthopedic disabilities (short leg, in a brace), with resulting poor balance and physical limitations, and learning disabilities (the result of childhood meningitis). His physician had advised the school that he should not engage in competitive contact sports or any forced exertion. Despite his condition and the school's knowledge of it and the physician's advice, the student's fifth-grade teacher, who also supervised recess, required him (and others) to engage in a "gut run" as punishment for speaking while in line. The "gut run" obliged a student to run a 350-yard sprint in less than two minutes. While taking his punishment, the student suffered cardiac arrhythmia and died.

The court held that the school district and the teacher are liable under the substantive due process provision of the Fourteenth Amendment (no state shall deprive a person of life without due process of law). This case, the court reasoned, was unlike *DeShaney* in two respects. First, here the district and its employee (teacher) acted deliberately; in *DeShaney*, the social services agency acted negligently. Second, here the district had custody over the student; in *DeShaney*, the social services agency did not.

The Michigan case sends a strong warning, especially if it is seen in light of the Maryland case (counselor has duty to prevent suicide) and the Kansas case (school district is liable for action of its contract transportation provider). These three cases signal courts' willingness to impose liability, not under IDEA, but under other legal principles, where school districts clearly and directly cause harm to their students. It is increasingly prudent, therefore, for districts to avoid all procedures that put students at any risk. These include corporal punishment, which is not prohibited under the Eighth Amendment (*Ingraham v. Wright*), the use of aversive interventions, and the use of unsupervised employees.

Granting Tuition

Courts generally will not award tuition if the parents unilaterally place a child in a private program. The reason for this rule is the provision of the IDEA that requires the provision of a "public" education, i.e., one at public expense and in public programs. Underlying this reason is the general understanding that public funds should not be spent for private education. There is an explicit exception in the IDEA for children who are placed in private schools by their LEAs or with the consent of their LEAs.

On the other hand, recovering tuition the child's parents have paid to a private school is a viable remedy when there is proof that the public schools have denied the child an appropriate education and there is no unilateral placement before exhaustion of administrative remedies or without notice to the school.

The U.S. Supreme Court ruled, in the 1985 case *School Committee of the Town of Burlington v. Department of Education of Massachusetts*, that courts may order school districts to reimburse tuition to parents who make a private school placement in order to obtain an appropriate education for their children. By making such a placement, parents do not waive their rights to seek reimbursement. In addition, courts must determine that the private school placement, not the placement of the proposed IEP, is appropriate. Without making that determination, courts may not order tuition reimbursement. The Supreme Court noted that tuition reimbursement is not an award of damages, since reimbursement merely requires the school district to pay belatedly what it should have paid all along.

The rule can adversely affect an LEA. Thus, in *Parks v. Parkovic* the court held that a disabled child and his parents were entitled to a preliminary injunction to prevent the state from refusing to pay tuition in a private school placement that the LEA and state agreed was appropriate. The injunction assures the child's continued placement and the provision of necessary services. The LEA and state may not agree to a placement and then refuse to fund it on the ground that the facility is not approved or the placement is inappropriate. Once they decide on the placement, they must fund it because the child is entitled to a free education.

Likewise, *Leo P. v. Board* charged the LEA with tuition at a private school. The LEA had agreed to private school placement for one academic year plus the summer after it. After the new academic year began, and while the child was still in private placement, the LEA refused payment on the basis that its own program was appropriate. The court held that the LEA must continue to pay tuition during due process and appeals. The LEA had failed to act timely to object to the private school (acting after the school year had begun).

If it is impossible for a court to determine, on the record before it, the effect of residential placement on learning disabled children and if it appears that IEPs for the children would not provide them an appropriate education, it is correct for the children to continue to be educated in a residential facility while new IEPs are developed.[13]

Some cases—apparently a minority—have reached an opposite result from the stay-put rule established by the cases noted above. They have created an exception to the stay-put rule for cases involving risk to the child's health or school district bad faith.[14] In addition, school districts may not unilaterally stop paying tuition. For example, once a court has determined that an LEA is responsible for paying for the costs of residential placement that it recommends, no subsequent change in the student's placement may be made solely on account of the cost of the placement. Changes may occur only upon recommendation of the pupil personnel team, made prior to the change.[15] Also, by illustration, *Grymes v. Madden* held that parents are entitled to tuition reimbursement (for private school placement made before they began due process) during pendency of due process appeal.[16]

By the same token, a parent who must spend funds to obtain related services that the school district agreed to provide in the child's IEP is entitled to recover the costs of the services when the school later refused to pay for them. The district's refusal to comply with its IEP agreement is the basis for the parent's recovery. Also, tuition reimbursement is a proper remedy where the schools illegally suspended a child and the parents incurred educational expenses during the period of suspension.[17]

There have been many recent cases on the award of tuition. The basic rule still is that private school placement unilaterally made by parents is not reimbursable by the schools. Thus, if a school offers an appropriate IEP and placement, it is not required to reimburse the parents who place the child in a private school (*Rouse v. Wilson*), and the parents' decision to make such a placement is at their own risk (*Evans v. District No. 17*).

Moreover, the parents' rights to reimbursement, if they are entitled to it at all, are not unlimited. Although the LEA must reimburse for tuition paid for a child with learning disabilities during the period that the LEA proposed the child be placed in a program for children with emotional disturbance (i.e., in an inappropriate program), once the school changes its recommendations and offers an LD placement, the parents' rights to reimbursement terminate (*Hudson v. Wilson*). The LEA does not have an unlimited obligation. Once it cures its default, it puts an end to its obligation of reimbursement.

Similarly, the parents' rights to reimbursement are available only if the parents notify the schools that they seek private placement (*Evans v. District No. 17, Garland Independent School District v. Wilks*, and *Quackenbush v. Johnson City School District*). The reason for this result is that compliance with the procedural safeguards of the IDEA is a prerequisite for achieving a free apppropriate public education. It is essentially unfair to require the schools to pay tuition if they do not comply but to allow parents to recover tuition costs when they do not comply.

It is perfectly clear that the LEA's procedural failures constitute denial of an appropriate education if the failures are so great that the student is functionally or actually excluded from an appropriate program, as seen in *Board of Education of County of Cabell v. Dienelt*. In that case, the LEA failed to conduct triennial reevaluations; did not notify the student's parents of their rights; failed to use an interdisciplinary team to evaluate the student; failed to conduct proper evaluations (that is, those tailored to the student's disabilities); drafted an IEP before the student had been evaluated; and failed to provide an appropriate curriculum. In that case and probably because of the egregious noncompliance by the LEA with the IDEA, the court awarded damages to the parents for their lost wages when they were seeking to have the LEA comply with the IDEA.

Finally, the LEA is not required to pay tuition for placement in an "unapproved" school. The IDEA itself provides that special education and related services are those that are provided by programs that meet the standards of the state education agency. If a school is not on the SEA's approved list, it cannot—because of the definition in the IDEA of a free appropriate public education—be considered appropriate. Thus, the parents may not recover tuition for the child enrolled in that school (*Schimmel v. Spillane*).

The cases that grant the parents the right to recover tuition for private school placement continue to make some points very clear. The *Burlington* case held that the plaintiff (parent) may recover tuition from the LEA or SEA for private school placement that the parent initiates if the plaintiff can show that the LEA placement was not an appropriate one (does not meet the *Rowley* standard for an appropriate education).

To claim tuition reimbursement, however, the plaintiff need not exhaust the administrative remedies under the IDEA before making the placement. To require the plaintiff to exhaust the remedies before making the placement would deny the student an appropriate education.

But parents who make a private school placement—whether before or after a due process hearing—do so at their peril. If a court determines that the parent-selected placement is not appropriate and that the LEA-offered placement and program are appropriate, the parents will not be entitled to tuition reimbursement.

Although the parents are not required to exhaust their administrative remedies before making the placement, they are required to notify the LEA that they intend to make a private school placement and to request tuition reimbursement. This notice gives the LEA an opportunity to cure any default in its program or placement, or both, for the student and to propose a new program, placement, or both.

Moreover, after making the placement, the parents must file a due process hearing or a lawsuit seeking reimbursement of the tuition, and they should do so annually (for each school year). Otherwise, they waive their right to tuition reimbursement for the present school year and for future ones, too.

Also, the parents may recover tuition only if the private program and placement are appropriate under the IDEA and the LEA program or placement are not. Thus, parents have to prove two facts—that the private program and placement are appropriate and that the LEA program and placement are not.

This is a high standard of proof and does not allow the courts to balance the relative appropriateness of the private and LEA programs or placements against each other. In other words, the courts may not say that the private program and placement are more appropriate than the LEA program and placement and award tuition reimbursement on that basis. The courts are required to deal straight up with the absolute standard—appropriate or not. A balancing of appropriateness is not permissible.

If, however, the parents are entitled to tuition reimbursement, they may recover the full tuition and other educational expenses. They are not limited to recovering only the tuition and other expenses that represent the relative appropriateness of the private school over the LEA placement or program. In short, there is no "comparative negligence" or "proportionate damage" approach.[18]

THE HANDICAPPED CHILDREN'S PROTECTION ACT: REVERSING SMITH V. ROBINSON

After the Court's decision in *Smith v. Robinson*, the advocates for students with disabilities and many members of Congress realized the need for legislation to overturn *Smith* and to make it clear that the IDEA permits the awarding of attorneys' fees to a prevailing party. They were motivated not only by the desire to seek clarity in the IDEA but also by a recognition that all of the IDEA's rights are meaningless without effective enforcement techniques. When a student's family cannot afford a lawyer to help enforce the IDEA, an effective enforcement technique is missing.

Accordingly, Senator Weicker (Connecticut), joined by Senator Harkin (Iowa) and other members of the Senate Subcommittee on the Disability Policy, introduced legislation to overturn *Smith*. Their bill was successful and eventually was enacted as the Handicapped Children's Protection Act of 1986, P.L. 99-372 (HCPA).

The HCPA provides that in any action or proceeding brought under the IDEA, a court may award reasonable attorneys' fees as part of the costs to the parents or guardian of a disabled child or youth who is the prevailing party. Fees are to be based on the rates prevailing in the party's community for the kind and quality of services rendered. No bonus or multiplier (e.g., three times the actual fee) is allowable.

There are some exceptions to the right to recover attorneys' fees. No fees may be awarded after the time the LEA makes a written offer of settlement to the parents or guardian if (a) the offer is timely (according to the Federal Rules of Civil Procedure or within ten days before an administrative procedure—due process hearing—begins), (b) the offer is not accepted within ten days after it is a made, and (c) the court or administrative-hearing officer finds that the relief finally obtained is not more favorable to the parents or guardian than the offer of settlement. Notwithstanding these exceptions, fees may be awarded if the parents or guardian prevail and if they are substantially justified in rejecting the settlement offer.

The court may reduce the fees if the parent or guardian unreasonably protracts the final resolution of the controversy, if the amount of the fees unreasonably exceeds the prevailing rate in the community, or if the time spent and legal services rendered were excessive in light of the nature of the action or proceeding. None of these reduction provisions applies if the court finds that the LEA itself unreasonably protracted final resolution of the controversy or if there was a violation of Section 615 of the IDEA. (Section 615 contains the procedural safeguards, particularly those relating to due process hearings. Thus, if an LEA effectively denies the parents or guardian an opportunity for due process hearings, it may not later complain if the court awards attorneys' fees that were incurred because there were no opportunities for due process hearings and the matter had to be taken directly to court.)

The HCPA applies retroactively to all actions or proceedings that were pending on July 4, 1984, the date of the decision in *Smith v. Robinson*. Naturally, several issues have arisen under the HCPA, and the courts have been involved in litigation over it. One question is whether the retroactivity provision is constitutional. Most courts hold that the HCPA is not unconstitutional. Congress has the power to make laws retroactive as long as it is absolutely clear about its intent to do so. Congress has the power to enforce the Fourteenth Amendment; the IDEA is enacted to enforce that amendment; and the HCPA is enacted to enforce the IDEA. Thus, retroactivity is constitutional.[19]

Similarly, the HCPA's retroactivity provision allows a Section 504 claim to be heard if it, too, was pending when HCPA was pending (*Board v. Diamond*). And if there also was pending a claim under Section 1983 of the Civil Rights Act, that claim can go forward and attorneys' fees can be awarded if the party prevails on that (and on a Section 504) claim (*Robinson v. Pinderhughes*).

The courts also have considered cases relating to the amount of the fees authorized by the HCPA. Some LEAs have argued that the fees should be proportional to the relief that the parents or guardian obtained—the less the relief, the less the fee. That argument has been rejected by *Rollison v. Biggs*, reasoning that the awarding of fees in a civil rights case is determined according to the public benefit created by the litigation.

May the fees be increased because of the SEA's or LEA's delay in complying with payment of the awarded fees? Yes, according to *Rollison v. Biggs* and *Moore v. D.C. Board of Education.*

May fees be awarded for work done in connection with a trial as well as in connection with the appeal? Yes, under *Board v. Diamond.*

May fees be awarded for work done solely in the due process hearing? Yes, under *USD No. 259 v. Newton, Burpee v. Manchester School District, Michael F. v. Cambridge School District,* and *School Board of the County of Prince William v. Malone,* but no, according to *Rollison v. Biggs.*

Often a case is concluded when the parties enter into a *consent decree* (as in *PARC*). Under a consent decree, the parties agree that a certain order shall be entered by a court, and the court agrees to enter such an order. Unlike the usual case, cases with a consent decree have been resolved largely by the parties themselves, with the court adopting (in whole or large part) their agreement. Typically, court orders are adversary—not agreed to by the parties. May fees be awarded for consent decree cases? Yes, under *Barbara R. v. Tirozzi.*

If a parent or guardian enters into a settlement agreement with an LEA or an SEA and the agreement does not provide for attorneys' fees, the fees may not be recovered under the HCPA (*Abu-Sahyun v. Palo Alto Unified School District*).

Finally, only attorneys, not "lay advocates," may be paid under the HCPA, which speaks only about attorneys' fees and not about any other kind of fees (*Arons v. New Jersey State Board of Education*).

Courts have been busy in interpreting the HCPA. In addition to the preceding cases, the courts have dealt more recently with the following matters and cases. The "prevailing party" rule (the parents in a due process hearing or judicial trial are entitled to attorneys' fees if they "prevail" against the school or state) means that the parents must succeed on any significant issue in litigation that achieved some of the benefit the party sought in bringing the hearing or lawsuit (*Texas State Teachers' Association v. Garland Independent School District* and

Kattan v. District of Columbia) or caused major legislative changes (*Holmes v. Sobol*). The key is whether the parents' action caused the defendant school or state to take some action to satisfy the parents' demand and that action altered the status quo (*Harris v. McCarty* and *Borgna v. Binghampton City School District*). Alternatively stated, the key is whether the parents achieved their paramount purpose in bringing the lawsuit and obtained a victory on a significant issue (*Joiner v. District of Columbia*) or even where the parents obtained a slight change in the defendant's behavior or the student's evaluation, program, placement, or provision of free appropriate public education (*Howey v. Tippecanoe School Corporation*). The parents may recover attorneys' fees even if they do not prevail in an administrative hearing if, later, they prevail in court (*Moore v. District of Columbia*).

The degree of the parents' success does not determine whether the parents are entitled to recover the attorneys' fees, but it does affect the size of the recovery. The most important factors in determining the size of the award are the time and labor of the attorney, the customary fee for similar services, the amount of money (or its equivalent) involved in the case, the results the attorney obtained, and the attorney's ability and experience. In addition to these criteria, a court may consider any special circumstances that make the award of counsel fees unjust, such as the school district being blameless if it simply follows state regulations that deny the student's rights under the statute. That is, the state regulations forbade the school district from holding a hearing, thus the district should not be required to pay attorneys' fees and the student and parent may seek them from the state but not from the local district (*Independent School District No. 623 v. Digre*).

Parents must be careful to claim the attorneys' fees and to put the state or school district on notice that they intend to claim them when they file their administrative hearing and law suit (*Rapid City School District No 51-4 v. Vahle*). They may recover the fees in a settlement agreement, even if the agreement is silent about fees, as long as they put the defendant on notice earlier that they would seek to recover the fees (*Barlow/Gresham Union High School District No. 2 v. Mitchell*).

Once parents and the school district reach a settlement, however, the parents may recover the attorneys' fees only for work performed before the settlement was reached (*Ramirez v. City of Manchester* and *Moore v. District of Columbia*). Clearly, parents may bring an independent law suit to recover fees that are due (*Ramirez* and *Moore*).

THE SUPREME COURT'S CONSERVATIVE APPROACH AND IDEA

The *Smith* case illustrates the Supreme Court's conservative or narrow approach in interpreting the IDEA. But *Smith* also is just one of many cases that illustrate the Court's "strict construction" approach to disability issues. It is important to understand not just *Smith* and its approach but also the more general doctrines that underlie that case and the Court's approach to the IDEA and other disability issues.

Although *Smith* was rendered in 1984, the Court previously had made it clear that it was not inclined to create new rights for people with disability. It had indicated, however, that it would enforce the rights that Congress created—if Congress would make it perfectly clear that it was creating new rights.

Pennhurst

The original case in the disability field was P*ennhurst State School (Pennhurst I) v. Halderman*, decided in 1981. In that case, the surface issue was whether the Developmental Disabilities Assistance and Bill of Rights Act (the "DD Act") created a right of residents of the Pennhurst state institution for people with mental retardation to live in the community. The DD Act provided:

> Congress makes the following findings respecting the rights of persons with developmental disabilities.
>
> (1) Persons with developmental disabilities have a right to appropriate treatment, services, and habilitation for such disabilities.
>
> (2) The treatment, services, and habilitation for a person with developmental disabilities should be designed to maximize the developmental potential of the person and should be provided in the setting that is least restrictive of the person's personal liberty.
>
> (3) The Federal Government and the States both have an obligation to assure that public funds are not provided to any institution . . . that—(A) does not provide treatment, services and habilitation which is appropriate to the needs of such person; or (B) does not meet the following minimum standards.

In *Pennhurst*, residents sued to be discharged and provided with community-based residences and services. They based their claims on alleged violations of a variety of federal and state laws: (1) the Eighth Amendment, prohibiting cruel and unusual punishment, and the Fourteenth Amendment, guaranteeing equal protection and due process; (2) Section 504 of the Rehabilitation Act, prohibiting discrimination solely on the basis of disability; (3) the DD Act, creating programs and stating that people with disabilities have rights to live in the least restrictive setting; and (4) state law.

The trial court found for the residents under the constitution, Section 504, and state law, but it did not rule on their rights under the DD Act. The court of appeals modified the trial court's order; it ruled that the DD Act had been violated, but it refused to consider the constitutional or the Section 504 claims. It also ruled that the state law had been violated.

The Supreme Court reversed the court of appeals, finding that the DD Act did not create any substantive right to residence in the least restrictive environment. The Supreme Court reasoned that the DD Act did not create such a right because Congress had not explicitly said that there is a right to community placement. Instead, Congress had declared only that there is a preference to such a placement, as a matter of federal policy.

The Supreme Court said:

> Turning to Congress' power to legislate pursuant to the spending power, our cases have long recognized that Congress may fix the terms on which it shall disburse federal

money to the States. [citations omitted] Unlike legislation enacted under § 5, however, legislation enacted pursuant to the spending power is much in the nature of a contract: in return for federal funds, the States agree to comply with federally imposed conditions. The legitimacy of Congress' power to legislate under the spending power thus rests on whether the State voluntarily and knowingly accepts the terms of the "contract." [citations omitted] There can, of course, be no knowing acceptance if a State is unaware of the conditions or is unable to ascertain what is expected of it. Accordingly, if Congress intends to impose a condition on the grant of federal moneys, it must do so unambiguously. [citations omitted] By insisting that Congress speak with a clear voice, we enable the States to exercise their choice knowingly, cognizant of the consequences of their participation.

Indeed, in those instances where Congress has intended the States to fund certain entitlements as a condition of receiving federal funds, it has proved capable of saying so explicitly. . . .

[T]he, specific language and the legislative history of § 6010 are ambiguous. We are persuaded that § 6010, when read in the context of other more specific provisions of the Act, does no more than express a Congressional preference for certain kinds of treatment. It is simply a general statement of "findings" and, as such, is too thin a reed to support the rights and obligations read into it by the court below. The closest one can come in giving § 6010 meaning is that it justifies and supports Congress' appropriation of money under the Act and guides the Secretary in his review of state applications for federal funds. [citations omitted] As this Court recognized [citations omitted], "Congress sometimes legislates by innuendo, making declarations of policy and indicating a preference while requiring measures that, though falling short of legislating its goals, serve as a nudge in the preferred directions." This is such a case.

On reconsideration of the case, the court of appeals held that state law created a right to community placement and rejected the state's argument that the Eleventh Amendment prohibited the federal court from enforcing a state-law claim against state officials. The court of appeals did not decide the other federal constitutional issues—namely, due process, equal protection, and cruel and unusual punishment.

The state again appealed the court of appeals judgment to the Supreme Court, which held in *Pennhurst II* that the Eleventh Amendment does, in fact, prohibit a person from suing a state official in federal court to enforce a right under state law. The importance of the Supreme Court's decision—prohibiting a person from requiring state officials to conform to state law by suing them in federal court—is twofold: (1) the decision reemphasized the Court's reluctance, first declared in *Pennhurst I*, to create rights unless the Congress and the states clearly agree that the rights exist; and (2) the decision created a precedent for other disability-rights cases, including *Dellmuth v. Muth*, decided in 1989.

Sovereign Immunity

The fundamental legal issue in *Pennhurst II* was whether a state, which may not be sued without its consent, agreed to be sued by participating in the DD Act. The Eleventh Amendment, as previously interpreted by the Court, effectively prevents a state from being sued without its consent. That result rests on the principle of *sovereign immunity*—the rule that the state (the sovereign) may not be sued (is immune) unless it consents to be sued. Thus, the issue was whether Pennsylvania could be sued in federal court simply because it took federal funds allocated to it under the DD Act.

To determine whether the state had waived its sovereign immunity and agreed to be liable to a suit, the Supreme Court began by stating the basic rule that a state's consent to be sued must be "unequivocally expressed." This rule is subject to another rule, however. The second rule is that Congress may override the state's sovereign immunity, which means that a state may be sued without its consent, if it does so by a law enacted to enforce the rights of citizens under the Fourteenth Amendment. But even this second rule is subject to the doctrine of "unequivocal expression."

Thus, the basic approach in interpreting the Eleventh and Fourteenth Amendments is to study the language that the state and Congress use. If the state is not unequivocally clear that it may be sued, or if the Congress is not equally clear that it overrides the Eleventh Amendment when it passes a law to enforce the Fourteenth Amendment, a state may defend against a suit by claiming the sovereign immunity defense. This is, after all, a basic tenet of the doctrine of federalism: A state's sovereign immunity extends not only to *whether* it may be sued, but also to *where* it may be sued (whether in federal court or not).

Given these precedents and the "unequivocal expression" rule of interpretation, the Court held in *Pennhurst II* that federal courts do not have jurisdiction to require that state officials and institutions comply with state law. The DD Act was not unequivocally clear that a state waives its sovereign immunity by taking federal funds under the DD Act. And no other act of the state indicated clearly and without any doubt that it had waived its immunity to be sued, much less to be sued in federal court.

Pennhurst I and *II* signaled a very important trend for the 1980s—the disinclination of the Supreme Court to be involved in cases that rest on constitutional issues and a very high reluctance to have federal courts, especially itself, involved in issues of state policy. After all, the fundamental issue underlying the legal issue of sovereign immunity and the approach to interpreting acts of Congress was the policy of deinstitutionalization. That policy—to close down the state institutions and create community-based placements for their residents—was a most controversial policy during the late 1970s and early 1980s. Indeed, it remains controversial even today. Advocates for and against deinstitutionalization were strong and numerous, and they all advanced various arguments for their cause. The matter was fundamentally one for state policy to resolve because the institutions were created and operated by the states, and much of the money to operate them was state money.

The way to keep the federal courts out of state policy issues was to limit the ability of plaintiffs (in *Pennhurst I* and *II*, its residents) who challenge state policy to use the federal courts to enforce claims that the state policy of institutionalization is illegal because it violates federal constitutional doctrines or federal statutes. The way to reach this result is to allow the state to defend against the lawsuit by claiming sovereign immunity from suit in federal court. And, ultimately, the way to reach the result that the state may defend on the ground of sovereign immunity is to interpret the DD Act in a strict, narrow way, requiring a clear and unequivocal expression of congressional intent that the state may be sued. If Congress wants the state to be sued so that the federal courts will have jurisdiction over challenges to state policies, state officials, and state expenditure decisions, Congress must be crystal clear about its intent.

Federalism

The Supreme Court's reluctance to have federal courts become involved in state policy and expenditure decisions, and its inclination to use the principle of federalism as a way of keeping the federal courts out of state policy matters, was demonstrated again in *Smith v. Robinson*. As pointed out earlier, the Court ruled that Congress intended the IDEA to be the exclusive remedy because it was a comprehensive scheme of enforcement for violations under the IDEA.

In *Smith*, one sees again the Court's reluctance to have federal courts dragged into the state policy-making and policy-enforcing arena. The fundamental issue in *Smith* was not the IDEA and rights to attorneys' fees. That was the legal issue, true. But the fundamental issue was again the federal courts' potential involvement in policy making. Thus, the challenge for the Court was to find a way out of deciding the issue of attorneys' fees and the allocation of federal and state IDEA dollars (since a finding that the plaintiff could recover attorneys' fees necessarily creates a claim on special education dollars to pay the fees).

If, in *Smith*, the Court could determine that there is no right to attorneys' fees, on the basis that the IDEA is not unequivocally clear that there is a right to them, it could avoid a decision about allocation of federal/state special education funds and the related policy problems of how much money shall be spent to educate children with disabilities and how it shall be spent.

As in *Pennhurst I* and *II*, so in *Smith*: The Court sought to avoid an issue of state policy by using the statutory interpretation doctrine of "unequivocal expression." More than that, however, resulted from *Pennhurst I* and *II* and from *Smith*. Not only did the Court avoid having the federal courts decide these issues about rights and rights enforcement, but it also clearly conveyed to the residents of Pennhurst and the students in special education—that is, to people with disabilities—that they must go to Congress and state legislatures to create rights and obtain the means to enforce rights. This is the result when the Court basically says that the federal courts will not deal with federal and state policy issues unless the Congress and states make it crystal clear that people with disabilities may sue in federal court to enforce rights that are intricately involved with controversial policy issues.

In effect, the Court says: If people with disabilities want new rights created or existing ones interpreted in their favor when the existing ones are subject to more than one interpretation, they may not look to the federal courts for help but must return to the legislatures for help. It is in the legislatures—in Congress and state legislatures—after all, that the original rights under the DD Act and the IDEA were created, and it is there, not in court, where the ambiguities must be resolved. Moreover, it is in Congress and the state legislatures that people with disabilities must resolve the fundamental policy issues—namely, how many rights do people with disabilities have, what are those rights, how and by whom will they be funded, and at whose disadvantage do those rights and their enforcement exist?

In the Court's view, as expressed in *Pennhurst I* and *II*, and in *Smith*, the policy issues should be resolved under the democratic majoritarian process—the process of open debate by those seeking rights and those affected by the creation of rights. Not only does majoritarian democracy require this result, but so too does the principle of federalism. After all, the Court is saying, the federal government, in the guise of the federal courts, should not require states to make certain policy decisions. To do so would be to have a federal government absolutely supreme over state governments. It would wipe out the opportunity and rights of states and their citizens to decide issues that are closer to them than to the federal government.

Antidiscrimination

The approach to statutory and constitutional interpretation that the Court followed in *Pennhurst I* and *II* and in *Smith* is consistent with the approach it used in other important civil rights cases involving hard issues of public policy.

Conrail and Grove City. In two cases decided in 1984, *Conrail v. Darrone* and *Grove City College v. Bell*, the Court again faced difficult policy issues. In *Conrail*, the question involved the extent to which the antidiscrimination provision of the Rehabilitation Act could be applied to a public agency—namely, the Consolidated Railroad system—and in *Grove City*, the extent to which the antidiscrimination provisions of the Civil Rights Act, prohibiting discrimination based on gender, could be applied to a private college that received some federal funds.

In both cases, then, the basic issue was essentially a policy issue—namely, the extent of federal antidiscrimination statutes. Alternatively stated, the issue was the extent to which quasi-public entities such as Conrail or fundamentally private agencies such as Grove City College could be required to accommodate people in minority status (disabled or female), sometimes at the expense of other people and, in the case of Grove City College, in violation of its organizing principles and underlying values.

In *Conrail v. Darrone*, the first issue was whether the antidiscrimination provision of the Rehabilitation Act—Section 504—authorized a disabled person (and, after his death, his estate) to sue the railroad for discrimination on the basis of disability. The second issue was, if a suit is permitted by Section 504, whether the suit is restricted only to discrimination related to employment. The Court held that Section 504 authorizes the lawsuit and that any lawsuit under Section 504 may extend beyond discrimination in employment. Thus, Section 504 allows a plaintiff to sue for discrimination in employment and in any activities other than employment.

The Court gave four reasons for this result. First, the language of Section 504 contains no limitation of suits to employment discrimination only. Second, the legislative purpose clearly was to allow suits for employment discrimination, as this was. Third, the Court defers to executive agency interpretations. Finally, the statute is a broadly remedial one that permits the use of Section 504 to enforce discrimination in "all programs receiving federal financial assistance." Note the Court's careful attention to the statutory language, the clearly expressed congressional intent, and then to other criteria for deciding the scope of Section 504.

In *Grove City*, however, the result was different. There the Court had to construe the meaning of Title IX (sex discrimination) as applied to a college that receives no federal financial assistance other than student loan funds. The narrow issue was whether the college is a program or activity that receives federal financial assistance. The Court held that the college is a recipient and based this result on the language of the statute, the broad remedial scope of Title IX, congressional intent, and agency interpretation (all the same considerations as in *Conrail*).

But that result—that the college is a recipient—did not dispose of the issue of whether Title IX applied to all of the college's activities or just to those of the financial aid office that administered the student loan funds. The issue then was whether the "program or activity" subject to Title IX is the entire college or just part of it.

The Court held that Title IX is "program-specific," applicable only to the student aid office. Again, the basis of the decision is the language and the congressional intent (the same factors as in *Conrail*'s decision). The federal financial assistance was earmarked for the college's financial program. It was not a general underwriting of anything except the college's ability to award financial aid.

By holding that the "program or activity" language of the statute does not subject the college to "institutionwide coverage," the Court avoided the underlying issue: Does Title IX apply to all aspects of private education when only one aspect is federally aided? Alternatively stated, will the Court, or Congress, decide on the scope of antidiscrimination laws, and if the Court is not the body of government to do that, how may it avoid that task and remit the parties to the majoritarian processs? The answer is that the Court may construe the language of a statute in such a way as to avoid or limit its involvement in policy issues raised by an interpretation of the statute.

Atascadero. The trend of the cases, *Pennhurst I* (DD Act), *Pennhurst II* (Eleventh Amendment), *Conrail* (Sec. 504), and *Grove City* (Title IX), was against results that would involve the courts in the political thickets in policy making. This trend was restated in *Atascadero State Hospital v. Scanlon*, a 1985 decision.

There the issue was whether a disabled person may sue a state for enforcement of Section 504 rights, filing the action in federal courts, or whether the Eleventh Amendment bars such an action. The general rule is that the Eleventh Amendment bars a suit against a state. As noted earlier, however, there are two exceptions: A state may consent to suit, or the Congress may abrogate the Eleventh Amendment when it enacts legislation to enforce the Fourteenth Amendment. The Court said: "But because the Eleventh Amendment implicates fundamental constitutional balance between the federal government and the States, this Court consistently has held that these exceptions apply only when certain specific conditions are met."

These are the "unequivocal expression" or "overwhelming implication" rules. The Court found that the state constitution does not waive the state's right to not be sued in federal court, and the Rehabilitation Act does not clearly enough subject the state to suits in federal court. To quote the Court: "A general authorization for suit in federal court is not the kind of unequivocal statutory language sufficient to abrogate the Eleventh Amendment. When Congress chooses to subject the States to federal jurisdiction, it must do so specifically."

Here again, the Court gives a strict or narrow reading to the statute—one that is defensible, but one that enables it to avoid the basic policy issue, which is whether the individual may sue a state in federal court to enforce a claimed right against discrimination based on disability. And here again the Court remits the parties to the majoritarian process. It sends them back to Congress to determine whether it, not the Court, wants to take the position that receipt of federal funds subjects the state to suit in federal court.

DOT v. PVA. When the Court again had the opportunity to duck the policy issues of the scope of antidiscrimination legislation, it did so again, in the 1986 decision *United States Department of Transportation v. Paralyzed Veterans of America (DOT v. PVA)*. There, as in *Grove City*, the issue was the meaning of "program or activity." Although *DOT v. PVA* was a Section 504 case and *Grove City* was a Title IX case, there was no difference in the result, the Court holding in *DOT v. PVA* that the federal aid to airports does not entitle a plaintiff who has been discriminated against—not by the airports but by air-carriers—to use Section 504 to sue the carriers. Again, the Court's approach is language-based (the carriers are not "recipients") and intent-based (Congress intended to cover only recipients, not all who benefit, however indirectly, from federal financial assistance). But the Court also was concerned about opening floodgates of litigation. It announced the new criterion of the "contractual-manageability" ground (the states must be free to decide whether to take aid in exchange for their commitment not to discriminate, and the power of the courts to enforce that contract of money for pledge to not discriminate must be kept within "manageable bounds").

Summary of Policy Issues. As was to be expected, the Court's decisions in *Smith v. Robinson, Conrail, Grove City, Atascadero*, and *DOT v. PVA* did result in a revisiting of the policy issue, but in a different forum. The parties' surrogates—females (*Grove City*) and people with disabilities (*Smith, Conrail*, and *Atascadero*)—did seek remedies in Congress, and they succeeded. The HCPA, P.L. 99-372, reversed *Smith* and granted a right to attorneys' fees to a prevailing party in IDEA actions or proceedings. P.L. 99-506 reversed *Atascadero* and provided for Section 504 to be enforced against state defendants and states themselves in federal courts. And P.L. 100-259, the Civil Rights Restoration Act, made it clear that "program or activity" means *all* the operations of a recipient, both for Title IX and Section 504 purposes. And P.L. 99-435 reversed *DOT v. PVA*.

Dellmuth v. Muth. The Supreme Court confronted the issue of the "strict" or "conservative" reading of the IDEA and the Eleventh Amendment in its 1988–89 term. It had before it the case *Dellmuth v. Muth*, which raised two issues.

The first was whether parents who challenge a special education placement may sue the states for the cost of private education. This is a question to which the lower courts had answered both "yes" and "no." The Court's decision, "no," resolved the issue.

The second issue was whether the Eleventh Amendment bars the parents' lawsuits against the states. Alternatively stated, the issue was whether the IDEA sufficiently overrides the states' sovereign immunity (from suit without consent, as guaranteed by the Eleventh Amendment) in pursuance of Congress's power to enforce the Fourteenth Amendment. The Court held that the Eleventh Amendment does prohibit parents from suing states under the IDEA. It gave three reasons for this result:

1. There is no unmistakable and unambiguous expression of congressional intent to make the states subject to lawsuits.
2. The expression of such intent must be found in the text of the statute itself.
3. Congressional history may not be used to furnish evidence of such intent.

As disappointing as this result was for many people, it was not surprising, but the battle to overturn the *Dellmuth* decision continued.

The Supreme Court's 1989 decision in *Dellmuth v. Muth*, holding that a state cannot be sued under the IDEA and permitting parents and students to sue only the local educational agencies, was overturned in 1990 when Congress amended the Individuals with Disabilities Education Act (formerly the Education of the Handicapped Act). Under the 1990 amendment, it is clear that a student or parents may sue the state and the state educational agency as well as a local educational agency. Thus, the state's defense of sovereign immunity is no longer available. The 1990 amendments once again show that Congress is willing to confront the Court's conservatism, declare explicitly and unequivocally the rights of students with disabilities, and give the students the ability to enforce those rights in lawsuits against the states. The Court said, in effect, in *Dellmuth*, that, if people with disabilities want certain rights, they should seek them in Congress and require Congress to set out those rights in clear and unequivocal fashion. After *Dellmuth* was decided, that is exactly what advocates for the students did, with the result that the 1990 amendments overturned the *Dellmuth* decision and declared that the democratic majoritarian process was not only available to them but would support them against the Court's conservative approach.

The Americans with Disabilities Act (ADA) [Sec. 2(a)(7)] reverses another United States Supreme Court decision that had weakened the ability of individuals with disabilities to sue state or local governments. In *Cleburne Living Center, Inc. v. City of Cleburne* (discussed in chapter 3), the Court adopted the principle that courts may not give individuals with mental retardation any special protection from discrimination by state or local governments. The issue in the case was whether a city zoning ordinance discriminated against a group home for individuals with mental retardation and whether the courts must scrutinize the ordinance, to determine if it was discriminatory under the Fourteenth Amendment's equal protection clause, with more care than they would if the ordinance did not apply to those individuals. Alternatively stated, the issue was whether individuals with mental retardation (and, by inference, other disabilities) are entitled to be treated like persons of color and women, to whom the courts give special protection from discriminatory state and local government laws. The Court held that individuals with mental retardation were not entitled to special protection under the equal protection clause. The result of the *Cleburne* decision was to make it far more difficult for courts to strike down, on equal protection grounds, any state or local government laws that discriminate against individuals with disabilities. *Cleburne* adopted the proposition that a law will be upheld, even though it has a discriminatory impact, if there is any plausible reason for it. Unlike laws that discriminate against persons of color or women, laws that adversely affect individuals with disabilities do not require special justification and do not receive special scrutiny by the courts. Thus, *Cleburne* effectively prevented individuals with disabilities from using the equal protection clause when they attacked discriminatory laws.

The ADA has reversed this result by declaring [Sec. 2(a)(7)] that individuals with disabilities are a discrete and powerless minority. This congressional finding of fact makes it more likely now that individuals with disabilities will rely on the equal protection clause when suing to overturn discriminatory laws. In addition, the courts will be hard pressed to overturn a congressional finding of fact concerning individuals with disabilities and to ignore Congress's resulting mandate that they give special protection under the equal protection clause to individuals with disabilities and scrutinize very closely any state or local government laws that discriminate against them.

Another consequence of the ADA's overturning of Cleburne is that individuals with disabilities will now sue under federal statutes (such as ADA and IDEA) as well as under the equal protection clause. In order to win, they must prove two facts: (1) they suffered a violation of the statute and (2) they suffered still other damage or injury—over and above the damage under the statute. If they can prove a double injury, their remedies will be under the statute and under other federal law [Section 1983 (Civil Rights Act)]. In some cases, they will have different and cumulative remedies: the remedy under the statute (ADA gives certain remedies but does allow a court to award monetary damages) and under the equal protection clause and Civil Rights Act (which allow courts to award monetary damages). In sum, an individual with a disability now is in a much better position to enforce rights under IDEA and ADA than before. The statutory and constitutional remedies are available and the courts must very closely scrutinize the action of state and local governments (under the ADA's reversal of *Cleburne*).

Like the IDEA, the ADA [Sec. 502] makes it clear that a state is not immune from suit by an individual and cannot invoke a defense of "sovereign immunity." Under recent United States Supreme Court decisions, an individual may not sue a state for violating a federal statute unless the statute is explicit and crystal clear that the state is subject to a lawsuit. ADA satisfies the "explicitness" standard.

Also like the IDEA, the ADA [Sec. 505] makes it possible for an individual who prevails in a lawsuit under it to recover attorneys' fees incurred in the lawsuit.

The ADA, like the IDEA, lays down the general rule that individuals with disabilities must have administrative hearings ("exhaust their administrative remedies") before they may file a lawsuit in federal or state court.

Finally, the ADA [Sec. 513] encourages alternative means of resolving disputes, including settlement negotiations, conciliation, facilitation, mediation, fact-finding, mini-trial, and arbitration. Similarly, the IDEA encourages alternative dispute resolution in two respects: it permits the states to use them under Part B [Sec. 1415] and it even encourages their use under Part H [Sec. 1480]. In short, the IDEA and ADA adopt similar approaches to the principle of due process: the right to administrative hearings, with appeals to the courts; the right to sue under a statute (IDEA and ADA, respectively), as well as under the equal protection clause (with special protection to be given by the courts); and the right to recover attorneys' fees if successful in the lawsuit.

State and local educational agencies have sought to block federal enforcement of Section 504 and IDEA by many ways. In addition to claiming successfully that the state has sovereign immunity (*Dellmuth v. Muth*), they also have claimed that the U.S. Department of Education's Office of Civil Rights (OCR) has no power to investigate complaints that a local educational agency is violating Section 504 (Rehabilitation Act) by placing students in residential schools rather than more integrated schools. In *Freeman v. Cavazos*, the Eleventh Circuit Court of Appeals ruled that OCR may, indeed, investigate school districts and that the U.S. Department of Education may withhold federal funds from them if they violate Section 504.

NOTES

1. Frederick L. v. Thomas, and Panitch v. Wisconsin.
2. Panitch v. Wisconsin.
3. Frederick L. v. Thomas, and Panitch v. Wisconsin.
4. San Antonio v. Rodriguez may be explained partially on the basis that the Supreme Court was more worried about becoming embroiled in school financial issues and related matters of taxation for public services than in dealing with the difficult constitutional issues the case posed.
5. Reid v. Bd. of Ed. of City of N.Y., Rhode Island Society for Autistic Children, Inc. v. Rhode Island Bd. of Regents, Silva v. Bd. of Ed., and Tidewater Assn. for Autistic Children v. Tidewater Bd. of Ed.
6. Harrison v. Michigan, Florida ARC v. State Bd. of Ed., and Radley v. Missouri.
7. North Carolina ARC v. North Carolina.
8. North Dakota ARC v. Peterson.
9. Colorado ARC v. Colorado.
10. 20 U.S.C. Sec. 1232(g).
11. The other leading case is Anderson v. Thompson. Cases that concur with "no damages" include Flavin v. Connecticut State Bd., Stemple v. Bd. of Ed. of Prince George's County, Akers v. Bolton (holding that the Eleventh Amendment bars suit against the state and the IDEA does not authorize private damage remedy), Hessler v. State Bd. of Ed., Reineman v. Valley View Comm. School Dist., Jaworski v. Rhode Island Bd. of Regents (denying compensatory damages for violation of P.L. 94-142 but allowing nominal compensatory damages for violation of state procedural due process regulations), Dept. of Ed. v. Katherine Dorr, (Ruth Anne) M. v. Alvin I.S.D., Colin K. v. Schmidt, Foster v. D.C. Bd. of Ed., Hines v. Pitt County Bd. of Ed., Davis v. Maine Endwell Cent. School Dist., Newport-Mesa U.S.D. v. Hubert, Carter v. I.S.D., Dore T. v. Board of Education, Mark R. v. Bd., Calhoun v. Illinois State Bd., Stacey G. v. Pasadena I.S.D., Marvin H. v. Austin I.S.D., Scokin v. Texas, Sanders v. Marquette Public Schools, Christopher T. v. San Francisco U.S.D., Timms v.

Metro. School Dist., Christopher N. v. McDaniel, Max M. v. Thompson, and William S. v. Gill (damages only under Sec. 1983, not Sec. 504 or IDEA).

Ezratty v. Puerto Rico suggests that a state, simply by participating in the IDEA, does not thereby give its consent to be sued for monetary damages. Cases that also rely on the Eleventh Amendment approach—no consent to be sued for monetary damages simply by participating in the IDEA—include M.R. v. Milwaukee Public Schools, Miener v. Missouri, Stemple v. Bd. of Ed. of Prince George's County, Riley v. Ambach, Hark v. School Dist. of Philadelphia, and Anderson v. Thompson.

Powell v. Defoe held that parents are not entitled to damages under the IDEA for alleged negligent (mis)classification of the child; they are not entitled to damages under Section 504 for alleged misplacement in special education because there is no implied right of action under Section 504 when placement was made for bona fide educational reasons, in good faith, and not because of discrimination because of disability; and the Civil Rights Act (Sec. 1983) does not give parents basis for relief because the IDEA contains its own exclusive remedy.

A case that reached a similar result is D.S.W. v. Fairbanks North Star Borough School Dist., which held that students who claimed their school district had been negligent in classifying, placing, and teaching them may not sue the district under the IDEA for damages.

Other cases denying "malpractice" damages are Loughran v. Flanders, Smith v. Alameda County School Services Agency, Donohue v. Copiague Union Free School Dist., Doe v. Rockingham County School Bd., Christopher N. v. McDaniel, Brosnan v. Livonia Public Schools (negligent diagnosis of learning disability not actionable), and Lindsay v. Thomas (negligent diagnosis of learning disability not actionable under state law).

12. Jose P. v. Ambach, Marvin H. v. Austin, Manecke v. School Board, Quackenbush v. Johnson City School Board, Diane P. v. Alief I.S.D., Rose v. Nebraska, Fontenot v. Louisiana Board of Elementary and Secondary Education, Board of Education v. Diamond, Barbara R. v. Tirozzi, and Mrs. A. W. v. Tirozzi.

13. Colin K. v. Schmidt.

14. Bloomstrom v. Massachusetts Dept. of Ed. (entitlement to the portion of costs corresponding to the cost of an appropriate education); Walter v. Cronin (child's physical health and bad faith of LEA as exceptions to "stay-put" rule, per Anderson v. Thompson); New York City Bd. of Ed. v. Ambach (LEA delays); Doe v. Anrig and Lillian S. v. Ambach (both cases conclude that bad faith by school justifies court award of tuition reimbursement); Stacey G. v. Pasadena I.S.D. (unreasonable delay in evaluation, causing harm to child); William S. v. Gill (allowing tuition reimbursement in case where parents made unilateral private school placement when evidence indicated child's physical health would have been endangered by remaining in current placement). Anderson v. Thompson, Colin K. v. Schmidt, Jaworski v. Bd. of Regents, Foster v. D.C. Bd. of Ed., (Ruth Anne) M. v. Alvin I.S.D., Walter v. Cronin, Mountain View-Los Altos Union H.S. Dist. v. Sharron B.H., and Matthews v. Ambach. A case that explicitly rejects the "bad faith" doctrine is Sanders v. Marquette Public Schools.

15. Michael P. v. Maloney.

16. *Concur*: Stemple v. Bd. of Ed. of Prince George's County, Doe v. Anrig; Lillian S. v. Ambach; Abrahamson v. Hershman; VanderMalle v. Ambach, holding that LEA must continue to pay private placement costs pending new placement decision (triggered because state moved school from approved list of schools), where LEA made the initial placement.

17. Adams Cent. School Dist. v. Deist. *Concur*: Harris v. D.C. Bd. of Ed. and Dept. of Ed. v. Katherine Dorr.

18. Doe v. Smith, Gillette v. Fairland Board of Education, Matta v. Board of Education, Indian Hills Exempted Village Schools, Rapid City School District 51-4 v. Vahle, Brown v. Wilson County School Board, Kerr Center Parents Association v. Charles, Roland M. v. Concord School Committee, Norton School Committee v. Massachusetts Department of Education, and Hampton School District. v. Dobrowolski.

19. Rollison v. Biggs, Jackson v. Franklin County School Board, Board of Education of East Windsor Regional School District v. Diamond, Counsel v. Dow, Fontenot v. Louisiana Board of Elementary and Secondary Education, Yaris v. Special School District of St. Louis County, and Dodds v. Simpson.

For 1994 Update on Enforcement please see page 405.

10
Statutory Techniques

ENFORCEMENT

The donkey chasing a carrot while running from a possible beating with a stick is a familar image, and it is an appropriate one in the case of the IDEA because Congress seeks to achieve the education of disabled children through similar approaches. To enforce the six principles of the law—zero reject, nondiscriminatory evaluation, individualized appropriate education, placement in the least restrictive setting, protection of rights through due process, and parent participation in school decisions—Congress holds out the promise of federal funds to SEAs and LEAs while requiring certain behaviors under threat of withdrawal of federal funds.

On closer examination, however, the image is somewhat misleading, for it suggests that congressional altruism is tinged with more than a bit of cynicism. In fact, Congress legislates the establishment of effective special education programs and demands normal fiscal accountability for them. It is helpful to look at the IDEA in this light: Congress puts money where the problems are; it seeks ways to require that programs for disabled children be accountable to the Congress and to the intended beneficiaries of the IDEA; it imposes normal requirements of fiscal accountability to ensure that the federal funds are in fact used as they were intended to be used; and it empowers the appropriate federal officials and agencies to review, correct, and impose sanctions on noncomplying recipients.

PUTTING MONEY WHERE THE PROBLEMS ARE

In 1975, Congress found that there were more than eight million disabled children in the United States whose special education needs were not being fully met [Sec. 1400(b)(1) and (2)]. Having concluded that it is proper to see that all of those children have a free appropriate public education available to them [Sec. 1400(c)], it was logical for Congress to attempt to solve the national problem through already existing state and local governmental mechanisms. Through the use of those mechanisms—not by establishing separate and distinct federally operated programs of public education—Congress has traditionally sought to respond to educational needs.

Congress's initial step was to provide money for state and local school programs. The second step was to ensure that the public agencies would spend the money on the children for which it was intended. The third step was to ensure that the money would be shared between local and state agencies (that is, between the agencies most directly responsible for educating disabled children and the agencies with overall supervision and some direct responsibility). The techniques were: authorization of expenditures, appropriation of funds, and pass-through requirements. Before describing these principal techniques for putting federal funds where they are most needed, it is appropriate to recite some of the facts to which Congress was responding.

A Bit of History

In very general terms, financing for the education of disabled children is the stepchild of public school financing. Many disabled children were without programs because funds had not been appropriated. Others were fortunate enough to be admitted to programs (although some of their disabled peers were not), but these programs often were inadequately funded. The use of labels by special educators and others involved in serving disabled children put them into categories—a convenient practice for serving those children and receiving appropriations for them, but of no use to the disabled children who were not labeled and categorized. In many school districts, disabled children were not sought out through child census or child identification programs and therefore were excluded from school planning, programming, and appropriations.

Because of the lack of free public programs, parents frequently were forced into starting private school programs or buying into existing private programs. In either case, parents were required to make tuition payments that parents of nondisabled children did not have to make, and in some cases the programs were located far from the parents' homes or in residential institutions. Some states did decide to help defray the tuition for private schooling, but they often did not appropriate sufficient funds to meet the needs of all affected parents.

Unhappily, not all state institutions for disabled children provided them with an education. Centers for the mentally retarded and hospitals for the mentally ill were notoriously deficient in school programs, especially when compared to state schools for the deaf or blind. State governments were often organized in a way that prevented institutional school programs from being supervised by public school authorities. Departments of public instruction lacked jurisdiction over departments of social services or human resources, and they did not have the authority or the will to supervise other departments' education of disabled children.

Federal Funding Techniques

Authorization and Appropriation of Monies. Congress authorized the expenditure of federal funds for disabled children ages birth to twenty-one, inclusive. The authorized funds are allocated to the states through the SEAs and to local agencies through the LEAs and IEUs in each state. Each SEA must have its application for funds approved by the Office of Special Education and Rehabilitative Services. The LEAs and IEUs must have their applications approved by the SEAs [Secs. 1412, 1413, and 1414]. All authorizations for state and local appropriations are keyed to a formula. In the case of an LEA, the allocation is based on the number of disabled children in the state, aged three through twenty-one, who are receiving special education and related services, multiplied by 40% of the average per-pupil expenditure in the public elementary and secondary schools for the immediately preceding fiscal year. There is a special allocation for children from birth through age two, under Part H of the IDEA.

The *basis of the authorization* is the number of disabled children in all states. The *basis of the allocation* to each state is the number of disabled children in the state in proportion to the number in the United States. The *amount of the allocation* to each state is 40% of the average per-pupil expenditure for disabled children receiving special education and related services in all public elementary and secondary schools in the United States.

The following formula is used to compute the average per-pupil expenditure: The aggregate expenditures (without regard to source) for all LEAs in the United States (including the District of Columbia) are determined for the second fiscal year prior to the one for which the computation is being done. If satisfactory data for that year are not available, suitable data for the most recent preceding fiscal year may be used. That figure, along with any direct expenditures by the state for operation of the LEAs (without regard to their source), must be divided by the aggregate number of children in average daily attendance who were provided with free public education by the LEAs during that fiscal year [Sec. 300.701(c)]. The 12 and 2% ceilings, as well as the exclusions (disabled children funded under Section 121 of the Elementary and Secondary Education Act of 1965), apply—those children are not to be taken into consideration [Sec. 300.701(c)].

Pass-Through Requirements. Having devised a way to get money to the states, Congress had to make it trickle down to where the problems and the disabled children are—the LEAs. Congress accomplished this by requiring that the funds "pass through" the SEA to the LEAs. No more than 25% of the funds may be retained by the SEA. What is not retained by the SEA must be passed through to the LEAs. The SEA may, if it wants, pass through more than the statutory minimum [Secs. 1411(b)(1) and (c)(1) and 300.705 and .706].

To determine how much each LEA and IEU is entitled to receive from the SEA, Congress used a simple formula based on the proportionate population of each LEA and IEU to its SEA population. The funds are allocated in the same ratio to the total amount available for pass-through that the number of disabled children (aged three through twenty-one) receiving special education and related services in the LEA or IEU bears to the total number of disabled children in all LEAs and IEUs applying for funds [Secs. 1411(d) and 300.707]. If an SEA determines that an LEA is adequately providing a free appropriate education to all of the disabled children in its jurisdiction by using state and local funds otherwise available to it, the SEA may reallocate all or part of the funds the LEA would have received under the pass-through provisions. That allocation must be made to other LEAs that are not adequately providing such an education [Sec. 300.708].

"Average Expenditures"

The LEA and IEU entitlement depends on the number of disabled children in the state who receive special education and related services. This number is defined as the average number of children receiving those services on December 1 of the school year [Secs. 1411(a)(3) and 300.751]. LEA entitlement also depends on the average per-pupil expenditure in public elementary and secondary schools of the United States (defined previously under "Authorization and Appropriation of Monies").

Ceiling

Referring to Sections 1411(a)(5) and 300.702, the following children may not be counted in determining the LEA allotment:

- the number of disabled children in excess of the 12% limitation
- disabled children counted under Section 121 of the Elementary and Secondary Education Act (ESEA) of 1965 (called "Head Start disabled children")

Limitations on "Allowable" Administrative Costs

SEAs are limited in how they may use funds not passed through. They may not use more than 5% of the funds or $200,000, whichever is greater, for administrative costs related to Sections 1412 (state eligibility) and 1413 (state plans) [Secs. 1411(b)(2) and (c)(2) and 300.620 and .621]. The funds available to the SEA for administration may be spent only for the following "allowable costs" [Sec. 300.621]:

1. Administration of the annual program plan and for planning at the state level, including planning, or assisting in the planning of, programs or projects for the education of disabled children.
2. Approval, supervision, monitoring, and evaluation of the effectiveness of local programs and projects for the education of disabled children.
3. Technical assistance to local education agencies.
4. Leadership services for program supervision and management of special education activities for the disabled.
5. Other state leadership activities and consultative services.

The SEA must use the remainder of the funds (those not allocated to allowable costs of administration) to provide support and direct services for the benefit of disabled children in accordance with the service priorities [Sec. 1411(b) and (c)]. Section 300.370 defines support and direct services as follows:

1. "Direct services" provided to a disabled child directly by the State, by contract, or through other arrangements.
2. "Support services" include implementing the comprehensive system of personnel development, recruitment and training of hearing officers and surrogate parents, and public information activities relating to a free appropriate public education for disabled children.

In the fiscal years beginning in 1978, the amount SEAs spent from federal funds not passed through for support or direct services must be matched, "on a program basis," with state funds for the provision of support or direct services for the fiscal year involved. The matching funds may not be federal funds [Secs. 1411(c)(2)(B) and 300.371]. "Program basis" refers to the major programs such as personnel development and training hearing officers.

Disentitled LEAs

No LEA may receive funds under the following conditions: if it is entitled to less than seventy-five hundred dollars in any fiscal year; if it has not submitted an application that meets the requirements of Section 1414 (SEA applications); if it is unable or unwilling to establish programs of free appropriate education; if it is unwilling to consolidate with another LEA; or if it has one or more disabled children who can best be served by a state or regional center specially designed to meet their needs [Secs. 1411(c)(4) and 300.360]. If an LEA has no right to funds, the SEA must use the funds the LEA would otherwise receive to assure a free appropriate education to the disabled children in the LEA's jurisdiction [Sec. 300.360].

Funds for Territories and BIA

Congress also has provided for federal funds to Guam, American Samoa, the Virgin Islands, the trust territory of the Pacific Islands [Sec. 1411(e)], and the Bureau of Indian Affairs in the Department of the Interior [Sec. 1411(f)].

Ratable Reductions

If Congress does not appropriate enough funds for the states to receive what they are authorized to receive, there will be a ratable reduction in the amount each state receives [Sec. 1411(g)(1)]. By the same token, there will be a ratable reduction of funds available to LEAs [Secs. 1411(g)(2) and 300.703].

Research, Innovation, Training, and Dissemination Activities

Under Section 1424 of the Act, the secretary may make specific grants for the benefit of severely disabled children and youth. These are for research (to identify and meet the needs of disabled children), development or demonstration activities (new or improved methods, approaches, and techniques for the education and adjustment of disabled children), training (of personnel to work with them), and dissemination (of materials and information about their education).

Postsecondary Education Programs

Under Section 1424(a) of the Act, the secretary may make grants to or enter into contracts with SEAs, institutions of higher education, junior and community colleges, vocational and technical schools, and other nonprofit educational agencies for developing, operating, and disseminating programs in postsecondary, vocational, technical, continuing, and adult education.

In addition, the secretary may make grants to or enter into contracts with SEAs, LEAs, institutions of higher education, or other nonprofit agencies to strengthen and coordinate education, training, and related services for disabled youths. These contracts are for assistance in the transition from school to postsecondary education, vocational training, competitive employment, continuing education or adult services, and to stimulate programs for secondary special education.

Antidilution Provisions/Excess Costs

Recognizing that inclusion of disabled children would be necessary but insufficient to help them, Congress set out to make sure that federal funds would not be diluted—that it would get the biggest bang for its buck. It required LEAs and IEUs to assure the SEAs that federal funds would be spent only for "excess costs" related to child identification, confidentiality of records, and full-service goals (including personnel development, adherence to the service priorities, parent participation, and least restrictive placement). Congress also established a timetable for accomplishing the full-service goal and implementing that goal [Secs. 1414(a)(1) and 300.182–.186].

An LEA meets the excess-cost requirement if it spends a certain minimum amount of its *own* money on each disabled child. This does not include costs of capital outlay or debt expenditure. The purpose of the excess-cost requirement is to ensure that children served with federal funds have at least the same average amount spent on them (from sources other than federal funds) as on children in the school district as a whole.

The minimum amount that must be spent for educating disabled children is computed under a formula. Any costs that exceed the amount determined by the formula are excess costs (they exceed the minimum). Only if an LEA can prove that it has spent the minimum may it use IDEA funds to educate disabled children.

The minimum average amount is computed as follows: (1) The LEA adds all of its expenditures from the prior year, except capital outlay and debt service, for elementary or secondary students (depending on whether the minimum is being computed for elementary or secondary disabled children); (2) the following sums then are subtracted from that amount: (a) amounts spent from IDEA funds and Title I and Title VII of ESEA (1965) and (b) amounts from state and local funds spent for programs for disabled children, programs to meet the special educational needs of educationally deprived children, and programs of bilingual education; and (3) the resulting amount is divided by the average number of students enrolled in the LEA's elementary or secondary programs in the preceding year (depending on whether the minimum is being computed for an elementary or a secondary child). The following example of an elementary school computation comes from the comments on the regulation:

a. First, the local educational agency must determine its total amount of expenditures for elementary school students from all sources—local, State and Federal (including Part B)—in the preceding school year. Only capital outlay and debt service are excluded.

Example: A local educational agency spent the following amounts last year for elementary school students (including its handicapped elementary school students):

(1) From local tax funds	$	2,750,000
(2) From State funds		7,000,000
(3) From Federal funds		750,000
		10,500,000

Of this total, $500,000 was for capital outlay and debt service relating to the education of elementary school students. This must be subtracted from total expenditures:

	$10,500,000
	−500,000
Total expenditures for elementary school students (less capital outlay and debt service)	10,000,000

b. Next, the local education agency must subtract amounts spent for:

(1) Programs for handicapped children;

(2) Programs to meet the special educational needs of educationally deprived children; and

(3) Programs of bilingual education for children with limited English-speaking ability.

These are funds which the local educational agency actually spent, not funds received last year but carried over for the current school year.

Example: The local educational agency spent the following amounts for elementary school students last year:

(1) From funds under Title I of the Elementary and Secondary Education Act of 1965	$	300,000
(2) From a special State program for educationally deprived children		200,000
(3) From a grant under Part B		200,000
(4) From State funds for the education of handicapped children		500,000
(5) From a locally-funded program for handicapped children		250,000
(6) From a grant for a bilingual education program under Title VII of the Elementary and Secondary Education Act of 1965		150,000
Total		1,600,000

(A local educational agency would also include any other funds it spent from Federal, State, or local sources for the three basic purposes: handicapped children, educationally deprived children, and bilingual education for children with limited English-speaking ability.)

This amount is subtracted from the local educational agency's total expenditure for elementary school students computed above:

$$
\begin{array}{r}
\$10,000,000 \\
-1,600,000 \\
\hline
8,400,000
\end{array}
$$

c. The local educational agency next must divide by the average number of students enrolled in the elementary schools of the agency last year (including its handicapped students).

Example: Last year, an average of 7,000 students were enrolled in the agency's elementary schools. This must be divided into the amount computed under the above paragraph:

$$
\frac{\$8,400,000}{7,000 \text{ students}}
$$
$$
=\$1,200/\text{student}
$$

This figure is the minimum amount the local educational agency must spend (on the average) for the education of each of its handicapped students. Funds under Part B may be used only for costs over and above this minimum. In this example, if the local educational agency has 100 handicapped elementary school students, it must keep records adequate to show that it has spent at least $120,000 for the education of those students (100 students times $1,200/student), not including capital outlay and debt service.

This $120,000 may come from any funds except funds under Part B, subject to any legal requirements that govern the use of those other funds.

If the local educational agency has handicapped secondary school students, it must do the same computation for them. However, the amounts used in the computation would be those the local educational agency spent last year for the education of secondary school students, rather than for elementary school students. [Sec. 300.184]

The basic intent of the excess-cost provision is to ensure that SEAs and LEAs provide the same support for disabled children as for all other children and that IDEA funds are used to supplement the state and local commitment. The regulations stipulate that SEAs and LEAs may not use IDEA funds to pay *all* of the special education and related services given to a disabled child [Sec. 300.186]. The excess-cost requirement, however, does not prevent an LEA from using IDEA funds to pay for all of the costs directly attributable to the education of a disabled child in any of the age ranges three through five and eighteen through twenty-one if no local or state funds are available for nondisabled children in that age range. The LEA, however, must comply with the nonsupplanting and other requirements in providing the education and services.

In another step to prevent dilution, Congress required LEAs to give satisfactory assurances to the SEAs that federal funds received under the IDEA will be used to pay only the excess costs directly attributable to the education of disabled children, to supplement and increase the amount of state and local funds expended for the education of disabled children, and to provide services in program areas that are comparable to services provided to other disabled children in the LEA [Secs. 1414(a)(2) and 300.229–.231]. Congress also stipulated that LEAs required by state law to carry out a program for educating disabled children are entitled to receive pass-through payments for use in carrying out that program, but pass-through funds may not be used to reduce state and local expenditures for the program below the level of such expenditures in the preceding fiscal year. In effect, LEAs must maintain their effort in order to qualify for funds [Sec. 1414(f)].

Another antidilution provision prohibits SEAs from using federal funds to match other federal funds [Sec. 1414a]. In a sense, too, the requirement that private schooling be paid for by the LEA is an antidilution requirement.

Consolidated Applications

Some LEAs may not be eligible for funds because they do not generate seventy-five hundred dollars annually, because their application is not approvable, or because they are unable to establish and maintain programs of sufficient size and scope to effectively meet the educational needs of disabled children. To maintain control of these LEAs, Congress authorized SEAs to require consolidated LEA applications and to allocate funds to LEAs submitting a consolidated application [Secs. 1414(c) and 300.190-.192]. This provision clearly prevents LEAs from escaping the provisions of the Act.

SEA Direct Services

An SEA may provide direct services to disabled children, thus displacing an LEA's authority, if the LEA does not seek IDEA funds or submits an unapprovable application or if the SEA determines that the LEA is unable or unwilling to establish and maintain a free appropriate public education. If the LEA is unable or unwilling to be consolidated with another LEA in order to meet those requirements or has one or more disabled children who can best be served by a regional or state center, the SEA also can provide direct services [Secs. 1414(d) and 300.360]. In such instances, the SEA may use payments that would have gone to the LEA and may provide appropriate services at locations it considers appropriate (including regional or state centers), subject to the general requirements of the Act, including least restrictive placement. An LEA that is able but unwilling to comply with the Act would, of course, be subject to the sanctions of that Act. Moreover, it would be in violation of Section 504.

Through all of these measures, Congress has attempted to put its money where the problems are—in the local schools. It has authorized funds, provided for their allocation, required that they be shared by state and local agencies, mandated that they be spent for excess costs and not used in any manner that would dilute their intended effect, and closed the door to LEAs attempting to escape the requirements of the Act. Having done this much, Congress turned to the problem of making the recipients' programs effective and accountable.

EFFECTIVE SPECIAL EDUCATION

Congress's intent to provide a free appropriate public education to all disabled children [Secs. 1400(c) and 1401(18)] is accomplished through six techniques that are intended to enhance the effectiveness of SEA and LEA programs: (1) assistance and involvement in state and local programs; (2) state and local program conformity with other federal legislation affecting the disabled; (3) state and local program effectiveness; (4) state and local program accountability; (5) limitations on administrative costs to be charged against IDEA funds; and (6) sanctions. Although it is organizationally convenient to discuss each technique separately, they are inseparable as a means of accomplishing congressional intent.

Federal Assistance and Involvement in State and Local Programs

Recognizing that it was appropriate for the federal government to assist, assess, and assure the effectiveness of state and local agency programs for educating disabled children [Sec. 1400(c)], Congress, in Section 1402, first created the Bureau of Education for the Handicapped. (Now, BEH is the Office of Special Education Programs—OSEP). It was designated as the principal agency for administering and carrying out programs and projects to train teachers of the disabled and to conduct research in education and training [Sec. 1402].

To advance its role in IDEA programs, Congress required the secretary of education to assist states in implementing the IDEA by providing short-term training programs and institutes if necessary, disseminating information, and making sure that each state certified the number of children included in its child count [Sec. 1417(a)(1)]. The secretary was authorized to issue regulations for SEA financial reports [Sec. 1417(a)(2)], for implementation of the IDEA [Sec. 1417(b)], and to assure the confidentiality of information received from SEAs and LEAs [Sec. 1417(c)]. The secretary also may hire personnel to help execute the duties of that office [Sec. 1417(d)]. Congress provided for evaluation of SEA and LEA programs by requiring the secretary to measure and evaluate the impact of IDEA programs and the effectivensss of SEA efforts to furnish a free appropriate public education to disabled children [Sec. 1418(a)]. The secretary has the right to conduct studies, investigations, and evaluations to assure effective implementation of the IDEA [Sec. 1418(b)], and the duty to report certain data and results of evaluations to Congress [Sec. 1418(f)].

Congress empowered the secretary of education to authorize use of IDEA funds by SEAs and LEAs for acquiring equipment and constructing necessary facilities if he or she determines that a program for education of the disabled will be improved by the use of federal funds for those purposes [Sec. 1404]. In addition, the secretary may make grants to SEAs and LEAs to remove architectural barriers and alter existing buildings or equipment so that they may be used by disabled children [Sec. 1406].

Conformity with Other Federal Programs

Approaching implementation of the IDEA on several fronts, Congress required SEAs to make plans for the proper use of IDEA funds [Sec. 1413(a)(1)]. Programs and procedures assure that

SEAs, LEAs, and other political subdivisions (such as cities, counties, and special districts) use federal funds in a manner consistent with the goal of establishing a free appropriate education for disabled children [Sec. 1413(a)(2)].

In an effort to make the education of disabled people meaningful by providing them with job opportunities after they leave school, Congress ordered the secretary to make sure that each recipient of IDEA funds make "positive efforts" to employ and advance in employment qualified disabled individuals in programs assisted by those funds [Sec. 1405]. This requirement is consistent with other federal legislation prohibiting employment discrimination against otherwise qualified disabled individuals (Secs. 101, 501, 503, and 504, Rehabilitation Act Amendments).

Program Effectiveness

Although the regulations just described will contribute to the free appropriate education of disabled children, nothing can accomplish that goal better than making SEA and LEA programs effective. Unless those programs deliver effective special education services to disabled children, federal, state, and local funds will not have been wisely spent, the hopes of consumers and educators will be crushed, discriminatory practices illegally foisted upon the disabled will not be fully redressed, and the notion that disabled children are not worth the investment of substantial amounts of time, money, and energy will not be dispelled.

To ensure program effectiveness, Congress first required special education programs to be appropriate to the child and individualized, for full benefit. Second, it required public school personnel to become more competent in educating and training disabled children through personnel development programs [Secs. 1413(a)(3), 1414(a)(C)(i), and 300.380–.387]. Third, it limited the number of children who may be counted as disabled for IDEA purposes (the "exclusion" and "ceiling"). Fourth, it extended the IDEA to private programs and established single-agency responsibility. Finally, it required both OSEP and SEAs to create procedures for at least annual evaluation of the effectiveness of state and local programs [Sec. 1413(a)(11)].

Program Accountability

Program accountability is another means of helping special education do the job it is designed to do. The techniques for accomplishing this end are multifaceted. Among them are requirements for single-agency responsibility, SEA preemption, LEA consolidation, public notice of LEA and SEA programs, parental access to records, and requirements that SEAs and LEAs provide information or assurances to OSEP or to the SEA, as appropriate [Secs. 1413, 1414, 1417, and 1418].

Accountability is also advanced by creation of advisory panels [Secs. 1413(a)(12) and 300.650], establishment of timetables for implementation of the Act, and formulation of full-service goals. The provisions for program evaluation are also a means of producing program accountability.

Limitations on Administrative Costs

By limiting the amount of administrative costs that SEAs or LEAs can charge against IDEA funds [Sec. 1411(b)(2), (c)(2), and (e)(3)], and by other techniques designed to put the money where the problems are, Congress clearly intends that programs for the disabled be made as effective as possible, as well as accountable for how they operate.

Sanctions

It might become necessary to apply stronger measures to recipients of IDEA funds if they do not comply with requirements of the Act. Accordingly, Congress provided four types of sanctions:

1. In spite of provisions dealing with exclusion, ceiling, and nondiscriminatory classification of students, children still might be erroneously classified as eligible so that the LEA could count them for receipt of federal funds. Obviously, the LEA should not receive federal funds for such children. Congress required the state plan to contain policies and procedures for seeking to recover federal funds available under the Act that are allocated for incorrectly classified children [Secs. 1413(a)(5) and 300.141].
2. An SEA may refuse to approve an LEA application that does not meet the requirements of Section 1414(a), setting out the contents of the LEA application, including child census, confidentiality, full-service goals, and related assurances [Secs. 1414(b)(1) and 300.193]. If, after reasonable notice and opportunity for a hearing, an SEA determines that an LEA has failed to comply with any requirement set forth in an SEA-approved application, the SEA must take one of two steps: (a) withhold payments to the agency until satisfied that the default has been cured; or (b) take the determination into account in reviewing any later application the LEA or IEU might make. It might even take both steps. In any event, the noncomplying agency must give public notice that it is subject to sanction [Secs. 1414(b)(2)(A) and (B) and 300.194].
3. If, after providing reasonable notice and an opportunity to be heard, the secretary of education finds that an SEA or LEA has failed to comply substantially with any provision of Section 1412 (SEA eligibility) or Section 1413 (state plan), or has failed to comply with any provision of the Act or with any requirements set forth in an SEA-approved application from an LEA, he or she must withhold any further payments to the state and may stop further payments to the state of disabled education funds under his or her jurisdiction, granted pursuant to Section 121 and ESEA and the Vocational Education Act.

   The secretary may limit the withholding of federal funds to specific programs or projects under the state plan [Sec. 1416] or portions of the state plan that are affected by the noncompliance. He or she also may order SEAs not to make further payments to noncomplying LEAs and may continue to withhold funds until the noncompliance is ended. A noncomplying SEA or LEA must give public notice of the sanction [Sec. 1416(a)]. (Sections 300.580 and .589 govern Department of Education sanction procedures.)

4. After exhausting all statutory appeals, any aggrieved party in a due process hearing has the right to bring a civil action in a state or United States district court concerning the identification, evaluation, or educational placement of a child, or the provision of a free appropriate public education to a child [Sec. 1415(e)(2)].

FISCAL ACCOUNTABILITY

Another way to accomplish the major principles of the Act is to require fiscal accountability of SEAs and LEAs. The Act imposes fiscal accountability in a variety of ways. It requires the state plan to set forth policies and procedures to assure that federal funds are spent according to provisions of the Act [Secs. 1413(a)(1) and 300.112].

In order to trace the expenditures and determine if the funds have been spent in accordance with the Act, Sections 1413(a)(6), (9), and (10) require public control of federal funds, prohibit co-mingling or supplanting by the state [Sec. 300.145], and require the state to impose fiscal control and fund accounting procedures. Section 1414(a)(2) requires LEAs to give assurances of public control of funds. The requirement of fiscal control by the state also applies to the LEAs [Sec. 1413(a)(10)].

SECTION IV

Free Appropriate Public Education and the American Value System

11
Objections to the IDEA and Answers to Them

A person with even the most casual knowledge about the IDEA can recognize that it makes revolutionary changes in the education of disabled children and in the relationships between the individuals and interest groups involved in educating them. No law as complex and innovative as the IDEA can escape severe criticisms. They come from sources such as the regular education constituency, administrators, and teacher associations and unions. They are based on educational and ethical grounds. And they can all be answered more or less satisfactorily.

This chapter gives the most common objections and some of the answers to them. Because the history of the IDEA, its implications, and some methods of implementation have already been discussed, the objections and answers will be concise, although more complete statements could be given. The purpose of this book, and particularly this chapter, is *not* to justify the IDEA in terms of how it has been implemented, nor to describe its implementation. Accordingly, the objections are not answered in terms of how schools and other agencies have responded since the IDEA became effective. I seek to set out the objections and answers. Readers must look elsewhere for data on implementation.

Objection 1: Congress requires compliance, but it does not appropriate sufficient funds. He (or she) who regulates should appropriate.

Answer: The education of disabled children is an obligation that each state has assumed for itself in its constitution or mandatory education laws. It is not an obligation that the federal government initially or traditionally has undertaken. The federal government seeks to help the states comply with their own self-imposed responsibilities. Its presence is designed to underwrite some, but not all, of the costs of special education that state and local governments have inadequately funded in the past. Nonetheless, it is true that the federal authorization for IDEA (the amount that Congress says it may spend) has not been equalled by the appropriation (the amount of money that Congress actually sets aside for the IDEA each year). Indeed, the IDEA has caused the state and local school authorities to substantially increase their funding for special education. Yet the federal share has not kept pace with what the federal government may spend if it wants to.

Objection 2: Educating disabled children is too expensive.

Answer: Although it may cost more to educate disabled children than nondisabled children, the states have a constitutional duty to do so. Federal funds help state and local education agencies comply with that duty. The costs of educating disabled children required additional tax levies, and present state and local educational funds have been reallocated. Funds spent on the far more costly task of maintaining disabled persons in institutions during the school-age years and afterwards can be reduced and diverted to educating them. The long-term cost of maintaining disabled people at public expense is far greater than the short-term cost of educating them when they are children. Indeed, the costs of educating a child with a disability increase in proportion to the severity of the child's disability. Still, there is abundant evidence that all children with disabilities can be workers, and the long-term benefit therefore justifies the short-term cost.

Objection 3: Granted, it is cheaper in the long run to educate a disabled person than to have the state pay for lifetime care, but state and local education agencies look only to their own funds and have little concern about the wider fiscal benefits of educating a disabled person.

Answer: Short-sightedness is common among all agencies of government, but it is not forgivable. The IDEA addresses the wider concerns through provisions allowing SEAs to use funds not passed through to LEAs for service contracts with state and private agencies, requiring state and local agencies (other than educational ones) to educate disabled children in their care or custody and providing increased levels of federal funds.

The 1988 amendments to the Social Security Act, entitled The Medicaid Catastrophic Health Amendments Act, provide the SEA and LEA with a pool of funds for educating children who have severe health-related disabilities, essentially by allowing IDEA and Medicaid funds to be combined to provide related services. These amendments reduce the burden on the education budget and partially answer the objection.

Objection 4: The IDEA requires funding of *related services*, which are not really *special education* services.

Answer: The related services are essential to the appropriate education of a disabled child. Without them, special education is an inadequate education.

Objection 5: Requiring SEAs and LEAs to provide related services will encourage them to create their own capacities to furnish those services, in spite of the fact that other agencies (such as mental health, social services, or human resources) have the necessary capacities. The resulting interagency competition will dilute already inadequate state fiscal and personnel resources.

Answer: Through the state plan and single-agency responsibility, SEAs can orchestrate the efforts of various agencies so that they cooperate rather than compete.

Objection 6: The IDEA tips the scales of state–federal relationships so drastically toward the federal that state and local discretion in the education of disabled children is all but eliminated. This represents an intolerable intrusion on the concepts of federalism and state and local autonomy in education.

Answer: The IDEA is a formula-grant act that does not require the states to participate. Moreover, state and local autonomy has permitted the states to fail in their legal duties to educate disabled children. Were it not for such massive failure, federal regulations governing the use of federal funds would not be necessary. The federal government must correct violations of citizens' Fifth and Fourteenth Amendment rights. To that end, it can legislate even without appropriating funds.

Objection 7: The requirement for single-agency responsibility runs against the grain of the Tenth Amendment, which provides that states retain powers not specifically delegated by the U.S. Constitution to the federal government.

Answer: As a condition for allocating federal funds to states that seek them, the federal government constitutionally may require administrative convenience through the single-agency device. Moreover, the single-agency requirement seals service gaps that previously excluded disabled children from a free appropriate education.

Objection 8: The IDEA represents an unwarranted shift in educational philosophy, requiring individualized education when, as a rule, mass education has been acceptable.

Answer: There is no shift in philosophy—only an extension of the accepted philosophies of education. Individualized education is necessary if disabled children are to be adequately educated (that is, if public policy is to be accomplished).

Objection 9: The law omits the gifted child, whose educational needs are clearly exceptional.

Answer: Gifted children have not been subjected to the same discrimination and violation of their constitutional rights as have disabled children. Federal programs already provide funds for their education. And, like the nondisabled child, they have been receiving at least a minimum level of education.

Objection 10: The IDEA should not authorize SEAs and LEAs to provide education to disabled children during the preschool years because those children are better dealt with by health and social service systems, not school systems. In addition, the IDEA should not authorize SEAs and LEAs to provide education to disabled children who are over the age of majority (usually eighteen) and in transition from school to adult services or postsecondary education because those children are better dealt with by existing service systems, such as vocational rehabilitation, developmental disabilities programs, mental health and mental retardation programs, social and human services programs, and institutions of higher education, including the vocational and technical institutes.

Answer: The schools are one part—and a very important part—of the system of services that federal, state, and local governments have created for people with disabilities. As part of that system, schools have legitimate roles to perform. In the case of preschool children, they can and should work with other service providers to assure that the children are prepared for elementary school. When other service providers do not furnish preschool training, the schools themselves may do so, benefiting both the children and the schools themselves.

In the case of young adults, the schools also can and should work with other service providers to assure that the young adults are moved effectively from their secondary education programs into postsecondary education or adult services. Schools have an important role to play in the transition of students into other service systems. That role includes providing transition services (which other service systems may not provide) so that students' educations are made most effective.

Objection 11: The IDEA creates a special law for special (disabled) people, thus contradicting one of its own principles—the integration of all students. Its concepts are internally inconsistent.

Answer: If disabled people are to be included in the benefits of a public education, integration through least restrictive appropriate placement and equal opportunities (the same as extended to nondisabled students) are a must. The longstanding and severe discrimination against disabled people justifies remedial legislation that redistributes public benefits in compliance with federal and state constitutional requirements and laws. Both integration and preferential treatment of disabled persons is justified in light of past wrongs and within the principles of distributive justice.

Objection 12: The IDEA places unwarranted emphasis on disabled children by putting an inordinate amount of public resources behind their education. More to the point, it says that disabled students are entitled to more of society's benefits than other children, thereby misconstruing the contribution—the "return"—that disabled children will make to society.

Answer: The issue of competing equities—who is to be inconvenienced so that the needs of disabled students may be met, and to what degree they are to be inconvenienced— is at the heart of all legislation that advances the interests of any minority group, whether the group is characterized by race, sex, disability, or some other trait. The answers have not yet been generally articulated, but in the case of the IDEA, they can be easily set forth.

The Act corrects massive past discrimination; it redresses the balance of fiscal equities by providing a limited portion of the additional costs of educating disabled children; it requires only that LEAs spend at least the same amount on disabled children as on nondisabled ones; it cures the imbalance of educational equities by enabling many disabled persons to make substantial contributions to society through the requirement that they be given education for work and equal educational opportunities; and it institutionalizes values that the majority holds dear. It is not likely to overbalance the competition for equities or put children with disabilities in a position of significant advantage.

Objection 13: Leaving aside the issue of competing equities, the IDEA grants to the disabled special rights, such as the right to an IEP and individualized appropriate education.

Answer: Although nondisabled students do not have the same legal claims as the disabled, they have generally received a far more appropriate education. The Act extends to the disabled the soundest current educational principles, including least restrictive appropriate placement, individualized programming, and procedural safeguards. It may, and indeed should, set the stage for nondisabled students to receive those same benefits. It can help special educators make important contributions to the education of all children.

Objection 14: The IDEA sets a policy that is simply disagreeable. Disabled children really should not be educated. They should be placed in institutions or special schools with their own kind.

Answer: Besides the fact that the states have a legal obligation to educate disabled children and have violated the state and federal constitutional rights of those children, it is definitely in the public interest to educate them outside institutions whenever possible. Only with education can the disabled contribute to society rather than be dependent on it. All the evidence shows that they can learn if appropriately trained, and appropriate training usually occurs outside of institutions.

Objection 15: The IDEA imposes such an excessive administrative burden that it will divert educators from their proper role—educating disabled children. Bureaucrats will devise coping behaviors, resulting in mere paper compliance with the law.

Answer: Although more paperwork is required, *better* paperwork is also called for, and SEAs and LEAs may charge some administrative costs against federal funds. Some educators may take approaches that undermine or diminish children's rights under the law, but this reaction certainly will not be universal. The required personnel development programs for preservice and inservice personnel and federal and state technical assistance should make the administrative "costs" more manageable. Educators' time should be increasingly available for the actual education of disabled students. Moreover, much of the administrative burden is created by the states themselves.

Objection 16: The state will simply certify to the federal government that the public agencies have complied with the IDEA when, in fact, they have not.

Answer: The IDEA is full of accountability devices that consumers and the OSERS may invoke if they believe that noncompliance exists. The Act's sanctions are strong enough to induce the states to comply.

Objection 17: To avoid certifying that something is true when it is not, states will try to reduce their responsibilities under the Act. They will lower their program standards to a level at which they will become relatively meaningless for disabled children.

Answer: An appropriate education entails not only compliance with state standards but also the avoidance of functional exclusion. Disabled children may invoke (and have invoked) the procedural safeguards, including their right to sue in federal or state courts, to ensure that they are not denied an appropriate education even though their educational program may comply with state standards.

Objection 18: In an effort to make compliance easier, educators will write IEPs that call for easily obtainable goals and objectives.

Answer: Although educators may seek to minimize IEP goals and objectives, parents and other participants at IEP conferences can see to it that the IEP is realistic.

Objection 19: A child's failure to achieve the goals and objectives set forth in the IEP does not make the educators liable. The IEP is really not a technique for holding educators accountable.

Answer: The Act has procedural safeguards that allow parents to raise the issue of the school's failure to write an IEP, and courts may hold the schools as well as individual educators liable for failing to write an IEP. The claim of such a case would be that the schools and educators failed to perform a statutory duty owed to the child, not that they or the child failed to perform as the IEP required. This is the *Rowley* process definition of appropriate education. Moreover, the *Rowley* substantive definition of appropriate education (that there be an educational benefit for the student) ensures that the educators can be held accountable.

Objection 20: The procedural safeguards of the IDEA are inconsistent with procedural safeguards under the laws of many states. The IDEA creates confusion and conflicts with some state laws.

Answer: The IDEA is a federal law that rightly seeks uniformity in its application and interpretation. For this reason, it is appropriate to include a single set of procedural safeguards. Although the safeguards in the IDEA may differ slightly from, or even conflict in some respects with, state laws, they reflect the basic provisions of case law and of state law to a surprisingly accurate degree. The differences or conflicts are minimal.

Objection 21: The costs of complying with the procedural safeguards are high and may require that funds be diverted from the education of disabled children to pay for the safeguards.

Answer: The safeguards are an integral part of the legislation. Without them, there would be no way to make the schools accountable or enable them to do their jobs properly. The safeguards do require administration, time, and personnel, but they are indispensable to the statutory guarantee of a free appropriate education. Compliance with child census, nondiscriminatory evaluation, the IEP, and other provisions is a means of forestalling due process hearings.

In states where similar safeguards have been in the law for several years, the number of cases has been well below educators' fearful expectations, and not all were decided against the schools. Educators are far from defenseless in due process hearings.

Objection 22: The IDEA requires the schools to answer to too many masters. There is an excess of "enforcers."

Answer: Although both the OSERS in the Department of Education and the Office for Civil Rights have enforcement powers (as do hearing officers and courts), the principles of *res judicata* (the same matter has been adjudicated before) and the *stare decisis* (the precedent for this case has been set by an earlier case with similar facts involving the same issue of law) can prevent duplication of enforcement. For that matter, educators' compliance is the best guarantee against sanctions.

Objection 23: The IDEA creates potential liability for school systems and educators. Both institutional and personal liability are likely. Educators may start to practice "defensive education," just as some physicians practice defensive medicine and some mental health professionals practice defensive treatment.

Answer: The IDEA may encourage the practice of defensive education, but it is more likely to require and enable educators to do what they have been trained to do and should have been doing all the time—giving each disabled child a free appropriate public education. The Act takes the best practices of special education and writes them into the law, thereby both requiring and enabling educators to practice as professional standards require. Moreover, the requirements for IEPs, nondiscriminatory testing, and parent participation should actually forestall lawsuits against educators if they comply with those requirements. The due process hearing itself can protect educators against later liability if they comply with the orders of hearing officers.

Objection 24: The IDEA is a lawyer's dream, creating a multitude of potential lawsuits against educators and schools.

Answer: Certainly, litigation is necessary to enforce the IDEA and to define or refine the rights of disabled children under it. But litigation also can show school systems how to carry out their obligations and give them desirable political clout in dealing with state and local funding sources. Moreover, the duties and the potential liabilities litigation creates exist independently of the IDEA. They are based on federal and state constitutional claims and state mandatory education laws.

Objection 25: The requirement of least restrictive appropriate placement guarantees some form of educational integration, but it does not and cannot guarantee social integration or a change in attitudes about the disabled.

Answer: Not only does school integration lead to social integration (to the extent that any student chooses to make friends with any other student, disabled or not), but it also has long-term social integration effects. It positively influences the attitudes of nondisabled toward disabled people.

Objection 26: The requirement for nondiscriminatory evaluation cannot always be satisfied, and the requirement institutionalizes the undesirable practice of classifying and labeling children.

Answer: The nondiscriminatory evaluation techniques found to be effective with disabled children in some minority populations can be adapted for use with disabled children in other minority populations. Moreover, classification itself is not entirely invidious. It does have educational benefits. The nondiscriminatory testing requirement attempts to encourage fairness in evaluation procedures and assumes, with justification, that fair procedures will yield acceptable results.

Objection 27: The requirement for parental consent to initial evaluation and nondiscriminatory testing may prevent school psychologists from testing a child and thereby deny the child the educational opportunities needed.

Answer: The school may invoke due process hearings if the parents refuse to consent to an initial evaluation. The requirement for fair testing procedures does not prevent testing. It requires testing to be accurately and appropriately performed. If anything, it results in greater accuracy in tests and a better basis for judgments by school personnel.

Objection 28: Realizing that a child who is designated *disabled* has substantial rights, schools may be reluctant to classify a child as disabled and might instead treat him or her as nondisabled, perhaps to the child's detriment.

Answer: Although this may occur, at least the child would not suffer the stigma of being labeled *disabled*. The child's parents may, of course, invoke a due process hearing if the school refuses to identify or evaluate their child or if it refuses to grant an appropriate education.

Objection 29: The practice described in Objection 28 would leave the "hardest" cases in special education and remove the "best" children from programs for the disabled.

Answer: If this occurs, it may prove to be consistent with the principle of least restrictive appropriate placement, thus making special education programs and classes truly special. This reflects the service priorities Congress set forth for the expenditure of IDEA funds. Also, some disabled children are not so different from nondisabled children—in the way they learn, the rate at which they learn, or the methods they need to be taught with—that they should be left out of the mainstream.

Objection 30: Teachers are inadequately prepared to implement the law. This is especially so of "regular" teachers.

Answer: SEAs have the responsibility and available federal funds to carry out preservice and inservice personnel development programs.

Objection 31: Although SEAs have the authority for personnel development, the law does not make any demands on colleges or universities that engage in teacher training. It does not require them to change their preservice curriculum to enable future regular and special educators to carry out provisions of the law such as least restrictive placement.

Answer: Congress could extend the regulations to colleges and universities receiving federal funds, but it chose not to impose requirements on them, singling out the SEAs as the agency responsible for statewide implementation. The SEAs may contract with colleges and universities for preservice and inservice training. And colleges and universities are funded under the IDEA for personnel development, research, and demonstration projects directed at implementing the IDEA.

Objection 32: The law requires too much of the schools, which must cope with severe personnel shortages in some school programs and inadequately trained personnel throughout.

Answer: The personnel development mandate should ease those immediate concerns, and the requirements for long-range planning (full-service goals), child census, and the ability of SEAs to contract with colleges and universities also will help schools with implementation. The Act simply requires schools to do what they were supposed to be doing all along.

Objection 33: Personnel problems are serious enough in metropolitan areas, but they are extreme in rural areas. In fact, rural school systems have a hard time complying with the law.

Answer: In addition to the provisions of the IDEA just mentioned in reply to Objection 32, the Act provides for consolidated grant applications, which should be especially appropriate for rural areas. The Act also provides for direct services by the SEAs and optional purchase of services from private agencies, colleges, and universities.

Objection 34: The IDEA creates unequal services for disabled children by setting priorities for some but not for others.

Answer: First-priority children are entitled to the first priority in the use of IDEA funds because they must be included in school programs. Equal protection and zero reject demand no less. Second-priority children are entitled to the second priority because the inadequate education they receive amounts to functional exclusion and may be tantamount to no education at all. Disabled children who are not in the first or second priorities do not have the same needs as other disabled children. School systems are already serving them better than the children in the first two priorities.

Objection 35: The IDEA creates artificial ceilings for the classification of disabled children for federal funding purposes. For example, some school systems typically have more learning disabled children than 2% of all their children.

Answer: The ceilings place reasonable limits, based on available data, on the responsibility of the federal government to fund state and local programs. Open-ended funding would be disastrous. At present, a school may serve more than the number of children covered by the federal ceilings by using its own funds. The ceilings force the school systems to adhere to the priorities by counting only the most needy children as eligible for federal funds.

Objection 36: The foregoing criticisms all make the point that the IDEA goes too far in regulating and falls short in appropriating. More money is needed to educate disabled children, and the IDEA does not provide enough.

Answer: The federal presence is designed to assist states in complying with *self-imposed* laws. Without the ceilings there would be an unlimited—and unrealistic—federal obligation. The IDEA is a remarkable beginning, one of the most important federal education laws ever enacted. It builds on case law, sets forth rights and techniques for securing those rights, commits the federal government to the education of disabled children, moves them into the mainstream of the schools, and gives them a means of joining the mainstream of society.

Objection 37: The IDEA does not create in-school advocacy systems despite ample evidence that child advocacy with school systems is necessary for the implementation of children's rights.

Answer: Although it does not create a single formal advocacy system within the schools, the IDEA does offer many techniques for monitoring, such as the procedural safeguards, parent participation, and administrative sanctions.

Objection 38: Whether the IDEA goes too far or not far enough in creating rights for disabled children is beside the point. What is important is whether the law overpromises and underperforms, creates unintended consequences (negative reactions to disabled children), or acts as a proper vehicle for interpreting and applying educational principles.

Answer: The IDEA is based on court decisions and congressionally gathered data that prove that disabled children have suffered longstanding and severe discrimination in the public schools. It promises them a redress of their grievances and follows up that promise with federal funds, accountability techniques, and the requirement of sound educational principles. Of course there will be negative reaction to any act that regulates, especially if it affects the traditionally sacrosanct practices of state and local schools. The IDEA, however, can positively shape attitudes about disabled children, show the schools how to perform duties they must perform as a matter of state law, provide financial support to the schools, and make important contributions to the education of nondisabled children. The educational practices that it mandates are sound and have been sound for a long time. If, for some reason, they *are* found to be unsound after careful research and review, they can be deleted from the law, but there is no present reason to change them.

Objection 39: The "bottom line" is not the IDEA or the cases—it is the values they enforce. Simply stated, the Act and the cases do not articulate the values of the majority.

Answer: The objection is untrue, as the next chapter will demonstrate.

12

Underlying Beliefs
and Values in
Right-to-Education Laws

No radical change of public policy occurs and is sustained unless there are generally accepted beliefs to support the change. This is particularly true of the right-to-education movement, and although our beliefs and values may not have been well articulated in the past,
they do exist and can be put forward.

To make clear the underlying beliefs and values in the right-to-education movement, this
chapter first reviews the role of law in the right-to-education cases. It then examines the dual
system of law to which children and adults with disabilities had been subjected and the ob-
jectionable principle that sustained that dual sustem. Third, it discusses briefly the civil rights
movement that began in 1954 with the Supreme Court's decision in *Brown v. Board of Education* and the meaning of that movement for disabled children and youth. Fourth, it sets
forth the basic concepts that underlie the right-to-education movement, explains the inter-
active relationship of political ideologies, human service and special education concepts,
and legal principles, and shows how the interaction of these ideas gave support to the right-
to-education movement. Fifth, it discusses the techniques of law reform, followed by, sixth,
a discussion of the nature of law reform in the context of the right to education for disabled
children and youth, and how advocates have resorted to federal and state legislatures, executive agencies, and courts to secure equal educational opportunities. Seventh, it sets forth
the underlying beliefs in special education law (the so-called right-to-education credo).
Eighth, it defines the law, the underlying beliefs and values, and shows how they are har-
monized through the IDEA. Finally, it describes the trade-offs that are made to obtain certain results in the education of disabled children.

ROLE OF LAW

It should be obvious by now that the role of law in our society is basically twofold. First, the law seeks to regulate the affairs of individuals in relation to each other. Consider how the IDEA does this. The IDEA makes it possible for parents, school personnel, and disabled children to have certain regularized relationships with each other, mainly through the principles of nondiscriminatory evaluation, appropriate and individualized education, least restrictive placements, due process, and parent participation. In each of these principles, the IDEA sets forth certain rules that parents, school personnel, and disabled children must follow to assure the child's education. In this way, the IDEA regulates the relationships of individuals to each other.

Second, the law seeks to regulate the affairs of an individual to his or her government. The IDEA does this in the same way that it regulates the affairs of individuals to each other, but simply by substituting the SEA or LEA for school personnel. Here, too, the IDEA emphasizes procedures and processes. And, to make those procedures and processes meaningful, the courts have interpreted them and other relevant laws (e.g., the Civil Rights Act and Section 504 of the Rehabilitation Act), thereby regulating the relationships of the governed (parents and children) to the government (SEA and LEA).

In these respects, then, the IDEA is very traditional. This is so even though its provisions may have seemed (or still may seem) to be thoroughly innovative, even radical.

DUAL SYSTEM OF LAW

The fact that the right-to-education movement for disabled children had to begin in the courts and be legitimized by Congress attests to a distressing historical fact: People with disabilities have been treated as second-class citizens in America. Not only has popular and some professional opinion usually treated them as less worthy of protection and improvement, but the law itself also has perpetuated the same treatment and a wrong idea—that those who are less able are indeed less worthy.

In the area of education, the right-to-education cases (especially the early ones) and IDEA frontally respond to this odious notion. For example, it was not uncommon for SEAs and LEAs to exclude disabled children from school. Hence we have the zero-reject principle. It was not uncommon for SEAs and LEAs to discriminate against disabled children in testing and classification, often for reasons wholly unrelated to the educational capacities of those children. Hence we have the nondiscriminatory evaluation principle. It was not uncommon for SEAs and LEAs to fail to provide disabled children an appropriate education, particularly with nondisabled children. Hence we have the principles of appropriate, individualized education, and least restrictive environment. Finally, there was precious little due process and parent participation in the education of disabled children. Hence we have the necessity for those two principles.

Because public and some professional opinion so influenced the law that the principle of "less able is less worthy" became the rule, it was necessary to make a radical and complete rejection of that principle. The right-to-education cases and the IDEA do this by affirming another principle: *Less able does not mean less worthy.*

LAW REFORM MOVEMENT

Brown v. Board of Education, the 1954 Supreme Court decision holding that separate education of the races in public education is inherently unequal and therefore forbidden by the equal protection doctrine, lighted the way for development of widespread civil rights reforms. The law's attention was drawn to segregation of people by race, first in public schools and then in public accommodations (such as restaurants and buses). Next, the law was broadened to protect students and minors generally so that they would have the same or substantially the same rights as adults have under the federal Constitution. At nearly the same time, the rights of persons charged with crimes were expanded under constitutional doctrines. Finally, the civil rights movement reached out to protect women and aliens from practices and laws that treated them discriminatorily.

The eighteen years from 1954 until 1972—the time span between *Brown* and the *PARC* and *Mills* decisions—represented a long time for disabled people who were victims of discrimination. Today, children and adults with disabilities, their families, and the professionals who serve them owe a tremendous debt to the civil rights frontiersmen who radically changed the meaning of the Constitution, particularly the equal protection and due process provisions of the Fourteenth Amendment. Without those constitutional pioneers and their risk-taking clients, the legal groundwork for the right-to-education movement would not have been laid and the "silent revolution" in education would have been much longer in coming.

The *Brown* decision was more than a landmark in the development of the law and the application of constitutional principles. It was a landmark, as chapters 1 through 3 showed, because it had such a profound and long-lasting influence on the law's application to other minority groups, including in particular those with disabilities. But *Brown* also reflected a developing moral sentiment—one not universally held but one that at least the Court's members and some others believed needed to be articulated. This sentiment was that segregation by race was ethically intolerable. Today, many people who challenge segregation by disability or other indicia of inferiority also premise their arguments on moral and ethical grounds. Finally, *Brown* stimulated an inchoate political movement and gave first voice to a renaissance in political ideology—an ideology of equality in opppportunity. In these three regards, *Brown* was a progenitor of the right-to-education movement on behalf of children with disabilities. Just how this is so is the topic of the next section.

NATURE AND SOURCES OF RIGHT-TO-EDUCATION POLICY

One of the remarkable aspects of the civil rights movement was the interaction of political beliefs and constitutional doctrines. It is not appropriate here to say which came first—the political belief or the legal doctrine. It is important, however, to note that there was a happy and necessary coincidence of doctrine.

Egalitarianism, Equal Protection, and Due Process

The belief in egalitarianism (that all citizens are inherently equal and should be treated that way) was the corollary of the constitutional doctrines of equal protection (equally situated people should be treated equally, as a general rule) and due process (governments may not act arbitrarily, treating some people one way and others another way, without reason). Egalitarianism held that it is not consistent with the democratic principles upon which this country was founded for blacks and whites to be treated differently (by being segregated), for women to be barred from various occupations, or for children to be without legal protection. The equal protection and due process doctrines held that the Constitution prohibits such discrimination against racial and other minorities.

In the right-to-education movement, there was a similar convergence of beliefs and ideologies. But there was more—the infusion of certain concepts of human services and special education. Thus, the right-to-education movement rests on three separate but complementary grounds: political egalitarianism, constitutional equal protection and due process, and the human services and special education doctrines of normalization and integration/least restriction/mainstreaming.

Egalitarianism holds that all citizens, and hence all children and youth, are essentially equal and should be treated that way. In education, this came to mean that disabled children should have the right to a free appropriate public education—which is what most nondisabled children obtain from the political process as a matter of right. *Equal protection* and *due process* hold, respectively, that governments may not treat essentially similar people differently or arbitrarily (i.e., without sufficient reason to make the distinctions). In education, these doctrines came to mean that disabled children may not be excluded from education. They, like nondisabled children, constitute a "class" of similar people— namely, students—each of whom is capable of learning. Accordingly, it is arbitrary, and therefore a violation of equal protection and due process, to treat one group of students (those who are disabled) different from another (those who are not) by denying them educational opportunities that are less than comparable to those of nondisabled children.

Just as egalitarianism gave impetus to the doctrine of equal educational opportunity, and just as the equal protection and due process doctrines gave a legal underpinning for equal educational opportunity, so, too, did certain human service and special education doctrines support the political and legal doctrines and receive legitimacy from them in turn. These doctrines were normalization and integration/least restriction/mainstreaming.

Normalization and Integration/Least Restriction/Mainstreaming

Normalization is a principle that came to America from the Scandinavian countries and was articulated here by Wolf Wolfensberger, now a professor of special education at Syracuse University. In his first formulation, normalization meant making the lives of mentally retarded people as normal as practicable. The principle of normalization sought to create human service systems, including special education, that were as normal as practicable for the clients in those systems. In his second formulation, normalization has given way to a new principle—*social role valorization:* the creation, support, and defense of "valued social roles" for disabled people and others who are at risk of social devaluation.[1] Both principles seek to reduce or prevent the overt signs and differentness that may devalue a person in the eyes of others and to change societal perceptions and values in regard to such a person so that his or her disability is no longer devalued.

The doctrine of *integration/least restrictive alternative/mainstreaming* really is three separate concepts rolled into one. As chapter 6 of this book shows, the legal doctrine of least restrictive alternative placement in education attempts to maximize the disabled student's education as well as the opportunity to associate with nondisabled students and adults. Similarly, chapter 6 describes mainstreaming as a related concept, one that addresses the placement of disabled students into educational settings—classes, other activities, and buildings—with nondisabled students. Both doctrines emphasize the integration of disabled and nondisabled students, and both regard integration as a strategy for educating disabled students.

It should be obvious that normalization/social role valorization and integration/least restriction/mainstreaming are powerfully related to political egalitarianism and constitutional equal protection. Like egalitarianism and equal protection, these two human service concepts seek equal educational opportunities for disabled students. They promote equal treatment when such treatment will render equal opportunities, and they seek unequal treatment when that kind of treatment is necessary to render equal educational opportunities. They also affirm that disabled students are not so different from, and actually are so much like, nondisabled students that it is not justified to treat them less favorably by segregating them and providing them with less than comparable educational opportunities.

For those who believe in the education of disabled students, it is fortunate that the climate of the 1970s was such that it was possible and even desirable as a matter of national politics to extend the benefits of egalitarianism to disabled students. Likewise, it was a happy matter that the courts had developed the equal protection and due process doctrines in such a way that they could be brought to bear on the education of disabled children and that the children's advocates could persuade the courts to apply the constitutional precedents of the civil rights movement in creative and positive ways to the education of disabled students.

Finally, it also was a matter of extreme good luck that human services and special education programs were developing and accepting ideologies that welcomed and were accommodating to these political and constitutional ideologies. The trio of ideologies—egalitarianism, equal protection and due process, and normalization and integration—were ideally suited to each other. They supported each other, complemented each other, and drove the law and the right-to-education movement in the same direction, toward enactment of the IDEA.

RELATIONSHIP OF THE RIGHT-TO-EDUCATION MOVEMENT TO OTHER FEDERAL POLICIES AND LAWS

During the same time that political, constitutional, and human service ideologies were converging to create the theoretical underpinnings of the right-to-education movement and the IDEA, other important legal developments were affecting people with disabilities. These were largely complementary of the right-to-education ideologies; they were based in major part on the same constitutional principles; and they were reflected in various federal laws.

To understand how these separate movements—the right-to-education movement and the "general-rights" movement—developed, it will be helpful to review the four major forces that influenced federal laws, including the IDEA. It then will be useful to consider the major concepts of the federal laws and their relationship to the IDEA, and also to consider the laws' relationships to the four motivating forces behind them.

Forces Influencing Federal Laws

Four major forces influence the enactment of federal laws. The first is the constitutional doctrine of *equal protection*, with its corollaries of egalitarianism (a political doctrine), normalization (a human services doctrine), and due process (with its insistence on fair procedures and its assumption that, generally, fair procedures will produce or tend to produce fair or acceptable results). This book has explained in detail how these doctrines have influenced and been reflected in the IDEA (see especially chapters 1 through 8).

The second major force is *social altruism*. This refers to the concern that most people have, and that the IDEA clearly has, for ameliorating the effects of a disability through provision of a free appropriate public education. The power of the federal government to enact the IDEA is based on the Constitution, but the power of the states to have their own education laws and carry out the federal law in cooperation with the federal government rests on their inherent powers of *parens patriae*. This is a centuries-old legal doctrine that asserts that government is responsible for taking care of those who, because of their youthfulness (status as minors), disability (having a handicap), or vulnerability (such as being victims of abuse or neglect), cannot take care of themselves without assistance from the government. Literally, *parens patriae* means "parent/father of the country," referring to the state as the father of the citizens. Clearly, the IDEA seeks to ameliorate the effects of a disability and to ensure that the former discrimination in education to which children with disabilities were subjected is not repeated.

The third major force is *deinstitutionalization*, more recently characterized as anti-institutionalization. Deinstitutionalization has sought to prevent people from being placed in institutions (such as those for people with mental retardation or other developmental disabilities or those for people with mental illness). It also has sought to change those institutions so that those who are placed there do not have to experience the horrid conditions that existed in the early 1970s, when deinstitutionalization became a federal and state goal. Finally, it has sought to prevent people from being placed in institutions in the first place by providing them with the necessary and appropriate services in home or community settings.

The IDEA is linked to the deinstitutionalization movement by its zero-reject principle (ensuring that the state and local education agencies serve all children, regardless of the type or extent of their disabilities); its principle of appropriate education (ensuring that services, whenever provided, are suitable and educationally beneficial); its least restrictive placement/environment principle (ensuring that, to the maximum extent appropriate, children with disabilities are educated in regular schools, regular classrooms, or other integrated settings and programs); and its twin principles of accountability—procedural due process and parent participation (ensuring that the schools be made accountable for their actions). Indeed, the IDEA has had a profound effect on many state institutions, enabling many children who otherwise would be placed or kept in those institutions to be educated in the community. As chapter 6 points out, however, the effect of the IDEA on the institutions is not as wholesome as it ought to be: Schools and parents still seek institutional placement, and courts are still inclined to grant it.

The fourth and final impetus for federal legislation is the desire to *rebalance power* between people with disabilities and the professionals who serve them. As this book has indicated, there is a long and unsavory history of discrimination in education against people with disabilities. Those who had the power to educate persons with disabilities (the state and local school authorities) often did not exercise that power to include them in an appropriate education but, rather, to exclude them from any education at all or to provide only a barely appropriate education. The IDEA accordingly seeks to change the relationship between the education officials, who have had power, and the students with disabilities and their parents, who have not had power. Its six principles all work toward that goal, as explained in detail previously in this book.

Major Concepts of the Federal Laws

As Turnbull and Barber indicated in their discussion of federal laws affecting adults with developmental disabilities,[2] these motives—the impetus in federal laws—are reflected in various concepts that underlie not only the IDEA but other federal laws as well. But to merely acknowledge that four major forces have been influencing the enactment of federal laws is not enough. It is important also to consider the major concepts of those federal laws and (a) their relationships to the IDEA and (b) their connections to those four major forces.

Normalization. The doctrines of normalization, social role valorization, integration, mainstreaming, and the least restrictive alternative are reflections of the constitutional doctrine of equal protection (see chapter 6), of altruism (an effort to bring persons with disabilities into a more "normal" way of life, where they can be more valued as contributing citizens), and of deinstitutionalization (an effort to provide community-based, integrated education instead of programs in segregated institutional settings). The fourth major principle of the IDEA—that of education in the least restrictive environment—sets forth the presumption that children with disabilities will be educated to the maximum extent appropriate with children who do not have disabilities.

Unity and Integrity of Families. Many federal laws seek to keep families together, recognizing that the family is the most important and the basic structure of civilization. In the IDEA, the effort to maintain the family's participation in the student's education is the sixth major principle: parent participation. And the principle of the least restrictive alternative also is relevant to this effort in that it seeks to have children with disabilities educated in the community and thereby in settings where they can continue to live with their families. Moreover, the provision in the IDEA for home-based education as an alternative in the continuum of services is an explicit recognition of the desirability of having children educated in the care of their families so that families may stay unified and not have to place the child into an institution.

Accountability and Due Process. The Constitution provides for procedural safeguards, and the IDEA simply describes those safeguards as applicable to the education of children with disabilities (see chapter 7). Moreover, the 1986 enactment of the Handicapped Children's Protection Act, overturning *Smith v. Robinson* and granting the prevailing party in a due process hearing or appeal from such a hearing the right to recover attorneys' fees, is a more recent statement of the concept of accountability and due process.

Advocacy and Advocates. Accountability and due process will not be obtained unless parents and students with disabilities have advocates. The IDEA's procedural safeguards (e.g., the right to a surrogate parent, the right of natural and surrogate parents to consent to certain procedures such as the initial evaluation and placement and to have a due process hearing if they and the schools disagree about the child's right to a free appropriate public education, and the right to recover counsel fees if prevailing in due process hearing or appeal—see chapter 7) are explicit recognitions that advocacy and advocates are essential to the child's educational rights' enforcement.

Consent, Choice, and Client Participation. It is a hallmark of constitutional government in this country that government exists by and with the consent of the governed. The IDEA recognizes that special education, as a service of the government, should be consistent with the principle of government by consent, and it therefore provides for the consent of parents for initial evaluation and placement, their and the student's participation in certain evaluations and in the development of the student's educational program through the right to an IEP, and the family's right to be involved in the development of early education programs for the child through the individualized family service plan (described in chapters 3 and 5).

Individualization. The due process principle requires that government make individual determinations when allocating benefits and burdens and eschews the "meat ax" approach of treating all students with disabilities exactly alike. The principle of individualization is reflected in the IEP and IFSP.

Developmental Model. The developmental model recognizes that all people with disabilities, no matter the nature or extent of their disabilities, have inherent capacities, including the ability to learn and be educated. *PARC v. Commonwealth*, discussed in detail in chapters 2 and 3, is explicit about that capacity, finding that all children with mental retardation can learn. And the IDEA, which rests on and was greatly influenced by *PARC* (see chapters 1 through 3), reflects the developmental model, too, through its principles of zero reject and appropriate education, especially as designed and carried out by the IEP and IFSP.

Economic Productivity. Madeleine Will, assistant secretary of education from 1983 through 1989, has often said that the implied promise of special education is a job. Granting that her statement is accurate and no responsible people dispute it, the IDEA clearly seeks to build the capacities of people with disabilities so that they may take their place in the workforce of America. It does this not only by the general principles of zero reject, nondiscriminatory evaluation, appropriate education, and least restrictive placement, but it does so also by the specific provisions for incentive grants for transition (see chapter 5), by providing for the education of youth up to age 21 (see chapter 3), and by provisions for the employment of people with disabilities in special education programs (see chapter 10).

Prevention, Cure, and Amelioration. A large number of disabilities, and many of the conditions that aggravate a disability, are caused by social or environmental conditions. Only a few disabilities are "organic" and caused by biological or inherent conditions in a person. Because of this, many federal laws seek to prevent, cure (absolutely reverse), or ameliorate (reduce the effects of) a disability. Clearly, the IDEA is consistent with those laws. By its principle of zero reject, it seeks to open the doors of education and its ameliorating effects to all children. By its principles of appropriate education and the least restrictive environment, it seeks to provide educational benefit in the community instead of deprivation—absolute or relative, it does not matter—by institutional placement. By its principle of parent participation, and especially through the IFSP for children from birth through age two and the provision of some related services for families, it seeks to ensure that families themselves receive some benefits from the child's education and that their circumstances, which sometimes can add to the child's disability, receive some attention, too.

TECHNIQUES AND NATURE OF LAW REFORM

Notwithstanding the convergence of ideologies and the recent history of the civil rights movement, the right-to-education movement did not happen and indeed could not have happened without the skills of the many advocates who understood how to change the laws that barred disabled children from equal educational opportunities. Those advocates were led at first by parents whose mentally retarded and otherwise disabled children successfully sued the states for their rights to an education (such as in *PARC* and *Mills*) and then were joined by the Council for Exceptional Children (CEC). Above all, they knew that they must master the techniques of, and control the nature of, law reform.

To achieve the right-to-education movement's goals of a free and appropriate public education for all disabled children, it was necessary to have a general purpose. That purpose was to change the nature of the public schools so that there would be no more second-class students, so that the dual system of education would be abolished. This goal required two strategies: (1) to chip away at and eventually dismantle the restrictions that the states' laws and the schools' practices and policies imposed on disabled children (chapters 2 though 8 describe those pre-IDEA practices in detail; they consisted by and large of pure and functional exclusion and misuse of classification procedures); and (2) to create rights, such as the rights to zero-reject laws, nondiscriminatory evaluation, and individualized appropriate education.

The first technique was (and almost always is) negative in nature; it seeks to tear down that which time, tradition, and law have created. The second technique was (and also almost always is) positive; it seeks to replace the destroyed system with something more accommodating and effective. Simply accomplishing the dismemberment of a system would be a half measure only. The right-to-education movement required that something of value replace the old. That is why the right-to-education movement not only made illegal the old ways but also enacted new ones.

Since the object (with its two strategies) was to abolish the dual system and replace it with a system of equal educational opportunities, the techniques for achieving that object had to include a sophisticated understanding of the meaning of *equal educational opportunities*. Advocates had to begin by explaining equal educational opportunity for disabled children. As chapter 3 shows, equality for disabled students consists of three sub-types:

1. It is possible to obtain equal educational opportunities for some disabled students by treating them exactly like nondisabled students. Educating an orthopedically impaired student in the same academic classes as nondisabled students is an example of "pure equal treatment" (assuming the school is barrier-free).
2. It is possible to obtain equal educational opportunities for other disabled students by treating them substantially like nondisabled students but also by making simultaneous accommodations to them. For example, educating a deaf child in the same classroom as

children who do not have a hearing deficiency may require only a few adaptations by the teacher or school system.

3. It is possible to obtain equal educational opportunities for still other students by treating them very differently, but not less effectively, than nondisabled students. For example, educating severely disabled students in separate classes, using a different curriculum and different methods of instruction, may provide those students with educational opportunities that, for them, are comparable to the opportunities provided to nondisabled students who are educated in their own classes with a different curriculum and different methods of instruction.

Thus, the first technique for the right-to-education movement was to develop and announce a well-thought-out concept of equal educational opportunity.

Next, advocates in the right-to-education movement had to target their efforts on all branches of federal and state government. In this respect, they adopted a bifurcated approach: They pursued law reform from federal and state governments alike. They knew they had to achieve a uniform, national result—one that secured equal educational opportunities to all disabled children, without regard to where they lived or by which government they were served. This required reforms at both levels of government. At the federal level, for example, advocates sought enactment of the 1973 and 1975 amendments to the Education of the Handicapped Act (see chapter 2 for a discussion of the IDEA's history). At the state level, they pursued mandatory education laws and the enforcement of existing ones.

As just suggested, the most obvious forums for the federal/state approach to a uniform, national result were the *elected legislatures*—the Congress in the federal route and the state legislatures in the state route. Advocates therefore sought passage of laws, appropriation of money to carry out the laws, and implementation of those laws at state and local levels. Legislatures, then, were a collective forum in which the right-to-education movement had to be established.

A second forum was directly related to the first—the *executive agencies* of the federal government (the Department of Health and Human Services and the Department of Education) and the executive agencies of the states (the state departments of education or public instruction). The executive agencies, after all, are charged with implementing the laws that the legislatures enact. They do this by issuing regulations and guidelines, providing technical assistance, and performing monitoring and overseeing functions. Clearly, such complex legislation as the IDEA required detailed regulations. For example, the IDEA itself has little in it concerning the principle of the least restrictive education of disabled children. By contrast, the regulations implementing the IDEA itself are quite specific and broad in setting forth the way in which the principle is to be carried out.

Finally, advocates had to resort to the courts to establish the educational right of disabled children, either as a matter of federal constitutional law or as a matter of state educational law. In addition, advocates sought judicial relief when state education agencies were reluctant or recalcitrant in carrying out state laws.

Thus, advocates had to adopt a *bifurcated* approach—to seek the educational rights of disabled children by federal and state routes. And they had to adopt an *integrated* approach—to seek those rights in the legislatures, executive agencies, and courts of the federal and state forums. Only by taking this *comprehensive* approach would they be able to achieve their complex goals.

But advocates were obliged to use still another technique of law reform. It was to obtain both substantive and procedural reforms in the education laws of the federal and state governments. By *substantive* reforms, they had in mind, and eventually obtained, law that created a new body of rights for disabled children. For example, the zero-reject principle is a substantive reform. It creates a right to a free public education for all disabled children. Likewise, the principles of nondiscriminatory evaluation, appropriate education, least restrictive environment, due process, and parent participation are substantive in nature. Each grants to disabled children certain rights that SEAs and LEAs are obliged to satisfy. There are correlating rights (for the students) and duties (upon the SEAs and LEAs).

By *procedural* reforms, the advocates wanted, and also eventually obtained, laws that specify how the substantive rights are to be carried out and made effective. For example, the zero-reject principle becomes effective when SEAs and LEAs conduct an annual census of disabled children. The nondiscriminatory evaluation principle is made effective through multifaceted testing. The appropriate education principle is carried out when IEPs are developed for each student. The least restrictive alternative placement rule is satisfied when the child receives a placement that is both educationally effective and more integrated than not with nondisabled students. And, of course, the due process and parent participation principles are complied with when certain procedures (e.g., notice, consent, access to records, and impartial hearings) are made available.

Clearly, then, it was imperative for advocates to pursue and secure their goal by a well-grounded understanding of how schools operate and can be made to operate, and by an equally sophisticated understanding of how law can be created to affect schools' operations. In summary, the techniques of law reform were exceedingly complex. They entailed:

- *bifurcated* advocacy at both the federal and the state levels;
- *comprehensive* and *integrated* advocacy in all three forums of law making (legislative, executive, and judicial); and
- a highly developed understanding of the *substantive* and *procedural* approaches to law reform.

All of this was undergirded by a well-developed *definition* of equal educational opportunity as the concept applies to disabled students.

Given this background to the right-to-education movement, it is now appropriate to set forth the IDEA's underlying beliefs (credo), their relationship to the law and values, and their implementation at law.

THE UNDERLYING BELIEFS:
A RIGHT-TO-EDUCATION CREDO

We believe that education makes a difference in a person's life. That was one of the foundations of *Brown v. Board of Education* and is supported by the six principles of the IDEA.

We know and believe that disabled children can profit from an education appropriate to their capacities. Hence, the IDEA and the case law grant each disabled child the right to a suitable education. In the case of the IDEA, an affirmative duty to hire disabled people is also imposed on the public schools.

We also believe in equity—that is, in equal educational opportunity. Thus, the IDEA and the cases grant the right of education to all disabled students.

We believe in the value of an education for all people—the universality of education. Accordingly, the IDEA and case law grant the right to an education to all disabled students.

Most of us believe that governmental benefits should not be parceled out on the basis of the recipients' unalterable characteristics. We believe that such a practice says something demeaning and invidious about the person who is denied benefits, and it places the government in the position of causing that person to feel and act inferior simply because he or she is different from those who are receiving the benefits. Our acceptance of this belief is seen in racial discrimination cases and in both criminal and civil law where a person is denied benefits because he or she is indigent, an alien, a member of one sex or the other, or disabled. In the case of the disabled, the right-to-education cases and the IDEA challenge the old distribution of governmental benefits (education) and attempt to redistribute them more equitably. They attack a system of distribution founded on the false premise that persons who have disabilities are expendable and that the bulk of benefits in education should be given to the most meritorious (where merit was measured by intelligence or conformity to the nondisabled norm).

We believe in the essential sameness of all persons. Grounded in concepts of normalization, egalitarianism, and equal protection, this belief leads us to assert that students with disabilities are no less worthy of constitutional protection and statutory benefits than are students without disabilities. Although people may be classified, their rights to an education should not be denied because of a classification. The principle of free appropriate public education for *all* disabled children illustrates this belief.

We also believe that the economic investment of furnishing a person with disabilities an education appropriate to his or her needs will yield long-term returns in the increased productivity and decreased dependency of that person. On humanitarian grounds, we also point out that students with disabilities have been seriously shortchanged in the competition for governmental benefits. Each principle of the right-to-education movement attests to this belief.

We believe that the longstanding state and local neglect of the educational claims of children who have disabilities, with its ample evidence, will not be abated in the foreseeable future. We even believe that it will be permanent. For that reason, permanent federal funding and control are amply justified.

We believe that because we choose who governs us we have the right to ask our representatives to be accountable to us. To that end, the IDEA and case law require several types of accountability.

We believe that people should treat each other fairly and decently and that government should deal fairly and decently with the governed. Alternatively stated, we believe that a fair process of governing will produce fair and acceptable results—thus, the IDEA and the case law requiring that procedural safeguards be made available to disabled students and their parents.

We believe that the best government is one we can influence or affect. We believe in participatory democracy in the education of children, and the IDEA may well be the highwater mark of participatory democracy in public education.

The IDEA translates our beliefs into public policy for the education of disabled children, assigns legal rights that reflect our collective decency, and defines and refines our relationships to each other and among the governments and the governed.

THE LAW, OUR BELIEFS, AND OUR VALUES

More often than not, our beliefs harmonize with our values. In this respect, and particularly in the right-to-education movement, the word *value* has a familiar meaning. A value is something we, as individuals and as a society, highly prize and cherish. It is something we do not want to be without and we do not want others to be without. In a constitutional sense, a value is a "fundamental interest."[3] There are many values, and the right-to-education movement reflects at least four of them.

1. We do not want to be without access to courts or other forums for the peaceful solution of our differences with others. Expressed in another way, we do not want to be without a way of being heard and heeded when we have disagreements with others. Access to the courts as an avenue for redress of grievances is constitutionally required and is provided in the IDEA and in the right-to-education cases through requirements for procedural due process.
2. We do not want to be denied a right to participate in self-government. Thus, the right to vote is constitutionally protected, and the right to participate in school (as a "government") is provided for in the IDEA and the case law under the concept of parental participation.
3. We do not want to be without the opportunity to acquire property or fulfill ourselves. The principles of substantive due process guarantee us these opportunities as a matter of constitutional law, and the IDEA and the case law address them through the requirements of nondiscriminatory evaluation (protection from classifications that inevitably forestall or retard the opportunities of disabled children to develop to their maximum potential) and least restrictive appropriate placement (protection from programs that will have equally debilitating results).

4. We do not want our unalterable traits, such as race, gender, ancestry, or place of birth, to be used as a basis for government distribution of benefits. Thus, the IDEA and the case law provide for free appropriate public educational opportunities for all disabled students.

PUTTING OUR BELIEFS AND VALUES TO WORK: CONCEPTS INTO LAW

It is remarkable to see how effectively the IDEA puts our beliefs and values to work for the education of disabled children. The Act shows how we develop our resources to allow our beliefs and values to flourish. This function is performed by the requirements for IEPs, personnel development, OSERS technical assistance, parent involvement, full-service goals, timelines for educating disabled children of certain ages, the child census, priorities for the use of funds, early intervention programs, and affirmative action in employing the disabled.

The IDEA also shows how we allocate status to people as a reflection of our values and beliefs.[4] We allocate power to disabled children through provisions such as permanent funding of the IDEA, service priorities, zero-reject principles, and least restrictive placement requirements. We distribute power to their parents through participation in IEP conferences, procedural safeguards, membership on advisory panels, and participation in developing state and local plans. Finally, we allocate status to educators through requirements for personnel development, by legitimizing the truly special functions of special education (through the service priorities), and by changing the roles of educators with respect to each other (through the principle of least restrictive placement).

The IDEA changes not only the status or power of people involved in the right-to-education movement, but also the procedures by which power and status are allocated. That is the ultimate meaning of the procedural safeguards and parent participation provisions.

The IDEA changes more than the procedures. It changes the very rights that government distributes, the beneficiaries of those rights, and the methods of distributing them. It guarantees a free appropriate public education to *all* disabled children, changes the nature of their education so that it will be appropriate to them, prefers some disabled children over others (the service priorities), grants rights to parents of disabled children, and demonstrates that federal funds are a means of enforcing those rights (by funding the excess costs of educating disabled children, requiring the pass-through of funds, setting limits on administrative costs that may be charged against federal funds, and making federal funding permanent).

A Concluding Note

It is always somewhat risky to try to tie up so many divergent points as have been made in this chapter. But it is equally risky to leave them to stand on their own, without a concluding note. To introduce that concluding note, it helps to ask a simple question: Where did the IDEA originate, where has it been, and where is it going?

Where did it originate? It originated with the articulation of legal, political, and human service values, ideologies, and principles. These were, in a nutshell, equal protection, due process, egalitarianism, normalization, and integration.

What happened with these articulated values? They became the underlying principles of various federal and state laws, notably the IDEA, the Rehabilitation Act, and the Developmental Disabilities Assistance and Bill of Rights Act, and their respective regulations.

Laws without funds, however, are rather toothless. And so it was that the special education programs' effectiveness depended on appropriations by Congress and state and local government. The same was—and always will be—true with respect not only to the IDEA but also the Rehabilitation Act and the DD Act.

At least two other ingredients are necessary to bring life into the law and to give effect to its language and values. Those are changed behaviors by professionals and, of course, by people with disabilities and their families. It is beyond argument that the law has changed professional behavior, individual capacities, and the expectations and lives of people with disabilities and their families.

Finally, the power to enforce the laws is requisite. Just as rights often run with revenues, so do rights depend on their enforcement. Just how well the courts have enforced the IDEA is a matter of some dispute.

To summarize: Values are translated into laws and regulations; laws and regulations are implemented with funds; laws, regulations, and funds are made effective when professionals, people with disabilities, and their families change their behaviors; and the proper interpretation of values and laws and the careful monitoring of practices is the role of enforcement techniques.

The IDEA—it should be clear by now—follows this paradigm of legal reform. Its values (chapters 1, 2, 11, and 12) are reflected in the law through the six principles (chapters 3 through 8) and the provision of funds to carry them out (chapter 10). These legal principles have changed professional practice and the way of life of people with disabilities, their families, and people without disabilities—the "norms and forms" of society. Withal, there are various ways of enforcing the law (chapters, 7, 8, 9, and 10).

The IDEA and the case law thus perfectly illustrate the unique role of law and lawmakers in changing existing institutions of society and building new ones, in changing the "norms and forms" of society, in which the norm was second-class citizenship of disabled people and the form was discrimination in education. But these laws are not without their detractors.

Some people argue that society has paid in the redistribution of governmental power over the education of disabled children. The balance of power now clearly rests with the federal government, and the principles and values of local autonomy in education have been diminished. But that is not an argument unique to the IDEA and the right-to-education cases. Indeed, *Brown* had a remarkable effect on public education by federalizing it in an important respect. *Brown* made clear *where* the schools were to educate children: Blacks and whites were to be educated together. In special education, *PARC* and *Mills* specified *which* children were to be educated and the terms of their education. *Rowley* federalized public education by setting out the general principles of curriculum for disabled students: The curriculum must be comparable to that for nondisabled students and developed through a specified process (the IEP). *Tatro* federalized public education by specifying the principles governing the indispensible accessories of a disabled child's education—the related services the school must furnish. Yet, *PARC, Mills, Rowley, Tatro,* and a host of other special education cases must be seen in the light of *Brown*'s initial federalization of education. It undoubtedly is true that the IDEA has further federalized education, but it did so upon the precedent of *Brown* and other federal legislation.

Others also argue that society has legislated a change in the competition for equities and weighted the law in favor of disabled children by requiring state and local education agencies to make their own investments in the education of those children (by way of the excess-cost provision). But the IDEA and the cases interpreting it simply help the states do what they already had agreed to do by enacting their own constitutions and public education laws. That was to educate *all* children, without regard to their disabilities. In a very real sense, the states already had provided disabled children with leverage in the competition for funds by assuring them as a matter of state law that they would receive an education. The IDEA and the cases do have the effect, however, of making the states live up to their promises. They put some bite into the teeth of the states' laws so that disabled children now can partake of the same meal—education—furnished to other children.

Still others say that we have given advocates for disabled children a quantum increase in ammunition. They contend that the "first-generation" issues—whether all disabled children have a right to an appropriate education at public expense—have faded and been replaced by "second-generation" issues dealing with the specifics of the right to a free appropriate public education. They further contend that the second-generation cases show that disabled children have too many rights, especially in comparison to nondisabled children.

A Caveat

A brief answer is that it is quite true that disabled children and their advocates still have powerful arrows in their quivers—namely the IDEA itself, its regulations, and the precedents of the many cases decided in their favor. This means that, as advocates select their ammunition to advance the claims of disabled children in second-generation matters, they must be on their guard as to the forums they choose for their battlegrounds and the issues around which battle is joined. This is so because they would not want to add fuel to an unnecessary backlash by overzealously implementing the rights of disabled children. Nor would they want to cause the IDEA's underlying beliefs and values to be denied by those in the majority (the nondisabled) whose very beliefs, values, and attitudes are so crucial to the success of the law and the acceptance of children with disabilities.

Accordingly, advocates for disabled children must: (1) continually articulate the beliefs and values that are the foundations for the IDEA and the case law, (2) be willing and able to say that the educational rights of disabled children should be made available to nondisabled children as well, and (3) be able to arouse the sympathetic imagination of nondisabled people so that *their* claims to better educational opportunities will be supported by, and give support to, the claims of disabled children.

Zero reject and protection from functional exclusion, individualized appropriate education, nondiscriminatory and nonstigmatizing classification procedures and placement, rights to procedural safeguards, and the rights of participation are six principles that are supported by widely and deeply held beliefs and values. They are, however, more than that. They have a touch of justice, and no child—disabled or nondisabled—has a monopoly on justice.

NOTES

1. Wolfensberger, "Social Role Valorization: A Proposed New Term for the Principle of Normalization," *Mental Retardation* 21(Dec. 1983):224.

2. Turnbull and Barber, "Federal Laws and Adults with Developmental Disabilities," in Summers (Ed.), *The Right to Grow Up* (Baltimore, MD: Paul H. Brookes, 1986).

3. Michelman, "Foreword: On Protecting the Poor through the Fourteenth Amendment," *Harvard Law Review* 83(1969):7.

4. *See* Gil, *Unravelling Social Policy* (Cambridge, MA: Schenkman, 1977).

APPENDIX A

BROWN V. BOARD OF EDUCATION

(excerpts from the Supreme Court's unanimous opinion, with only Footnote 11 included)

OLIVER BROWN, et al., Appellants,

v.

BOARD OF EDUCATION OF TOPEKA, Shawnee County,
Kansas, et al. (No. 1.)

Mr. Chief Justice Warren delivered the opinion of the Court.

These cases come to us from the States of Kansas, South Carolina, Virginia, and Delaware. They are premised on different facts and different local conditions, but a common legal question justifies their consideration together in this consolidated opinion.[1]

In each of the cases, minors of the Negro race, through their legal representatives, seek the aid of the courts in obtaining admission to the public schools of their community on a nonsegregated basis. In each instance, they had been denied admission to schools attended by white children under laws requiring or permitting segregation according to race. This segregation was alleged to deprive the plaintiffs of the equal protection of the laws under the Fourteenth Amendment. ...

The plaintiffs contend that segregated public schools are not "equal" and cannot be made "equal," and that hence they are deprived of the equal protection of the laws. ...

The most avid proponents of the post-War Amendments undoubtedly intended them to remove all legal distinctions among "all persons born or naturalized in the United

States." Their opponents, just as certainly, were antagonistic to both the letter and the spirit of the Amendments and wished them to have the most limited effect. What others in Congress and the state legislatures had in mind cannot be determined with any degree of certainty.

An additional reason for the inconclusive nature of the Amendment's history, with respect to segregated schools, is the status of public education at that time.[4] In the South, the movement toward free common schools, supported by general taxation, had not yet taken hold. Education of white children was largely in the hands of private groups. Education of Negroes was almost nonexistent, and practically all of the race were illiterate. In fact, any education of Negroes was forbidden by law in some states. Today, in contrast, many Negroes have achieved outstanding success in the arts and sciences as well as in the business and professional world. It is true that public school education at the time of the Amendment had advanced further in the North, but the effect of the Amendment on Northern States was generally ignored in the congressional debates. Even in the North, the conditions of public education did not approximate those existing today. The curriculum was usually rudimentary; ungraded schools were common in rural areas; the school term was but three months a year in many states; and compulsory school attendance was virtually unknown. As a consequence, it is not surprising that there should be so little in the history of the Fourteenth Amendment relating to its intended effect on public education.

In the first cases in this Court construing the Fourteenth Amendment, decided shortly after its adoption, the Court interpreted it as proscribing all state-imposed discriminations against the Negro race.[5] The doctrine of "separate but equal" did not make its appearance in this Court until 1896 in the case of Plessy v. Ferguson, ... involving not education but transportation.[6] ... In more recent cases, all on the graduate school level, inequality was found in that specific benefits enjoyed by white students were denied to Negro students of the same educational qualifications. ... In none of these cases was it necessary to reexamine the doctrine to grant relief to the Negro plaintiff. And in Sweatt v. Painter ..., the Court expressly reserved decision on the question whether Plessy v. Ferguson should be held inapplicable to public education.

In the instant cases, that question is directly presented. Here, unlike Sweatt v. Painter, there are findings below that the Negro and white schools involved have been equalized, or are being equalized, with respect to buildings, curricula, qualifications and salaries of teachers, and other "tangible" factors.[9] Our decision, therefore, cannot turn on merely a comparison of these tangible factors in the Negro and white schools involved in each of the cases. We must look instead to the effect of segregation itself on public education.

In approaching this problem, we cannot turn the clock back to 1868 when the Amendment was adopted, or even to 1896 when Plessy v. Ferguson was written. We must consider public education in the light of its full development and its present place in American life throughout the Nation. Only in this way can it be determined if segregation in public schools deprives these plaintiffs of the equal protection of the laws.

Today, education is perhaps the most important function of state and local governments. Compulsory school attendance laws and the great expenditures for education both demonstrate our recognition of the importance of education to our democratic society. It is required in the performance of our most basic public responsibilities, even service in the armed forces. It is the very foundation of good citizenship. Today it is a principal instrument in awakening the child to cultural values, in preparing him for later professional training, and in helping him to adjust normally to his environment. In these days, it is doubtful that any child may reasonably be expected to succeed in life if he is denied the opportunity of an education. Such an opportunity, where the state has undertaken to provide it, is a right which must be made available to all in equal terms.

We come then to the question presented: Does segregation of children in public schools solely on the basis of race, even though the physical facilities and other "tangible" factors may be equal, deprive the children of the minority group of equal education opportunities? We believe that it does.

In Sweatt v. Painter ..., in finding that a segregated law school for Negroes could not provide them equal educational opportunities, this Court relied in large part on "those qualities which are incapable of objective measurement but which make for greatness in a law school." In McLaurin v. Oklahoma State Regents, ... the Court, in requiring that a Negro admitted to a white graduate school be treated like all other students, again resorted to intangible considerations: "... his ability to study, to engage in discussions and exchange views with other students, and, in general, to learn his profession." Such considerations apply with added force to children in grade and high schools. To separate them from others of similar age and qualifications solely because of their race generates a feeling of inferiority as to their status in the community that may affect their hearts and minds in a way unlikely ever to be undone. The effect of this separation on their educational opportunities was well stated by a finding in the Kansas case by a court which nevertheless felt compelled to rule against the Negro plaintiffs:

"Segregation of white and colored children in public schools has a detrimental effect upon the colored children. The impact is greater when it has the sanction of the law; for the policy of separating the races is usually interpreted as denoting the inferiority of the Negro group. A sense of inferiority affects the motivation of a child to learn. Segregation with the sanction of the law, therefore, has a tendency to [retard] the educational and mental development of Negro children and to deprive them of some of the benefits they would receive in a racial[ly] integrated school system."[10]

Whatever may have been the extent of psychological knowledge at the time of Plessy v. Ferguson, this finding is amply supported by modern authority.[11] Any language in Plessy v. Ferguson contrary to this finding is rejected.

We conclude that in the field of public education the doctrine of "separate but equal" has no place. Separate educational facilities are inherently unequal. Therefore, we hold that the plaintiffs and others similarly situated for whom the actions have been brought are, by reason of the segregation complained of, deprived of the equal protection of the laws guaranteed by the Fourteenth Amendment. This disposition makes unnecessary any discussion whether such segregation also violates the Due Process Clause of the Fourteenth Amendment.[12] ...

NOTES

11. K.B. Clark, Effect of Prejudice and Discrimination on Personality Development (Midcentury White House Conference on Children and Youth, 1950); Witmer and Kotinsky, Personality in the Making (1952), ch VI; Deutscher and Chein, The Psychological Effects of Enforced Segregation: A Survey of Social Science Opinion, 26 J Psychol 259 (1948); Chein, What are the Psychological Effects of Segregation Under Conditions of Equal Facilities?, 3 Int J Opinion and Attitude Res 229 (1949); Brameld, Educational Costs, in Discrimination and National Welfare (MacIver, ed., 1949), 44-48; Frazier, The Negro in the United States (1949), 674-681. And see generally, Myrdal, An American Dilemma (1944).

APPENDIX B

SOUTHEASTERN COMMUNITY COLLEGE V. DAVIS

SOUTHEASTERN COMMUNITY COLLEGE

v.

FRANCIS B. DAVIS.

Mr. Justice Powell delivered the opinion of the Court.

This case presents a matter of first impression for this Court: Whether § 504 of the Rehabilitation Act of 1973, which prohibits discrimination against an "otherwise qualified handicapped individual" in federally funded programs "solely by reason of his handicap," forbids professional schools from imposing physical qualifications for admission to their clinical training programs.

I

Respondent, who suffers from a serious hearing disability, seeks to be trained as a registered nurse. During the 1973-1974 academic year she was enrolled in the College Parallel program of Southeastern Community College, a state institution that receives federal funds. Respondent hoped to progress to Southeastern's Associate Degree Nursing program, completion of which would make her eligible for state certification as a registered nurse. In the course of her application to the nursing program, she was interviewed by a member of the nursing faculty. It became apparent that respondent had difficulty understanding questions asked, and on inquiry she acknowledged a history of hearing problems and dependence on a hearing aid. She was advised to consult an audiologist.

On the basis of an examination at Duke University Medical Center, respondent was diagnosed as having a "bilateral, sensori-neural loss." App. 127a. A change in her hearing aid was recommended, as a result of which it was expected that she would be able to detect sounds "almost as well as a person would who has normal hearing." App. 127a-128a. But this improvement would not mean that she could discriminate among sounds sufficiently to understand normal spoken speech. Her lipreading skills would remain necessary for effective communication: "While wearing the hearing aid, she is well aware of gross sounds occurring in the listening environment. However, she can only be responsible for speech spoken to her, when the talker gets her attention and allows her to look directly at the talker." App. 128a.

Southeastern next consulted Mary McRee, Executive Director of the North Carolina Board of Nursing. On the basis of the audiologist's report, McRee recommended that respondent not be admitted to the nursing program. In McRee's view, respondent's hearing disability made it unsafe for her to practice as a nurse.[1] In addition, it would be impossible for respondent to participate safely in the normal clinical training program, and those modifications that would be necessary to enable safe participation would prevent her from realizing the benefits of the program: "To adjust patient learning experiences in keeping with [respondent's] hearing limitations could, in fact, be the same as denying her full learning to meet the objectives of your nursing programs." App. 132a-133a.

After respondent was notified that she was not qualified for nursing study because of her hearing disability, she requested reconsideration of the decision. The entire nursing staff of Southeastern was assembled, and McRee again was consulted. McRee repeated her conclusion that on the basis of the available evidence, respondent "has hearing limitations which could interfere with her safely caring for patients." App. 139a. Upon further deliberation, the staff voted to deny respondent admission.

Respondent then filed suit in the United States District Court for the Eastern District of North Carolina, alleging both a violation of § 504 of the Rehabilitation Act of 1973, 87 Stat. 394, as amended. 29 U.S.C. § 794,[2] and a denial of equal protection and due process. After a bench trial, the District Court entered judgment in favor of Southeastern. 424 F. Supp. 1341 (1976). It confirmed the findings of the audiologist that even with a hearing aid respondent cannot understand speech directed to her except through lipreading, and further found that,

> "[I] in many situations such as an operation room, intensive care unit, or post-natal care unit, all doctors and nurses wear surgical masks which would make lip-reading impossible. Additionally, in many situations a Registered Nurse would be required to instantly follow the physician's instructions concerning procurement of various types of instruments and drugs where the physician would be unable to get the nurse's attention by other than vocal means." *Id.,* at 1342.

Accordingly, the Court concluded that:

> "[Respondent's] handicap actually prevents her from safely performing in both her training program and her proposed profession. The trial testimony indicated numerous situations where [respondent's] particular disability would render her unable to function properly. Of particular concern to the court in this case is the potential danger to future patients in such situations." *Id.,* at 1345.

Based on these findings, the District Court concluded that respondent was not an "otherwise qualified handicapped individual" protected against discrimination by § 504. In its view, "[o]therwise qualified, can only be read to mean otherwise able to function sufficiently in the position sought in spite of the handicap, if proper training and facilities are suitable and available." *Ibid.* Because respondent's disability would prevent her from functioning "sufficiently" in Southeastern's nursing program, the Court held that the decision to exclude her was not discriminatory within the meaning of § 504.[3]

On appeal, the Court of Appeals for the Fourth Circuit reversed. 574 F. 2d 1158 (1978). It did not dispute the District Court's findings of fact, but held that the Court had misconstrued § 504. In light of administrative regulations that had been promulgated while the appeal was pending, see 42 Fed. Reg. 22676 (May 4, 1977),[4] the appellate court believed that § 504 required Southeastern to "reconsider plaintiff's application for admission to the nursing program without regard to her hearing ability." *Id.*, at 1160. It concluded that the District Court had erred in taking respondent's handicap into account in determining whether she was "otherwise qualified" for the program, rather than confining its inquiry to her "academic and technical qualifications." *Id.*, at 1161. The Court of Appeals also suggested that § 504 required "affirmative conduct" on the part of Southeastern to modify its program to accommodate the disabilities of applicants, "even when such modifications become expensive." *Id.*, at 1162.

Because of the importance of this issue to the many institutions covered by § 504, we granted certiorari. 439 U.S. _____ (1979). We now reverse.[5]

II

This is the first case in which this Court has been called upon to interpret § 504. It is elementary that "[t]he starting point in every case involving the construction of a statute is the language itself." *Blue Chip Stamps* v. *Manor Drug Stores,* 421 U.S. 723, 756 (1975) (Powell, J., concurring); see *Greyhound Corp.* v. *Mt. Hood Stages, Inc.,* 437 U.S. 322, 330 (1978); *Santa Fe Industries, Inc.* v. *Green,* 430 U.S. 462, 472 (1977). Section 504 by its terms does not compel educational institutions to disregard the disabilities of handicapped individuals or to make substantial modifications in their programs to allow disabled persons to participate. Instead, it requires only that an "otherwise qualified handicapped individual" not be excluded from participation in a federally funded program "solely by reason of his handicap," indicating only that mere possession of a handicap is not a permissible ground for assuming an inability to function in a particular context.[6]

The court below, however, believed that the "otherwise qualified" persons protected by § 504 include those who would be able to meet the requirements of a particular program in every respect except as to limitations imposed by their handicap. See 574 F. 2d. at 1160. Taken literally, this holding would prevent an institution from taking into account any limitation resulting from the handicap, however disabling. It assumes, in effect, that a person need not meet legitimate physical requirements in order to be "otherwise qualified." We think the understanding of the District Court is closer to the plain meaning of the statutory language. An otherwise qualified person is one who is able to meet all of a program's requirements in spite of his handicap.

The regulations promulgated by the Department of Health, Education, and Welfare (HEW) to interpret § 504 reinforce, rather than contradict, this conclusion. According to these regulations, a "[q]ualified handicapped person" is, "[w]ith respect to postsecondary and vocational education services, a handicapped person who meets the academic and technical standards requisite to admission or participation in the [school's] education program or activity...." 45 CFR § 84.3 (k)(3) (1978). An explanatory note states:

> "The term 'technical standards' refers to *all* nonacademic admissions criteria that are essential to participation in the program in question." 45 CFR pt. 84, App. A, at p. 405 (emphasis supplied).

A further note emphasizes that legitimate physical qualifications may be essential to participation in particular programs.[7] We think it clear, therefore, that HEW interprets the "other" qualifications which a handicapped person may be required to meet as including necessary physical qualifications.

III

The remaining question is whether the physical qualifications Southeastern demanded of respondent might not be necessary for participation in its nursing program. It is not open to dispute that, as Southeastern's Associate Degree Nursing program currently is constituted, the ability to understand speech without reliance on lipreading is necessary for patient safety during the clinical phase of the program. As the District Court found, this ability also is indispensable for many of the functions that a registered nurse performs.

Respondent contends nevertheless that § 504, properly interpreted, compels Southeastern to undertake affirmative action that would dispense with the need for effective oral communication. First, it is suggested that respondent can be given individual supervision by faculty members whenever she attends patients directly. Moreover, certain required courses might be dispensed with altogether for respondent. It is not necessary, she argues, that Southeastern train her to undertake all the tasks a registered nurse is licensed to perform. Rather, it is sufficient to make § 504 applicable if respondent might be able to perform satisfactorily some of the duties of a registered nurse or to hold some of the positions available to a registered nurse.[8]

Respondent finds support for this argument in portions of the HEW regulations discussed above. In particular, a provision applicable to postsecondary educational programs requires covered institutions to make "modifications" in their programs to accommodate handicapped persons, and to provide "auxiliary aids" such as sign-language interpreters.[9] Respondent argues that this regulation imposes an obligation to ensure full participation in covered programs by handicapped individuals and, in particular, requires Southeastern to make the kind of adjustments that would be necessary to permit her safe participation in the nursing program.

We note first that on the present record it appears unlikely respondent could benefit from any affirmative action that the regulation reasonably could be interpreted as requiring. Section 84.44 (d)(2), for example, explicitly excludes "devices or services of a personal nature" from the kinds of auxiliary aids a school must provide a handicapped individual. Yet the only evidence in the record indicates that nothing less than close, individual attention by a nursing instructor would be sufficient to ensure patient safety if respondent took part in the clinical phase of the nursing program. See 424 F. Supp., at 1346. Furthermore, it also is reasonably clear that § 84.44 (a) does not encompass the kind of curricular changes that would be necessary to accommodate respondent in the nursing program. In light of respondent's inability to function in clinical courses without close supervision, Southeastern with prudence could allow her to take only academic classes. Whatever benefits respondent might realize from such a course of study, she would not receive even a rough equivalent of the training a nursing program normally gives. Such a fundamental alteration in the nature of a program is far more than the "modification" the regulation requires.

Moreover, an interpretation of the regulations that required the extensive modifications necessary to include respondent in the nursing program would raise grave doubts about their validity. If these regulations were to require substantial adjustments in existing programs beyond those necessary to eliminate discrimination against otherwise qualified individuals, they would do more than clarify the meaning of § 504. Instead, they would constitute an unauthorized extension of the obligations imposed by that statute.

The language and structure of the Rehabilitation Act of 1973 reflect a recognition by Congress of the distinction between the evenhanded treatment of qualified handicapped persons and affirmative efforts to overcome the disabilities caused by handicaps. Section 501 (b), governing the employment of handicapped individuals by the Federal Government, requires each federal agency to submit "an affirmative action program plan for the hiring, placement, and advancement of handicapped individuals...." These plans "shall include a description of the extent to which and methods whereby the special needs of handicapped employees are being met." Similarly, § 503 (a), governing hiring by federal contractors, requires employers to "take affirmative action to employ and advance in employment qualified handicapped individuals...." The President is required to promulgate regulations to enforce this section.

Under § 501 (c) of the Act, by contrast, state agencies such as Southeastern are only "encourage[d]...to adopt such policies and procedures." Section 504 does not refer at all to affirmative action, and except as it applies to federal employers it does not provide for implementation by administrative action. A comparison of these provisions demonstrates that Congress understood accommodation of the needs of handicapped individuals may require affirmative action and knew how to provide for it in those instances where it wished to do so.[10]

Although an agency's interpretation of the statute under which it operates is entitled to some deference, "this deference is constrained by our obligation to honor the clear meaning of a statute, as revealed by its language, purpose and history." *International Brotherhood of Teamsters v. Daniel,* 439 U.S. ____, ____ n. 20 (1979). Here neither the language, purpose, nor history of § 504 reveals an intent to impose an affirmative action obligation on all recipients of federal funds.[11] Accordingly, we hold that even if HEW has attempted to create such an obligation itself, it lacks the authority to do so.

IV

We do not suggest that the line between a lawful refusal to extend affirmative action and illegal discrimination against handicapped persons always will be clear. It is possible to envision situations where an insistence on continuing past requirements and practices might arbitrarily deprive genuinely qualified handicapped persons of the opportunity to participate in a covered program. Technological advances can be expected to enhance opportunities to rehabilitate the handicapped or otherwise to qualify them for some useful employment. Such advances also may enable attainment of these goals without imposing undue financial and administrative burdens upon a State. Thus situations may arise where a refusal to modify an existing program might become unreasonable and discriminatory. Identification of those instances where a refusal to accommodate the needs of a disabled person amounts to discrimination against the handicapped continues to be an important responsibility of HEW.

In this case, however, it is clear that Southeastern's unwillingness to make major adjustments in its nursing program does not constitute such discrimination. The uncontroverted testimony of several members of Southeastern's staff and faculty established that the purpose of its program was to train persons who could serve the nursing profession in all customary ways. See, *e.g.,* App. 35a, 52a, 53a, 71a, 74a. This type of purpose, far from reflecting any animus against handicapped individuals, is shared by many if not most of the institutions that train persons to render professional service. It is undisputed that respondent could not participate in Southeastern's nursing program unless the standards were substantially lowered. Section 504 imposes no requirement upon an educational institution to lower or to effect substantial modifications of standards to accommodate a handicapped person.[12]

One may admire respondent's desire and determination to overcome her handicap and there well may be various other types of service for which she can qualify. In this case, however, we hold that there was no violation of § 504 when Southeastern concluded that respondent did not qualify for admission to its program. Nothing in the language or history of § 504 reflects an intention to limit the freedom of an educational institution to require reasonable physical qualifications for admission to a clinical training program. Nor has there been any showing in this case that any action short of a substantial change in Southeastern's program would render unreasonable the qualifications it imposed.

V

Accordingly, we reverse the judgment of the court below, and remand for proceedings consistent with this opinion.

So ordered.

NOTES

1. McRee also wrote that respondent's hearing disability could preclude her practicing safely in "any setting" allowed by "a license as L[icensed] P[ractical] N[urse]." App. 132a. Respondent contends that inasmuch as she already was licensed as a practical nurse, McRee's opinion was inherently incredible. But the record indicates that respondent had "not worked as a practical nurse except to do a little bit of night duty," App. 32a, and had not done that for several years before applying to Southeastern. Accordingly, it is at least possible to infer that respondent in fact could not work safely as a practical nurse in spite of her license to do so. In any event, we note the finding of the District Court that "a Licensed Practical Nurse, unlike a Licensed Registered Nurse, operates under constant supervision and is not allowed to perform medical tasks which require a great degree of technical sophistication." 424 F. Supp., 1341, 1342-1343 (EDNC 1976).

2. The statute provides in full:"No otherwise qualified handicapped individual in the United States, as defined in section 706 (6) of this title, shall, solely by reason of his handicap, be excluded from the participation in, or be denied the benefits of, or be subjected to discrimination under any program or activity receiving Federal financial assistance *or under any program or activity conducted by any Executive agency or by the United States Postal Service. The head of each such agency shall promulgate such regulations as may be necessary to carry out the amendments to this section made by the Rehabilitation, Comprehensive Services, and Developmental Disabilities Act of 1978. Copies of any proposed regulation shall be submitted to appropriate authorizing committees of the Congress, and such regulation may take effect no earlier than the thirtieth day after the date on which such regulation is so submitted to such committees.'* The italicized portion of the section was added by § 119 of the Rehabilitation, Comprehensive Services, and Developmental Disabilities Act of 1978, 92 Stat. 2982. Respondent asserts no claim under this portion of the statute.

3. The District Court also dismissed respondent's constitutional claims. The Court of Appeals affirmed that portion of the order, and respondent has not sought review of this ruling.

4. Relying on the plain language of the Act, the Department of Health, Education, and Welfare (HEW) at first did not promulgate any regulations to implement § 504. In a subsequent suit against HEW, however, the United States District Court for the District of Columbia held that Congress had intended regulations to be issued and ordered HEW to do so. *Cherry* v. *Mathews,* 419 F. Supp. 922 (1976). The ensuing regulations currently are embodied in 45 CFR pt. 84.

5. In addition to challenging the construction of § 504 by the Court of Appeals, Southeastern also contends that respondent cannot seek judicial relief for violations of that statute in view of the absence of any express private right of action. Respondent asserts that whether or not § 504 provides a private action, she may maintain her suit under 42 U.S.C. § 1983. In light of our disposition of this case on the merits, it is unnecessary to address these issues and we express no views on them. See *Norton* v. *Mathews,* 427 U.S. 524, 529-531 (1976); *Moor* v. *County of Alameda,* 411 U.S. 693, 715 (1973); *United States* v. *Augenblick, 393* U.S. 348, 351-352 (1969).

6. The Act defines "handicapped individual" as follows:"The term 'handicapped individual' means any individual who (A) has a physical or mental disability which for such individual constitutes or results in a substantial handicap to employment and (B) can reasonably be expected to benefit in terms of employability from vocational rehabilitation services provided pursuant to subchapters I and III of this chapter. For the purposes of subchapters IV and V of this chapter, such term means any person who (A) has a physical or mental impairment which substantially limits one or more of such person's major life activities, (B) has a a record of such an impairment, or (C) is regarded as having such an impairment." Section 7 of the Rehabilitation Act of 1973, 87 Stat. 359, as amended, 88 Stat. 1619, 89 Stat. 2, 29 U.S.C. § 706 (6).This definition comports with our understanding of § 504. A person who has a record of or is regarded as having an impairment may at present have no actual incapacity at all. Such a person would be exactly the kind of individual who could be "otherwise qualified" to participate in covered programs. And a person who suffers from a limiting physical or mental impairment still may possess other abilities that permit him to meet the requirements of various programs. Thus it is clear that Congress included among the class of "handicapped" persons covered by § 504 a range of individuals who could be "otherwise qualified." See S. Rep. No. 1297, 93d Cong., 2d Sess., 38-39 (1974).

7. The note states:"Paragraph (k) of § 84.3 defines the term 'qualified handicapped person.' Throughout the regulation, this term is used instead of the statutory term 'otherwise qualified handicapped person.' The Department believes that the omission of the word 'otherwise' is necessary in order to comport with the intent of the statute because, read literally, 'otherwise' qualified handicapped persons include persons who are qualified except for their handicap, rather than in spite of their handicap. Under such a literal reading, a blind person possessing all the qualifications for driving a bus except sight could be said to be 'otherwise qualified' for the job of driving. Clearly, such a result was not intended by Congress. In all other respects, the terms 'qualified' and 'otherwise qualified' are intended to be interchangeable." 45 CFR pt. 84, App. A, at p.405.

8. The court below adopted a portion of this argument: "[Respondent's] ability to read lips aids her in overcoming her hearing disability; however, it was argued that in certain situations such as in an operating room environment where surgical masks are used, this ability would be unavailing to her. "Be that as it may, in the medical community, there does appear to be a number of settings in which the plaintiff could perform satisfactorily as an RN, such as in industry or perhaps a physician's office. Certainly [respondent] could be viewed as possessing extraordinary insight into the medical and emotional needs of those with hearing disabilities. "If [respondent] meets all the other criteria for admission in the pursuit of her RN career, under the relevant North Carolina statutes, N.C. Gen. Stat. §§ 90-158, *et seq.,* it should not be foreclosed to her simply because she may not be able to function effectively in all the roles which registered nurses may choose for their careers." 574 F. 2d 1158, 1161 n. 6 (CA4 1978).

9. This regulation provides in full:"(a) *Academic requirements.* A recipient [of federal funds] to which this subpart applies shall make such modifications to its academic requirements as are necessary to ensure that such requirements do not discriminate or have the effect of discriminating, on the basis of handicap, against a qualified handicapped applicant or student. Academic requirements that the recipient can demonstrate are essential to the program of instruction being pursued by such student or to any directly related licensing requirement will not be regarded as discriminatory within the meaning of this section. Modifications may include changes in the length of time permitted for the completion of degree requirements, substitution of specific courses required for the completion of degree requirements, and adaptations of the manner in which specific courses are conducted. "(d) *Auxiliary aids.* (1) A recipient to which this subpart applies shall take such steps as are necessary to ensure that no handicapped student is denied the benefits of, excluded from participation in, or

otherwise subjected to discrimination under the education program or activity operated by the recipient because of the absence of educational auxiliary aids for students with impaired sensory, manual, or speaking skills. "(2) Auxiliary aids may include taped texts, interpreters or other effective methods of making orally delivered materials available to students with hearing impairments, readers in libraries for students with visual impairments, classroom equipment adapted for use by students with manual impairments, and other similar services and actions. Recipients need not provide attendants, individually prescribed devices, readers for personal use or study, or other devices or services of a personal nature." 45 CFR § 84.44.

10. § 115(a) of the Rehabilitation Act of 1978 added to the 1973 Act a section authorizing grants to state units for the purpose of providing "such information and technical assistance (including support personnel such as interpreters for the deaf) as may be necessary to assist those entities in complying with this Act, particularly the requirements of § 504." 92 Stat. 2971, codified at 29 U.S.C. § 775. This provision recognizes that on occasion the elimination of discrimination might involve some costs; it does not imply that the refusal to undertake substantial changes in a program by itself constitutes discrimination. Whatever effect the availability of these funds might have on ascertaining the existence of discrimination in some future case, no such funds were available to Southeastern at the time respondent sought admission to its nursing program.

11. The Government, in a brief *amicus curiae* in support of respondent, cites a report of the Senate Committee on Labor and Public Welfare on the 1974 amendments to the 1973 Act and several statements by individual Members of Congress during debate on the 1978 amendments, some of which indicate a belief that § 504 requires affirmative action. See Brief for the Government as *Amicus Curiae* 44-50. But these isolated statements by individual Members of Congress or its committees, all made after the enactment of the statute under consideration, cannot substitute for a clear expression of legislative intent at the time of enactment. *Quern* v. *Mandley,* 436 U.S. 725, 736 n. 10 (1978); *Los Angeles Dept. of Water & Power* v. *Manhart,* 435 U.S. 702, 714 (1978). Nor do these comments, none of which represents the will of Congress as a whole, constitute subsequent "legislation" such as this Court might weigh in construing the meaning of an earlier enactment. Cf. *Red Lion Broadcasting Co.* v. *FCC,* 395 U.S. 367, 380-381 (1969). The Government also argues that various amendments to the 1973 Act contained in the Rehabilitation Act of 1978 further reflect Congress' approval of the affirmative action obligation created by HEW's regulations. But the amendment most directly on point undercuts this position. In amending § 504, Congress both extended that section's prohibition of discrimination to "any program or activity conducted by any Executive agency or by the United Postal Service" and authorized administrative regulations to implement only *this amendment.* See n. 2, *supra.* The fact that no other regulations were mentioned supports an inference that no others were approved. Finally, we note that the assertion by HEW of the authority to promulgate any regulations under § 504 has been neither consistent nor long-standing. For the first three years after the section was enacted, HEW maintained the position that Congress had not intended any regulations to be issued. It altered its stand only after having been enjoined to do so. See n. 4, *supra.* This fact substantially diminishes the deference to be given to HEW's present interpretation of the statute. See *General Electric Co.* v. *Gilbert,* 429 U.S. 125, 143 (1976).

12. Respondent contends that it is unclear whether North Carolina law requires a registered nurse to be capable of performing all functions open to that profession in order to obtain a license to practice, although McRee, the Executive Director of the state Board of Nursing, had informed Southeastern that the law did so require. See App. 138a-139a. Respondent further argues that even if she is not capable of meeting North Carolina's present licensing requirements, she still might succeed in obtaining a license in another jurisdiction. Respondent's argument misses the point. Southeastern's program, structured to train persons who will be able to perform all normal roles of

a registered nurse, represents a legitimate academic policy and is accepted by the State. In effect it seeks to ensure that no graduate will pose a danger to the public in any professional role he or she might be cast. Even if the licensing requirements of North Carolina or some other State are less demanding, nothing in the Act requires an educational institution to lower its standards.

APPENDIX C

BOARD V. ROWLEY

(excerpts from Court's majority opinion only; concurring and dissenting opinions are omitted, as are some footnotes from the majority opinion)

BOARD OF EDUCATION OF THE HENDRICK HUDSON CENTRAL SCHOOL
DISTRICT BD. OF ED., WESTCHESTER COUNTY, ET AL., PETITIONERS
v.
AMY ROWLEY, BY HER PARENTS AND NATURAL GUARDIANS,
CLIFFORD AND NANCY ROWLEY, ETC.

Justice Rehnquist delivered the opinion of the court.

I

The Education for All Handicapped Children Act of 1975 (Act), 20 U.S.C. § 1401 *et seq.*, provides federal money to assist state and local agencies in educating handicapped children, and conditions such funding upon a State's compliance with extensive goals and procedures. The Act represents an ambitious federal effort to promote the education of handicapped children, and was passed in response to Congress' perception that a majority of handicapped children in the United States "were either totally excluded from schools or [were] sitting idly in regular classrooms awaiting the time when they were old enough to 'drop out.' " H.R. Rep. No. 94-332, p. 2 (1975). The Act's evolution and major provisions shed light on the questions of statutory interpretation which is at the heart of this case.

Congress first addressed the problem of educating the handicapped in 1966 when it amended the Elementary and Secondary Education Act of 1965 to establish a grant program "for the purpose of assisting the States in the initiation, expansion, and improvement of programs and projects ... for the education of handicapped children." Pub. L. No. 89-750, § 161, 80 Stat. 1204 (1966). That program was repealed in 1970 by the Education for the Handicapped Act, Pub. L. No. 91-230, 84 Stat. 175, Part B of which established a grant program similar in purpose to the repealed legislation. Neither the 1966 nor the 1970 legislation contained specific guidelines for state use of the grant money; both were aimed primarily at stimulating the States to develop educational resources and to train personnel for educating the handicapped.[1]

Dissatisfied with the progress being made under these earlier enactments, and spurred by two district court decisions holding that handicapped children should be given access to a public education,[2] Congress in 1974 greatly increased federal funding for education of the handicapped and for the first time required recipient States to adopt "a goal of providing full educational opportunities to all handicapped children." Pub. L. 93-380, 88 Stat. 579, 583 (1974) (the 1974 statute). The 1974 statute was recognized as an interim measure only, adopted "in order to give the Congress an additional year in which to study what if any additional Federal assistance [was] required to enable the States to meet the needs of handicapped children." H.R. Rep. No. 94-332, *supra,* p. 4. The ensuing year of study produced the Education for All Handicapped Children Act of 1975.

In order to qualify for federal financial assistance under the Act, a State must demonstrate that it "has in effect a policy that assures all handicapped children the right to a free appropriate public education." 20 U.S.C. § 1412(1). That policy must be reflected in a state plan submitted to and approved by the Commissioner of Education,[3] § 1413, which describes in detail the goals, programs, and timetables under which the State intends to educate handicapped children within its borders. §§ 1412, 1413. States receiving money under the Act must provide education to the handicapped by priority, first "to handicapped children who are not receiving an education" and second "to handicapped children ... with the most severe handicaps who are receiving an inadequate education," § 1412(3), and "to the maximum extent appropriate" must educate handicapped children "with children who are not handicapped." § 1412(5).[4] The Act broadly defines "handicapped children" to include "mentally retarded, hard of hearing, deaf, speech impaired, visually handicapped, seriously emotionally disturbed, orthopedically impaired, [and] other health impaired children, [and] children with specific learning disabilities." § 1401(1).[5]

The "free appropriate public education" required by the Act is tailored to the unique needs of the handicapped child by means of an "individualized educational program" (IEP). § 1401(18). The IEP, which is prepared at a meeting between a qualified representative of the local educational agency, the child's teacher, the child's parents or guardian, and, where appropriate, the child, consists of a written document containing

> "(A) a statement of the present levels of educational performance of the child, (B) a statement of annual goals, including short-term instructional objectives, (C) a statement of the specific educational services to be provided to such child, and the extent to which such child will be able to participate in regular educational programs, (D) the projected date for initiation and anticipated duration of such service, and (E) appropriate objective criteria and evaluation procedures and schedules for determining, on at least an annual basis, whether instructional objectives are being achieved." § 1401(19).

Local or regional educational agencies must review, and where appropriate revise, each child's IEP at least annually. § 1404(a)(5). See also §§ 1413(a)(11), 1414(a)(5).

In addition to the state plan and the IEP already described, the Act imposes extensive procedural requirements upon States receiving federal funds under its provisions. Parents or guardians of handicapped children must be notified of any proposed change in the "identification, evaluation, or educational placement of the children of the provision of a free appropriate public education to the child," and must be permitted to bring a complaint about "any matter relating to" such evaluation and education. § 1415(b)(1)(D) and (E).[6] Complaints brought by parents or guardians must be resolved at "an impartial due process hearing," and appeal to the State educational agency must be provided if the initial hearing is held at the local or regional level. § 1415(b)(2) and (c).[7] Thereafter, "[a]ny party aggrieved by the findings and decisions" of the state administrative hearing has "the right to bring a civil action with respect to the complaint ... in any State court of competent jurisdiction or in a district court of the United States without regard to the amount in controversy." § 1415(e)(2).

Thus, although the Act leaves to the States the primary responsibility for developing and executing educational programs for handicapped children, it imposes significant requirements to be followed in the discharge of that responsibility. ...

II

This case arose in connection with the education of Amy Rowley, a deaf student at the Furnace Woods School in the Hendrick Hudson Central School District, Peekskill, New York. Amy has minimal residual hearing and is an excellent lipreader. During the year before she began attending Furnace Woods, a meeting between her parents and school administrators resulted in a decision to place her in a regular kindergarten class in order to determine what supplemental services would be necessary to her education. Several members of the school administration prepared for Amy's arrival by attending a course in sign-language interpretation, and a teletype machine was installed in the principal's office to facilitate communication with her parents who are also deaf. At the end of the trial period it was determined that Amy should remain in the kindergarten class, but that she should be provided with an FM hearing aid which would amplify words spoken into a wireless receiver by the teacher or fellow students during certain classroom activities. Amy successfully completed her kindergarten year.

As required by the Act, an IEP was prepared for Amy during the fall of her first-grade year. The IEP provided that Amy should be educated in a regular classroom at Furnace Woods, should continue to use the FM hearing aid, and should receive instruction from a tutor for the deaf for one hour each day and from a speech therapist for three hours each week. The Rowleys agreed with the IEP but insisted that Amy also be provided a qualified sign-language interpreter in all of her academic classes. Such an interpreter had been placed in Amy's kindergarten class for a two-week experimental period, but the interpreter had reported that Amy did not need his services at that time. The school administrators likewise concluded that Amy did not need such an interpreter in her first-grade classroom. They reached this conclusion after consulting the school district's Committee on the Handicapped, which had received expert evidence from Amy's parents on the importance of a sign-language interpreter, received testimony from Amy's teacher and other persons familiar with her academic and social progress, and visited a class for the deaf.

When their request for an interpreter was denied, the Rowleys demanded and received a hearing before an independent examiner. After receiving evidence from both sides, the examiner agreed with the administrators' determination that an interpreter was not necessary because "Amy was achieving educationally, academically, and socially" without such assistance. App. to Pet. for Cert. F-22. The examiner's decision was affirmed on appeal by the New York Commissioner of Education on the basis of substantial evidence in the record. ... Pursuant to the Act's provision for judicial review, the Rowleys then brought an action in the United States District Court for the Southern District of New York, claiming that the administrators' denial of the sign-language interpreter constituted a denial of the "free appropriate public education" guaranteed by the Act.

The District Court found that Amy "is a remarkably well-adjusted child" who interacts and communicates well with her classmates and has "developed an extraordinary rapport" with her teachers. 483 F. Supp. 528, 531. It also found that "she performs better than the average child in her class and is advancing easily from grade to grade," *id.*, at 534, but "that she understands considerably less of what goes on in class than she would if she were not deaf" and thus "is not learning as much, or performing as well academically, as she would without her handicap," *id.*, at 532. This disparity between Amy's achievement and her potential led the court to decide that she was not receiving a "free appropriate public education," which the court defined as "an opportunity to achieve [her] full potential commensurate with the opportunity provided to other children." *Id.*, at 534. According to the District Court, such a standard "requires that the potential of the handicapped child be measured and compared to his or her performance, and that the remaining differential or 'shortfall' be compared to the shortfall experienced by nonhandicapped children." *Ibid.* The District Court's definition arose from its assumption that the responsibility for "giv[ing] content to the requirement of an 'appropriate education'" had "been left entirely to the federal courts and the hearing officer." *Id.*, at 533.[8]

A divided panel of the United States Court of Appeals for the Second Circuit affirmed. The Court of Appeals "agree[d] with the [D]istrict [C]ourt's conclusions of law," and held that its "findings of fact [were] not clearly erroneous." 632 F. 2d 945, 947 (1980).

We granted certiorari to review the lower courts' interpretation of the Act. 454 U.S.— 1981. Such review requires us to consider two questions: What is meant by the Act's requirement of a "free appropriate public education?" And what is the role of state and federal courts in exercising the review granted by §1415 of the Act? We consider these questions separately.[9]

III

A

This is the first case in which this Court has been called upon to interpret any provision of the Act. As noted previously, the District Court and the Court of Appeals concluded that "[t]he Act itself does not define 'appropriate education,'" 483 F. Supp., at 533, but leaves "to the courts and the hearing officers" the responsibility of "giv[ing] content to the requirement of an appropriate education." *Ibid.* See also 632 F. 2d, at 947. Petitioners contend that the definition of the phrase "free appropriate public education" used by the courts below overlooks the definition of that phrase actually found in the Act. Respondents agree that the Act defines "free appropriate public education," but contend that the statutory definition is not "functional" and thus "offers judges no guidance in their consideration of controversies involving the 'identification, evaluation, or educational placement of the child or the provision of a free appropriate public education.' " Brief for Respondents 28. The United States, appearing as *amicus curiae* on behalf of the respondents, states that "[a]lthough the Act includes definitions of 'free appropriate public education' and other related terms, the statutory definitions do not adequately explain what is meant by 'appropriate.' " Brief for United States as *Amicus Curiae* 13.

We are loath to conclude that Congress failed to offer any assistance in defining the meaning of the principal substantive phrase used in the Act. It is beyond dispute that, contrary to the conclusions of the courts below, the Act does expressly define "free appropriate public education":

> "The term 'free appropriate public education' means *special education* and *related services* which (A) have been provided at public expense, under public supervision and direction, and without charge, (B) meet the standards of the State educational agency, (C) include an appropriate preschool, elementary, or secondary school education in the State involved, and (D) are provided in conformity with the individualized education program required under section 1414(a)(5) of this title." § 1401(18) (emphasis added).

"Special education," as referred to in this definition, means "specially designed instruction, at no cost to parents or guardians, to meet the unique needs of a handicapped child, including classroom instruction, instruction in physical education, home instruction, and instruction in hospitals and institutions." § 1401(16). "Related services" are defined as "transportation, and such developmental, corrective, and other supportive services ... as may be required to assist a handicapped child to benefit from special education." § 1401(17).[10]

Like many statutory definitions, this one tends toward the cryptic rather than the comprehensive, but that is scarcely a reason for abandoning the quest for legislative intent. Whether or not the definition is a "functional" one, as respondents contend it is not, it is the principal tool which Congress has given us for parsing the critical phrase of the Act. We think more must be made of it than either respondents or the United States seems willing to admit.

According to the definitions contained in the Act, a "free appropriate public education" consists of educational instruction specially designed to meet the unique needs of the handicapped child, supported by such services as are necessary to permit the child "to benefit" from the instruction. Almost as a checklist for adequacy under the Act, the definition also requires that such instruction and services be provided at public expense and under public supervision, meet the State's educational standards, approximate the grade levels used in the State's regular education, and comport with the child's IEP. Thus, if personalized instruction is being provided with sufficient supportive services to permit the child to benefit from the instruction, and the other items on the definitional checklist are satisfied, the child is receiving a "free appropriate public education" as defined by the Act.

Other portions of the statute also shed light upon congressional intent. Congress found that of the roughly eight million handicapped children in the United States at the time of enactment, one million were "excluded entirely from the public school system" and more than half were receiving an inappropriate education. Note to §1401. In addition, as mentioned in Part I, the Act requires States to extend educational services first to those children who are receiving no education and second to those children who are receiving an "inadequate education." § 1412(3). When these express statutory findings and priorities are read together with the Act's extensive procedural requirements and its definition of "free appropriate public education," the face of the statute evinces a congressional intent to bring previously excluded handicapped children into the public education systems of the States and to require the States to adopt *procedures* which would result in individualized consideration of and instruction for each child.

Noticeably absent from the language of the statute is any substantive standard prescribing the level of education to be accorded handicapped children. Certainly the language of the statute contains no requirement like the one imposed by the lower courts—that States maximize the potential of handicapped children "commensurate with the opportunity provided to other children." 483 F. Supp., at 534. That standard was expounded by the District Court without reference to the statutory definitions or even to the legislative history of the Act. Although we find the statutory definition of "free appropriate public education" to be helpful in our interpretation of the Act, there remains the question of whether the legislative history indicates a congressional intent that such education meet some additional substantive standard. For an answer, we turn to that history.[11]

B

(i). As suggested in Part I, federal support for education of the handicapped is a fairly recent development. Before passage of the Act some States had passed laws to improve the educational services afforded handicapped children,[12] but many of these children were excluded completely from any form of public education or were left to fend for themselves in classrooms designed for education of their nonhandicapped peers. The House Report begins by emphasizing this exclusion and misplacement, noting that millions of handicapped children "were either totally excluded from schools or [were] sitting idly in regular classrooms awaiting the time when they were old enough to 'drop out.'" H.R. Rep. No. 94-332, *supra,* at 2. See also S. Rep. No. 94-168, p. 8 (1975). One of the Act's two principal sponsors in the Senate urged its passage in similar terms:

> "While much progress has been made in the last few years, we can take no solace in that progress until all handicapped children are, in fact, receiving an education. The most recent statistics provided by the Bureau of Education for the Handicapped estimate that … 1.75 million handicapped children do not receive any educational services, and 2.5 million handicapped children are not receiving an appropriate education." 121 Cong. Rec. 19486 (1975) (remarks of Sen. Williams).

This concern, stressed repeatedly throughout the legislative history,[13] confirms the impression conveyed by the language of the statute: By passing the Act, Congress sought primarily to make public education available to handicapped children. But in seeking to provide such access to public education, Congress did not impose upon the States any greater substantive educational standard than would be necessary to make such access meaningful. Indeed, Congress expressly "recognize[d] that in many instances the process of providing special education and related services to handicapped children is not guaranteed to produce any particular outcome." S. Rep. No. 94-168, *supra,* at 11. Thus, the intent of the Act was more to open the door of public education to handicapped children on appropriate terms than to guarantee any particular level of education once inside.

Both the House and the Senate reports attribute the impetus for the Act and its predecessors to two federal court judgments rendered in 1971 and 1972. As the Senate Report states, passage of the Act "followed a series of landmark court cases establishing in law the right to education for all handicapped children." …

Mills and *PARC* both held that handicapped children must be given *access* to an adequate, publicly supported education. Neither case purports to require any particular substantive level of education.[15] Rather, like the language of the Act, the cases set forth extensive procedures to be followed in formulating personalized educational programs for handicapped children. See 348 F. Supp., at 878-883; 334 F. Supp., at 1258-1267.[16] The fact that both *PARC* and *Mills* are discussed at length in the legislative reports[17] suggests that the principles which they established are the principles which, to a significant extent, guided the drafters of the Act. Indeed, immediately after discussing these cases the Senate Report describes the 1974 statute as having "incorporated the major principles of the right to education cases." S. Rep. No. 94-168, *supra,* at 8. Those principles in turn became the bases of the Act, which itself was designed to effectuate the purposes of the 1974 statute. H.R. Rep. No. 94-332, *supra,* at 5.[18]

That the Act imposes no clear obligation upon recipient States beyond the requirement that handicapped children receive some form of specialized education is perhaps best demonstrated by the fact that Congress, in explaining the need for the Act, equated an "appropriate education" to the receipt of some specialized educational services. ...

It is evident from the legislative history that the characterization of handicapped children as "served" referred to children who were receiving some form of specialized educational services from the States, and that the characterization of children as "unserved" referred to those who were receiving no specialized educational services. ... By characterizing the 3.9 million handicapped children who were "served" as children who were "receiving an appropriate education," the Senate and House reports unmistakably disclose Congress' perception of the type of education required by the Act: an "appropriate education" is provided when personalized educational services are provided.[21]

(ii).   Respondents contend that "the goal of the Act is to provide each handicapped child with an equal educational opportunity." Brief for Respondents 35. We think, however, that the requirement that a State provide specialized educational services to handicapped children generates no additional requirement that the services so provided be sufficient to maximize each child's potential "commensurate with the opportunity provided other children." Respondents and the United States correctly note that Congress sought "to provide assistance to the States in carrying out their responsibilities under ... the Constitution of the United States to provide equal protection of the laws." S. Rep. No. 94-168, *supra,* at 13.[22] But we do not think that such statements imply a congressional intent to achieve strict equality of opportunity or services.

The educational opportunities provided by our public school systems undoubtedly differ from student to student, depending upon a myriad of factors that might affect a particular student's ability to assimilate information presented in the classroom. The requirement that States provide "equal" educational opportunities would thus seem to present an entirely unworkable standard requiring impossible measurements and comparisons. Similarly, furnishing handicapped children with only such services as are available to non-handicapped children would in all probability fall short of the statutory requirement of "free appropriate public education"; to require, on the other hand, the furnishing of every special service necessary to maximize each handicapped child's potential is, we think, further than Congress intended to go. Thus to speak in terms of "equal" services in one instance gives less than what is required by the Act and in another instance more. The theme of the Act is "free appropriate public education," a phrase which is too complex to be captured by the word "equal" whether one is speaking of opportunities or services.

The legislative conception of the requirements of equal protection was undoubtedly informed by the two district court decisions referred to above. But cases such as *Mills* and *PARC* held simply that handicapped children may not be excluded entirely from public education. ... The right of access to free public education enunciated by these cases is significantly different from any notion of absolute equality of opportunity regardless of capacity. To the extent that Congress might have looked further than these cases which are mentioned in the legislative history, at the time of enactment of the Act this Court had held at least twice that the Equal Protection Clause of the Fourteenth Amendment does not require States to expend equal financial resources on the education of each child. *San Antonio School District v. Rodriguez,* 411 U.S. 1 (1975); *McInnis v. Shapiro,* 293 F. Supp. 327 (ND Ill. 1968), *aff'd sub nom, McInnis v. Ogilvie,* 394 U.S. 322 (1969).

In explaining the need for federal legislation, the House Report noted that "no congressional legislation has required a precise guarantee for handicapped children, i.e. a basic floor of opportunity that would bring into compliance all school districts with the constitutional right of equal protection with respect to handicapped children." H.R. Rep. No. 94-332, *supra,* at 14. Assuming that the Act was designed to fill the need identified in the House Report—that is, to provide a "basic floor of opportunity" consistent with equal protection—neither the Act nor its history persuasively demonstrates that Congress thought that equal protection required anything more than equal access. Therefore, Congress' desire to provide specialized educational services, even in furtherance of "equality," cannot be read as imposing any particular substantive educational standard upon the States.

The District Court and the Court of Appeals thus erred when they held that the Act requires New York to maximize the potential of each handicapped child commensurate with the opportunity provided nonhandicapped children. Desirable though that goal might be, it is not the standard that Congress imposed upon States which receive funding under the Act. Rather, Congress sought primarily to identify and evaluate handicapped children, and to provide them with access to a free public education.

(iii). Implicit in the congressional purpose of providing access to a "free appropriate public education" is the requirement that the education to which access is provided be sufficient to confer some educational benefit upon the handicapped child. It would do little good for Congress to spend millions of dollars in providing access to a public education only to have the handicapped child receive no benefit from that education. The statutory definition of "free appropriate public education," in addition to requiring that States provide each child with "specially designed instruction," expressly requires the provision of "such ... supportive services ... as may be required to assist a handicapped child *to benefit* from special education." § 1401(17) (emphasis added). We therefore conclude that the "basic floor of opportunity" provided by the Act consists of access to specialized instruction and related services which are individually designed to provide educational benefit to the handicapped child.[23]

The determination of when handicapped children are receiving sufficient educational benefits to satisfy the requirements of the Act presents a more difficult problem. The Act requires participating States to educate a wide spectrum of handicapped children, from the marginally hearing-impaired to the profoundly retarded and palsied. It is clear that the benefits obtainable by children at one end of the spectrum will differ dramatically from those obtainable by children at the other end, with infinite variations in between. One child may have little difficulty competing successfully in an academic setting with nonhandicapped children while another child may encounter great difficulty in acquiring even the most basic of self-maintenance skills. We do not attempt today to establish any one test for determining the adequacy of educational benefits conferred upon all children covered by the Act. Because in this case we are presented with a handicapped child who is receiving substantial specialized instruction and related services, and who is performing above average in the regular classrooms of a public school system, we confine our analysis to that situation.

The Act requires participating States to educate handicapped children with nonhandicapped children whenever possible.[24] When that "mainstreaming"preference of the Act has been met and a child is being educated in the regular classrooms of a public school system, the system itself monitors the educational progress of the child. Regular examinations are administered, grades are awarded, and yearly advancement to higher grade levels is permitted for those children who attain an adequate knowledge of the course material. The grading and advancement system thus constitutes an important factor in determining educational benefit. Children who graduate from our public school systems are considered by our society to have been "educated" at least to the grade level they have completed, and access to an "education" for handicapped children is precisely what Congress sought to provide in the Act.[25]

C

When the language of the Act and its legislative history are considered together, the requirements imposed by Congress become tolerably clear. Insofar as a State is required to provide a handicapped child with a "free appropriate public education," we hold that it satisfies this requirement by providing personalized instruction with sufficient support services to permit the child to benefit educationally from that instruction. Such instruction and services must be provided at public expense, must meet the State's educational standards, must approximate the grade levels used in the State's regular education, and must comport with the child's IEP. In addition, the IEP, and therefore the personalized instruction, should be formulated in accordance with the requirements of the Act and, if the child is being educated in the regular classrooms of the public education system, should be reasonably calculated to enable the child to achieve passing marks and advance from grade to grade.[26]

D

In assuring that the requirements of the Act have been met, courts must be careful to avoid imposing their view of preferable educational methods upon the States.[29] The primary responsibility for formulating the education to be accorded a handicapped child, and for choosing the educational method most suitable to the child's needs, was left by the Act to state and local educational agencies in cooperation with the parents or guardian of the child. The Act expressly charges States with the responsibility of "acquiring and disseminating to teachers and administrators of programs for handicapped children significant information derived from educational research, demonstration, and similar projects and [of] adopting, where appropriate, promising educational practices and materials." Section 1413(a)(3). In the face of such a clear statutory directive, it seems highly unlikely that Congress intended courts to overturn a State's choice of appropriate educational theories in a proceeding conducted pursuant to § 1415(e)(2).[30]

We previously have cautioned that courts lack the "specialized knowledge and experience" necessary to resolve "persistent and difficult questions of educational policy." *San Antonio School District v. Rodriguez*, 411 U.S. 1, 42 (1973). We think that Congress shared that view when it passed the Act. As already demonstrated, Congress' intention was not that the Act displace the primacy of States in the field of education, but that States receive funds to assist them in extending their educational systems to the handicapped. Therefore, once a court determines that the requirements of the Act have been met, questions of methodology are for resolution by the States.

V

Entrusting a child's education to state and local agencies does not leave the child without protection. Congress sought to protect individual children by providing for parental involvement in the development of State plans and policies, *supra,* at 4-5 and n. 6, and in the formulation of the child's individual educational program. As the Senate Report states:

> "The Committee recognizes that in many instances the process of providing special education and related services to handicapped children is not guaranteed to produce any particular outcome. By changing the language [of the provision relating to individualized educational programs] to emphasize the process of parent and child involvement and to provide a written record of reasonable expectations, the Committee intends to clarify that such individualized planning conferences are a way to provide parent involvement and protection to assure that appropriate services are provided to a handicapped child." S. Rep. No. 94-168, *supra,* at 11-12. See also S. Conf. Rep. No. 94-445, p. 30 (1975); 45 CFR §121a.345 (1980).

As this very case demonstrates, parents and guardians will not lack ardor in seeking to ensure that handicapped children receive all of the benefits to which they are entitled by the Act.[31]

NOTES

4. Despite this preference for "mainstreaming" handicapped children—educating them with nonhandicapped children—Congress recognized that regular classrooms simply would not be a suitable setting for the education of many handicapped children. The Act expressly acknowledges that "the nature or severity of the handicap [may be] such that education in regular classes with the use

of supplementary aids and services cannot be achieved satisfactorily." § 1412(5). The Act thus provides for the education of some handicapped children in separate classes or institutional settings. See *ibid.;* § 1413(a)(4).

6. The requirements that parents be permitted to file complaints regarding their child's education, and be present when the child's IEP is formulated, represent only two examples of Congress' effort to maximize parental involvement in the education of each handicapped child. ...

15. The only substantive standard which can be implied from these cases comports with the standard implicit in the Act. *PARC* states that each child must receive "access to a free public program of education and training *appropriate to his learning capacities*," 334 F. Supp., at 1258, and that further state action is required when it appears that "the needs of the mentally retarded child are not being *adequately* served," *id.,* at 1266. (Emphasis added.) *Mills* also speaks in terms of "adequate" educational services, 348 F. Supp., at 878, and sets a realistic standard of providing *some* educational services to each child when every need cannot be met.

21. In seeking to read more into the Act than its language or legislative history will permit, the United States focuses upon the word "appropriate," arguing that "the statutory definitions do not adequately explain what [it means]." Brief for the United States as *Amicus Curiae* 13. Whatever Congress meant by an "appropriate" education, it is clear that it did not mean a potential-maximizing education.

The term as used in reference to educating the handicapped appears to have originated in the *PARC* decision, where the District Court required that handicapped children be provided with "education and training appropriate to [their] learning capacities." 334 F. Supp., at 1258. The word appears again in the *Mills* decision, the District Court at one point referring to the need for "an appropriate educational program," 348 F. Supp., at 879, and at another point speaking of a "suitable publicly-supported education," *id.,* at 878. Both cases also refer to the need for an "adequate" education. See 334 F. Supp., at 1266; 348 F. Supp., at 878.

The use of "appropriate" in the language of the Act, although by no means definitive, suggests that Congress used the word as much to describe the settings in which handicapped children should be educated as to prescribe the substantive content or supportive services of their education. For example, § 1412(5) requires that handicapped children be educated in classrooms with nonhandicapped children "to the maximum extent appropriate." Similarly, § 1401(19) provides that, "whenever appropriate," handicapped children should attend and participate in the meeting at which their IEP is drafted. In addition, the definition of "free appropriate public education" itself states that instruction given handicapped children should be at an "appropriate preschool, elementary, or secondary school" level. § 1401(18)(C). The Act's use of the word "appropriate" thus seems to reflect Congress' recognition that some settings simply are not suitable environments for the participation of some handicapped children. At the very least, these statutory uses of the word refute the contention that Congress used "appropriate" as a term of art which concisely expresses the standard found by the lower courts.

23. This view is supported by the congressional intention, frequently expressed in the legislative history, that handicapped children be enabled to achieve a reasonable degree of self sufficiency. After referring to statistics showing that many handicapped children were excluded from public education, the Senate Report states: "The long range implications of these statistics are that public agencies and taxpayers will spend billions of dollars over the lifetimes of these individuals to maintain such persons as dependents and in a minimally acceptable lifestyle. With proper education services, many would be able to become productive citizens, contributing to society instead of being forced to remain burdens. Others, through such services, would increase their independence, thus reducing their dependence on society." S. Rep. No. 94-168, *supra,* at 9. See also H.R. Rep. No. 94-332, *supra,*

at 11. Similarly, one of the principal Senate sponsors of the Act stated that "providing appropriate educational services now means that many of these individuals will be able to become a contributing part of our society, and they will not have to depend on subsistence payments from public funds." 121 Cong. Rec. 19492 (1975) (remarks of Sen. Williams). See also 121 Cong. Rec. 25541 (1975) (remarks of Rep. Harkin); 121 Cong. Rec. 37024-37025 (1975) (remarks of Rep. Brademas); 121 Cong. Rec. 37027 (1975) (remarks of Rep. Gude); 121 Cong. Rec. 37410 (1975) (remarks of Sen. Randolph); 121 Cong. Rec. 37416 (1975) (remarks of Sen. Williams).

The desire to provide handicapped children with an attainable degree of personal independence obviously anticipated that state educational programs would confer educational benefits upon such children. But at the same time, the goal of achieving some degree of self sufficiency in most cases is a good deal more modest than the potential-maximizing goal adopted by the lower courts.

Despite its frequent mention, we cannot conclude, as did the dissent in the Court of Appeals, that self sufficiency was itself the substantive standard which Congress imposed upon the States. Because many mildly handicapped children will achieve self sufficiency without state assistance while personal independence for the severely handicapped may be an unreachable goal, "self sufficiency" as a substantive standard is at once an inadequate protection and an overly demanding requirement. We thus view these references in the legislative history as evidence of Congress' intention that the services provided handicapped children be educationally beneficial, whatever the nature or severity of their handicap.

25. We do not hold today that every handicapped child who is advancing from grade to grade in a regular public school system is automatically receiving a "free appropriate public education." In this case, however, we find Amy's academic progress, when considered with the special services and professional consideration accorded by the Furnace Woods school administrators, to be dispositive.

29. In this case, for example, both the state hearing officer and the District Court were presented with evidence as to the best method for educating the deaf, a question long debated among scholars. See Large, Special Problems of the Deaf Under the Education for All Handicapped Children Act of 1975, 58 Washington U.L.Q. 213, 229 (1980). The District Court accepted the testimony of respondents' experts that there was "a trend supported by studies showing the greater degree of success of students brought up in deaf households using [the method of communication used by the Rowleys]." 483 F. Supp., at 535.

30. It is clear that Congress was aware of the States' traditional role in the formulation and execution of educational policy. "Historically, the States have had the primary responsibility for the education of children at the elementary and secondary level." 121 Cong. Rec. 19498 (1975) (remarks of Sen. Dole). See also *Epperson v. Arkansas,* 393 U.S. 97, 104 (1968) ("[b]y and large, public education in our Nation is committed to the control of state and local authorities").

31. In addition to providing for extensive parental involvement in the formulation of state and local policies, as well as the preparation of individual educational programs, the Act ensures that States will receive the advice of experts in the field of educating handicapped children. As a condition for receiving federal funds under the Act, States must create "an advisory panel, appointed by the Governor or any other official authorized under State law to make such appointments, composed of individuals involved in or concerned with the education of handicapped children, including handicapped individuals, teachers, parents or guardians of handicapped children, State and local education officials, and administrators of programs for handicapped children, which (A) advises the State educational agency of unmet needs within the State in the education of handicapped children, [and] (B) comments publicly on any rules or regulations proposed for issuance by the State regarding the education of handicapped children." § 1413(a)(12).

APPENDIX D

IRVING ISD V. TATRO

(excerpts from the majority opinion, in which all members of the Court joined and agreed that "related services" include clean intermittent catheterization)

IRVING INDEPENDENT SCHOOL DISTRICT

v.

TATRO ET UX, INDIVIDUALLY AND AS NEXT FRIENDS
OF TATRO, A MINOR

Chief Justice Burger delivered the opinion of the Court.

We granted certiorari to determine whether the Education of the Handicapped Act or the Rehabilitation Act of 1973 requires a school district to provide a handicapped child with clean intermittent catheterization during school hours.

I

Amber Tatro is an 8-year-old girl born with a defect known as spina bifida. As a result, she suffers from orthopedic and speech impairments and a neurogenic bladder, which prevents her from emptying her bladder voluntarily. Consequently, she must be catheterized every three or four hours to avoid injury to her kidneys. In accordance with accepted medical practice, clean intermittent catheterization (CIC), a procedure involving the insertion of a catheter into the urethra to drain the bladder, has been prescribed. The procedure is a simple one that may be performed in a few minutes by a layperson with less than an hour's training. Amber's parents, babysitter, and teenage brother are all qualified to administer CIC, and Amber soon will be able to perform this procedure herself.

In 1979 petitioner Irving Independent School District agreed to provide special education for Amber, who was then three and one-half years old. In consultation with her parents, who are respondents here, petitioner developed an individualized education program for Amber under the requirements of the Education of the Handicapped Act, 84 Stat. 175, as amended significantly by the Education for All Handicapped Children Act of 1975, 89 Stat. 773, 20 U.S.C. §§ 1401(19), 1414(a)(5). The individualized education program provided that Amber would attend early childhood development classes and receive special services such as physical and occupational therapy. That program, however, made no provision for school personnel to administer CIC....

This case poses two separate issues. The first is whether the Education of the Handicapped Act requires petitioner to provide CIC services to Amber. ... States receiving funds under the Act are obliged to satisfy certain conditions. A primary condition is that the state implement a policy "that assures all handicapped children the right to a free appropriate public education." 20 U.S.C. § 1412(1). Each educational agency applying to a state for funding must provide assurances in turn that its program aims to provide "a free appropriate public education to all handicapped children." § 1414(a)(1)(C)(ii).

A "free appropriate public education" is explicitly defined as "special education and related services." § 1401(18).[5] The term "special education" means

> "specially designed instruction, at no cost to parents or guardians, to meet the unique needs of a handicapped child, including classroom instruction, instruction in physical education, home instruction, and instruction in hospitals and institutions." §1401(16).

"Related services" are defined as

> "transportation, and such developmental, corrective, and other *supportive services (including* speech pathology and audiology, psychological services, physical and occupational therapy, recreation, and *medical* and counseling *services, except that such medical services shall be for diagnostic and evaluation purposes only) as may be required to assist a handicapped child to benefit from special education,* and includes the early identification and assessment of handicapping conditions in children." §1401(17) (emphasis added).

The issue in this case is whether CIC is a "related service" that petitioner is obliged to provide to Amber. We must answer two questions: first, whether CIC is a "supportive servic[e] ... required to assist a handicapped child to benefit from special education; and second, whether CIC is excluded from this definition as a "medical servic[e]" serving purposes other than diagnosis or evaluation.

A

The Court of Appeals was clearly correct in holding that CIC is a "supportive servic[e] ... required to assist a handicapped child to benefit from special education."[6] It is clear on this record that, without having CIC services available during the school day, Amber cannot attend school and thereby "benefit from special education." CIC services therefore fall squarely within the definition of a "supportive service."[7]

As we have stated before, "Congress sought primarily to make public education available to handicapped children" and "to make such access meaningful." *Board of Education of Hendrick Hudson Central School District v. Rowley,* 458 U.S. 176, 192 (1982). A service that enables a handicapped child to remain at school during the day is an important means of providing the child with the meaningful access to education that Congress envisioned. The Act makes specific provision for services, like transportation, for example, that do no more than enable a child to be physically present in class, see 20 U.S.C. § 1401(17); and the Act specifically authorizes grants for schools to alter buildings and equipment to make them accessible to the handicapped, § 1406; see S. Rep. No. 94-168, p. 38 (1975); 121 Cong. Rec. 19483-19484 (1975) (remarks of Sen. Stafford). Services like CIC that permit a child to remain at school during the day are no less related to the effort to educate than are services that enable the child to reach, enter, or exit the school.

We hold that CIC services in this case qualify as a "supportive servic[e] ... required to assist a handicapped child to benefit from special education."[8]

B

We also agree with the Court of Appeals that provision of CIC is not a "medical servic[e]," which a school is required to provide only for purposes of diagnosis or evaluation. See 20 U.S.C. §1401(17). We begin with the regulations of the Department of Education, which are entitled to deference.[9] See, *e.g., Blum v. Bacon,* 457 U.S. 132, 141 (1982). The regulations define "related services" for handicapped children to include "school health services," 34 CFR §300.13(a) (1983), which are defined in turn as "services provided by a qualified school nurse or other qualified person," §300.13(b) (10). "Medical services" are defined as "services provided by a licensed physician." §300.13(b)(4).[10] Thus, the Secretary has determined that the services of a school nurse otherwise qualifying as a "related service are not subject to exclusion as a "medical service," but that the services of a physician are excludable as such.

This definition of "medical services" is a reasonable interpretation of congressional intent. Although Congress devoted little discussion to the "medical services" exclusion, the Secretary could reasonably have concluded that it was designed to spare schools from an obligation to provide a service that might well prove unduly expensive and beyond the range of their competence.[11] From this understanding of congressional purpose, the Secretary could reasonably have concluded that Congress intended to impose the obligation to provide school nursing services.

Congress plainly required schools to hire various specially trained personnel to help handicapped children, such as "trained occupational therapists, speech therapists, psychologists, social workers and other appropriately trained personnel." S. Rep. No. 94-168, *supra,* at 33. School nurses have long been a part of the educational system, and the Secretary could therefore reasonably conclude that school nursing services are not the sort of burden that Congress intended to exclude as a "medical service." By limiting the "medical services" exclusion to the services of a physician or hospital, both far more expensive, the Secretary has given a permissible construction to the provision.

Petitioner's contrary interpretation of the "medical services" exclusion is unconvincing. In petitioner's view, CIC is a "medical service," even though it may be provided by a nurse or trained layperson; that conclusion rests on its reading of Texas law that confines CIC to uses in accordance with a physician's prescription and under a physician's ultimate supervision. Aside from conflicting with the Secretary's reasonable interpretation of congressional intent, however, such a rule would be anomalous. Nurses in petitioner's school district are authorized to dispense oral medications and administer emergency injections in accordance with a physician's prescription. This kind of service for nonhandicapped children is difficult to distinguish from the provision of CIC to the handicapped.[12] It would be strange indeed if Congress, in attempting to extend special services to handicapped children, were unwilling to guarantee them services of a kind that are routinely provided to the nonhandicapped.

To keep in perspective the obligation to provide services that relate to both the health and educational needs of handicapped students, we note several limitations that should minimize the burden petitioner fears. First, to be entitled to related services, a child must be handicapped so as to require special education. See 20 U.S.C. § 1401(1); 34 CFR § 300.5 (1983). In the absence of a handicap that requires special education, the need for what otherwise might qualify as a related service does not create an obligation under the Act. See 34 CFR § 300.14, Comment (1) (1983).

Second, only those services necessary to aid a handicapped child to benefit from special education must be provided, regardless how easily a school nurse or layperson could furnish them. For example, if a particular medication or treatment may appropriately be administered to a handicapped child other than during the school day, a school is not required to provide nursing services to administer it.

Third, the regulations state that school nursing services must be provided only if they can be performed by a nurse or other qualifed person, not if they must be performed by a physician. See 34 CFR §§ 300.13(a), (b)(4), (b)(10) (1983). It bears mentioning that here not even the services of a nurse are required; as is conceded, a layperson with minimal training is qualified to provide CIC. See also *e.g., Department of Education of Hawaii v. Katherine D.,* 727 F. 2d 809 (CA9 1983).

Finally, we note that respondents are not asking petitioner to provide *equipment* that Amber needs for CIC. Tr. of Oral Arg. 18-19. They seek only the *services* of a qualified person at the school.

We conclude that provision of CIC to Amber is not subject to exclusion as a "medical service," and we affirm the Court of Appeals' holding that CIC is a "related service" under the Education of the Handicapped Act.[13]

NOTES

10. The regulations actually define only those "medical services" that *are* owed to handicapped children: "services provided by a licensed physician to determine a child's medically related handicapping condition which results in the child's need for special education and related services." 34 CFR § 300.13(b)(4) (1983). Presumably this means that "medical services" *not* owed under the statute are those "services by a licensed physician" that serve other purposes.

11. Children with serious medical needs are still entitled to an education. For example, the Act specifically includes instruction in hospitals and at home within the definition of "special education." See 20 U.S.C. §1401(16).

12. Petitioner attempts to distinguish the administration of prescription drugs from the administration of CIC on the grounds that Texas law expressly limits the liability of school personnel performing the former, see Tex. Educ. Code Ann. §21.914(c) (Supp. 1984), but not the latter. This distinction, however, bears no relation to whether CIC is a "related service." The introduction of handicapped children into a school creates numerous new possibilties for injury and liability. Many of these risks are more serious than that posed by CIC, which the courts below found is a safe procedure even when performed by a 9-year-old girl. Congress assumed that states receiving the generous grants under the Act were up to the job of managing these new risks. Whether petitioner decides to purchase more liability insurance or to persuade the state to extend the limitation on liability, the risk posed by CIC should not prove to be a large burden.

13. We need not address respondents' claim that CIC, in addition to being a "related service," is a "supplementary ai[d] and servic[e]" that petitioner must provide to enable Amber to attend classes with nonhandicapped students under the Act's "mainstreaming" directive. See 20 U.S.C. § 1412(5)(B). Respondents have not sought an order prohibiting petitioner from educating Amber with handicapped children alone. Indeed, any request for such an order might not present a live controversy. Amber's present individualized education program provides for regular public school classes with nonhandicapped children. And petitioner has admitted that it would be far more costly to pay for Amber's instruction and CIC services at a private school, or to arrange for home tutoring, than to provide CIC at the regular public school placement provided in her current individualized education program. Tr. of Oral Arg. 12.

GLOSSARY

affirmed (aff'd.)   a word that indicates in a citation to a case that a higher court has agreed with the result, and usually the reasoning, of a lower court and approved the judgment of the lower court. Sometimes a higher court can affirm part of a lower court's judgment and reverse part of it, depending on the nature of the judgment.

amicus curiae   a Latin term indicating an individual or organization that is neither plaintiff nor defendant in a civil case but, because of special expertise or interest, is allowed by a court to become involved in the case as a "friend of the court." The involvement usually consists of submitting a brief (written presentation) containing supporting legal arguments and special facts to the court.

appeal   the process whereby a court of appeals reviews the record of proceedings and judgment of a lower court to determine if errors of law or fact were made which might lead to a reversal or modification of the lower court's decision. If substantial errors are not found, the lower court's decision will be affirmed. If they are, its decision will be reversed or modified.

C.F.R.   an abbreviation for *Code of Federal Regulations,* a publication of the U.S. government that contains the regulations of the executive agencies of government (e.g., U.S. Department of Education) implementing laws (statutes) passed by Congress (e.g., P.L. 94-142).

cert. den.   an abbreviation that indicates in a citation to a case that a higher court (usually, the Supreme Court) has declined to order a lower court to send the case to it for review. By contrast, *cert. granted* means the higher court has ordered a lower court to send a case to it for review.

certiorari (cert.)   a Latin term that indicates in a citation to a case that an order from an appeals court (usually, the Supreme Court) to a lower court has been entered, either requiring or declining to require the lower court to send up a case for review. The right-to-education cases decided by the U.S. Supreme Court usually go to that court on a petition (request) for *certiorari* by one of the parties (and the Court sometimes grants the request and orders the lower court to send the case to it for review).

civil case   a lawsuit brought by one or more individuals to seek redress of some legal injury (or aspect of an injury) for which there are civil (non-criminal) remedies. In right-to-education cases, these remedies are based on the federal or state constitutions, federal or state statutes, or federal or state agency regulations, or a combination of federal and state constitutions, statutes and regulations. Right-to-education cases are always civil suits.

class action   a civil case brought on behalf of the plaintiffs who are named in the suit, as well as on behalf of all other persons similarly situated, to vindicate their legally protected interests. *Mills v. D.C. Board of Education* was brought on behalf of 12-year-old Peter Mills and six other school-age children who were named in the complaint, as well as all other exceptional children in the District. By contrast, *Board v. Rowley* was not a class action lawsuit because it was brought on behalf of only one person, who sued to protect only her rights, not the rights of other people.

competing equities   a term describing a situation in which two or more people or groups of people have rights or privileges that cannot be fully satisfied without infringing on the rights or privileges of each other. For example, children with disabilities have some rights to be integrated with nondisabled children, but nondisabled children also have rights to an education that is not disrupted by children with disabilities (see chapter 6). In such a case, the competing equities of both children must be weighed against each other and a decision made by a court or other policy maker as to which claims prevail. Another way of thinking about competing equities is to ask: Whose rights or privileges are to be reduced for the benefit of other people?

complaint   a legal document submitted to the court by plaintiffs, in which they inform the court and the defendants that they are bringing a lawsuit and set out the underlying reasons for which they sue and the relief they want.

concur   a term that indicates in a citation to a case that one court agrees with the judgment of another and follows the precedent of that court's decision.

consent agreement   an out-of-court agreement reached by the parties to a suit, which is formally approved by the court. In *Pennsylvania Association for Retarded Children v. Pennsylvania,* a court entered an order that it adopted pursuant to a consent agreement between plaintiffs and defendants.

constitutional right   a legal right based on provisions of the U.S. Constitution or a state constitution. Equal protection and due process of law are the federal constitutional rights most relevant to the right to education. The Fourteenth Amendment applies to state (and therefore, local) governments and guarantees the rights of due process and equal protection. (See chapters 2 through 8.)

damages   money awarded by a court to someone who has been injured (the plaintiff), which must be paid by the one who is responsible for the injury (the defendant).

de facto   a Latin term that means, literally, "by reason of the fact." Integration by race and disability now is required by law (*de jure* integration), but may not actually occur in some schools or among some students (*de facto* segregation).

defendant   the person against whom a lawsuit is brought for redress of a violation of one or more of a plaintiff's legally protected interests.

defense   a reason cited by a defendant why a lawsuit against him or her is without merit or why he or she is not responsible for the injury or violation of rights as alleged by the plaintiff.

de jure   a Latin term that means, literally, "by law." Segregation of the schools by race or disability was required by laws of some states; thus, *de jure* segregation was enforced. Present law requires de jure integration.

dicta   a Latin term describing language in a judicial opinion that is not essential to the disposition of the case or to the court's reasoning and that is regarded as gratuitous. *Dicta* are persuasive but not binding on other courts, whereas the court's holding and reasoning are.

discovery the process by which one party to a civil suit can find out about matters relevant to the case, including information about what evidence the other side has, what witnesses will be called, and so on. Discovery devices for obtaining information include depositions and interrogatories to obtain testimony, requests for documents or other tangibles, and requests for physical or mental examinations.

due process of law a right to have any law applied by the federal or state government reasonably and with sufficient safeguards, such as hearings and notice, to ensure that an individual is dealt with fairly. Due process is guaranteed under the Fifth and Fourteenth Amendments to the federal Constitution.

EHLR an abbreviation for the works of a commercial publisher that report the opinions and judgments of many of the special education cases decided by state and federal courts in reports cited as *Education for the Handicapped Law Reporter (EHLR)*. In this book, the citation is stated in this way: *EHLR* 552:104—indicating that the report begins at section 552 of *EHLR* and at page 104. The case name precedes the *EHLR* citation, and the abbreviation of the court and date of judgment are set out in parentheses after the page reference.

Eighth Amendment the Eighth Amendment to the federal Constitution guarantees that the federal government will not impose a cruel and unusual punishment upon conviction of a crime. The amendment does not forbid the use of corporal punishment on students. It is not a factor in right-to-education cases.

en banc a Latin term referring to a situation in which a court consisting of more than one member (such as the federal appeals courts) hears a case with all of its members present at the hearing and participating in the decision. Usually, federal courts of appeals are divided into panels (or groups) of judges; a panel hears a case and normally makes the judgment of the court by itself, without participation of the other members of the court. Sometimes, however, a case is so difficult or important that all members of the court hear the case and decide the outcome. The court then sits *en banc*—all together.

equal protection of law a right not to be discriminated against for any unjustifiable reason, such as because of race or handicap. Equal protection is guaranteed under the Fourteenth Amendment. (See chapters 2 and 3)

et seq. a Latin term that means "and following" (*et* means "and"; *seq.* is an abbreviation for *sequens*, which means "following"). The phrase always follows a noun (e.g., Vol. 20, United States Code, Sections 1401 *et seq.*—hence, "and the following sections").

ex rel. a Latin term that indicates a lawsuit is brought on behalf of one person by another (e.g., the attorney general of a state may sue on behalf of an individual; thus, the case is captioned *"State of Kansas, ex rel. Jane Doe, an incompetent, v. Superintendent, State Hospital"*). The lawsuit normally is one in which the state attorney general seeks to vindicate a legal position that is favorable to the state and its citizens on behalf of a person not able to bring a lawsuit directly.

expert witness a person called to testify because he or she has a recognized competence in an area. For example, experts in the *PARC* right-to-education case had doctoral degrees in the field of special education, were authors of numerous professional publications pertaining to exceptional children, and were consultants to advisory committees on education.

F. 2d an abbreviation, in a citation to a lawsuit's reported judgment and order, that indicates that the case was decided by a federal court of appeals and is reported in a certain volume of the reports of the federal courts of appeals (shown as "Cir." for Circuit Court(s) of Appeal(s)). The volume of the reports precedes the *F. 2d (Federal Report, 2d Series)* designation; the page at which the report begins follows the *F. 2d* designation; and the identity of the court and the date of the judgment are set out in parentheses after the page number. Thus, *Smuck v. Hobson,* 408 F. 2d 175 (D.C. Cir. 1969), shows that the appellate judgment (in the case involving school classification practices of the District of Columbia Board of Education) is reported at volume 408 of the *Federal Reports, 2d Series,* beginning at page 175, and is a decision of the federal court of appeals (D.C. Circuit Court of Appeals) for the District of Columbia in 1969.

F. Supp.   an abbreviation, in a citation to a lawsuit's reported judgment and order, that indicates that the case was decided by a federal trial court (a "district" court) and is reported in a certain volume of the reports of the federal trial courts. The volume of the reports precedes the *F. Supp. (Federal Supplement)* designation; the page at which the report begins follows the *F. Supp.* designation; and the identity of the court and the date of the judgment are set out in parentheses after the page. Thus, in *PARC v. Commonwealth of Pennsylvania,* 343 F. Supp. 279 (E.D. Pa. 1972), the case is reported at volume 343 of the *Federal Supplement,* beginning at page 279, and is a decision of the federal district court for the Eastern District (section) of Pennsylvania in 1972.

Fed. Reg.   an abbreviation for *Federal Register,* a daily publication of Congress that contains the text of new laws and regulations and comments by members of Congress on matters of public policy.

Fifth Amendment   the amendment to the federal Constitution that guarantees that the rights of life, liberty, and property will not be taken from a citizen by the federal government without due process of law. Due process guarantees apply to state and local governments under the Fourteenth Amendment.

First Amendment   the amendment to the federal Constitution that guarantees free speech, assembly, worship, and petition for redress of grievances.

Fourteenth Amendment   the amendment to the federal Constitution that applies to the states (not the federal government, which is bound by the first 10 amendments) and guarantees the rights of due process and equal protection to the citizens of each state.

in re   a Latin term in a captioned title of a case that indicates "in the matter of" and always is followed by the name of a party to a lawsuit (e.g., *In Re: John Doe, a minor*—here, the caption/title to the lawsuit reads "in the matter of John Doe, a minor/child").

infra   a Latin word in a citation to a case that indicates that the same case is referred to in a later part of the same article, chapter, book, judicial opinion, or other writing (e.g., the court may refer to the *Rowley* case, *infra,* meaning later, or, literally, within, its opinion).

injunctive relief   a remedy granted by the court forbidding or requiring some action by the defendant. Injunctive relief includes temporary restraining orders and preliminary and final injunctions. The difference among these types of relief is that they are issued for varying lengths of time, at various stages of the litigation process, and on the basis of varying degrees of proof.

judgment   an order by a court after a verdict has been reached. The judgment declares the relief to be granted.

on remand   a reference in a citation to a case that indicates that a lower court has entered a judgment, for at least a second time, when it received the case from a higher court with a judgment and order to act in a particular way (e.g., the court's initial judgment is appealed, the appeals court enters a judgment to reverse in part and affirm in part and directs the lower court to change its original order, and the lower court then does so when the case is "on remand" to it from the higher court).

parens patriae   a Latin term that means, literally, "father of the country," and that refers nowadays to the doctrine that a state may act in a paternalistic way on behalf of its citizens, especially those who are children or who are mentally disabled and therefore less effective than other people in protecting themselves. The *parens patriae* doctrine justifies compulsory education, which is regarded as beneficial to children and the state alike but, because of its benefit to children, can be required for their own good.

per curiam   a Latin term in a citation to a case that refers to the judgment of a court entered "by the court" (rather than by a judge who writes the opinion for the court). *Per curiam* cases normally do not have opinions of the judges, only the court's disposition of the case (e.g., affirmed, petition denied, etc.).

P.L.   an abbreviation for "Public Law," referring to a statute passed by Congress as a public law. Every public law has a number that follows the P.L. designation—thus, P.L. 94-142 refers to Public Law 142 of the 94th Congress.

plaintiff   a person who brings a suit to redress a violation of one or more of his or her legal rights.

precedent   a decision by a judge or court that serves as a rule or guide to support other judges in deciding future cases involving similar or analogous legal questions. In the early right-to-education cases, courts cited some famous education decisions as precedents, including *Brown v. Board of Education,* outlawing segregated schools, and *Hobson v. Hansen,* outlawing the track system in the District of Columbia. Just as *PARC* and *Mills* were cited as precedent by other courts for finding a constitutional right to education, so *Rowley* is now cited on various legal issues (see chapter 5).

private action   a case brought on behalf of one or more individuals to vindicate violation of their own legally protected interests. As distinguished from a class action, where the relief applies to all persons similarly situated or within the class represented by the plaintiffs (e.g., *PARC*), any relief granted in private action applies only to those plaintiffs actually before the court (e.g., *Rowley*).

procedural right   a right that relates to the process of enforcing substantive rights or to obtaining relief, such as the right to a hearing, the right to present evidence in one's defense, and the right to counsel.

quid pro quo   a Latin term that literally means "something for something" and indicates an exchange of money and/or goods (e.g., a school district provides inservice training in exchange for—as a *quid pro quo* for—state aid to defray expenses).

relief   a remedy for some legal wrong. Relief is requested by a plaintiff, to be granted by a court, against a defendant.

reversed (rev'd.)   a word that indicates in a citation to a case that a higher court has overturned the result, and usually the reasoning, of a lower court and entered (or ordered the lower court to enter) a different judgment. Sometimes a higher court can reverse part of a lower court's judgment and affirm part of it, depending on the nature of the judgment.

settlement   an out-of-court agreement among parties to a suit, which resolves some or all of the issues involved in a case.

statutory right   a right based on a statute or law passed by a unit of federal, state, or local governments (see chapter 1).

sub nom.   a Latin abbreviation in a citation to a case that indicates the case was decided by another court under a different name (*sub* meaning "under," and *nom.* being an abbreviation for the Latin word *nomine,* meaning "name").

substantive right   a right such as the right to an education, usually granted by statutes and constitutions.

supra   a Latin word in a citation to a case that indicates that the same case has been referred to in an earlier part of the same article, chapter, book, judicial opinion, or other writing. It means the opposite of *infra.*

U.S.   an abbreviation, in a citation to a decision of the U.S. Supreme Court, that indicates that a judgment of that Court is reported at a certain volume of the *United States Reports,* which contain only the judgments and other orders of the U.S. Supreme Court. The volume number precedes the *U.S.* designation, the page number follows it, and the date of judgment is set out in parentheses after the page reference.

U.S.C. (also U.S.C.A.)   an abbreviation for *United States Code,* an official publication of the United States government (or *United States Code Annotated,* a commercial publication) that contains the codified acts of Congress.

U.S.L.W.   a commercial publication that reports the judgments of various courts in *United States Law Week.* The volume of *USLW* precedes the USLW designation, and the page of the report follows it, with the identity of the court and date of judgment set out in parentheses after the page number.

vacated   an abbreviation that indicates in a citation to a case that a higher court has set aside the judgment of a lower court.

verdict   a decision by a judge or jury in favor of one side or the other in a case.

TABLE OF CASES

CASE INDEX

INDEX

A

Ability grouping, 96-98
Accountability
  federal laws and, 308
  fiscal, 287
  single-agency responsibility and, 43, 48
  through advisory panels, 285
ADA. *See* Americans with Disabilities Act
  (ADA)
Administrative costs, 278-279, 286
Administrative remedies, 217-219
Advisory panels, 231
Advocacy
  bifurcated, 312
  comprehensive and integrated, 312
  federal laws and, 308
  need for, 109
  parental, 74
Affirmative action, 47-48
Ages-certain requirements, 39-40
Aging out
  availability of services for, 42-43
  of severely disabled children, 46
AIDS, 107
  coverage by ADA of individuals with, 25
  exclusion of individuals with, 61-63
  location issues for students with, 62-63
  nature and effects of, 60
  special education as disabled for individuals
    with, 59-61
AIDS-related complex (ARC), 60, 61

Air conditioning, 147
Aliens, 35
American Association on Mental Retardation
  (AAMR), 102, 114
American Psychiatric Association, 102
Americans with Disabilities Act (ADA) (P.L.
  101-336)
  employment discrimination protection under,
    25-26
  enforcement procedures and remedies for,
    28-29
  function of, 38, 128-129
  general coverage of, 24, 87
  importance of, 23, 29, 131-132
  protected individuals under, 24-25, 271
  public accommodations and services operated
    by private entities and, 26-27
  public services and state/local governments
    and, 26
  significance for families of, 232-234
  telecommunications services under, 27-28
  transportation for disabled and, 27
Annual program plan, 20
Anti-institutionalization movement, 163, 307
Appellate courts, 6
Appropriate education
  availability of related services and, 144-149
  definitions of, 47, 182-183
  determination of, 131-132, 172
  expert judgment and, 142-143
  federal legislation and, 124-131

1994 UPDATE

This supplement to *Free Appropriate Public Education: The Law and Children with Disabilities* (4th ed.) covers cases reported in volumes 18, 19, and 20, *Individuals with Disabilities Education Law Reporter* (*IDELR*), beginning at Vol. 18, No. 10, March 6, 1992, and continuing through Vol. 20, No. 10, February 10, 1994. All references are to Vol. 18, 19, or 20 of *IDELR* (for example, 18/945 indicates that the case is reported in Vol. 18 at page 945).

CHAPTER THREE: ZERO REJECT (ZR)

Age for Terminating Services

The issue of "older students' entitlement" has been the topic of several lawsuits. At the heart of the issue is this: May a state limit services to students in special education who are over the age of eighteen on the basis that it limits services to students who are in regular education and over that age? In the *Merrifield* case, the court held that the state may impose that limit; when the state receives IDEA funds, it agrees to serve students in special education until they are twenty-one unless a state law establishes an earlier age disqualification.

A case that changed the result in *Merrifield* is *Tuttle v. Evans* (*IDELR* 18/945, Cir. Ct. Shelby Co., Ind., Oct. 1991), affirmed by the Indiana Court of Appeals (613 N.E. 2d 854, 1993). The court ruled that students may not be excluded between their eighteenth and twenty-second birthdays if they have not graduated; the state's constitution and special education law as well as IDEA and Section 504 prohibit their disqualification by reason of age.

Expulsion and Continued Services

The Assistant Secretary of OSERS has ruled that, while expelled, a student who has a disability and who was expelled but not on account of his disability is entitled to continued special education services. The opinion was challenged as being a legislative rule, not an agency interpretation of existing rules—as, in effect, legislation, not regulation. The District Court held the OSERS policy to be legislation and invalid (*Metropolitan School District of Wayne Township v. Davila*, 770 F. Supp. 1331, S.D. Ind. 1990); the Court of Appeals reversed (969 F. 2d 485, 7th Cir., 1992), and the school district has asked the U.S. Supreme Court to review that decision.

When a teacher and school administrator have reasonable cause to believe that a special education student is concealing drugs in his clothing, they may require him to undergo a strip search and search of his clothing without violating his constitutional rights to privacy, so long as the strip search is conducted in private, by people who are of the same sex as the student, permits the student to wear other clothing during the search but after the administrators visually inspect his naked body, and is based on reasonable grounds (sufficient under the 4th Amendment's guarantee against unreasonable searches and seizures) (*Cornfield v. Consolidated High School Dist. No. 230*, 991 F. 2d 1316, 7th Cir., 1993).

Public/Private School Tuition Reimbursements

Until a recent U.S. Supreme Court decision, it was unclear whether an SEA or LEA could be required to pay for tuition in a school that the state had not accredited.

Courts had generally disapproved payment to those schools. For example, in one case, the result was that a court may not order reimbursement of tuition paid to a school that the state does not certify or accredit, but it also may still order judgment for parents (the type and extent of which will be determined after another hearing on IEP) if the court finds that the LEA's proposed program does not meet the *Rowley* educational benefit standard (*Straube v. Florida Union Free School District*, IDELR 18/617, S.D. N.Y., 1991). In a later decision in the same case, the court ruled that if the private school is not on the SEA's approved list and the LEA cannot provide free appropriate public education (FAPE), then the SEA must take steps to secure conditional approval of the private school (*Straube*, IDELR 19/131, S.D. N.Y., 1992).

These two decisions preceded the Supreme Court's decision in *Florence County School District Four v. Carter* (IDELR 20/532, U.S. Sup. Ct., 1993). There the Court held that parents may be awarded reimbursement for private school placement costs, even though the private school does not have or meet state accreditation standards, if they meet the following tests: the public school placement is not appropriate; the private school placement is appropriate in that it is reasonably calculated to provide an educational benefit to the student; and the costs assessed by the private school are reasonable. In this case, the Court reasoned that IDEA's requirement (that placement must meet the state's standards) cannot be applied to parental, unilateral placements; it would be inconsistent with IDEA's goals to forbid parents from placing their child at a private school that otherwise (except for accreditation) offers an appropriate education simply because the school lacks the state's stamp of approval. Moreover, the parental right of placement, established in the *Burlington* case, would be a nullity and mean nothing if the parent could not make a private school placement. Finally, IDEA's requirement that a student's education be provided under public supervision and that the student's IEP be developed and annually reviewed by a local agency does not apply because it cannot feasibly be met in the case of a unilateral parental placement; for that reason, these requirements do not apply to such a placement.

Placement at a private school and payment of its tuition by an LEA is appropriate only when it is the sole educational setting that is reasonably calculated to provide educational benefit and when the student and parents agree to attendance at that school (if they do not agree that the student will attend, then they recover no tuition for attendance at another school unless a court orders tuition payment) (*Brown v. County Bd. of Ed.*, *IDELR* 18/670, Va. Ct. App., 1992).

Where a student's original placement is inappropriate and the alternative placement is appropriate, reimbursement is warranted, even if the parents did not give sufficient notice (*Northeast Central School Dist. v. Sobol*, *IDELR* 18/1219, N.Y. Ct. App., 1992).

Where in-state programs can be appropriately designed to meet the needs of children and be made available at no cost to their parents, the IDEA does not require SEAs or LEAs to use public funds to pay for private out-of-state schools (*Dreher v. Amphitheater U.S.D.*, *IDELR* 19/315, D. Ariz., 1992).

Tuition reimbursement is denied when the LEA offers an appropriate education (AE) that complies with *Rowley* and that is more integrated (least restrictive environment, LRE) than the private school in which the parents placed the student. When AE and LRE exist together in the LEA, even though the private school placement may be superior to the LEA's, then IDEA does not require public funding of a superior program, only that an LEA offer an appropriate one (*Doe v. Bd. of Ed. of Tullahoma City Schools*, *IDELR* 18/1089, E.D. Tenn., 1992).

It is proper for a court to balance academic progress with associational rights under the LRE doctrine and to refuse a private school placement and tuition reimbursement when the LEA program is less restrictive and still provides academic benefit; a balance between the two (AE and LRE) is required (*Amann v. Stow School System*, *IDELR* 19/618, 1st Cir., 1992).

Although a private school might be ideal for a student, still tuition reimbursement is denied when the LEA can provide FAPE under *Rowley* (*Lenn v. Portland School Committee*, *IDELR* 19/615, D. Me., 1992).

A student with severe emotional and behavioral disabilities should be placed in an LEA's program, not a psychiatric facility, where that placement will yield an academic benefit for the student and the student will have the opportunity to associate with nondisabled peers and participate more fully in the community (*Teague Indep. Sch. Dist. v. Todd L.*, *IDELR* 20/259, 5th Cir., 1993).

When a student's disruptive and violent behavior persists in a day school and in homebound placements, even after the LEA has made efforts to support the student in those placements, the LEA may place the student in a residential program, and, indeed, the LRE principle not only does not forbid that placement but requires it (*Johnson v. Westmoreland County Sch. Bd.*, *IDELR* 19/787, E.D. Va., 1993).

If a school district has to pay for the costs of a residential placement in order to provide an appropriate education, it also must pay the transportation and caretaker costs for the student who is transported from home to the school to attend the school's day program (while awaiting admission to the residential program) (*Ojai Unified Sch. Dist. v. Jackson*, *IDELR* 20/354, 9th Cir., 1993).

When an LEA agrees or is ordered to pay the tuition of students placed by it in a private school (to provide them with an appropriate education), it may not choose to pay less than the full tuition rate (*Fisher v. District of Columbia*, *IDELR* 20/419, D.D.C., 1993).

A federal court of appeals has confirmed and adopted the policy set out in an OSEP memorandum opinion. The OSEP opinion held that an LEA is not required to provide related services to all students placed by parents in private schools; an LEA may elect which of the parentally placed students it wishes to serve and which services it wishes to make available to them. The OSEP opinion is *Letter to Livingston* (*IDELR* 17/523; OSERS 1991); the district court opinion is in *Tribble v. Montgomery Co. Bd. of Ed.* (*IDELR* 19/102, M.D. Ala., 1992); and the 11th Circuit Court of Appeals decision, reversing the district court and affirming OSEP, is *Tribble v. Montgomery Co. Bd. of Ed.* (*IDELR* 20/661, 1993).

Where parents want their child placed in a private school and the school agrees that out-of-school placement is warranted but offers instead to place the student into a state facility for people with mental retardation and autism, the parents bear the burden of proof to convince the court that the public facility and the program there are not reasonably calculated to offer educational benefit (*Gill v. Stafford Co. School Bd.*, *IDELR* 18/522, Va. Cir. Ct., 1992).

In order to secure private school tuition reimbursement, the parents must go to a due process hearing first and may not go directly to federal court (*Straube v. Florida Union*, *IDELR* 19/131, 493, S.D. N.Y., 1992).

If a parent requests a due process hearing for one school year, based on inappropriate education, and a due process hearing officer rules in favor of the parents for that year, and in the next year the parents also have another due process hearing, the due process hearing officer in the next year must affirm the first hearing officer's decision unless there are new facts showing a change of circumstance in the child or the private placement. Hence, if the first officer upheld tuition reimbursement for one year, the second officer must do so for the second (*Edwards-White v. D.C.*, *IDELR* 18/899, D. D.C., 1992).

Procedural errors were not sufficient to warrant finding that an LEA denied FAPE; accordingly, tuition reimbursement was denied (*Ash v. Lake Oswego School Dist.*, *IDELR* 19/482, 9th Cir., 1992 [cites *Hall v. Vance Co.* for proposition that procedural failure can result in denial of FAPE]; *Amann v. Stow Sch. System*, *IDELR* 19/618, 1st Cir., 1993). See also cases on "process definition," under Appropriate Education.

SEA Responsibility

The SEA is more than a regulatory and pass-through agency; it has duties under IDEA to ensure that the rights of students are protected regardless of the actions of LEAs. Accordingly, the pervasive problems in the state's education system, including in particular the unreasonable delays in placing students in appropriate private placements, violate IDEA, and the SEA must prepare a plan of correction (*Cordero v. Pa. Dept. of Ed., IDELR* 18/1099, M.D. Pa., 1992, and *IDELR* 19/623, M.D. Pa., 1993).

Compensatory Education

Compensatory education is available to a man, age twenty-seven, if he can prove that he was denied appropriate education during the time he was enrolled in an LEA (*Pihl v. Massachusetts Dept. of Educ., IDELR* 20/668, 1st Cir., 1993). Here, the district court has yet to hold that the man was denied an appropriate education; the court of appeals decision was simply that, if he can prove the denial, he is entitled to compensatory education.

Where an LEA takes reasonable steps to integrate a student, evaluate and even pay for an independent evaluation, provide supportive services in the regular program (but not all the services the family wants), the district is not liable for providing compensatory education because some related services were withheld (*Jeanette H. v. Pennsbury School District, IDELR* 18/1087, E.D. Pa., 1992, cf. *Murphy v. Timberlane*, p. 5).

Compensatory education is awardable where the LEA allegedly denied a "basic floor of opportunity" under *Rowley* and the parents are not required to allege bad faith by the LEA, since, under *Burlington*, tuition reimbursement cases do not require that kind of showing and compensatory education is equivalent to tuition reimbursement (*McManus v. Wilmette School District 39 Bd. of Ed., IDELR* 19/485, N.D. Ill., 1992; *Harris v. D.C. Bd. of Ed., IDELR* 19/105, D. D.C., 1992; *Manchester School District v. Christopher B., IDELR* 19/389, D. N.H., 1992, reverses earlier ruling).

When a student is "truant" for two years because his parents have withdrawn him from the LEA as a consequence of their dispute with the LEA about an appropriate education, the student still is entitled to two years of compensatory education and the district may not rely on the defense that it made a "good faith" effort during those two years to offer an appropriate program (*Murphy v. Timberlane Regional Sch. Dist., IDELR* 19/846, D. N.H., 1993). (Note: this case seems out of line with other compensatory education cases where a good faith defense is allowed.)

A defense of laches is available to an LEA faced with a compensatory education claim (in this case no laches found), but the laches also must prejudice the LEA (*Murphy v. Timberlane Regional School District, IDELR* 19/128, 1st Cir., 1992).

Qualification for Services

Students who qualify for special education or who already have been placed in special education retain their IDEA rights even though they have been adjudicated as juvenile offenders and placed in a state's juvenile corrections or criminal justice system (*Donnell C. v. Illinois State Bd. of Educ.*, *IDELR* 20/514, N.D. Ill., 1993).

Sports Participation

Where a state scholastic athletic association rule prohibits a transfer student from participating in interscholastic football for a year after he transfers from one school district to another, a student with a disability who has transferred from one school district to another to secure an appropriate education does not experience discrimination and may not sue for a civil rights violation when the association's rule is applied to him (as to all other transfer students) (*Crocker v. Tennessee Secondary Sch. Athletic Assn.*, *IDELR* 19/663, 6th Cir., 1993).

The "Establishment Clause"

Three cases recently have dealt with the issue of whether federal (IDEA) or state funds may be spent by a state or local educational agency to pay for special education services provided on the grounds of religious schools or by faculty at those schools. The establishment clause forbids a state-established or sponsored religion.

The U.S. Supreme Court recently held that the establishment clause does not forbid a student from receiving, at public expense, related services while enrolled in a parochial school. The Court reasoned that the service itself is "neutral," that is to say, it is part of a government program (IDEA) that is not skewed toward a religion (*Zobrest v. Catalina Foothills Sch. Dist.*, *IDELR* 19/921, U.S. Sup. Ct., 1993).

In the *Zobrest* case, the district and circuit courts held that the establishment clause is violated when a deaf student needs day-long interpreter help and when the parochial school that he attends inextricably intertwines its secular education and religious training. In order for federal aid (IDEA) to be available to the student at a parochial or other religious school, the aid must have a clearly secular and separable purpose (*Zobrest*, *IDELR* 18/1187, 9th Cir., 1992). The Supreme Court's decision opened the doors to students who are placed in parochial schools and receive any special education or related services provided to them there by the parochial school.

The test is one of "skewing"—the placement or service does not violate the establishment clause if the service is religiously neutral and is provided as part of a general public program. Does the service or the public program tilt (skew) the public funding toward the religion? Alternatively stated, is the service or public program so intertwined with the religious mission of the school that the service or public program advances or furthers the school's religious mission?

The skewing test was the implicit basis on which the court prohibited IDEA placement in a parochial school in *Wright v. Saco School Department* (*IDELR* 18/505, Me. Sup. Ct., 1991), where the court concluded that the establishment clause is violated when the school site cannot be religiously neutral. As in *Zobrest*, the degree of involvement of the parochial program in the student's education was determinative.

A New York state court reached the same result in *Grumet v. New York State Education Department* (*IDELR* 18/855, N.Y. Supreme Court, Albany County, 1992), when the state legislature redrew school district lines in order to create a school district exactly contiguous with the boundaries of a separate religious community. Under this redistricting, public money would fund the education of only the religious community's children.

After the U.S. Supreme Court's *Zobrest* decision, the New York State Court of Appeals held that legislation that created a distinct school district solely to accommodate a separatist religious community had the effect of advancing a religious belief and was deliberately skewed toward that belief (*Grumet v. Board of Education of Kiryas Joel Village Sch. Dist.*, *IDELR* 20/149, N.Y. Ct. App., 1993). The U.S. Supreme Court heard the case in March 1994 and will issue a decision by July 1994.

Still, some parochial-school services are permissible, even before and especially after the *Zobrest* decision. For example, a special education student is entitled to publicly paid transportation (a related service) between her parochial school and her special education classes at a public school (*Felter v. Cape Girardeau Sch. Dist.*, *IDELR* 19/764, E.D. Mo., 1993).

Similarly, a student is entitled to publicly paid special education in a parochial school; the purpose of the private school placement is to provide special education (basic life skills) that could not be provided in a public school setting, not to provide religious instruction (*Day v. Radnor Township Sch. Dist.*, *IDELR* 19/806, E.D. Pa., 1993).

CHAPTER FOUR:
NONDISCRIMINATORY EVALUATION (NDE)

An LEA that violates the student's due process and procedural safeguard rights (not having a school district representative at the IEP meetings) may not make a change of placement; the NDE and IEP process must be met before change in program or placement occurs (*Smith v. Henson*, *IDELR* 18/897, D. D.C., 1992; *P.J. v. State of Conn. Bd. of Ed.*, *IDELR* 18/1010, D. Conn., 1992).

Likewise, when an LEA fails to develop a student's IEP properly, in that not all of the required individuals are present (here, the student's classroom teacher or representative of a private school where he had been unilaterally placed by his parents), the LEA may not refuse to reimburse private school tutoring because a FAPE cannot be provided when the process is so flawed (*W.B. and B.G. v. Board of Trustees of Target Range School District No. 23*, *IDELR* 18/1019, 9th Cir., 1992).

An LEA must consider an independent evaluation of a student in determining whether he has a specific learning disability (SLD), but having done that and having evaluated the student itself, it may determine the student does not have an SLD, relying on the expert evaluations, expert testimony, and the preponderance of the evidence before it (*Kelby v. Morgan Hill Unified District*, *IDELR* 18/831, 9th Cir., 1992).

If a school district's mandatory reevaluation process risks the mental health of a student with a learning disability, the district violates the student's constitutional rights to privacy and has no independent absolute right to its own reevaluation of the student. An independent reevaluation, secured by the parents, should be considered by the district (*Andress v. Cleveland Independent School District, IDELR* 20/743, E.D. Tex., 1993).

A school district that has agreed to pay for an out-of-district placement must conduct a comprehensive psychological evaluation of a student (and incorporate the evaluation results into the student's IEP) if the student's parent wants to place him back in the district's program (*Dale v. West Central School District 49-7, IDELR* 20/427, D. S.D., 1993).

CHAPTER FIVE: APPROPRIATE EDUCATION (AE)

Appropriate Education: The *Rowley* Benefit Rule

Courts consistently hold that an LEA must develop an IEP and placement reasonably calculated to benefit a student and that, if the IEP and placement meet that test, then the LEA satisfies the *Rowley* standard of an appropriate education and a least restrictive placement. The LEA's IEP and placement will prevail over a residential placement if both offer benefit. Benefit exists when a student makes progress toward IEP goals while enrolled in an LEA program. Both academic and nonacademic benefit are to be considered by an LEA in designing the student's IEP and placement. The fact that the student also makes progress while in a private or residential program does not mean that the LEA program is not appropriate; it can be, just as the private or residential program can be appropriate. A dispute over methodology (usually the dispute revolves around the type of communications training for students with hearing loss, but also includes disputes about the methodology for educating children with autism) is not one for the courts to resolve as long as the LEA's chosen methodology provides benefit. A student is not entitled to the optimal or most appropriate program and placement. The cases are *Lewis v. School Bd. of Loudoun County* (*IDELR* 19/712, E.D. Va., 1992); *Swift v. Rapides Parish Pub. Sch. Sys.* (*IDELR* 19/771, W.D. La., 1993); *Peterson v. Hastings Pub. Sch.* (*IDELR* 20/252, D. Neb., 1993); *Lenn v. Portland Sch. Comm.* (*IDELR* 20/342, 1st Cir., 1993); *Fuhrmann v. East Hanover Bd. of Ed.* (*IDELR* 19/1065, 3d Cir., 1993); *Delaware County Intermediate Unit #25 v. Martin K.* (*IDELR* 20/363, E.D. Pa., 1993); *Bonnie Ann F. v. Calallen Indep. Sch. Dist.* (*IDELR* 20/736, S.D. Tex., 1993); *Blickle v. St. Charles Community Unit Sch. Dist. No. 303* (*IDELR* 20/168, N.D. Ill., 1993); and *Brougham v. Town of Yarmouth* (*IDELR* 20/12, D. Me., 1993).

Related Services

"Related services" does not include a full-time nurse who spends the bus time and school time with the student, who performs suctioning of a tracheotomy tube and feeding via a nasogastric tube, who is performing essentially medical services on a constant basis, whose services are required to help ensure life-saving procedures, who is one of three nurses in a rural district that consists of 75,000 students in ninety different schools, and whose services cost $30,000 annually. Also, the student had homebound services, an IEP, and other related services sufficient to ensure educational benefit under *Rowley*, and the nursing services were essentially medical (*Granite School District v. Shannon M.*, *IDELR* 19/772, D. Utah, 1992).

Where the psychiatric hospitalization of a student was for basically educational reasons, where the LEA failed to follow procedural safeguards in classification (and failed to classify the student as having a severe emotional disability), and where the parents' unilateral placement of the student in a psychiatric hospital in order to avoid the student's expulsion from school was the only resource the parents had to secure any services, the LEA is responsible for paying the hospital costs and must reimburse the parents (*Babb v. Knox Co. School System*, *IDELR* 18/1030, 6th Cir., 1992).

"Process Definition"

An LEA may not try to remove a student from a residential program (where it is paying the tuition) and place the student in its district program without first assessing whether the district is capable of implementing the student's IEP (*Day v. Radnor Township Sch. Dist.*, *IDELR* 19/799, E.D. Pa., 1993).

Similarly, an LEA must conduct a nondiscriminatory evaluation when a student enters the district from an out-of-state program and may not simply offer an "interim IEP" (resource room and regular education modifications) and insist that the student be withdrawn from the present out-of-state residential placement; the IDEA procedures must be followed (NDE and then IEP) (*Salley v. St. Tammany Parish School Board*, *IDELR* 19/520, E.D. La., 1993).

Similarly, a student is entitled to have a complete IEP, not just an "interim IEP," when entering a school district for the first time, even if the development of a permanent IEP requires the district to convene an IEP team during the summer (*Myles S. v. Montgomery County Bd. of Educ.*, *IDELR* 20/237, N.D. Ala., 1993).

State Law and Maximum Development; Higher Standard

Although Tennessee law required LEAs to provide special education and related services "sufficient to meet the needs and maximize the capabilities of handicapped children," a court has refused to interpret the law as setting a higher standard than the IDEA "appropriate education" standard. There have been no previous interpretations of the state law by state courts, there are two diametrically opposed federal court interpretations of the law, there is no legislative history to prove that the legislature intended to set a higher standard, there is no executive agency regulation stating that the law creates a higher standard, and the district had offered an IEP that met the "benefit" rule and was in the least restrictive environment (*Doe v. Board of Educ. of Tullahoma City Sch.*, *IDELR* 20/617, 6th Cir., 1993).

CHAPTER SIX:
LEAST RESTRICTIVE ENVIRONMENT (LRE)

The doctrine of the least restrictive alternative was established by the U.S. Supreme Court's interpretation of the federal constitution. Having established the doctrine, the Court and only the Court can interpret it. Unfortunately, the Court has decided to make a significant retreat from the LRE doctrine. In *Heller v. Doe* (__ U.S. __, 113 S. Ct. 2637, 125 L. Ed. 2d 257, 1993) the Court had to decide whether the state of Kentucky has to use the least restrictive means for achieving its goals of involuntarily committing to a mental retardation facility those individuals with mental retardation who are dangerous to themselves or others.

The issue arose when advocates for people with mental retardation challenged Kentucky's statute on the basis that it sets up one procedure for involuntary commitment of individuals with mental illness and another for involuntary commitment of individuals with mental retardation. The procedure for committing the former is more difficult than the procedure for committing the latter.

The Court held that the statute does not treat unequally these two groups of individuals; Kentucky has plausible reasons for creating a double standard. Moreover, said the Court, "(w)e do not require Kentucky to have chosen the least-restrictive means of achieving its legislative end (*San Antonio Independent School Dist. v. Rodriquez*, 411 U.S. 1, 93 S. Ct. 1278, 36 L. Ed. 2d 16, 1973). [The *Rodriquez* case held that students in relatively poor school districts are not unequally treated in comparison to students in relatively rich school districts when the state allocates the same amount of money to each district. The state's choice of how to fund public education is not subject to an equal protection attack since there is no right to education in the federal constitution and some reason why the state would choose equal funding even if it results in unequal benefit—the richer districts get richer.] As long as Kentucky 'rationally advances a reasonable and identifiable governmental objective, we must disregard' the existence of alternative methods of furthering the objective that we, as individuals, perhaps would have preferred."

This language—no requirement of a least restrictive approach as long as a state "rationally advances a reasonable and identifiable governmental objective"—cuts to the very heart of the LRE doctrine. If the Court's future decisions about the LRE doctrine are as absolutist as this language, then IDEA's LRE principle will rest entirely on Congress's wishes, not on the constitution, and thus could be repealed by Congress by an amendment to IDEA.

As noted in the section on tuition reimbursements under Zero Reject, the cases on tuition reimbursement essentially balance the student's rights to an appropriate education with the student's rights to an education in the least restrictive environment. Accordingly, a school district is required only to provide an appropriate education, not an ideal one unless state law sets a higher standard (such as education to the maximum of a student's potential).

Where a student's IEP is not reasonably calculated to provide FAPE, and where the student's institutionalization is based on educational reasons that are quite apart from medical reasons for placement, the LEA must take steps to find a suitable residential placement and must pay for all costs except that its exposure to medical costs is for diagnostic and evaluative services only (*Pamela B. v. Longview School District*, IDELR 18/514, W.D. Wash., 1992).

If, however, a student can benefit from a residential placement nearer to the family's home, then an LEA must change the student's placement from a residential school farther away from home to one closer to home (*Remis v. New Jersey Dept. of Human Resources*, IDELR 19/879, D. N.J., 1993).

A leading case on LRE is the *Oberti* decision. There, the court issued two separate decisions.

In the first decision in the *Oberti* case, the court held that the criteria for determining whether a child with mental retardation and communication disabilities (age seven) should be included in a regular education placement with supportive services are (a) whether, and to what extent, the student can be included into the matrix of regular class, and (b) what supplementary aids are necessary to accomplish this result.

In the second decision in the *Oberti* case, the court held that where a student is not so disruptive as to constitute danger or harm to other students, where he will benefit from inclusive education with support, where other students will benefit from having him there, and where the provision of supplementary aids and services will enable inclusive education, then the LEA must provide those aids and services and the child should be included in regular programs (*Oberti v. Bd. of Ed.*, IDELR 19/423, D. N.J., 1992).

Just as *Oberti* sends a strong inclusion message, consistent with the decisions in *Greer* and *Daniel R.R.* (both cited above or in the text), so does *Statum v. Birmingham Pub. Sch. Bd. of Educ.* In this case the court ordered an LEA to place into regular education a student who has severe mental retardation and physical disabilities (*IDELR* 20/435, N.D. Ala., 1993). The student had been in a regular placement, with supplementary aids and services, the year before (as a kindergarten student) and had benefited from that placement and program. The court held that the student should be in a regular education first-grade placement and program, with supports, and set out these criteria for removing the student from the regular to a self-contained placement and program. The LEA failed to prove that:

- the self-contained program would enhance the student's education to any significant degree.
- the student's IEP goals and objectives could not be implemented within the regular classroom with supplementary aids and services.
- the implementation would have an adverse effect on the other students in that program.

- the costs of the supplementary aids and services would impair the district's ability to educate other special education students.

Since the district could not prove any of these matters, it was not justified in removing the student from the regular program and withdrawing support from the student there.

An LEA may not place a nine-year-old child with moderate mental retardation in a special education classroom and also regular education classroom, with the time divided equally between the two, but instead must place the child in the regular classroom with supportive services. There are four factors relevant to determining the appropriate level of integration (*Bd. of Ed. of Sacramento USD v. Holland*, E.D. Cal., 1992; affirmed, *IDELR* 20/812, 9th Cir., 1994):

1. Education benefits of the integrated setting compared with those of the segregated setting.
2. The nonacademic benefits of interaction with nondisabled peers.
3. The effect of the child's presence in the regular education program on the teacher and other students.
4. Costs of supplementary services required to maintain the child in the integrated placement.

An LEA is correct in placing a sixteen-year-old student with Down syndrome into a program for moderately mentally retarded students where he will receive vocational training and everyday survival skills instead of functional academics, where the student had derived little, if any, benefit from the placement in the mild-mental retardation program (*Chris C. v. Gwinett County School District*, *IDELR* 18/710, N.D. Ga., 1992).

Slight deviations from exact procedures in developing a student's IEP did not adversely affect the appropriateness of the student's education nor the parent's rights to participate in the IEP's development, and the student's IEP itself was reasonably calculated to benefit him, even though it did not call for him to be graduated; the fact that a segregated private school offers a somewhat better and more appropriate education is not enough to require the LEA to pay tuition there (*Livingston v. Desoto Co. School District*, *IDELR* 18/656, N.D. Miss., 1992).

Greer v. Rome City (cited in my text in the chapter on LRE) (762 F. Supp. 936, 950 F. 2d 688, 1991) is reinstated after being withdrawn (withdrawn at 956 F. 2d 1025, *IDELR* 18/831; reinstatement, *IDELR* 19/100, 11th Cir., 1992).

CHAPTER SEVEN: PROCEDURAL DUE PROCESS

Standard of Review

A parent has the right to present witnesses in a judicial hearing (at a federal district court); the *Rowley* standard of de novo review not only allows but also requires a court to hear from expert witnesses before making a judgment (cases cited on judicial deference to experts) (*Carroll v. Metropolitan Government of Nashville and Davidson Co.*, *IDELR* 18/579, 6th Cir., 1992; *Lenn v. Portland Sch. Comm.*, *IDELR* 20/342, 1st Cir., 1993).

Tuition Payment During Due Process or Litigation: The Stay-Put Rule

Parents lived in State A, had a son in private school in State B with an IEP from State A and approval of and payment of school tuition by State A. When the parents moved to State C, that state refused to pay the tuition of the school, saying that the movement into State C constituted an initial application for services and that the stay-put rule was not applicable. The parents sued for continued tuition and were granted a temporary restraining order that required State C to continue to pay tuition. A continuation of services already established, though by State A, is a continuation and the stay-put rule applies (*Lyons v. Town of Yarmouth*, *IDELR* 18/671, D. Me., 1992).

Likewise, during the pendency of a due process hearing, parents are entitled to a temporary restraining order prohibiting an LEA from terminating a student's private school placement (*Carl B. v. Mundelein Sch. Dist. 120 Bd. of Educ.*, *IDELR* 20/263, N.D. Ill., 1993) and to continued payment of tuition (*Woods v. New Jersey Dept. of Educ.*, *IDELR* 20/439, 3d Cir., 1993).

Similarly, an LEA must pay for the tuition of a student whom the parents unilaterally placed in a private school where the district's program was found to be inappropriate by a hearing officer and where the parents asked for a hearing on the district's proposed placement (*Pomona Unified Sch. Dist. v. Nelson*, *IDELR* 19/903, C.D. Cal., 1993).

An SEA may not change a child's placement and is bound by the stay-put rule where for five years it had treated a student as a resident of the district; now, after it had treated a student as a resident of the district and expels the child and claims that the child is no longer a resident (and therefore the LEA may expel with impunity), it must continue to serve the student (*C.A. v. Christina School District*, D. Del., 1992).

But, the stay-put rule does not bar a state school for the blind from changing its criteria for admission and, after change, transferring a student from that school to a community school where the student is twenty years old, has made no progress in the state school, and is entitled to a less segregated placement (*Sherri A.D. v. Kirby*, *IDELR* 19/339, 5th Cir., 1992).

Exhaustion of Administrative Remedies

Parents still must exhaust their administrative remedies and have the burden of proving the LEA's action makes exhaustion futile (*Stauffer v. William Penn Sch. Dist.*, *IDELR* 20/508, E.D. Pa., 1993).

Free Transcript

An indigent parent who is acting as her own attorney in an IDEA action against an LEA is entitled to both an electronic tape-recorded record of the due process hearing and a written transcript of the same hearing, but the right to the written transcript exists under federal law relating to indigents who represent themselves (in forma pauperis), not under IDEA (*Militello v. Board of Educ. of City of Union City*, *IDELR* 19/657, D. N.J., 1992).

Choice of Administrative Procedures

When a parent sues an LEA for IDEA rights, the parent must use IDEA's procedures and may not rely on a state's administrative procedures act or antidiscrimination law's procedures (*Jenkins v. Carney-Nadeau Pub. Sch.*, *IDELR* 20/249, Mich. Ct. App., 1993).

Statute of Limitations

The cases go in two directions. Some adopt the state's administrative procedures act statute of limitations; typically, that statute of limitations requires a party to file for a due process hearing or an appeal from a hearing (local or state level) within 30 and 120 days. Others adopt a more liberal statute of limitations and allow an appeal to be filed within the time set for lawsuits between parties who allege a wrong (tort), breach of contract, or civil rights violation. Typically, these statutes require a party to file for a due process hearing or appeal within 180 days and three years. The best advice is this: file as early as possible so you will not be tripped up by a statute of limitations defense.

It is proper for a court to impose a 30-day statute of limitations under IDEA by borrowing that limitation from the most analogous state laws (*Valerie J. v. Derry Coop. Sch. Dist.*, *IDELR* 20/334 and 431, D. N.H., 1993). Similarly, a court in another state borrowed from that state's most analogous statute of limitations and imposed a 45-day limitation on IDEA claims, but imposed a three-year limitation for Section 504 civil-rights violations actions (*Wills v. Ferrandino*, *IDELR* 20/603, D. Conn., 1993).

If, however, a state changes its period of limitations for IDEA actions but the parents are not informed of the change and would be barred under the earlier and shorter limitations, it is only equitable to let them rely on the later and longer limitations period (*Hebert v. Manchester N.H. Sch. Dist.*, *IDELR* 20/747, D. N.H., 1993).

CHAPTER EIGHT: PARENT PARTICIPATION

The school district where the parent who has custody of a child (pursuant to a valid divorce decree and agreement) lives is the school district that is responsible for the student's special education costs, not the district where the noncustodial parent lives (*George H. & Irene L. Walker Home for Children, Inc. v. Town of Franklin*, *IDELR* 20/665, Mass. Sup. Judicial Court, 1993).

CHAPTER NINE: ENFORCEMENT

Contempt of Court

A state is not in contempt of court where, in carrying out a consent decree requiring certain individualized treatment programs for residents of a state mental retardation facility, 1:1 staffing, and protection from unreasonable risks to personal safety, the state had taken reasonable efforts to protect its clients from harm, even though some of the specific conditions of the consent decree had not been met. Substantial good faith compliance is a sufficient defense in contempt hearings (*United States of America v. State of Oregon, IDELR* 18/753, D. Ore., 1991).

Damage

Sometimes, parents and students will not seek damages under IDEA but, instead, under state statutory or common law. The usual result has been unfavorable, with most courts ruling that a cause of action for educational malpractice does not exist and thus damages are not available. This majority trend is seen in *Rich v. Kentucky Country Day* (*IDELR* 18/607, Ky. Ct. App., 1990), where the court adopted the majority line of cases and held that there is no right to a cause of action in educational malpractice against public or private schools. Suits in educational malpractice would lack a satisfactory standard of care for measuring an educator's conduct, would produce inherent uncertainty in determining the cause and nature of any damages, would result in an ensuing flood of litigation, and would force courts to "blatantly" interfere with the internal workings of schools. The earlier cases established a rule against damages (*Meiner v. Missouri, Loughran v. Flanders*). Increasingly, however, the courts are prone to award damages to students or parents who seek that remedy in special education cases.

General Rule Under IDEA: Start Over. Normally, and without any doubt, IDEA gives a remedy of "Start Over." That is to say, a court will order an LEA to restart the NDE, IEP/AE, LRE, PDP, or PP process all over again if the agency has made a mistake in the process and the mistake impairs the student's IDEA rights.

Newer Rule Under IDEA: Other Remedies. Under the Supreme Court's decision in the *Burlington* case, a second remedy was created: reimbursement of tuition to parents who paid private tuition in order to secure an appropriate education that an LEA was not providing.

It was not much of a step for the courts to go from a tuition reimbursement remedy to a compensatory education remedy. The two remedies are essentially alike; both reimburse the student or parents for denial of IDEA rights during the time the student was entitled to them.

Nor was it much of a step for the courts to order extended school years for some students—a sort of "compensatory" relief so that they would not regress, to compensate for their extreme disabilities.

Resistance to New Remedies.

No Cause of Action. Given these four remedies (start over, tuition reimbursement, compensatory education, and extended school year), the argument by the LEAs and SEAs was this, in a word: "enough." They based their argument on the Supreme Court's decision in *Smith v. Robinson* (denying attorney fees because IDEA establishes a comprehensive, exclusive scheme of remedies). If attorney fees cannot be "read into" IDEA (before Congress expressly allowed for them under the Handicapped Children's Protection Act), then surely other damages could not be read into the IDEA as well.

The usual line of cases denying IDEA damages is followed in *Valerie v. Derry* (*IDELR* 18/1107 and 18/1108, U.S.D.Ct., N.H., 1992), where a federal court reaffirmed its earlier decisions that monetary damages are available only under Section 504.

Another case denying damages, but under Section 1983, is *Dorothy J. v. Little Rock School District* (*IDELR* 18/235, U.S.D.Ct., E.D. Ark., 1992), where the court ruled that a school district and a state human services agency were not liable to a student with mental disabilities who was attacked and raped by a ward of the state department of human services. The court reasoned that the attack was by an individual, not a person acting on behalf of a state or under color of law; that there was no "custodial relationship" between the attacked student/victim and the state agency, giving rise to a duty on the state agency to protect the victim; that this is true even when the state agency knew of the attacker's propensity for aggression; and that there was such a remote connection between the attacking student, the government agency, and the victim that the victim may not sue the state agency.

A similar result was obtained in *D.R. v. Middle Bucks Area Vocational Technical School* (*IDELR* 18/108, U.S.D.Ct., E.D. Pa., 1992). There, two female students, one of whom has a physical disability, were assaulted physically and sexually by several male students. They sued the school to recover damages for violation of their constitutional rights (as in *Dorothy J.*, above, they said they have constitutional rights to be protected from abuse during the school day). The court ruled that they may not recover; there was not a custodial relationship (as in *Waechter*) between the students and the school and thus the school had no duty to protect. Moreover, the school did not create or exacerbate the danger posed by male students, and, finally, the victims' injuries did not result from any policy, custom, or practice established by state officials.

Similarly, in *Robbins v. Maine School Administrative District No. 8* (*IDELR* 19/384, U.S.D.Ct., Maine, 1992) a court denied recovery to students suing under Section 1983, who claimed they were subjected to physical and emotional assaults while placed in a self-contained classroom at a regional special education facility. The court found that the district had *not*, with deliberate indifference to the consequences, established a policy, practice, or custom that directly inflicted injury, and that mere nonfeasance was insufficient to constitute the necessary degree of "state action."

Note that these three cases all involve the same basic tests: custodial relationships, state action, disregard of consequences, and existence of a policy-practice-custom that will lead to injury. Also, these courts hold that nonfeasance—failure to act—is not sufficient to make a state liable. There must be a "state-created danger," per the U.S. Supreme Court's decision in *DeShaney v. Winnebago County Dept. of Social Service* (*IDELR* 489, U.S. 189, 1989). Unless a student or parents can prove that danger by showing that these other facts exist, the student or parents will not recover and the district/school will not be liable.

Defense of Sovereign Immunity. A valid defense to any Section 1983 case is "sovereign immunity." Under that doctrine, a state official, acting under color of law and consistent with his duties, is immune from a lawsuit so long as his conduct does not violate "clearly established statutory or constitutional rights of which a reasonable person would have known" (*Harlow v. Fitzgerald*, 457 U.S. 800, 1982; *Mitchell v. Forsyth*, 472 U.S. 511, 1985), "whether the legal norms allegedly violated by the defendant were clearly established at the time of the challenged actions or . . . whether the law clearly proscribed the actions the defendant claims he took."

A case that allowed the parents to try to recover under Section 1983, when the defendants claimed sovereign immunity defense, is *Taylor v. Honig* (*IDELR* 19/472, 9th Cir., 1992). The parents claimed that the state education agency deliberately sabotaged their son's IEP and that the state's placement of him in a juvenile facility, although permissible under IDEA, in this case caused him to experience cruel and unusual punishment in contravention of the 8th Amendment. Although admitting that the evidence was "thin," the court allowed the parents' lawsuit to go forward and overruled the "sovereign immunity" defense. There seemed to be enough evidence that the state and its physicians were deliberately indifferent to his physical and mental health needs, violating the standard in *Estelle v. Gamble* (429 U.S. 97, 1976).

In another case, however, the same court held that a school district's staff is not liable, and may assert the sovereign immunity defense, when it improperly tested and diagnosed a student and, on the basis of the tests and diagnosis, refused to admit the student to special education (*Planells v. San Francisco Unified School District, IDELR* 19/477, 9th Cir., 1992).

Likewise, *Norris v. The Board of Education of Greenwood Community School Corporation* (*IDELR* 19/361, S.D. Ind., 1992) held that a student may not recover against a school district and its officials for failing to diagnose the student's special education needs in violation of IDEA, state law, and the federal constitution. The defendants are entitled to sovereign immunity.

Minority Trend for Damages Under Federal Law: "Over and Above." Yet, as the cases in the text (Chapter 9) show, the courts are beginning to allow damages. They do so when the student has a claim for relief and remedies "over and above" those he has under IDEA. Thus, the student can get damages under Section 1983 for harm he suffered while he was a student under IDEA and in addition to any remedies he gets under IDEA, so long as the harm is additional to the harm he experiences under IDEA.

An example of the courts' tendency to allow students to recover under Section 1983 in limited circumstances is *Sean R. v. Board of Education* (*IDELR* 19/173, U.S.D.Ct., D.

Conn., 1992). There, a student recovered for breach of privacy when a school district disclosed the student's school records without the student's or parents' consent. Under FERPA, which protects the privacy of school records, the student has a reasonable expectation of privacy. Since IDEA incorporates FERPA, a violation of FERPA is a violation of IDEA. When the school violates FERPA, it also violates IDEA. But since there is no remedy under IDEA, there must be one under other law. FERPA does not provide one; thus, Section 1983 should and, under this court's decision, does.

In *John and Kathryn G. v. Board of Education of Mt. Vernon* (*IDELR* 18/1026, U.S.D.Ct., S.D. N.Y., 1992), parents of a child with a learning disability sued the school district under IDEA, Section 504, and Section 1983, claiming that they are entitled to monetary damages because the district failed for four years to identify the student's disabilities and then failed to provide an appropriate education under IDEA. The court ruled that the parents may hold the school liable under Section 504 only if they can show that the school acted in bad faith in not diagnosing the student (or otherwise responding to his apparent or known/identified disability), citing *Monahan v. State of Nebraska* (687 F. 2d 1164, 8th Cir., 1982). The court also ruled that the parents do not need to show bad faith, however, to sue under Section 1983, only that the district failed to diagnose when it reasonably knew or should have known that the student had a disability, the failure to diagnose being a denial of access to the procedural safeguards of IDEA and the substantive benefits of IDEA. The parents may recover monetary damages under Section 1983 and most likely under Section 504 because of the Supreme Court's 1992 decision in *Franklin v. Gwinette County Public Schools* (112 S. Ct. 1028), holding that monetary damages are available under T. IX, sex discrimination prohibited, of the Education Act Amendments of 1972, even though the statute does not specifically authorize them. This is so because Section 504, like T. IX, is an antidiscrimination law.

Similarly, *Ali v. Wayne-Westland School District* (*IDELR* 19/511, U.S.D.Ct., E.D. Mich., 1992) allowed a student to sue and recover damages under Sections 504 and 1983 when he was injured in a chemistry lab experiment and when he proved that the school should have recognized that he had a learning disability (but failed to recognize that disability). The same case, however, disallowed the student's claim of negligence, based on state law.

In the only case to date in which a court allowed a student to recover not only actual damages but also punitive damages, an LEA, SEA, and state human services department had failed to fund the residential component of the student's out-of-state school tuition. IDEA allows a court to "grant such relief as (it) determines appropriate" (20 U.S.C. Sec. 1415 (e)(2)); in this court's judgment, that included punitive damages against the LEA or SEA.

Minority Trend for Damages Under State Law. In addition, courts are beginning to explore new "education malpractice" cases. The *Waechter* case ("gut run"), the Maryland case of a counselor who did not try to prevent a suicide (*Eisel*), and the Kansas case of a school bus driver (*Kansas Trust Co.*) all allow damages where the student is in special education and suffers harm from the LEA's actions and where there is no clear remedy under IDEA or even a clear violation of IDEA. In a sense, these are not IDEA cases, they are instead pure malpractice cases, but they are important for special education professionals, LEAs, and parents and students nonetheless.

In *Hendrickson v. Spartenburg County School District No. Five* (*IDELR* 18/857, S. C. Ct. App., 1992), the issue of teacher competence and injury to students arose with a result favorable to students. A court allowed a district to dismiss a teacher for slapping a student and for failing to manage and supervise a class. (Note: where teacher incompetence threatens injury to a student, a school district had better act to insulate the student from the teacher.)

Some subsequent cases continue this trend. In *Haley v. McManus* (*IDELR* 18/815, La. Ct. App., 1st Cir., 1991), a state appeals court awarded damages to a student with ADD who experienced a petit mal epileptic seizure, and was hospitalized for treatment for the seizure, when the teacher whipped the student with his belt. (Note: this case is very much like the *Waechter* case, where prior knowledge of student's disability, the foreseeability of harm from punishment, the fact of physical custody and oversight of the student by the teacher, and the extreme intervention/punishment by the teacher were controlling factors.)

In *Doe v. Escambia* (*IDELR* 18/1286, Fla. Dist. Ct. App., 1st Dist., 1992), a school district was held liable for violating state statutory law and common law when it failed to provide adequate supervision of a special education student who was taken from the school grounds and raped by several male students. This case did not involve IDEA rights, but state statutory and common law rights.

A case that does not follow the trend to grant liability is *Hunter v. Carbondale Area Sch. Dist.* (*IDELR* 20/503, M.D. Pa., 1993), where a court held that a district does not owe a duty to protect a special education student from a death-causing assault that occurred after school hours and away from the school grounds.

Grooms v. Marlboro (*IDELR* 18/825, S.C. Ct. App., 1992) allowed parents of a child with mental retardation to sue the school district for negligent supervision when the school district allowed the student to "skip" classes when he was "too disruptive" to the class and, during his absence, assigned the school janitor to supervise the student. During one of those janitorial supervisions, the boy began to wrestle with another, the janitor did not intervene, and the boy suffered severe head injuries. The school district had no discretion—and thus was not immune under the "discretionary function" theory used in the Ohio school bus case cited in my text. Instead, the school district had a mandate to supervise properly and thus was discharging a mandatory, not a discretionary, duty, and thus was under a duty to supervise properly, as in the Kansas case cited in my text. (Note: this is another case like *Waechter*, with somewhat the same factors coming into play.)

Likewise, an LEA can be held liable if it fails to protect students from teachers. The LEA's liability is under Section 1983 of the Civil Rights Act, which gives a student a right of action and damages if a state or any of its employees deprives the student of any of his or her legal rights—such as rights under the Constitution to freedom from invasion of one's personal security through sexual abuse or rights under state or federal statutes. The leading cases are *D.R. v. Middle Bucks Area Vocational Technical School* (972 F. 2d 189, 3d Cir., 1992; cert. den., 113 S. Ct. 1045, 1993), *Black v. Indiana Area School Dist.* (985 F. 2d 707, 3d Cir., 1993), and *Stoneking v. Bradford Area School Dist.* (882 F. 2d 720, 3d Cir., 1989).

Relying on those cases, a federal court in the 3d Circuit has held that a school district may be held liable to a student for its failure to supervise a teacher who the district knows or has reason to know subjects the students to physical or emotional abuse (here, sexual and physical abuse) (*C. M. v. Southeast Delco School Dist.*, *IDELR* 19/22, E.D. Pa., 1993, and *K.L. v. Southeast Delco School Dist.*, *IDELR* 20/244, E.D. Pa., 1993). The district has an affirmative action to protect students against its employees; a district that tolerates, condones, or encourages unconstitutional behavior by a teacher (assault on a student) is liable. The key to the liability is the duty of a district to supervise an employee who stands in a particularly sensitive relationship to students. Moreover, if the district has notice or reasonably is held to having notice that an employee is invading a student's privacy, and if the student thereby is harmed and the district does nothing to prevent the harm, not only is the district liable but so too are the district's superintendent and other senior officers; they are not entitled to any qualified immunity defense. The district's and officers' liability does not include, however, liability for any of the teacher's actions toward students who have graduated. Post-graduation behavior is not state action because the teacher is not a state employee (that is, is not acting as a teacher—because the students have graduated).

It is not surprising, in light of these decisions, that a state court has allowed a jury to award damages to a student and against a teacher who deliberately refused to let the student take tests orally instead of in writing. The student's IEP called for oral testing, and the teacher knew of the IEP accommodation to the student's learning disability (*Doe v. Withers*, *IDELR* 20/422, W. Va. Cir. Ct., 1993).

Nor is it shocking that a state court has held that a school district is not liable to a bus driver whom it fires because he sexually abused special education students on his bus (*Heslop v. Board of Education, Newfield Cent. Sch. Dist.*, *IDELR* 20/317, N.Y. App. Div., 1993).

In *Beede v. Town of Washington School District* (*IDELR* 18/1295, U.S.D.Ct., Vt., 1992), a student refused to attend speech therapy classes as a kindergarten student. Despite indications of the fact that she needed a behavioral evaluation (because she did not attend speech therapy classes), the LEA refused to provide such an evaluation and in fact two years later terminated her from special education. The court held that she may sue for a violation of her IDEA procedural rights (violation of the parents' rights to an IEP meeting, reevaluation, and notice before special education services are terminated), a usual "start over" or "restart" remedy. In addition, the court also allowed the parents' claims for Section 1983, Section 504, and IDEA violations to go forward to a hearing—possibly allowing them to get an "over and above" remedy for IDEA, Section 1983, and Section 504 violations.

In *Squiers v. Sierra Nevada* (*IDELR* 18/648, Nev. Sup. Ct., 1991), the state's highest court declined to rule whether parents have a right to sue for educational malpractice, but did allow the parents to sue for a breach of contract against a private school that had guaranteed that it would make certain, particularized services available to their son and also had made specific representations concerning the quality of the school program. (Note: the breach of contract theory is relatively novel and a backdoor way into allowing damages for educational defaults, whether or not the defaults are called malpractice.)

The "discretionary function" defense was successful in *Bencic v. City of Malden* (*IDELR* 18/625, Mass. App. Ct., Middlesex, 1992), where the court ruled that it was within a district's discretion to provide a student with an IEP, and, when there were no IEP and no program for behavioral management, the district is not liable to another student when a special education student attacks him and injures him.

A similar defense was available to a school principal, school nurse, and special education director who were sued when a school aide improperly catheterized a student. The Alabama Supreme Court held that these three individuals were protected from liability for improperly training and supervising a classroom aide. The doctrine of "discretionary function" immunity protects them from a lawsuit because supervision and training require constant decision making and the exercise of judgment on their part—the more a person has to exercise judgment, the more the person is engaged in a discretionary function and is immune. The aide, however, is not immune and may be held liable for improper catheterization (*Nance v. Matthews*, *IDELR* 20/3, Ala. Supreme Court, 1993).

Liability for Student Behavior. IDEA takes into account that it may not be appropriate (and consistent with IDEA) to place a student with disabilities into a mainstream/regular setting if the student may jeopardize other students (so-called danger to others exception to the rebuttable presumption in favor of least restrictive placement; see Chapter 6 of my text). If a district follows that presumption and has no reason to believe that the special education student will be aggressive to nondisabled students, then the school district does not violate the constitutional due process rights (life, liberty, property) of a nondisabled student who is attacked by the student with disabilities (*Cohen v. School District of Philadelphia*, *IDELR* 18/911, U.S.D.Ct., E.D. Pa., 1992).

A case that follows the traditional "no damages" line and applies it to student, not school, behavior is *Rankins v. Aytch* (*IDELR* 18/635, La. Ct. App., 2d Cir., 1991). In this instance a state appeals court held that, under state law, parents and teachers of a student with severe emotional disabilities, who had been acting out and aggressive at the time the teachers placed her forcibly on the school bus, are not liable to the bus driver whom the student attacked because they did not have reasonable grounds to think that the student would attack the driver.

Attorney Fees

Under the Handicapped Children's Protection Act, a court may award attorney fees to the parents or student who prevails in any action against the LEA or SEA and may charge those fees to the "losing" LEA or SEA. The cases are *Aranow v. D.C. Board of*

Education (*IDELR* 18/577, D. D.C., 1992); *Krichinsky v. Knox County Schools* (*IDELR* 18/1085, 6th Cir., 1992); *Board v. Redovian* (*IDELR* 18/1092, U.S.D.Ct., N.D. Ohio, 1992); *Borengasser v. Arkansas Bd. of Educ.* (*IDELR* 20/70, 8th Cir., 1993); *Lawyer v. Chesterfield County Sch. Bd.* (*IDELR* 20/173, E.D. Va., 1993); *Felter v. Cape Girardeau Sch. Dist.* (*IDELR* 20/434, E.D. Mo., 1993); *Witty v. Dukakis* (but attorney must assert right to fee recovery on a timely basis—he who waits is lost) (*IDELR* 20/517, 1st Cir., 1993); *Phelan v. Bell* (*IDELR* 20/528, 6th Cir., 1993); *S-1 v. State Bd. of Educ. of N.C.* (attorney fees awarded for work done before case became moot) (*IDELR* 20/609, 4th Cir., 1993); and *Brown v. Griggsville Community Unit Sch. Dist. No. 4* (fees are awardable but in this case they were not earned—the mere filing of a due process hearing request did not cause the LEA to change the student's placement; instead the reevaluation of the student was the cause) (*IDELR* 20/758, 7th Cir., 1993).

Generally, courts have interpreted HCPA broadly, allowing attorney fees for work done in mediation (*Masotti v. Tustin Unified School District Board of Education*, *IDELR* 19/480, C.D. Cal., 1992), for work done to secure a temporary restraining order (*Capielo v. D.C. Board of Education*, *IDELR* 18/620, D. D.C., 1992), for work done to monitor a school district after the parents sued and won and a court entered an order requiring the district to undertake certain activities (*Mason v. Kaagan*, U.S.D.Ct., D. Vt., 1992), and for not only attorney fees but also expert witness fees (*Aranow v. D.C. Bd. of Ed.*, supra).

Where a parent's lawsuit caused a state to enact a new law that grants, by legislation instead of by judicial order, essentially what the parent wants, the parent may recover attorney fees (*Grinsted v. Houston County Sch. Dist.*, *IDELR* 20/339, M.D. Ga., 1993).

But the amount of fees is proportional to the amount of success the parents achieve—the more success, the more they are entitled to all of their attorney fees (*Fenneman v. Gorham Superintending Sch. Comm.*, *IDELR* 19/666, D. Me., 1992; *Hunger v. Leininger*, *IDELR* 19/776, N.D. Ill., 1993; *Lawyer v. Chesterfield County Sch. Bd.*, *IDELR* 20/173, E.D. Va., 1993).

The prevailing rate for an out-of-state attorney is the rate in that attorney's jurisdiction, not the rate in the jurisdiction where the case is tried (*Mr. W. v. Malito*, *IDELR* 19/901, C.D. Ill., 1993).

If an attorney represents himself, he or she surrenders the right to recover attorney fees (*Rappaport v. Vance*, *IDELR* 19/770, D. Md., 1993). The exception to that rule is this: if the law (about self-representation and attorney fee recovery) is unsettled at the time the attorney represents himself, then it is permissible to award him attorney fees (*Kattan v. District of Columbia*, *IDELR* 20/23, D.C. Cir., 1993).

But an attorney may not bill for both his work and his law clerks' work—duplicative billing is not allowed (*Hall v. Detroit Pub. Sch.*, *IDELR* 20/18, E.D. Mich., 1993).

If, however, parents unreasonably protract the litigation (*Johnson v. Bismarck*, *IDELR* 18/571, 8th Cir., 1992), or if they fail to reserve the attorney fees as part of a settlement with an LEA (*Fischer v. Rochester Community Schools*, U.S.D.Ct., E.D. Mich., 1992), or where they simply fail to make a case (*Wheeler v. Towanda School Dist.*, *IDELR* 18/637, 3d. Cir., 1992), then the courts will not award attorney fees.

Attorney-Client Privilege

Where a state allows "lay advocates" to represent parents and students in IDEA administrative hearings, the communications between the parents and the lay advocate are privileged, just as they would be if they were communications between a parent and a licensed lawyer representing the parent or student (*Woods v. New Jersey Dept. of Educ.*, *IDELR* 19/1092, D. N.J., 1993).

Section 504 and IDEA

Although the U.S. Department of Education, Office of Civil Rights, takes the position that Section 504 (prohibiting discrimination based solely on disability) requires the same kind of response to a student's needs as IDEA (*Letter to Zirkel*, *IDELR* 20/134), a federal court disagrees and has ruled that a student who is not eligible for IDEA (the student has Attention Deficit Disorder, which is now, in 1994, an IDEA disability, U.S.C.) is entitled to only a reasonable accommodation to overcome any LEA discrimination, not to the same procedures and benefits granted by IDEA. Section 504 does not necessarily require as much as IDEA, and if the discrimination can be eliminated by services that fall short of IDEA, then that is sufficient under Section 504 (*Lyons v. Smith*, *IDELR* 20/164, D. D.C., 1993).